Upon this rock I will build my church;
and the gates of hell shall not prevail against it.

MATTHEW 16:18 KJV

The story of the Church is a story of many resurrections.

JOHN CALVIN

The Church is in an excellent state when it is supported only by God.

BLAISE PASCAL

There is but one way of recovering the idea of the Church.
It is by regaining, on a scale worthy of it,
the evangelical faith which made and makes the Church always.

PETER T. FORSYTH

The Real Church is the assembly which is called, united,
held together and governed by the Word of her Lord,
or she is not the Real Church.

KARL BARTH

I believe we are now in a struggle for the soul of the church,
for faithfulness to the Scriptures, and for continuity
with the creedal and confessional traditions of the church.

CARL BRAATEN

Other Books by Donald G. Bloesch

CENTERS OF CHRISTIAN RENEWAL

THE CHRISTIAN LIFE AND SALVATION

THE CRISIS OF PIETY

THE CHRISTIAN WITNESS IN A SECULAR AGE

CHRISTIAN SPIRITUALITY EAST AND WEST (COAUTHOR)

THE REFORM OF THE CHURCH

THE GROUND OF CERTAINTY

SERVANTS OF CHRIST (EDITOR)

THE EVANGELICAL RENAISSANCE

WELLSPRINGS OF RENEWAL

LIGHT A FIRE

THE INVADED CHURCH

JESUS IS VICTOR! KARL BATH'S DOCTRINE OF SALVATION

THE ORTHODOX EVANGELICALS (COEDITOR)

ESSENTIALS OF EVANGELICAL THEOLOGY, VOL. 1: GOD, AUTHORITY AND SALVATION

ESSENTIALS OF EVANGELICAL THEOLOGY, VOL. 2: LIFE, MINISTRY AND HOPE

THE STRUGGLE OF PRAYER

FAITH & ITS COUNTERFEITS

IS THE BIBLE SEXIST?

THE FUTURE OF EVANGELICAL CHRISTIANITY

CRUMBLING FOUNDATIONS

THE BATTLE FOR THE TRINITY

A HERMENEUTICS OF ULTIMACY: PERIL OR PROMISE? (COAUTHOR)

FREEDOM FOR OBEDIENCE

THEOLOGICAL NOTEBOOK VOL. 1

THEOLOGICAL NOTEBOOK VOL. 2

A THEOLOGY OF WORD & SPIRIT

HOLY SCRIPTURE

GOD THE ALMIGHTY

JESUS CHRIST: SAVIOR & LORD

EVANGELICAL THEOLOGY IN TRANSITION: THEOLOGIANS IN DIALOGUE
   WITH DONALD BLOESCH (COAUTHOR)

THE HOLY SPIRIT

REINHOLD NIEBUHR'S APOLOGETICS

·CHRISTIAN FOUNDATIONS·

THE
CHURCH

SACRAMENTS, WORSHIP, MINISTRY, MISSION

DONALD G. BLOESCH

INTERVARSITY PRESS
DOWNERS GROVE, ILLINOIS 60515

InterVarsity Press
P.O. Box 1400, Downers Grove, IL 60515-1426
World Wide Web: www.ivpress.com
E-mail: mail@ivpress.com

InterVarsity Press® is the book-publishing division of InterVarsity Christian Fellowship/USA®, a student movement active on campus at hundreds of universities, colleges and schools of nursing in the United States of America, and a member movement of the International Fellowship of Evangelical Students. For information about local and regional activities, write Public Relations Dept., InterVarsity Christian Fellowship/USA, 6400 Schroeder Rd., P.O. Box 7895, Madison, WI 53707-7895, or visit the IVCF website at <www.ivcf.org>.

Scripture quotations, unless otherwise noted, are from the Revised Standard Version of the Bible, *copyright 1946, 1952, 1971 by the Division of Christian Education of the National Council of the Churches of Christ in the U.S.A., and are used by permission.*

"The Cambridge Declaration" on pp. 288-94 is reprinted by permission of the Alliance of Confessing Evangelicals, 1716 Spruce St., Philadelphia, PA 19103.

"The Gospel of Jesus Christ: An Evangelical Celebration" on pp. 295-305 is reprinted by permission of the Committee on Evangelical Unity of the Gospel, P.O. Box 5551, Glendale Heights, IL 60139-5551.

I wish to thank the Copyright Company of Nashville, Tenn., for granting permission to quote from the song "As the Deer" by Martin Nystrom, which appears in Maranatha! Music Praise Hymns and Choruses (1997); and Music Services, Inc. for allowing me to quote from the song "The Only One" by Eddie Espinosa.

Chapter nine, "The Demise of Biblical Preaching," is an expanded version of an article published under the same title in Touchstone *8, no. 4 (Fall 1995), and is used by permission.*

Cover illustration: Guy Wolek

ISBN 0-8308-1416-7

Printed in the United States of America ∞

Library of Congress Cataloging-in-Publication Data

Bloesch, Donald G., 1928-
  The Church: sacraments, worship, ministry, mission / Donald G.
Bloesch
    p. cm.—(Christian foundations)
Includes bibliographical references and indexes.
  ISBN 0-8308-1416-7 (cloth: alk. paper)
  1. Church. I. Title.
BV600.3 .B57 2002
262—dc21

2002007425

| **P** | 18 | 17 | 16 | 15 | 14 | 13 | 12 | 11 | 10 | 9 | 8 | 7 | 6 | 5 | 4 | 3 | 2 | 1 |
| **Y** | 16 | 15 | 14 | 13 | 12 | 11 | 10 | 09 | 08 | 07 | 06 | 05 | 04 | 03 | 02 |

*Dedicated to the
memory of
Philip Schaff*

Acknowledgments ——————————————————— 11
Abbreviations ———————————————————— 12
Preface ———————————————————————— 13

1 Introduction ——————————————————— 17
Differing Theological Perspectives ————————— 19
Need for a Theological Balance —————————— 23

2 Continuing Issues in Ecclesiology ——————— 27
Authority and Infallibility ——————————————— 30
Reinterpreting the Church's Mission ———————— 32
Quandary over Worship ———————————————— 35
Marks and Signs ——————————————————— 39
Christian Unity ———————————————————— 41

3 The Church in the Plan of Salvation ————— 46
Roman Catholic Theology ——————————————— 47
Martin Luther ———————————————————— 48
John Calvin ————————————————————— 50
Emil Brunner ————————————————————— 51
Karl Barth —————————————————————— 53
Thomas F. Torrance —————————————————— 56
The Redemptive Community ————————————— 58
The Church's Mandate ———————————————— 62
Mary: A Type of the Church —————————————— 64

4 The Church and the Kingdom ————————— 69
Two Sides of the Church ———————————————— 70
The Kingdom in the Making —————————————— 76
The Kingdom and World History ———————————— 78

5 Authority in the Church ——————————— 82
Papalism versus Conciliarism ————————————— 83
Biblicism versus Ecclesiasticism ———————————— 86
Experientialism versus Rationalism —————————— 93
The Church Militant and Triumphant ————————— 96

6 Marks of the Church ———————————— 99
The Catholic Consensus ———————————————— 100
Practical Marks ———————————————————— 103

Marks of the False Church ———————— 109
Word and Spirit ———————————— 113

7 Worship in Spirit and Truth———————— 116
Worship in Biblical Perspective ————————— 118
God Transcendent ————————————— 122
Word and Image ————————————— 126
The Crisis in Spirituality ————————————— 130
True Spirituality ————————————— 131
Appendix A: Contemporary Worship ———————— 135
Appendix B: An Evangelical Order of Worship ——————— 141
Appendix C: A Reformed Worship Center ————————— 143

8 Rethinking Sacraments———————————— 147
Sacramental Understanding in Christian History ——————— 148
Holy Baptism ————————————— 154
Holy Communion ————————————— 160
Confession ————————————— 165
Word and Sacrament ————————————— 172
Appendix D: An Ecumenical Consensus? ———————— 175

9 The Demise of Biblical Preaching ———————— 178
A Legacy in Peril ————————————— 179
Aberrations After the Reformation ————————— 180
Toward the Recovery of Biblical Preaching ——————— 184
Postscript ————————————— 187

10 A Socio-Theological Typology———————— 189
A Typology of Religious Association ———————— 190
A Theological Interpretation ————————————— 193
Learning from the Sects ————————————— 195
Epilogue ————————————— 198
Appendix E: Further Thoughts on Sects and Cults ————— 201

11 The Diversity of Ministries———————————— 204
Protestant Religious Orders ————————————— 211
Women in Ministry ————————————— 218
Marriage and Celibacy ————————————— 228

12 The Gospel in a Syncretistic Age———————— 235
Troeltsch's Theology of Religious History ——————— 240

Moltmann's Global Theology ———————— 244
The Church's Apostolic Mission ———————— 246

13 Toward the Reunion of the Churches ———— 252
The Trauma of the Reformation ———————— 253
The Retreat from Ecumenicity ———————— 255
Evangelical-Catholic Unity ———————— 257
The Ecumenical Imperative ———————— 262

14 A Confessing Church ———————————— 265
The Meaning of a Confessing Church ———————— 266
Types of Confession ———————————— 268
Hallmarks of a True Confession ———————— 270
A Confessing Church versus a Cultural Church ———— 273
The Work of a Confession ———————————— 278
Appendix F: The Voice of Orthodoxy ———————— 280
Appendix G: The Meaning of the Gospel ———————— 283

Appendix 1: The Cambridge Declaration ———————— 288
Appendix 2: The Gospel of Jesus Christ:
An Evangelical Celebration ———————— 295
Notes ———————————————————— 306
Index of Names ———————————————— 341
Index of Subjects ———————————————— 345
Index of Scripture ———————————————— 349

Acknowledgments

I wish to thank the following people for helping me gain information for the recent volumes of my Christian Foundations series: Mark Achtemeier and Gary Hansen of the theology and history division of the Dubuque Seminary faculty; Joel Samuels, Anastasia Bissell and Paul Waelchli of the University of Dubuque Library; John Rush and David MacLeod of Emmaus Bible College; Charlene Swanson of the Bethel Seminary library; and Ethel Bloesch of the University of Iowa Library. I remain indebted to my wife Brenda for her diligent copyediting and research and to Debbie Lovett for her careful typing.

Abbreviations for Biblical Translations

KJV	King James Version
NKJ	New King James Version
NIV	New International Version
REB	Revised English Bible
NLT	New Living Translation
NJB	New Jerusalem Bible

(Note: Bible references not otherwise indicated are from the Revised Standard Version.)

Preface

In trying to forge an evangelical theology of the church, I have been alert to the peril of individualism in which the quest of the solitary individual for union with the eternal (prominent in Platonism and Neoplatonism) eclipses the biblical vision of a community gathered together to hear the Word of God and to minister to the needs of the saints. The penetration of individualism into the life of the church is much more apparent in the revival tradition of Protestantism than in the Reformation tradition. Indeed in this past century theologians in both Lutheran and Reformed camps have produced significant treatises on the church. I am thinking here of scholars like P. T. Forsyth, Emil Brunner, G. C. Berkouwer, T. F. Torrance and Dietrich Bonhoeffer. In my doctrine of the church I have drawn on these and other scholars, but I have also sought to relate to the concerns of the great mass of believers who stand in the traditions of evangelical revivalism, Puritanism and Pietism with their emphasis on personal decision and the experiential appropriation of the truth of faith. We must resist the ideology of individualism, but we must also be wary of the ideology of collectivism. We enter the church one by one but never apart from the hearing of the gospel and the prayers of the faithful. We are not born into the church by virtue of having Christian parents. Nor are we guaranteed membership in the family of God by the ritual of baptism. We are reborn into the kingdom of God through the mediation of the church, through its proclamation and its sacraments as the Spirit acts upon them. Faith and baptism sets us on the way, but we persevere through communion with the whole company of the saints—on this side and on the other side of the grave.

In this book I have sought to steer a middle way between pietism and enthusiasm on the one hand and sacramentalism and sacerdotalism on the other. The dire need today is for both *reformation* in the light of the Word of God and *revival* through the outpouring of the Spirit of God. The truth of the gospel must be discovered anew, not simply in abstract thought but in personal experience. This gospel must be confessed in the face of the principalities and powers of the age, though this confession must not be reduced to a ritual performance, but must constitute a genuine witness of faith. We need to make tangible contact with the realities we purport to believe in, yet we are also obliged to reflect on the significance of these realities for the life of the church. Christian experience and the Christian mind go together, though in certain stages of the church's pilgrimage one may have to be stressed more than the other.

An evangelical theology will be both a theology of Christian renewal and a theology of the Word of God. It will seek not only a sound and true interpretation of the mysteries of faith but also a mystical participation in these mysteries. Theologians show their evangelical credentials or lack thereof in the way in which they preach and pray. If their preaching takes the form of kerygmatic proclamation rather than pedagogy and if their prayers consist not in vain repetition but in heartfelt supplication and intercession, then they can indeed be considered evangelical in the sense of being true to the gospel.

My theology has on occasion been described as an ecumenical orthodoxy, and I have approved this appellation so long as its meaning is not a return to past formulations but a drawing upon the past in shaping a new future. An ecumenical orthodoxy holds to the unfolding of scriptural truth in church tradition. It acknowledges that the Spirit has been active in guiding the church to a true perception of the meaning and impact of the biblical revelation. But we would also do well to consider that scriptural truth has been compromised and distorted in church tradition. We should always view tradition critically, though never iconoclastically. It behooves us to discriminate between what is true and false in church tradition. We must not read Scripture through the eyes of "the great tradition" but assess the great tradition in light of the infallible standard for faith and practice—the confluence of the Word and Spirit.

In preference to an ecumenical orthodoxy I espouse an evangelical neo-orthodoxy whose aim is to give a fresh interpretation of age-old truths for our time and place in history. The church fathers put Scripture over their own interpretations and traditions, and we must do likewise. A theology of Word and Spirit will not simply repeat the precepts of the scriptural revelation but will confess the faith anew in the light of this revelation. It will seek a contemporary reaffirmation of old truths, one that is based on the Bible, illumined by the Spirit and appropriated in the evangelical experience of an awakened heart.

As an evangelical theologian who tries to remain open to the new wind of the Spirit, I do not see my task as the demolishment of liberal theology. Nor am I engaged in the wholesale repudiation of the liberal heritage. Liberal theology arose as an often valid protest against imbalances in orthodoxy. Its roots are not primarily in unbelief but in the searchings of faith that regrettably were increasingly severed from their biblical moorings. Where liberal theology went astray was in its attempt to find the answer to the human predicament in culture rather than in the mystery of God's self-condescension in Jesus Christ, in experience rather than historical revelation. It should be obvious that I am not a theological liberal (though some conservatives have labeled me as such), but I wish to have a liberal spirit in the sense of being self-critical. I am opposed to liberalism as an ideology but not to the liberal call for self-examination. A truly liberal spirit combined with a passion for the gospel leads to a creative and expansive orthodoxy in contrast to a narrow or constrictive orthodoxy. An orthodoxy that keeps itself open to revision in the light of the new truth disclosed by the Spirit in the Bible and in gospel preaching will play a pivotal role in the revivification of the church in our time.

·ONE·

INTRODUCTION

To know God is to be changed by God;
true knowledge of God leads to worship.

JOHN CALVIN

A theologian without faith is like a sky without a star,
a heart without a pulse, light without warmth,
a sword without edge, a body without soul.

PHILIP SCHAFF

The prime duty of the Church is not to impress,
or even to save, men, but to confess the Savior, to confess
in various forms the God, the Christ, the Cross that does save.

PETER T. FORSYTH

Talk about God has true content when it conforms
to the being of the Church, i.e., when it conforms to Jesus Christ.

KARL BARTH

The relation of theology to the church has long been disputed among theologians. On the one hand are those who claim that theology is primarily descriptive—either of states of human consciousness or of the symbols and concepts that have shaped Christian community. On the other hand are those who maintain that theology is basically the articulation of a commitment or experience that redeems and transforms. Theology thus becomes more existential than theoretical, more experiential than scientific.

In the age of Protestant orthodoxy the defenders of Reformation faith stressed the scientific and universal character of theology. With some plausibility they contended that the object of theological reflection is true and valid irrespective of the subjective response. They further argued that theology could be done by the unregenerate as well as the regenerate so long as we bring to the theological task the necessary tools of analysis and synthesis *(theologia irregenitorum)*. In reaction to the arid intellectualism spawned by this type of orthodoxy, the Pietists stressed the need for personal regeneration in fulfilling the theological task. One cannot truly know the revealed content of the faith without an experience of personal conversion.[1] Theology was redefined not simply as the doctrine of God but as "the doctrine . . . of living to God" or "working towards God" (William Ames).[2] Life, experience and commitment became the watchwords of theology rather than the triune being of God or the eternal decrees or the two natures of Christ.

Theology at its best has perceived that logos and praxis, Word and Spirit belong together. Doctrine without devotion is empty; devotion without doctrine is blind. If the goal of theology is simply to bring our thoughts into conformity with the mind of God we run the risk of rationalism or propositionalism. If our goal is solely to effect a change in life or character we are prone to reduce theology to ethicism and moralism. It is my thesis that a theology of the Christian life and a theology of the Word of God must be united. Word must never be separated from Spirit and vice versa. A dogmatic theology *(theologia dogmatica)* must at the same time be a theology of the spiritual life *(theologia vitae spiritualis)*. The proper milieu for the study of theology is not the university but the fellowship of the church. Our approach to the great doctrines that have formed the faith must not be purely historical but existential. One can know the revealed content of the faith only by participating in this truth through the mystical union engendered by faith. The key to right understanding of the story of faith is the practice of faith in daily life and in the context of a believing community. I am arguing not for dropping theology from the university curriculum but for allowing the teachers of theology in a secular milieu to be existentially committed to the truth of what they are teaching even while granting their students the right to differ and the freedom to come to their own conclusions.

Differing Theological Perspectives

Friedrich Schleiermacher (d. 1834) was among those who sought to correct a misguided rationalism in Christian theology and anchor faith in concrete religious experience. The object of faith is not propositional truths that come directly from God, nor is it an infinite being wholly outside life and experience. Instead, faith focuses upon the awareness of the self that it is upheld and sustained by the power of universal love. True religion is not assent to creeds or dogmas but a "sense and taste for the Infinite."[3] The church is not a divine institution on earth but "a communion or association relating to religion or piety."[4] Theology is done within the fellowship of faith; it does not imperialistically set forth ontological claims but assesses what is now believed and experienced in the faith community. "It expresses the feeling of the religiously moved Christian heart in the way possible and necessary at the given time."[5] The purpose of preaching is "not to instruct but to evoke a sense of the mystery of God."[6] Preaching is basically a "testimony . . . to one's own experience" rather than a definitive proclamation of truth revealed by God.[7] Schleiermacher's fundamental point of departure was not the revelation of God in holy Scripture but "the soul's experience of spiritual life within the Christian Church."[8] His method was not that of listening to God but of delving into the self and discovering the infinite in the finite.

Schleiermacher appears to bring together the existential and theoretical sides of Christian theology, but he sacrifices objective content for subjective illumination. The important thing is not knowledge of God but the consciousness of the presence of God. Doctrines are not articulations of revealed truth but "accounts of the Christian religious affections set forth in speech."[9] The primary subject matter of theology is not the gospel or the Word of God but the experience of the "World Spirit," particularly as we see this in Jesus Christ. Faith is a feeling of absolute dependence on God[10] rather than an acknowledgement of what God has done for us in Christ (as in Barth). In criticism of Schleiermacher, H. R. Mackintosh declares, "No emphasis on experience can hide from us the fact that only as taught by Christ, the Word of God addressed to us, can we distinguish within experience what is Christian from what is not."[11]

* * *

Reacting against Schleiermacher and neo-Protestantism in general, Karl Barth sought to recover the objective and transcendent dimensions of Christian faith, though these were always related to the subjective human response of faith and obedience.[12] Like Schleiermacher Barth was emphatic that theology can be done only within the confines of the church, but he insisted that the purpose of theology is to equip the ambassadors of Christ to confront the world with the claims of faith. Schleiermacher had described himself as "a pietist of a higher order" in that he tried to make the horizon of Christian faith more inclusive and more world-affirming. But in common with the Pietist movement he located Christian identity in an experience of Christ within us. Barth, to the contrary, returned to the Reformation criterion of a divine revelation that bursts into human life and experience from the beyond.

While fully cognizant of the perils of subjectivism and experientialism to which Pietism was vulnerable, Barth was equally adamant in resisting the rationalism that came to characterize scholastic orthodoxy, both of the Catholic and the Protestant variety. He was implacably firm in asserting that "dogmatics is quite impossible except as an act of faith, in the determination of human action by listening to Jesus Christ and as obedience to Him."[13] Our dogmatic efforts must always point beyond themselves to God's self-revelation in Christ as attested in holy Scripture. Barth regarded the church moreover as the product of our adoption into the family of God by the risen Lord rather than as the tangible expression of our embarking on a quest for unity with God. We cannot be faithful stewards of the mysteries of God unless we stand firm on the gospel of God revealed in the Bible and promised to the church. With Calvin and Luther, Barth acknowledged *sensus* and *experientia* to be "the presupposition of true theology."[14] Yet this is not an experience separated from revelation but the product of revelation. Barth sided with the Pietists over the orthodox in affirming a *theologia regenitorum* (theology of the regenerate). The theologian must be a person of faith if he or she is to expound the Word of God with credibility and integrity. Yet our exposition is not grounded in faith but in the revelation of God that precedes human effort and apprehension.

*　　*　　*

Evangelical Covenant theologian John Weborg is of special interest, since he speaks within the Pietist tradition but seeks to buttress his assertions by appeals to Catholic (especially patristic) theology.[15] Seizing on a distinction in Catholic liturgical tradition, Weborg offers a typology of *theologia prima* and *theologia secunda,* though he develops this in his own way.[16] *Theologia prima,* or primary theology, is speech to God, which may be formal or informal. "When it is informal, *theologia prima* breaks out in protest, praise, petition or penitence. It emerges at times as an acclamation of God's power or fidelity and at other times as an argument with God more than as an argument about God or for God."[17] *Theologia secunda* is secondary theology, signifying reflection on God and the revelation of God. *Theologia secunda* is as necessary as *theologia prima,* since we need to understand what we have experienced if we are to make sense of this experience and of life in general. "*Theologia prima* forestalls the intellectual security if not pride in *theologia secunda.* Even the most sophisticated propositional resolutions to theological problems have not made prayer obsolete."[18] *Theologia secunda,* on the other hand, "keeps *theologia prima* from being a prisoner to its own subjectivity and enriches the depth and breadth of its language and experience."[19]

The speech associated with *theologia secunda* is "more studied than spontaneous, more dogmatic than doxological. Instead of direct address in the first person, this type of theology speaks of God in the third person, and when careless in doing so, risks portraying God as an object."[20] The danger in *theologia secunda* is that faith will become purely theoretical and cerebral and the imaginative vision that propels faith will be overshadowed by a concern for precision and technical accuracy.

Weborg is insistent that the two types of theology belong together and both can become misleading in their own ways if separated. The hymns, prayers and liturgy of the church have a certain precedence over the creeds and tomes of the church, but the former demand articulation and interpretation if they are to keep the church faithful to its mandate to proclaim the gospel to a lost and despairing world.

How should the searching Christian respond to this typology? It has the merit of uncovering the ineradicable experiential dimension in the life and theology of the church. Where it might be subject to criticism is in its implied subordination of theology to spirituality, of logos to praxis. Weborg acknowledges that the two sides must always be held together, that experience always needs to be interpreted. A more serious omission is that he fails to point to the priority of divine revelation over both experience and theological reflection. The right order is neither from experience to reflection nor from reflection to experience. It is from divine revelation to human experience and reflection. Our authority does not lie in religious experience (as with Schleiermacher) but in the living Word of God—the object of our experience. And this Word cannot be encapsulated in the liturgy of the church or the creeds of the church, but it stands over and against both liturgy and creeds and thereby allows for these to be subjected to a criterion higher than both.[21] According to Catholic liturgical theologian David Power, "The value of the liturgical is its capacity to transmit that Christian experience, deeply felt and demanding, in which God makes his claim upon us."[22] From my perspective the purpose of liturgy is not to transmit a Christian experience but to serve the heralding of the Word of God, which is apprehended by faith and may involve experiences, but these are not the principal thing.

Weborg is profoundly correct in his assertion that theology must have a doxological dimension and that all true reflection must be grounded in prayer if it is to be fruitful and rewarding. *Theologia prima* is not the foundation for *theologia secunda,* however, but it is the correlate of *theologia secunda.* Pietism at its best perceived this truth, and it is to be hoped that if Weborg develops this typology in more depth, he will reason along similar lines.

Need for a Theological Balance

Theology is not autobiography: its object is not the faith journey of the Christian wayfarer. Nor is theology the systematizing of the teaching of the Bible.[23] The dogmatic task is not simply to ascertain what the prophets and apostles said but to determine what we must say now on the basis of their testimony. In fulfilling this task we not only engage in the study of Scripture but also try to fathom what the Spirit is saying in the Scripture and to the church in every age. Evangelical theology will always have two sides: the objective rendering of what is stated in Scripture and the subjective application of the truth-content of Scripture to the existential situation of the interpreter and hearer. Theology is done not simply by analyzing the data of the Bible but by opening ourselves to the meaning that is conveyed by the Spirit of God through Scripture and the ongoing commentary on Scripture. Our goal is not merely to repeat Scripture but to apply Scripture under the guidance of the Spirit to a new situation. Doing theology is being taught by God and being formed by God into fit instruments of his service. It involves an in-depth engagement with the Word of God animated by a zeal for the glory of God.[24]

Theology in this sense will always be undertaken in the church. Its goal is to enable people of faith to understand their faith more fully and therefore equip them to be more diligent witnesses to their faith in the world. Theology is not the dispassionate assembling and systematizing of biblical data but the effort of the community of faith to maintain the integrity of its witness in a secular or non-Christian milieu that will invariably be hostile to the claims of faith. With Barth and the Pietists I therefore affirm that the only valid theology is a *theologia regenitorum.*

The theological task can be fulfilled only through successfully averting the dual dangers of subjectivism and objectivism. The truth of faith is neither an internal experience nor an external axiom. Evangelical Christianity is neither experientialism nor propositionalism, though it necessarily has both an experiential and a propositional dimension.

In the area of ecclesiology the theologian should take care to avoid both individualism and institutionalism. The church is not an assembly of like-minded persons who have made similar decisions, but it is also not a divinely constituted religious institution whose rites automatically confer faith or guarantee salvation. It has power and insight, but only as these are given by the Spirit of God. The church through the Spirit is both the begetter of faith and the receiver of faith. Its own rites and ceremonies have little value except when they are used by the Spirit to instruct and edify the saints, that is, those who believe in Jesus Christ as Lord and Savior.

The role of experience in theology has special import in this discussion. Faith transcends experience because its object is the living Word of God, who is prior to our experience of him. Yet faith is never entirely bereft of experience because we could not be engrafted into the body of Christ without experiencing this new birth in some vital way. Experience is the medium of faith but not the source of faith. I here fully agree with Congregational theologian P. T. Forsyth:

> It is not the *sense* of the experience that is the main matter, but the *source* of the experience, and its content. It is not our experience we are conscious of—that would be self-conscious piety—but it is Christ.[25]

It was fashionable in the circles of neo-orthodoxy to downplay the role of experience because experience in itself is irremediably equivocal and ambiguous. Yet without experience Christianity is reduced to ideas. Revelation then becomes a purely rational event, a communication of one mind to another. Forsyth gives us this timely admonition:

The once-born are the chief spiritual peril in the Church, the religious-minded without the religious experience, with a taste for religion but no taste of it, who treat Christianity as an interpretation of life rather than a recasting of the soul, and view the Church as the company of the idealists rather than the habitation of the Spirit."[26]

In this discussion we should keep in mind that the experience involved in the decision of faith is not religious experience as such but the evangelical experience of an awakened heart. It is the experience of being convicted of sin and rising to new life in Christ through the gift of the Holy Spirit. It is the experience of being filled with the joy of salvation and sustained by the assurance of the forgiveness of sins. It is the experience of finding the peace of God that passes all understanding. It is the experience of walking and living in the freedom of the Spirit.

Yet there is another side of the Christian life. Sometimes God hides himself from us even when we continue in the life of faith. On occasion God may withdraw his gracious presence to test us or to discipline us but always with the view to making us stronger. Experience will surely be there at the beginning of faith—when we embark on our spiritual journey—but it will more than likely recede as we grow in faith. Even the most godly Christians sometimes have to pass through a dark night of the soul where they have to believe against all reason, sight and understanding.[27] Dietrich Bonhoeffer wisely observes: "We will not be saved by experiences but by grace, not even through an *experience of grace* but by grace alone. Grace is more than what we 'experience' of it. Grace has to be *believed.*"[28] We are justified by grace alone, but this grace needs to be received by faith, and this reception is not merely intellectual but also experiential. Yet it is an experience of being taken out of ourselves into the promises of Christ that never deceive, not of being led more deeply into ourselves (as in mysticism). Experience is not the beginning of faith, but the beginning of faith will involve an experience—of the gravity of our sin and of the blessedness of Christ's redemption. Luther could appeal not only to Scripture but also to experience: "This I have not only from the Scriptures but also from experience, for the name of Christ often helped me when nobody else could. So I've had words and deeds in my favor, Scriptures and experience, and God gave me both in abundance."[29]

A theology of Word and Spirit will be a theology of the church on the march against the principalities and powers of the world. We are to stand firmly on the Word and move forward in the power of the Spirit as we bring the claims of Christ to a lost and despairing humanity. The gates of hell will not prevail against the church because Christ is more powerful than the devil (Mt 16:18). The grace that comes to us from the Holy Spirit cannot be permanently resisted or thwarted. The coming of the kingdom of Christ brings an end to the dominion of the kingdoms of this world. This is why the church can face the future with confidence and hope, knowing that God will resolutely work out his purposes even in the midst of tribulation and death. God is not the direct cause of everything that happens (this would be metaphysical determinism), but God is present in all the events that constitute world history, guiding them toward fulfillment in his eschatological kingdom. Not all things that happen are in accord with God's ultimate will, but everything is made to serve the mystery of redemption by God's beneficent foresight and superintending guidance and direction.

·TWO·

CONTINUING
ISSUES IN
ECCLESIOLOGY

A Christian optimism has grown up which had begun . . . to dream
of a speedy unity of the Churches without a prime regard to their belief.
PETER T. FORSYTH

The immediate, primary task of the Church is not to preach and to fight
for a social programme, but to preach the message
of redemption and eternal life.
EMIL BRUNNER

The Bible needs the church as its bulwark. How else will it be preserved,
translated, interpreted and proclaimed?
CLARK PINNOCK

To avoid confusing the Spirit and the Church,
it would be better not to speak of the Church as a "divine" reality.
HANS KÜNG

T he debate in contemporary theology revolves more and more
around the role of the church in the economy of salvation. It
is increasingly recognized that the Reformation itself was
propelled by deep divisions concerning the identity and mission of the
church. The developing scholarly consensus today is calling into question the traditional model of the church as institution and sacrament.[1]
Scholars like Emil Brunner, Jürgen Moltmann, Hans von Campen-

hausen, Hans Küng, Leonardo Boff and Elisabeth Schüssler Fiorenza contend that the original Pauline view was that of the church as a charismatic fellowship. The idea of a sacramental, sacerdotal and hierarchical church came later. Fiorenza is adamant that it is not "cultic priesthood" that is decisive for the ministry of the church but the gifts of the Spirit: "All members of the Christian community are called to exercise their 'spiritual gifts' for the building up of the 'body of Christ,' the Christian community."[2]

Other voices, however, are striving to recover the traditionalist Catholic conception of the church as a divine-human organism that imparts the mysteries of salvation through its certified representatives. Roman Catholic theologian Henri de Lubac argues that

> if Christ is the sacrament of God, the Church is for us the sacrament of Christ; she represents him, in the full and ancient meaning of the term, she really makes him present. She not only carries on his work, but she is his very continuation, in a sense far more real than that in which it can be said that any human institution is its founder's continuation.[3]

The traditionalist or sacerdotal model of the church is also being embraced by a growing number of Protestant scholars intent on forging ties with Roman Catholicism and Eastern Orthodoxy. Kevin Offner contends that for the Bible to be rightly understood it must be interpreted through the lens of the historic church. The church, moreover, speaks "through God-appointed authorities—popes, bishops, presbyters down through the ages, who, under God, have written creeds and formed ecumenical councils."[4]

A closely related question is whether the church is a veritable means of grace or simply a sign of grace that has already been actualized in the life, death and resurrection of Jesus Christ. The later Karl Barth rejects the idea of the church as a means of grace and regards Jesus Christ as the only sacrament of the church. The church is portrayed no longer as a sacramental community but as a servant community, which unites service and proclamation. It is not a channel or mediator of grace but a herald of grace. Pannenberg too is reluctant to speak of the church as a means of salvation and instead regards the church as a proleptic sign of the coming glory of the kingdom.[5] Baptist theologian Clark Pinnock surprisingly takes the more traditionalist position by viewing the church and the sacraments as effectual signs and means of the salvific grace revealed in Jesus Christ. They do not possess divine powers in and of themselves, but they do so through the gift of the Holy Spirit.[6]

Another issue that is spurring debate is whether the church is an extension or continuation of the incarnation, a position advocated by Johann Adam Möhler, Thomas O'Meara and Henri de Lubac among many others.[7] Does the church perpetuate the incarnation or merely bear witness to it through its worship and proclamation?[8] Is the church a divine institution, the mystical body of Christ, or a community of pardoned sinners who are striving for righteousness through the strengthening power of the Holy Spirit? Roman Catholic theologians traditionally have focused on the purity and holiness of the church, but now there is growing recognition that the church consists of sinners who are only partially regenerated. Karl Rahner can speak of a "sinning Church." Hans Küng declares, "The real Church . . . is not only a Church composed of people, but of sinful people. The real Church is not only human, but also sinful."[9]

The enigmatic relationship between the church and the kingdom is also a matter of contention. Is the church an anticipatory sign of the kingdom or the embryo of the kingdom, a stage in its historical realization? Is the kingdom the animating principle of the church or the goal of the church, as Pannenberg expresses it? Dare we speak of the kingdom as hidden in the institutional forms of the historical church? From my perspective there is both continuity and discontinuity between the kingdom and the church, but we must insist that the kingdom of God is wider and deeper than the church as a historical institution. This does not imply, however, that the coming of the kingdom rests partly "in the potentialities and powers of the world religions."[10] At the same time, I concur with Barth that it is within the parameters of biblical faith to maintain that the kingdom of Christ is manifest in many cultural and religious achievements, though only those with the eyes of faith can properly discern the breadth of the Spirit of God's activity in the world outside the church.[11]

Authority and Infallibility

Theologians and denominations continue to be divided over the role of the church in determining what is authoritative for faith and morals. Traditionally Catholics and Eastern Orthodox have held that the church furnishes the right interpretation of Scripture, though Scripture as the depository of divine revelation must always be esteemed by the church. Reformation Protestants have contended that Scripture is over the church, since it was dictated by the Spirit of God. Moreover, Scripture interprets itself through the power of the Spirit, though the church has the critical role of communicating this interpretation to its people.

Today there is a catholicizing movement in Protestantism that seeks to recover the normative role of church tradition in the shaping of theological authority. Magazines like *Pro Ecclesia, Touchstone, The Evangelical Catholic* and *Lutheran Forum* are intent on uniting scriptural authority with that of the "great tradition" of the undivided church.[12] Scripture, it is said, should be read through the lens of the fathers and teachers of the church.[13] The question arises whether the scripture principle of evangelical Protestantism is being abandoned for the authority of sacred tradition.

In the developing ethos of postmodernism the idea of metaphysical foundations for faith is being challenged in light of the growing consciousness of the relativity of human knowledge and the equivocal character of human language. The gospel is still normative for those who stand in a particular community of faith, but it can no longer be presented as an ontological truth claim in the public arena. It can be appreciated for its role in facilitating the social cohesion of a particular people but not as a metaphysical first principle that is virtually exempt from cultural and historical conditioning.[14]

Just as the older liberal theology had questioned the infallibility of Scripture, so postmodernist theology questions the infallibility of the gospel itself. Creeds and confessions are considered useful in enabling a community of faith to identify itself, but they cannot be regarded as embodying the definitive expression of faith for any particular generation. The new mood is articulated by Yale theologian Miroslav Volf:

> Though God's revelation is complete and trustworthy, there is no such thing as an infallible interpretation of this revelation, no ecclesiastical truth of obligatory character for one's conscience, no ecclesiastical truth concerning what one is to believe and to do, and thus no ecclesiastical truth concerning who belongs to the church and who does not.[15]

Volf acknowledges that the church is obliged to make provisional judgments regarding the truth of its faith, but these should always be open to revision in light of new insights from the Spirit of God. On the Catholic side Hans Küng and Yves Congar prefer the term "indefectibility" to "infallibility," since the first connotes a church that remains in the truth despite the limitations and errors of its theologians and interpreters.[16]

Against such views Karl Barth is intent on preserving the idea of the infallibility of the church so long as we distinguish between the message of the gospel itself and the ongoing interpretations of this message in the history of God's people. As he phrases it:

> The Church is infallible, not because its pronouncements, which are of necessity humanly limited, possess as such inerrancy and perfection; but because by its pronouncements it bears witness to the infallible Word of God and gives evidence that it has heard that Word; because the Church, abandoning all its own wisdom, lets itself be taught by the Word of God.[17]

In my opinion the church can be considered a valuable aid in enabling seekers of truth to gain a deeper and truer perception of the truth, but only holy Scripture as it is interpreted by the Spirit can be viewed as the fount of eternal wisdom, the final norm for faith and practice. The church can bear a true witness to God's self-revelation in Christ but only insofar as it subordinates itself to Scripture and allows itself to be taught by the Spirit of God. The church can be a support for truth, but it is dangerously misleading to conceive of it as an incarnation of the truth. The church can be a helpful guide for people of faith, but it must never be thought of as a guarantee for knowing the truth. The church is not itself the kingdom of God but a poignant sign and witness of the inbreaking of the kingdom into human history. The church is our mother and teacher in the faith but only insofar as it is open to being corrected and reformed by the wisdom of the eternal God as we see this manifested and embodied in Jesus Christ. Our hope as Christians is not in the church, in its programs and strategies, in its pronouncements and decrees, but in its Lord and Master, Jesus Christ, who speaks to us through Scripture and the ongoing theological commentary on Scripture through the ages.

Reinterpreting the Church's Mission

With the rise of new schools of theology it is not surprising that the mission of the church is being drastically reinterpreted. Whereas traditional theology envisions the church's mission as the proclamation of the good news of redemption through the cross and resurrection of Christ, the new theology views it in terms of humanization and social liberation. For Eugene Bianchi the fundamental mission of the church is to overcome the alienations that presently divide a broken humanity.[18] According to Harvey Cox, "the church's task in the secular city is to be the *diakonos* of the city, the servant who bends himself to struggle for its wholeness and health."[19] Peter Hodgson gives voice to the pluralistic vision[20] that sees all religions as having a modicum of validity among their own people: "The ecclesial community encompasses a plurality of peoples and cultural traditions and is but one of several religio-cultural shapes assumed by what Christians call the kingdom of God but what other religions give other names."[21] "Christianity is only one of the great religious and ethical systems of humanity. . . . It cannot expect to evangelize or prevail over the others."[22] Indeed "all claims to superiority are parochial." "The survival of all may depend on finding new bases for spiritual unity that transcend anything we now know."[23]

Predictably the ministry of the church assumes a new role in contemporary theology. Instead of expounding scriptural truth, ministers now devote their energies to breaking down barriers that impede humanity's progress toward peace and justice. According to Hodgson our aim should be "the creation of a global religious consciousness and a partnership in the struggle against common threats—technological dehumanization, militarism, nuclear war, environmental destruction, uncontrolled population growth, poverty and starvation, political and economic oppression."[24] The minister ceases to be a proclaimer of a definite message and now becomes "a nurturer of ecumenical and world openness."[25]

In the perspective of the new spirituality apologetics is no longer demonstrating the superiority of the Christian religion or the validity of Christian truth claims but arguing for the viability of a new religious vision that fulfills rather than negates the religious aspirations of the whole of humanity. Because "there is no universal world court or absolute philosophy in which the rival truth claims can be adjudicated,"[26] we must strive for a consensus that allows each religion to develop in its own way but on the basis of a similar religious experience. Apologetics in the traditional sense is supplanted by dialogue in the quest for a more comprehensive religious vision.

Another emergent strand in academic theology reflects the impact of the New Age movement, in which the church's mission is privatized or spiritualized.[27] The kingdom of God is no longer an emerging reign of justice on earth but the transformation of religious consciousness. It is not a blueprint for a new social order but a call to turn inward and find peace through union with the all-encompassing spiritual presence. The church becomes a society of seekers for enlightenment as opposed to the company of the committed with a mission and message for the world. Whereas liberation and feminist theologies tend to politicize the church's mission, the New Age spiritualizes or privatizes this mission. Evangelical theology, from my perspective, insists that the church has a fundamentally spiritual mission; yet this is a mission that is realized not in withdrawal or detachment from the afflictions and conflicts of humanity but in the very midst of these afflictions. Those of us who stand with the faith of the Reformation acknowledge that the message of the gospel has profound social and political implications and ramifications; yet the gospel itself is not a political message but the power of redeeming transformation as we see this manifested in Jesus' life, death and glorious resurrection.

The evangelical movement today has admirably resisted the new trends in theology that reconceive the mission of the church as an exercise in social engineering. Yet in their worship and social programs evangelicals betray a subtle accommodation to the therapeutic culture of our time by reducing salvation to psychic wholeness and the church to a life support system in the quest for stability and peace in a world disintegrating into spiritual and moral chaos. This is not to deny that the gospel is a facilitator of psychic health and a healer of broken relationships, but the core of its message is reconciliation and redemption through the decisive action of God in the person of Jesus Christ recorded in the history contained in holy Scripture. Salvation is an objective accomplishment before it is a subjective experience.

The need today is neither for a therapeutic church nor for a political church but for a confessing church, one that will boldly confess the claims of Christ in the face of the heresies and heterodoxies of our age. A truly confessing church will eventually draw up a confession of faith that will pinpoint the areas of danger to the integrity of the church's message and mission. Confessions are not as such infallible, but they may infallibly express the will of God for a particular situation in the history of the church. In a time when the church's trumpet is becoming indistinct and its ministry is vacillating in confusion, prophets are needed who will make visible the lines between the church and the world. Dietrich Bonhoeffer aptly expresses my own sentiments: "There can only be a church as a Confessing Church, i.e., as a church which confesses itself to be for its Lord and against his enemies. A church without a confession or free from one is not a church, but a sect, and makes itself master of the Bible and the Word of God."[28]

The hope of the church today lies neither in a revamped apologetics nor in an innovative church growth program but in a vibrant confession of faith that cuts across all denominational and sectarian lines and that speaks to the burning issues of the time. Yet we must be alert to the omnipresent danger that such a confession of faith could itself become a springboard for sectarianism. We confess not articles of faith so much as the living Lord who alone is the object of faith. He alone is "the way, the truth, and the life" (Jn 14:6 REB), and the key to the authenticity of a confession is whether it truly points beyond itself to the "author and finisher of our faith" (Heb 12:2 KJV).[29]

Quandary over Worship

An emerging issue in both Protestant and Catholic churches is worship, particularly the service of worship. Whereas the Word and sacraments constituted the focal point of ministry in the past, the new emphasis is on personal sharing, visual aids and contemporary music. Instead of a careful exposition of God's Word, we are introduced to the spiritual journeys of people of faith. Drama begins to overshadow proclamation, and theatrics supplant liturgy, even in many so-called evangelical churches. Worship is transposed into entertainment, and the principal concern is to gain the attention of the audience rather than give glory to God by celebrating the great events of sacred history. Many churches are caught up in the church growth movement in which humanly contrived strategies take precedence over biblical fidelity and doctrinal purity. Some churches follow the Willow Creek experiment in creating seekers' services, which are designed to meet religious needs rather than proclaim a definite message.[30]

Some clergy in both liberal and evangelical churches are intent on revising worship by incorporating liturgies drawn from the past, including Catholic tradition. In my opinion a retreat into the past is not what is needed, since it may further isolate the church from the cultural arena. High church worship as such still envisages worship as performance, whereas biblical worship is fundamentally adoration and confession. The strength of the liturgical movement in the recent past has been its emphasis on the need for active participation in the worship celebration by the congregation. The danger in this movement has been its conversion of worship into prescribed rituals and formulas, thereby blocking the free movement of the Spirit in the congregation.[31]

Closely related to the erosion of theocentric worship in the church services of our day is the loss of sacramental reality, particularly evident in both conservative and mainstream Protestantism. Baptism is no longer an initiation into the mystical body of Christ through faith and repentance but now an outward profession of belief that certifies our agreement with the precepts of church tradition. Sacraments are no longer signs and means of grace but ordinances of the church that regulate the life of the church. Karl Barth in his earlier years lamented that the Reformed church had been misunderstood when it created the impression that it was a church bereft of sacraments, even a church inimical to sacraments.[32] P. T. Forsyth in early twentieth-century England astutely perceived, "A Church cannot . . . live without sacraments, which are 'essential means'; but still less can it live without sacramental souls, which are also ends in themselves."[33]

In Roman Catholicism the sacraments are presently being rethought to assign a greater role to human responsibility. They are increasingly seen not simply as causes of grace or carriers of grace but as signs of grace or as badges of spiritual commitment. Catholic theologians today are more and more reluctant to speculate on the metaphysical effects of sacramental action and instead view the sacraments as "expressions of what the Christian life is all about."[34] It is said that Scripture and rituals find their meaning only in being interpreted by the experience of the people of God.[35] The sacraments as traditionally understood become aids to salvation rather than conditions of salvation. Joseph Martos declares, "Christian initiation does not have to be restricted to baptism; there are other ways of entering, or entering more deeply into, the experience of salvation and community."[36]

Sacramental reality can be subverted by losing sight of the ineradicable relation between the sign and the thing signified in the worship celebration. When faith is viewed as mental assent to propositional truth, it presupposes that the truth of revelation is directly accessible to human reason, and there is no need for this truth to be mediated through an outward or sacramental sign. In rationalism the numinous and ecstatic aspects of worship are supplanted by a wholly cerebral understanding. But sacramental reality can also be subverted by ritualism, in which the sign becomes virtually identical with the thing signified. It is then no longer a means of grace but a cause of grace. Salvation is accomplished simply by the performance of the rite (ex opere operato) rather than imparted to people of faith through the rite.

Finally, we need to give serious attention to the demise of biblical preaching, which extends to Protestant as well as Catholic and Orthodox churches. Michael Green articulates the concerns of a growing number of church leaders and theologians:

> One of the great weaknesses in contemporary Christianity is the poverty of preaching. Many clergy consider it a chore, and many congregations complain if it lasts more than ten minutes. There seems to be little expectation that the Spirit of God might be present and active, to take home the words that one would hope have been prepared and prayed over in his presence, so that the message (or some part of it) becomes luminous, indeed life-changing, for one here and another there in the congregation.[37]

An Orthodox theologian confesses that apostolic fervor and the urgency of preaching are sadly lacking in his communion:

> The content of the Orthodox faith is evangelical, but the spirit and practice of the actual contemporary Orthodox experience is by and large not evangeli-

cal. Perhaps the most severe indictment against all of us is that a person can grow up in the Church and after years of training attain to priesthood and even episcopacy and still be conditioned by the idea that the Church *qua* Church can function only in terms of formal religiosity and human prudence, not in the spirit of Christ and the good news.[38]

Part of the problem lies in the loss of the gospel as the content of the sermon. Too often it is assumed that the role of the preacher is to make the faith palatable to its cultured despisers rather than simply expound the good news, which itself creates faith through the power of the Spirit. Even while recognizing the sad condition of the preaching ministry in his own communion, one Catholic parish priest shows that his understanding of the sermon still falls short of the biblical, kerygmatic model:

> I have to convince people that it is intellectually honest to believe in God, that belief is a tenable position. To do this, I may have to share a part of my own odyssey; I shall certainly have to make it plain that with all my shortcomings I am a person of faith, for faith is humanity's response to God's revelation of self.[39]

Increasingly Catholic and Orthodox theologians are rediscovering what the Protestant Reformers clearly grasped—that preaching has sacramental efficacy when it is solidly based on the Word of God and empowered by the Spirit of God.[40] Yet we must be careful not to identify the words of the pastor with the very Word of God itself. I here fully concur with Karl Barth: "However clearly and precisely the Gospel is preached, the divine incognito still remains. The pure, non-ecclesiastical Gospel is proclaimed by no human mouth."[41] This is why Barth could speak of both the impossibility and the necessity of preaching God's Word.[42] In and of ourselves we cannot proclaim the gospel of reconciliation and redemption with meaning and power, but filled with the Holy Spirit we can help to bring the words of Scripture to life as we obediently endeavor to find God's truth in the reading and study of the Scriptures.

Marks and Signs

The identity of the church as the people of God and the mystical body of Christ is hidden in the forms and rituals of the church's life. Even so, theologians through the ages have insisted that there are outward signs that attest the authenticity of any particular church body, and these continue to be a subject of dispute in academic theology.

Theology tends to divide on the question of whether the Spirit or the Word constitutes the basic evidence for the apostolicity and catholicity of the church. Irenaeus seemed to endorse a pneumatocentric theology when he declared, "Where the Church is, there is the Spirit of God; and where the Spirit of God is, there is the Church, and every kind of grace."[43] At the same time, he also contended that the Word and the Spirit are the two hands of the Father working together in an indissoluble unity. Moltmann is closer to a pneumatocentric perspective in his claim that "the church is present wherever 'the manifestation of the Spirit' takes place."[44] The Reformers and the tradition of Protestant orthodoxy were prone to uphold a logocentric theology in which the church receives its identity and mission from the Word. Calvin asserted, "God begets and multiplies his Church only by means of his word. . . . It is by the preaching of the grace of God alone that the Church is kept from perishing."[45] Wolfhart Pannenberg, on the other hand, avers that "the Reformation view of the church as a creation of the Word . . . stands in danger of a one-sided christological constriction" resulting in "a theocracy of proclamation."[46] The Reformation at its best stressed the dialectical inseparability of Word and Spirit, and Pannenberg acknowledges that the fuller Reformation perspective can be retrieved by stressing "the relation of Word to Spirit no less than that of Spirit to Word."[47]

Theologians from all communions generally endorse the classical marks of the church as contained in the Nicene Creed—oneness, holiness, catholicity and apostolicity. Contemporary theology, however, is not in agreement on the meaning of these marks. Does oneness refer to the church as an institution or to the invisible fellowship of the saints on earth and in heaven? Does apostolicity signify that the ministers of the church are linked to the apostles through a special rite of laying on of hands by bishops in an unbroken historical succession, or does it not refer to a continuity in the message of faith that was first articulated by the apostles? Nathaniel Micklem voices the concerns of many Protestants in his criticism of the Catholic conception of apostolic succession: "Our protest is not against that which episcopacy represents, but only against that view which would make Word and Sacrament contingent upon the office, not the office on the Word."[48]

Roman Catholic theologians are presently rethinking the marks of the church especially in the light of Vatican Council II. For Avery Dulles the unity or oneness that we attribute to the true church is not "the external unity" of a visible institution but rather "the interior unity of mutual charity leading to a communion of friends."[49] On catholicity Dulles maintains that what is most important is "not the accomplished fact of having many members or a wide geographical distribution, but rather the dynamic catholicity of a love reaching out to all and excluding none."[50] Walter Kasper articulates the vision of the church in the new Catholicism:

> The unity and catholicity of the Church are always and in every case still *in fieri;* they will always remain a task. The solution cannot lie either in mutual absorption or in simple integration of individual ecclesiastical communities, but only in the constant conversion of all—i.e., in the readiness to let the event of unity, already anticipated in grace and sign, occur ever and again in obedience to the one gospel as the final norm in and over the Church.[51]

The magisterial Reformation was inclined to define the church in terms of the right preaching of the Word and the right administration of the sacraments. Questions that forced themselves to the center of discussion in post-Reformation Protestantism include the extent of the efficacy of Word and sacraments in situations where faith is rare or nonexistent. Moreover, are there other marks besides the Word and sacraments that should be given special attention today?[52]

In the light of the Pentecostal awakening, the role of signs and wonders as attestations of the gospel has become a major theological issue. Is the message of the church validated by miraculous signs, including physical healings, or is the inward illumination of the Holy Spirit sufficient to make the message persuasive and authentic? P. T. Forsyth mirrors the Reformed distrust of dependence on signs and wonders: "They are tests of nature and not of faith, tests of feeling rather than insight, tests of empirical experience instead of soul experience, of success rather than of devotion."[53] Christoph Blumhardt by contrast is convinced that people on various stages of faith's journey need signs and wonders: "Even now, during this time when we must have patience and until the time when signs and wonders will be seen everywhere, until all the wretched are truly helped—in this time of battle, we need signs and wonders."[54] It is possible to argue on biblical grounds that signs and wonders may strengthen faith, but they do not demarcate the boundaries of the true church, since they are found in non-Christian religions as well.

Orthodox theologian Paul Evdokimov expresses a welcome reserve in delimiting the boundaries of the church so that the great host of humanity is summarily excluded: "We know where the Church is, but it is not for us to judge and to say where the Church is not."[55] The missionary proclamation must go out to the whole world, but we dare not presume on where or how the Spirit of God may work, nor should we deny that the hidden Christ may be at work in the most unexpected places in preparing people for the new dispensation of grace.

Christian Unity

The issue of Christian unity continues to be at the forefront in both academic theology and church life. Catholic scholars are beginning to question the traditional Catholic position that the way to unity lies through conversion to the Roman Catholic Church. They are recognizing that real unity involves the mutual conversion of the churches to Jesus Christ and his gospel.[56] Protestants for their part are acknowledging that individual conversion to Christ must be tied to integration in the life of the church. Evangelical Protestants are beginning to see that our overriding concern should be not denominational growth but a united evangelical witness before the world. Some evangelicals are coming to recognize that unity among ourselves is not enough: we must strive for evangelical-Catholic unity (including unity with the Orthodox churches). But whether this concern involves organizational unity is quite another question, and most evangelicals would disavow this as a legitimate goal.

Some who belong to the wider evangelical movement are presently engaged in dialogue with renewal-minded Roman Catholics and have published such documents as "The Gift of Salvation" (December 1997), which restates the doctrine of justification, seeming to affirm the basic vision of the Protestant Reformation.[57] These scholars have been criticized for overlooking crucial, substantial differences between the two communions, but I do not regard this criticism as entirely fair. Timothy George acknowledges that evangelicals do not have "unity of faith with the Church of Rome," but they do have a "unity in Christ" with Catholic believers.[58] The fact that evangelical and Catholic scholars could come to some kind of consensus on the doctrine of justification is encouraging, but I must caution that any enthusiasm is premature, since major differences remain between official Catholic teaching and the teaching of the Reformers on justification and many other doctrines, including papal infallibility, the immaculate conception of Mary, the assumption of Mary and eucharistic transubstantiation.

A growing number of Protestant church leaders and scholars are calling for integration with either the Church of Rome or the Eastern Orthodox Church. Richard Neuhaus, a convert from Lutheranism to Catholicism, is convinced that the rediscovery of the gospel of gratuitous justification by the Protestant Reformers can best be preserved in the Catholic Church, for the majority of Protestants, including Lutherans, have become entrapped by moralism and individualism. Lutheran pastor Jeffrey C. Silleck argues that "the churches of the reformation are not complete churches in and of themselves, but rather constitute only a confessing movement within the greater Christian family because of an emergency situation within that family."[59] For him as well as for many other high church Lutherans the gospel freedom of the Reformation lies in return to the mother church, for "Rome is theologically healthy, missiologically vital, truly catholic, truly diverse and increasingly evangelical."[60] Theologians Carl Braaten and Robert Jenson present the case for an evangelical catholicism that involves recognition of papal leadership and adoption of a liturgical rite of ordination in the apostolic succession.[61]

I propose an evangelical catholicism that seeks spiritual but not organizational unity with the Catholic churches. My mentors in this ecumenical task include Congregational theologian Peter T. Forsyth and Reformed theologian Philip Schaff.[62] Neither of these men was in favor of jettisoning the solid gains of the Protestant Reformation, including its appeal to holy Scripture over church tradition. For Schaff (d. 1893), the Reformation signifies the spiritual fulfillment of Catholicism, and any move toward Christian unity must acknowledge this momentous fact. Schaff perceived one flock but not one fold. True union is "inward and spiritual," not legal or administrative. Schaff acknowledged that the empirical church, time and again, has fallen away from the evangelical and apostolic witness of the New Testament. Yet even in its corruption the church stands as "bearer of all God's revelations, the channel of Christianity, the depository of all the life powers of the Redeemer, the habitation of the Holy Ghost."[63]

Peter T. Forsyth (d. 1921) sought to recover a high doctrine of the church for his time and yet held that the church is always under the gospel. There can be no unity at the deepest level that either willfully or unwittingly sacrifices truth for fraternity. Forsyth warned that "a Christian optimism has grown up" which dreams of "a speedy unity of the Churches without a prime regard to their belief."[64] He envisaged a church with universal claims and a global mission. "*Every soul is born for the Church. For every soul is born for society;* and it is also born for *redemption;* and therefore it is born for the *society of redemption.*"[65] According to Forsyth the unity of the church is based not on creedal formulas or sacramental rites but on Jesus Christ himself acting for our redemption in his cross and resurrection victory and ruling through the word that goes out from the mouth of his ambassadors and heralds. To find the key to Christian unity we must look to "the creative act of our moral redemption which creates our faith today and which created the Church at first; it is not in the traditional polity, creed or cultus we inherit."[66]

In our quest for Christian unity we must avoid a false romanticism that sounds the call for a return to "the great tradition" of the undivided church of the first five centuries.[67] While this church surely succeeded in preserving the truth of the original gospel, it also fell away from this truth at various points. Among these were its reduction of grace to energy infused by the Spirit and thereby open to control by the clerics of the church and its confounding of the eros of Greek philosophy with the New Testament agape. Nevertheless it was through the travails and conflicts of the patristic church that the doctrines of the two natures of Christ and the holy Trinity were articulated, which deservedly have normative status in all churches that bear the name of Christian. Today we should look not backward so much as forward—to the coming great church, a church unified in its mission to the unbelieving world and dedicated to the dawning of the social righteousness brought about by the Spirit of God in advancing the kingdom of God on earth. At the same time, in looking to the future we must constantly draw upon the wisdom of the past, yet always testing this wisdom in the light of the Word of God.

Whatever their doctrinal allegiance or ecclesiastical affiliation, all Christians should agonize over the continuing divisions that subvert Christian fellowship and undermine Christian mission. We must be willing to subject our provisional denominational loyalties to the new light that breaks forth from God's holy Word and be willing to place the cause of the kingdom above denominational expansion.

We must also be prepared to acknowledge that disunity among Christians not only undercuts our credibility in witnessing but also blurs our perception of the truth of the gospel. A cardinal reason why we as Christians still have difficulty in coming to an agreement on justification, the sacraments, the papacy, purgatory, etc. is that we live and function in separate communities of faith and therefore find it immensely difficult to identify with the concerns of others who stand in different traditions. It was Philip Schaff's genius that he transcended denominational parochialism and was thereby able to appreciate the valid contributions of a great number of Christian bodies—as disparate as the Roman Catholic Church and the Salvation Army.[68]

Neither Schaff nor Forsyth counseled church union on the basis of the least common denominator, for this would be a spurious unity indicating compromise on essentials. Compromise on Christian fundamentals is the surest way to create disunity. In seeking evangelical catholicity we must resist the allurements of a theological liberalism that is interested in forging a new faith rather than recovering the richness of the old faith. Forsyth's observation is still true: "The greatest issue for the moment is within the Christian pale; it is not between Christianity and the world. It is the issue between the theological liberalism (which is practically unitarian) and a free but positive theology, which is essentially evangelical."[69] Yet this does not mean that all those caught up in the liberal movement should be summarily excluded from the theological conversation. Nor does it deny that some of these voices are making bona fide claims, for this is precisely what makes heresy so beguiling. We can learn from those who are heterodox as well as those who are orthodox, recognizing that every heterodoxy contains a remnant of orthodoxy and every orthodoxy contains a grain of heresy. Our goal should be not to drive heretics out of the church but to forge a doctrinal consensus crossing all denominational lines and animated by faith in the living God. When the pulpits again sound the evangelical message of redemption through God's free grace revealed and conveyed through the atoning sacrifice of Christ on the cross and his glorious resurrection from the grave, the real heretics will to their dismay begin to discern a new spirit at work in the church and will then more likely than not leave the church voluntarily.

·THREE·

THE CHURCH IN THE PLAN OF SALVATION

Outside the Church no one can be saved. . . . Who is not
in this ark will perish in the flood.

VATICAN COUNCIL I

The Church is itself an integral part of the New Testament message.
The Church itself is a part of revelation—
the story of the whole Christ . . . and of the Holy Ghost.

GEORGES FLOROVSKY

The Church is not the continuation of Christ,
but His creation and His response.

PETER T. FORSYTH

The Church . . . attempts to be what in obedience to Jesus Christ
he calls her to be: the steward of his graces and
the proclaimer of his works and words.

HANS URS VON BALTHASAR

The current debate on the role of the church in the drama of salvation revolves around the question of whether the church plays a positive role in contributing to the efficacy of Christ's atoning death and resurrection. Is the church a veritable means of grace or only a testimony to grace (as in the later Barth)? Is there salvation outside the church in the hidden Christ who is presumably at work in all religions and cultures, or does Christ relate to us in a salvific way only through the ministrations of his church (the traditional Catholic view)?

Roman Catholic Theology

As Catholic tradition developed, salvation came to be seen less as a free gift of the Spirit and more as a grace created by the Spirit and infused into people of faith through the rites and sacraments of the faith community. The church became a realm of supernatural mediation, playing the pivotal role of binding and loosing through its exercise of the keys of the kingdom. Cyprian articulated what was to be normative in Catholic theology: "If someone has not the church for his mother, he has not God for his father."[1] Thus "there is no salvation outside the church."[2] This view has come under critical scrutiny in Catholic theology since the Second Vatican Council, which acknowledged that the Spirit of Christ works salvifically beyond the parameters of prescribed and officially sanctioned rites and ceremonies. Yet even in the new theology the church is envisioned as the redemptive agency of the Spirit by which seekers after truth are brought to the full realization of their salvation.[3]

The traditional view of the church was propounded by Karl Adam, who spoke of the church primarily as "an *institution for salvation*. She is not simply a community of salvation, a community, that is, which receives in faith the salvation of Christ and carries it out in herself. It is she who *gives* this salvation and makes the faithful members of Christ."[4] The church stands

> not only in a passive but also in an active relationship to Christ and the salvation He gives—always of course only as instrumental cause, as the visible earthly tool with which the Lord of Church, who won her by His Blood, pours the treasures of grace and love proceeding from the Trinity into the body of the Church.[5]

Pope John Paul II reminds us that although the church mediates

Christ's salvation, the source of this salvation is the grace of God. "People are saved *through* the Church, they are saved *in* the Church, but they always are saved *by the grace of Christ.*"[6] He reaffirms the Augustinian-Thomistic tradition that holds to the priority of grace over human striving and obedience: "All of the Church's children must remember that their privileged condition is not the result of their own merits, but the result of the special grace of Christ."[7]

In Roman Catholic theology people of faith cannot earn grace, but they can cooperate with grace and thereby contribute to grace's efficacy. In the words of Francis Fernandez, who here claims to be restating Thomas Aquinas's position: "They will be good collaborators with God's grace, for *the holy Spirit uses man as an instrument.* Then their works take on a divine effectiveness, like a tool which of itself is incapable of producing anything, but in the hands of a good craftsman can produce a masterpiece."[8]

From an evangelical perspective the problem with the Roman Catholic view even in its newer forms is that it seems to compromise the biblical doctrine of *solus Christus,* Christ alone as the Savior of the world. According to Fernandez we who are brothers of the suffering Christ can "together with him . . . save the world."[9] It also appears that in Roman Catholic theology grace is in the hands and power of the church. It is the church which through its rites and ceremonies communicates grace to its people. Thomas Torrance vigorously argues against this view on the grounds that grace "remains absolutely sovereign and transcendent in God's self-communication to us, and so retains its incomprehensibility and mystery as *grace.*"[10]

Martin Luther

Martin Luther challenged the Catholicism of his time by insisting that grace is not a fluid or power dispensed by the church but the free bestowal of the Spirit of God who nonetheless condescends to meet us wherever the Word is truly proclaimed and the sacraments rightly administered. The sacraments do not work automatically *(ex opere oper-*

ato), but they can have a powerful effect when they are united with the preaching of the Word and laid hold of by the Spirit as he communicates the meaning and impact of the Word to the hearts of believers. For Luther the Spirit freely binds himself to means of grace, particularly the preaching of the Word, to accomplish his goals in human life. The Spirit does not go before the Word but acts within the Word to seal in us the grace of regeneration: "For we must first hear the Word, and then afterwards the Holy Ghost works in our hearts; he works in the hearts of whom he will, and how he will, but never without the Word."[11]

The church is not created by individual believers but functions as the community of redemption by which people come to know about Christ and thereby receive the blessing of salvation. By directing us to Christ the church becomes a means or channel of salvation.

> He who wants to find Christ, must first find the church. How would one know Christ and faith in him if one did not know where they are who believe in him? He who would know something concerning Christ, must neither trust in himself nor build his bridge into heaven by means of his own reason, but he should go to the church; he should attend it and ask his questions there.[12]

Luther was adamant that God conveys his salvation through outward means—the word, the sacraments and the Christian life. To try to go to God directly through special illuminations and private revelations indicates an effort at self-salvation that contravenes the clear witness of holy Scripture. Luther did not deny that some Christians receive special illuminations from the Spirit of God, but he insisted that we must not put our trust in these things. He declared, "I have concluded a pact with my Lord God that He should not send me visions or dreams or even angels. For I am content with this gift which I have, holy Scripture, which abundantly teaches and supplies all things necessary both for this life and also for the life to come."[13] Luther warned against both enthusiasm on the left, which elevates religious experience over the Word, and sacerdotalism on the right, which binds the conscience to the dictates of the church. It is not we who find God either through the performance of rites and ceremonies or through mystical visions and raptures, but it is God who finds us through simple faith in the glorious redeemer, Jesus Christ, to whom we are introduced through the words of the preacher. Faith is attained not through descent into the self but rather through "hearing, learning and pondering the Gospel."[14] Faith transports us out of ourselves into the promises of Jesus Christ, which are found in holy Scripture and which never deceive.[15]

John Calvin

In common with Luther, Calvin propounded a theology of Word and Spirit in which the role of the Spirit is to illumine and bring home to us the meaning of the written Word of God. For both these scholars the content of the Bible is the living Christ who unites within himself the truth of the eternal Logos and the power and energy of the Spirit. Faith is an awakening worked within us by the Spirit to the truth enunciated and revealed in holy Scripture. It involves a conscious recognition and affirmation of Jesus Christ as Lord and Savior of the elect people of God. As Calvin phrased it, "The word is as necessary to faith, as the living root of the tree is to the fruit; because . . . none can trust in God but those who know his name."[16]

Calvin was adamant that salvation is found only in the church, the community where Christ is acknowledged and proclaimed. We are incorporated in the church through faith and baptism. Christ reaches out to us through visible signs and means, the most crucial being the preaching of the Word and the celebration of the sacraments. Yet God never imparts his power to these outward means but uses them to manifest his power. The power and efficacy of the Word and sacraments remain God's own. Moreover, while we are bound to the means of grace God himself is free to speak and move wherever he will, though when he acts it is always for the purpose of moving people toward faith in the Lord Jesus Christ.

For believers the church is necessary to introduce them to salvation and to preserve them in the faith once delivered to the saints. "Apart from the body of Christ and the fellowship of the godly, there can be no hope of reconciliation with God. Hence, in the Creed we profess to believe in 'The Catholic Church and the forgiveness of sins.'. . . Hence, also, a departure from the Church is an open renouncement of eternal salvation."[17]

The preacher himself can be considered a means of grace, since it is through his instrumentality that Christ bestows his blessings. The minister of the Word can even be said

> to save those whom he leads to the obedience of faith. So conducted indeed ought to be the ministry of our salvation, as that we may feel that the whole power and efficacy of it depends on God, and that we may give him his due praise; we ought at the same time to understand that preaching is an instrument for effecting the salvation of the faithful, and though it can do nothing without the Spirit of God, yet through his inward operation it produces the most powerful effects.[18]

Yet while Calvin staunchly affirmed the role of instruments or means of grace, he insisted that it is the Spirit alone who saves and redeems, though the Spirit acts in conjunction with and sometimes in and through outward instrumentality. He could even declare, "Our salvation is not only helped forward by God, but also . . . it is begun, continued and perfected by him, without any contribution of our own."[19] If we can be said to make a contribution, then this is solely because the Spirit has chosen us as his vessels to distribute the graces of the sacrifice and resurrection of Christ. The Spirit of God acts within us to achieve our salvation, and this grace is irresistible, meaning that all the credit or merit belongs to God.[20] Our faith and obedience are a result of God's eternal predestination, which we cannot effectively oppose, though we can willingly acclaim and celebrate.

Emil Brunner

While standing within the Reformed tradition Emil Brunner is severely critical of Calvin and Calvinism, especially of its dogma of double predestination and its implied determinism. He sees the history of the early church as a movement away from the gathered community of self-giving love to a hierarchical, sacerdotal community in which the grace of God is controlled by a spiritual elite.[21] Fellowship was replaced by institution and faith by creed and moral code. The *ecclesia,* a creation of the free movement of the Spirit, is both obscured and preserved by the dogmas and rites of the institutional church. Although recognizing the critical role of sacraments in the life of the church, Brunner is insistent that the sacraments do not produce community but are given to the community through the "Word and Spirit of Jesus Christ, which we receive in faith."[22]

In a marked departure from the Reformation, Brunner tends to separate the free movement of the Spirit from the preaching and reading of the Word. He contends that the Holy Spirit can operate "without the Word, by the dynamic energy which is proper to it. The propagation of Christianity takes place to a large extent more unconsciously than consciously, more involuntarily than voluntarily, and therefore silently rather than by speech."[23]

Brunner is not always clear regarding the precise relation of the Word and sacraments. It seems that for him the gift of the Holy Spirit is offered through the preaching of the Word but is more fully realized in sacramental celebration. "One can listen to the announcement of the divine Word without belonging to the community, without identifying oneself with it, abiding in it, and taking part in its life. The so-called sacraments are the *verbum communale,* the form of the Word through which the individual is really incorporated and made one with the community."[24] This is why he can declare that baptism is "not in the first instance a cognitive but a causative act," for in baptism we receive the gift of the Holy Spirit.[25] The sacraments are clearly subordinate to the treasure of the gospel, which the church is assigned to make known and proclaim, but they are necessary for the preservation of the church as a community. He can describe them as "the divinely given flying buttresses which save the Church from collapse."[26]

Brunner is very supportive of fellowships of renewal that often arise out of the church, sometimes in defiance of the church. These para-parochial fellowships can be regarded as new manifestations of the *ecclesia*, which is often stifled and impeded by outmoded institutional structures. He goes so far as to entertain the possibility that "it might be the will of God eventually to destroy the ancient churchly frame-work of the *Ecclesia* or at least—as is now already happening—to com-plete it by structures of a very different order."[27] Brunner confesses his admiration for the Oxford Group movement (later known as Moral Re-Armament) as a community of spiritual renewal that has brought new life and power to people of various faith backgrounds.[28]

> Ever and again in conferences and international gatherings one finds that people who at first knew nothing of Jesus Christ and experienced as Buddhists, Muslims or atheists the transformation of their lives, step by step in fellowship with these Christian friends of theirs learn to know Christ, read the Bible and begin to live in prayer, without thereby losing contact with their own religious national community. What is public in the Church, the proclamation of Christ, is here not public, is, so to speak, merely whispered in the ear; what here on the other hand is public, is what is never or seldom spoken of aloud in the Church, the changing of one's own life.[29]

It seems that for Brunner while the preaching of the Word and cele-bration of the sacraments are central in ecclesiology, they are not absolutely indispensable for the experience of new life in Christ, which can be communicated by the Spirit through new forms and structures that often speak to a new situation in the church and the culture. What is not expendable is the living Christ himself and the Spirit that goes out from him, and though traditional forms and structures may well be with us for some time, new wineskins are being created which will more readily carry the new wine of the gospel to an unbelieving world (cf. Mt 9:17; Lk 5:37-39).

Karl Barth

In his earlier writings, including the first volumes of the *Church Dog-matics*, Barth still held to a sacramental view of the church and the ordinances of baptism and the Lord's Supper. As he progressed in this monumental undertaking, however, Barth began to shift, emphasizing the ethical rather than the soteriological role of the church and sacraments. Jesus Christ himself became the only sacrament—the visible sign of invisible grace, and the church and ordinances became testimonies of grace rather than means of grace. Barth was quite firm that Jesus Christ alone is the mediator of salvation, and we are witnesses to this fact rather than co-mediators with Christ.

> The Church is neither author, dispenser, nor mediator of grace and its revelation. It is the subject neither of the work of salvation nor the Word of salvation. It cannot act as such. It cannot strut about as such, as though this were its calling. Its work and action in all forms, even in the best possibilities, stands or falls with the self-attestation and self-impartation of Jesus Christ Himself, in which it can only participate as assistant and minister.[30]

For Barth there can be a correspondence but not a coalescence between divine and human action.[31] The Bible is an echo and mirror of the Word of God but not a conduit of the Word. The church is a sign and witness of the truth of the gospel but not the embodiment of this truth. Nor is it an extension or continuation of Christ's incarnation but the fruit and consequence of the incarnation. The eucharist is not a duplication or repetition of the sacrifice on Calvary but a commemoration and proclamation of this sacrifice. Barth also had reservations on the theology of the imitation of Christ:

> I do not like this word "repetition." This is a term that is too coloured by its use in Roman Catholicism; they also think of an ethic of following in footsteps, repeating acts of Christ. But this is not the meaning of Paul. As disciples we are called to witness; we cannot do the same acts as Christ.[32]

Even so, Barth never broke completely with his earlier sacramental view, for he continued to hold that the sacramental sign in the ordinances of baptism and the Lord's Supper gives certainty of grace. It is not a cause of faith but a confirmation of faith. We do not need any "repetition or realisation of our redemption" for "Christ has achieved all of this perfectly once-for-all!"[33] A sacramental thrust can be discovered in his earlier *Göttingen Dogmatics*:

> The sign is no mere symbol of a presence of grace available always and everywhere. This sign is not exchangeable for another. The sign remains sign, but by the power of the Spirit it truly and effectively attests the grace of God in Christ, really confirms his presence to us.[34]

Barth was insistent that while personal faith is necessary in the plan of redemption it follows this redemption rather than realizes it. Both the act of faith and the observances of baptism and the Lord's Supper belong to the human response to God's gift of salvation in Jesus Christ rather than make this gift actual or effectual. Faith is not the cause of salvation but the sign that salvation has been fully accomplished and enacted in Jesus Christ.

Barth nonetheless made a prominent place for human response and obedience but not as causal elements in our salvation. We are not co-redeemers alongside of Christ but covenant partners with Christ in making his salvation known to the world. We are not dispensers of grace but ambassadors and heralds of grace as we seek to live out a life of costly discipleship under the cross. Yet there are passages in Barth in which he seemed to acknowledge that Christians can indeed play a positive role in bringing people into the kingdom through the word of their testimony.[35] We ourselves cannot save, but we can point others to the One who alone does redeem from sin, death and hell. Our witness can have soteriological significance when it comes alive through the power of the Spirit.

One common criticism of Barth is that he tended to sever the gift of grace from the sacramental acts that commemorate this grace. Dawn DeVries charges that "Barth's rhetoric" unlike that of Calvin "seems to suggest that God's appearance in the Word is an unpredictable, extrinsic occurrence. As does Zwingli, Barth argues that God is absolutely free, not committed in any respect to use instruments for communicating grace."[36] This may be somewhat of an overstatement, since

Barth attributed the inward certainty of our salvation that is imparted through sacramental observance to the work of the Holy Spirit within us. He also continued to perceive the preaching of the Word as an effective means of reaching the world of unbelief for the gospel, though this efficacy does not reside in the words that we employ but in the Spirit who speaks and acts in conjunction with our speaking. He could even make the surprising statement that "in the delivering of the Christian message it is also a matter of saving souls, of inviting and helping men to personal being, possession and capacity in the king-dom of grace and salvation, and therefore to participation in the supreme good and all the other goods which it includes."[37] Through our preaching and witness we can lead others into an experience of salvation, but it is Jesus Christ alone who procures salvation as an objective act that determines and shapes our lives. Personal conver-sion *(Bekehrung)* is a fruit and evidence of the conversion of the world to Christ *(Umkehr),* which occurred in his cross and resurrection vic-tory.

Thomas F. Torrance

Whereas Barth was prone to separate Spirit baptism and water bap-tism, Torrance stresses their inseparability, and this is also true of how he conceives of the church and the Lord's Supper. Yet he is profoundly convinced that the invisible reality of the living Word of God cannot be reduced to the visible reality of the church and the sacraments. Divine revelation must never be confused with the subjective consciousness of the church, nor should the Spirit ever be thought of as the immanent mind and soul of the empirical church. Torrance argues that "there is *one baptism* and *one Body* through the *one Spirit.* Christ and his Church participate in the one baptism in different ways—Christ actively and vicariously as Redeemer, the Church passively and receptively as the redeemed Community."[38] The sacraments do not as such contain or confer grace, but they are employed by the Spirit to direct us to the liv-ing Christ, the fount and source of all grace. Grace is not a created power that can be controlled and dispensed by the clerics of the church, but it is the living Christ himself reaching out to us through sacramental acts of celebration and adoration. Torrance disputes the Augustinian-Thomistic conception of supernatural grace and the church as "a realm of supernatural mediation between God and man, heaven and earth, eternity and time."[39] He complains that

> this supernatural grace was thought of as bestowed by God through the merits of Christ, on the ground of what he had done on our behalf, but it was not thought of as the direct self-communicating of God in his own life and reality through the Incarnate Son and in the Holy Spirit, so much as the communication of healing power which indirectly makes us participate in God. This is brought about by God's omnipotent causality in effecting finite mediations as a counter-part to supernatural grace through which it can take root in us and save us. Here, however, grace is not only distinguished from Christ but is an intermediary reality between God and man which holds God himself apart from us in his eternal immutability and impassibility while giving us a measure of indirect participation in the divine.[40]

Torrance upholds what he calls an interactionist-unitary view of reality as opposed to a dualistic view that separates the spiritual and the material, the eternal and the temporal. When God interacts with us he gives himself to us in such a way that we share in his own "inner life and light and love."[41] Yet "his activity never falls within our dividing or compounding or within our control in any way, for it rests wholly upon the free ground of God's self-existing and self-affirming being as Father, Son and Holy Spirit."[42]

Torrance is sharply critical of Karl Barth's return "to a sacramental dualism between water-baptism and Spirit-baptism, in which the meaning of baptism is found not in a direct act of God but in an ethical act on the part of man made by way of response to what God has already done on his behalf."[43] Torrance postulates "an even stronger unity between water-baptism and Spirit-baptism objectively determined by the saving act of God in the incarnate Son and by his direct act now through the Spirit."[44]

In his theology the divine reality is not wholly extrinsic to the creaturely structures that bring us into contact with this reality. The creaturely structures are made to participate in this reality through the action of the Spirit of God. "A true sign . . . has in it something of that which it signifies; it is analogous to the thing signified, and corresponds appropriately to its nature. In the ordinance of Christ, through His command and promise, the outward sign and the inward reality belong together as form and content of the sacramental communion."[45]

Torrance can be appreciated for firmly maintaining that it is not the ritual act itself that mediates grace, but through partaking in the ritual we are directed to the ontological ground of the ritual and of all creative life in the church—God's self-sacrifice for humanity in Jesus Christ. Yet when he contends that it is the sacrament of holy baptism that engrafts us into the body of Christ it seems that he lapses into a sacramental objectivism. The fuller Reformed view is that baptism functions in this way only when united with personal faith in the Lord Jesus Christ. Is not the decision of faith in the power of the Spirit as critical for our salvation as God's electing grace in Jesus Christ? Is not baptism of the Spirit a different action from water or sacramental baptism, even though the two are indissolubly related in the process of regeneration and redemption by which we are remolded in the image of Christ?

The Redemptive Community
The church can be thought of as a redemptive community but not in the sense of being in itself a redeeming force in the world. It is the community of the redeemed but not the source of redemption. It plays an important role in directing sinners to Christ, but its ministrations and rituals do not effect redemption. The church's actions take on redemptive significance because they are used by the Spirit to heal and transform lives. Yet the Spirit acts in his own way and time, sometimes not in and through but over and against the words and rites of the church.

In contrast to the traditional Roman Catholic view, I hold that the church is not a co-mediator with Christ but instead a receiver and reflector of his saving grace. To be sure, Catholic theologians point out that as people of faith we mediate *in* Christ, not *alongside* Christ. Yet they can also speak of Christ completing his atoning work in and through his members. In the Reformed view that I am enunciating Christ's atoning suffering is complete (Heb 9:25-28; 10:11-14), but the effects of his saving work are communicated to the world through his ambassadors and heralds. The church does not secure redemption, but by the power of the Spirit it communicates the fruits of redemption. The church does not itself absolve from sin, but it grants the assurance of God's forgiveness. In this understanding the church is a derivative light, not the source of light. It is the reflector of light, not the generator of light.

The church does not dispense grace but proclaims grace. In this role it may on occasion become the means through which people come to experience God's grace. It is certainly fallacious to argue that the church makes reparation for sin. The church cannot of itself bind and loose, but it can be the mouthpiece of Christ, who alone binds and looses. The church does not procure redemption, nor does it simply point to a redemption in the past. It is also misleading to speak of the church as re-presenting Christ's sacrifice in the Mass. What the church does is communicate the salvific effects of this sacrifice to its own people and to the world.

In this discussion it is important to make the distinction between the objective redemption accomplished by Christ on the cross and the subjective redemption accomplished by his Spirit working within us. The church does not have a creative role in procuring objective redemption. Instead, it is the receiver and beneficiary of this redemption. At the same time, the church does have a modest role in subjective redemption, not through its own resources and powers but through the condescension of the Holy Spirit who acts and speaks through his appointed representatives, yet always at his own discretion.

The Reformers were surely right in their protest against the notion that the church possesses a treasury of merits which it can transfer to us through works of penance that it prescribes. It has no treasury of merits on which to draw, but it can direct people to the merits of Jesus Christ, which alone can redeem from sin.

A careful observer will detect that my view on this question is close to that of Barth. Like him I do not believe that we are called to complete or add onto the salvific work of Christ on the cross. Our mission is to herald the good news of what God has done for us in Christ rather than to be co-redeemers with Christ in establishing his kingdom on earth. Yet in proclaiming the good news do not we become instruments of the Spirit of God, who seals the power of the gospel in our hearts through faith and repentance? We cannot be efficient causes of grace, but can we not be instrumental causes when we are acted upon by the Spirit in carrying forward the plan of salvation in history?

For Barth the human decision follows and corresponds to the divine act in Jesus Christ, manifested in the lives of his people by the Holy Spirit. Yet Barth is reluctant to speak of this human decision as the instrumentality by which salvific change is effected. For Barth baptism acknowledges and proclaims the crisis of salvation, but it does not bring it about. In his theology human action cannot duplicate or join with divine action, but it can correspond to divine action. In my view, which is here in accord with Calvin and Luther, divine action can employ human action as an instrument or medium. Christ alone saves those who are lost, but he may use us as his agents in bringing the benefits of his salvation to a despairing world. Christ alone saves from sin, death and hell, but we can be instruments in the Spirit's distribution of graces by directing people to Christ's salvation. Our mission is to "rescue the perishing" and "care for the dying" by presenting the claims of Christ to a suffering humanity.[46]

I see the church as having two sides—the divine and the human. It is both a sign and witness of grace and an agent in the Spirit's application of grace. It is both a gathered fellowship of believers and the mystical body of Christ. The sacraments are both a commemoration and celebration of grace and a means of grace. Christians are both heralds of the gospel and representatives of Christ to their neighbors. They are both ambassadors of righteousness and winners of souls. They are both servants of the Word and channels of the Word.

In a past controversy in the church I am closer to the Reformed than to the Lutheran view in affirming that the finite is not capable of the infinite *(finitum non capax infiniti)*. That is to say the finite in and of itself is not capable of apprehending or receiving or bearing the infinite. Yet the infinite is capable of the finite.[47] The almighty God is capable of reaching out through human means to touch his people and advance his kingdom. Because Christians can, through the power of grace, not only herald God's grace but also bear his grace and love, Luther was not wrong in describing Christians as "little Christs," though this must not be taken to mean that we are in any way extensions of Christ. With my Reformed forbears I contend that the relative cannot contain the absolute, but the absolute can enter into the relative so that people can really know and truly believe.

Catholic theology often leaves the impression that God is dependent on human means and channels in order to realize his purposes in the world. We see this elevation of the creaturely in these words of a mystical writer:

> Christ has no body now on earth but yours. No hands but yours. No feet but yours. Yours are the eyes through which his compassion must look out on the world. Yours are the feet with which he must go about doing good. Yours are the hands through which he must bless the world now.[48]

While this statement reflects the biblical truth that God uses human instrumentality, it obscures the complementary truth that God does not need human instrumentality. He can raise up sons of Abraham out of stones (Lk 3:8). Out of his generous love he allows us to have a role in fulfilling his mission on earth, but he does not really need us even in this respect. He calls us to be coworkers in carrying forward the drama of salvation in history, but we are always receivers of God's grace, never authors or creators of grace.

We are signs and witnesses, not causal agents in the sense of being collaborators with God in ushering in his kingdom of promise.[49] Our efforts do have abiding value when they are united with his work in extending the kingdom through Christian mission. We do not of ourselves contribute to the building of the kingdom, but we can hasten its coming by our prayers (2 Pet 3:12). We can proclaim that the kingdom of God is at hand and admonish both church and world to prepare themselves for this glorious and awesome event or series of events that constitutes the inbreaking of the eschatological reality of a new age.

We can take up the cross and follow Christ through the power of grace. We can share the fruits of Christ's cross and resurrection victory with others as we are led by the Spirit. Human effort follows divine grace and is sustained and perfected by this grace. Grace does not allow us to remain passive but makes us active in bearing witness to our faith through our words and our life. In this way we become means of grace to a graceless and ungodly world whose hope of salvation lies outside itself in the risen and ascended Christ.

What I am upholding is a monergy that embraces synergy. God's grace brings about the desired effect—faith and obedience, but it does this by animating and motivating the human subject to believe and obey. Synergism as such means that we contribute to our salvation through our own power, that God does some and we do some. We need to avoid both monergism and synergism by maintaining that God does all—but in and through human action. We believe and overcome through the power of grace, not through our own power—even in part. Some Catholic and Orthodox theologians would be open to this way of stating what is fundamentally a paradox to human understanding.[50]

The Church's Mandate

The mandate of the church includes the worship of God in the power of his grace. The church is not only a product of grace but also a celebrant of grace. Christians are summoned to works of piety—prayer, devotion, fasting, tithing, etc. There are duties that we owe to God alone, and there is a love that is to be given only to God—the adoring love, which is love united with faith.

In addition to being a worshiping community the church should also be a nurturing community. It not only offers up sacrifices of praise and thanksgiving to God but also trains and instructs the people of God to walk in his paths. The church is a teacher as well as a mother. It not only transmits the truth of faith to its people but also interprets this truth so that they can be disciples and ambassadors of the living Christ.

This brings us to the mandate of evangelism. The church is given the charge to be a witness and herald of God's grace. The people of God are called to utter the words of God and thereby communicate the salvific plan of God. Christians are agents of the Spirit in the fulfillment of the Great Commission to go into the whole world and make disciples of all nations (Mt 28:19-20; Mk 16:15; Lk 24:44-53; Acts 1:8).

Besides being a witness to what God has done for us in Christ, the church is also a channel of grace. Here we are confronted with its sacramental side. The church is an outward sign that conveys invisible grace—not through its own power but through the power of the Spirit who acts upon and within the church's preaching and celebration. The church not only points to a salvation beyond itself, but also communicates the fruits of this salvation, which include the forgiveness of sins and the new life in Christ. Our task as Christians is to make all people see "what is the plan of the mystery hidden for ages in God who created all things; that through the church the manifold wisdom of God might now be made known to the principalities and powers in the heavenly places" (Eph 3:9-10).

Again, the church will be a reflector of grace through the practice of Christian love. It is not only a sacramental institution but also a fellowship of love (koinonia), which ministers to the hurts of its people. It not only extends a helping hand to the person in need but embraces this person with a compassion the world does not know (cf. Lk 15:22-24).

As a fellowship of love the church is a bearer of grace and a vessel of grace. A church bereft of the fellowship of love is less than the church of the living God.

Finally, the church will be a servant of grace. It will be involved in works of mercy and works of justice. It not only builds up the saints but ministers to sinners outside its domain. The true church will be dedicated to both the worship of God and service to the world. It will manifest both adoring love to God and serving love to the neighbor in need.

The church is basically a life support system not only enabling its members to survive in a cruel and hostile world but also empowering them to prevail over the principalities and powers of the world. The foremost duty of the church is to glorify God through worship, service and proclamation. Forsyth says it well: "The prime duty of the Church is not to impress, or even to save, men, but to confess the Saviour, to confess in various forms the God, the Christ, the Cross that does save."[51] As we confess Christ as our Liberator, so we are liberated through the power of his Spirit.

The church has a spiritual mission with far-reaching political and cultural implications. Its principal concern is to bring people into a right relationship with God through the power of the Word and Spirit, but it will also be involved in teaching people to be agents of justice and righteousness in a basically unjust society. Its spiritual mission takes precedence over its cultural mandate, since being in Christ has priority over acting in Christ. Social reform that goes deeper than altering power structures in society has its roots in a transformation of consciousness that only the Word and Spirit bring about. The pathway to social reformation leads through personal transformation that is effected by the Spirit through the preaching of the gospel and the fellowship and prayers of the saints.

Mary: A Type of the Church

In catholic tradition Mary, the mother of Christ, is commonly regarded as a type or figure of the church, since she received the blessings of

God through her faith and obedience. The church is not the source of salvation but the receiver and proclaimer of salvation. So it is with Mary. She was the redeemed but not the redeemer. She was blessed because she believed, but she could not have believed unless she had been chosen for this momentous role of being the mother of God. Elizabeth exclaimed, "Blessed is she who has believed that what the Lord has said to her will be accomplished!" (Lk 1:45 NIV). Her belief did not cause the promise to be fulfilled, but it was the Spirit who fulfilled the promise by granting her faith, enabling her to conceive and give birth to the Messiah.

It is important to bear in mind that Mary was chosen before her response. Mary was not the arm of God's grace but the object of his grace. She was not only chosen to be the mother of Christ, but she was also given to John to be the mother of the church (Jn 19:26-27). Moreover, she was in the upper room when the Holy Spirit descended upon the apostles (Acts 1:14). With the others she was empowered to be a herald of God's grace to the world.

Ever since medieval times Mary has been acclaimed in the Roman church as the mediatrix and dispensatrix of all graces.[52] She has often been likened to the neck and Christ to the head, the inference being that we cannot reach the head except through the neck.[53] Mary thus becomes a co-redeemer with Christ. The Reformation protested against elevating Mary to a mediator alongside of Christ and proclaimed that our salvation is a work of Christ alone (solus Christus). Mary was seen as a sign and witness of grace, never as the source or fountain of grace. Yet various Reformers, including Luther, were remarkably open to the idea of Mary's spiritual motherhood. If Mary is chosen to be the mother of Christ, she becomes in a sense the mother of all those who are united to Christ by faith. Just as the role of the church is to receive, celebrate and proclaim, so Mary's role was likewise to receive and exult in Christ the Savior (Lk 1:48). Luther could declare, "Thus, Mary is the mother of Jesus, and the mother of us all. If Christ is ours, we must be where he is; and where he is we must be also, and all that he has must be ours, and his mother therefore also is ours."[54]

Max Thurian, who was for a time the theologian of the Taizé community,[55] makes a convincing case on the basis of biblical exegesis and exposition that Mary's role as our spiritual mother was already realized at the wedding feast at Cana where "Mary passes from the function of Mother of God to that of the type of the Church, from the human and spiritual role of the Mother of the Messiah, to the purely spiritual role of the believing woman in the Church. The Mother of God becomes the Believing Woman."[56] Then at the cross "in the very moment when Jesus, the new Moses, is going to die He commits Mary to John, that is to say he commits the Church to the faithful Apostle, as Moses had committed the people to Joshua in order that he might lead them into the Promised Land."[57]

In the fuller biblical vision the Holy Spirit is the mother of the church, for it was through the outpouring of the Spirit at Pentecost that the church was born. Also it is the Spirit who nurtures and consoles the faithful and who keeps us on the right paths. We are adopted into the family of God through faith, and faith is a gift of the Spirit. At the same time, the Spirit works through visible means and signs—preaching, prayer, acts of compassion, teaching—and Mary with all the saints of God presumably engages in these activities.

Yet it is dangerously misleading to argue, as do traditionalist Catholic theologians, that Mary or any of the saints are co-redeemers or co-mediators with Jesus. We do not "co-redeem with him," as Francis Fernandez alleges,[58] but we go before him as his messengers and follow him as his disciples. Like Mary we are servants of grace but not sources of grace. Mary was blessed because she believed, but her faith was a gift of God, not a meritorious work. Paul reminds us that we are saved only *by* grace but we are saved *through* faith (Eph 2:8). Faith is the medium of grace, the sign that grace is already at work, but it is not the condition for receiving grace. When grace falls on us we will then invariably believe. We do not contribute to our justification, but we bear witness to our justification and redemption by our faith and obedience. Before Mary believed she was already chosen for her special mission. She found favor with God (Lk 1:30) not because she was already holy but because she had been elected by God for a holy purpose. Mary simply acknowledged what had been foreordained to take place. She was a willing instrument in the hands of God, and she is therefore a model of faith.

It is well to note that the Reformers did not jettison all Marian doctrine, but they wished to give all the glory and credit for our salvation to Christ alone. They continued to affirm Mary's perpetual virginity, and Luther and Zwingli could still refer to Mary as mother of God. Luther was amazingly insistent on Mary's complete purity and contended that the first instant she began to live she was "without sin, adorned with the gifts of God."[59] The Swiss canton of Zurich, the home base of Zwingli, continued to celebrate the feast of the Assumption of Mary, and Bullinger, Zwingli's successor, held that Mary was taken up bodily into heaven.[60]

As evangelical Christians we are not obliged to accept any of these Marian doctrines unless we are firmly persuaded by the testimony of holy Scripture. Yet we should extol Mary as a model of faith, for Scripture clearly speaks of her in this way. We can also regard Mary as a mother in the church, since she is an example of faith for all believers. What saves is not her assent to God's grace but the evangelical proclamation that grace is poured out on all who believe. Because Mary served this proclamation in a special way she can be honored by the church.

There can be a place for Mariology in the theology of the church but not an independent Mariology.[61] Mariology should be subsumed under Christology, ecclesiology or hagiology, the doctrine of the saints. Mary is a model of holiness as well as of faith, but she was not sinless, for Scripture tells us that all mortals have sinned and fallen short of the glory of God (Rom 3:23). Mary needs to be redeemed as do all the saints of the church, and this is why she could hail the Messiah as "God my Savior" (Lk 1:47). The Catholic Church has in some instances allowed Mary to overshadow Christ in the plan of salvation, and this is especially true in much popular devotion. The Protestant descendents of the Reformation have virtually dismissed Mary as an active participant in the drama of salvation. An evangelical catholicity will acclaim Mary not as co-redemptrix and mediatrix of all graces but as mother of God and a mother in the faith through her witness and intercession for the church.

Though Mary's unique role in the communion of saints is often bypassed in Protestant liturgy and theology, it is sometimes recognized in the hymns of the church. For example, "Ye Watchers and Ye Holy Ones" by John Riley contains these words:

> O higher than the cherubim,
> > More glorious than the seraphim,
> > > Lead their praises, Alleluia!

> Thou bearer of the eternal Word,
> > Most gracious, magnify the Lord,
> > > Alleluia, Alleluia.[62]

The third and fourth verses contain invocations to the whole company of the departed saints.

Mary is to be honored not as an intermediary between Christ and his church but as the preeminent member of his church—his mother and our mother by faith. We do not need to go through her to reach Christ, but we have access to her and all the saints because we are mystically united with them through his Spirit. It is not theologically wise to invoke the saints in order to get the attention of God, but we can be buoyed up in the confidence that they are praying for us and for the advancement of the kingdom on earth.[63]

·FOUR·

THE CHURCH
AND THE
KINGDOM

Many whom God has, the church does not have;
and many whom the church has, God does not have.

AUGUSTINE

God's Kingdom is beyond the limitations of each
historical realization of Christian community.

WOLFHART PANNENBERG

History is no mere preparation for the Kingdom,
it is the Kingdom in the making.

PETER T. FORSYTH

The kingdom is not merely individual, but cosmic. . . .
Like a dragnet, it sweeps the nations in.

MICHAEL HORTON

The relation between the church and the kingdom has long occupied the attention of leading theologians in all denominations. Some have described the church as a sign of the kingdom, others as a means to the kingdom. Still others portray the church as the outward form of the kingdom, the herald of the kingdom, or an echo or mirror of the kingdom. Then there are those who create a hiatus between church and kingdom, viewing the latter as wholly future. One should keep in mind that these views are not necessarily mutually exclusive and that all may have some biblical support depending on how the church and the kingdom are defined.

It is my thesis that the church and the kingdom are inseparable, yet not identical. The kingdom inheres in the church but at the same time transcends the church. Pannenberg gives a timely warning that "the provisional character of every realization of Christian life at present easily escapes from Christian thought, when the fundamental difference between church and Kingdom is forgotten."[1] In Moltmann's view "the church in the power of the Spirit is not yet the kingdom of God, but it is its anticipation in history."[2] He sees the church as the vanguard of the kingdom but not as the exclusive agent of the kingdom.

In the traditions of mysticism and Pietism the temptation is to separate the transcendent reality of the kingdom from the outward forms and rituals that define the church. These movements are right in their aversion to reducing the kingdom to forms and rituals, but we need to remember that the kingdom is mediated to us through material means. Christoph Blumhardt is among those who are intent on maintaining the spiritual character of the kingdom while still strongly holding to its worldly relevance. For Blumhardt it is a disaster without equal if church forms are mistaken for the kingdom of God, if we focus our energies on buildings, altars and rituals, on creedal formulations, as if these outward things of earthly origin were the kingdom of God.[3]

Two Sides of the Church

In Christian tradition the distinction is frequently made between the visible and invisible church. The first is empirical and tangible, the second spiritual and transcendent. The essence as well as the goal of the visible church is the invisible church. At the same time, the latter comes to us only in the form of a visible community of believers. We have the spiritual only in the material, the eternal only in the temporal. Otherwise the invisible church becomes a Platonic ideal that towers above and exists independently of the earthly and the material. It may be more theologically appropriate to speak of the invisible church as the hidden church and the visible church as the manifest church.

Augustine often spoke as if the holy catholic church were a visible, historical institution. The kingdom of God or the invisible church is the city of God expanding its territory in the world through the power of the Word and Spirit. He declared, "The Church now on earth is both the kingdom of Christ, and the kingdom of heaven."[4] Yet he also maintained that the true church will encompass the elect of all ages. Even some of those who are outside the boundaries of the empirical church will be included in the kingdom of God, whereas some who are officially members of the church will be excluded if they lack true faith. Augustine acknowledged that there are wolves within the church and sheep without. He also distinguished between the church of faith and the church of sight, that of pilgrims who are exposed to danger and temptation and that of victorious saints who will reign with Christ in heaven.

Augustine's legacy is reflected in the theology of the Protestant Reformers, though they were adamant that when the Word of God is not proclaimed and faith is lacking the church is not present but only an empty shell. John Calvin envisioned a holy community where church and state would work together in maintaining a righteous social order, but this was not yet the kingdom of God, which will be inaugurated at the second coming of Christ. Luther held that God is Lord of all nations but not God of all nations.[5] Outside the church and the sacraments there is no sanctification.[6] If we are not in the kingdom of Christ we are then in the kingdom of Satan.

The distinction between the visible and invisible churches was underscored by Friedrich Schleiermacher who held that the first is "a divided church" while the second is "an undivided unity."[7] The first moreover is "always subject to error," while the second is "infallible."[8] In his theology "all errors that are generated in the Visible Church come to be removed by the truth which never ceases to work in it."[9] The kingdom is portrayed as wider and deeper than the invisible church and is virtually identified with the forward march of civilization.[10]

While Schleiermacher perceived an antithesis between the visible and invisible churches, Dietrich Bonhoeffer underlined their unity:

> Since the ascension, Christ's place on earth has been taken by his Body, the Church. The Church is the real presence of Christ. Once we have realized this truth we are well on the way to recovering an aspect of the Church's being which has been sadly neglected in the past. We should think of the Church not as an institution, but as a *person,* though of course a person in a unique sense.[11]

Yet Bonhoeffer was insistent that there is no "mystical fusion between Christ and his Church."[12] Instead "the Body of Christ has penetrated into the heart of the world in the form of the Church."[13] At the same time Christ remains Lord over his people. The living Word of God is not a creation of the church but instead the creator and ruler of the church. The church is the form of the body of Christ. It is in the church that we come to know Christ, and it is through the church that we are united to Christ in faith. "To be in Christ . . . means to be in the Church. But if we are in the Church we are verily and bodily in Christ."[14]

In Paul Tillich we see a vigorous attempt to distinguish the "Spiritual Community," the presence of Spirit in universal history, from the empirical church.[15] The invisible church is the spiritual essence of the visible church; it is not a reality beside the visible churches. The empirical church is the church in its manifestation in history. The invisible church is the church in its latency, which includes the whole human race as it exists in its openness to God, the infinite ground and source of its being. The empirical or visible churches participate in both the ambiguities of life in history and in the unambiguous life of the Spiritual Community, the power of the new being that is epitomized in Jesus Christ.

Karl Barth was intent on keeping the lines between the church and the kingdom intact. The church is not itself the kingdom of Christ, but it is included in the kingdom of Christ, which basically means the reign of Christ over humankind, both in its faith and its faithlessness. The mission of the church is to herald the coming of the kingdom, not to actualize this coming through its rites and ceremonies. It is God who actualizes his kingdom, and he does this through the gift of the Holy Spirit.[16] Because God's election reaches out to all and the atoning suffering of Christ is intended for all, all people are virtual members of the church. We become actual members of the church, however, only by the grace of adoption, which imparts to us faith in the living Christ. Markus Barth makes the daring claim that the church "includes . . . virtually all who are still unbelievers."[17]

I have already dealt with Emil Brunner's polarity of *ecclesia* and church, in which the latter is seen as a distortion and ossification of the power of Christian fellowship evident in the New Testament communities of faith.[18] Brunner expresses a growing consensus in modern theology: "The Church of faith extends far beyond the Church as a worshipping community; there are true members of the Church of faith who belong to no worshipping congregation, just as there are many members of the worshipping community who do not belong to the true Church."[19]

In Eastern Orthodoxy the overwhelming tendency is to equate a particular historical institution (the Orthodox church) with the kingdom of Christ or the mystical body of Christ. The church is not so much the human response to divine revelation as part of the content of this revelation (Georges Florovsky). Vladimir Lossky makes the audacious claim that "the Church is our nature recapitulated by Christ and contained within His hypostasis. It is a theandric organism, both divine and human."[20] According to Archimandrite Vasileios "the Church is God's Christ Himself, the Kingdom of God which 'is within us' (Lk 17:21). It is heaven on earth."[21] And in the words of Vladimir Rodzianko, "We, the Orthodox, do not distinguish the church and the kingdom. . . . The Kingdom and the Church and the body of Christ are one and the same thing."[22]

This triumphalist note is also apparent in Roman Catholic theology, though the Second Vatican Council was emphatic that the body of Christ is wider and deeper than any historical institution. Pope Pius XII on the other hand contended that the mystical body of Christ and the Catholic Church are "one and the same."[23] In his 1950 encyclical *Humani Generis* he unwittingly limited the body of Christ to Latin-rite, or Roman, Catholics.[24] When contemporary Catholic theologians like Karl Rahner and Hans Küng acknowledge that the empirical church is a church of sinners, they are clearly implying that the body of Christ and the Roman church are not the very same reality.

Representative of contemporary Reformed theology at its best is Thomas F. Torrance who, while holding to a high view of the church, nevertheless warns against the danger of self-deification.

> It must not be forgotten that the sole Object of dogmatic statements is the Datum of divine Revelation which does not cease to be God's own Being and Act in His Self-giving, and therefore is not something that passes over into the inner spiritual states of the Church's experience or into its historical consciousness and subjectivity. Dogmatic statements are not constructs out of the Church's acts of consciousness nor can they be reached by reading them off the subjective structures of the mind of the Church, for that would imply that the Truth of God is identical with the collective subjectivity of the Church or that the Holy Spirit is the immanent soul and mind of the historical Church impregnating it with the Truth of God. That would imply the identity of dogmas with Dogma, and a view of the Truth in which its essence is determined by its existence in the historical Church, as if the truth of a thing is not that it is what it is in God but only what it becomes in temporal tradition; but behind all this would lie a self-deification of the Church and an identification of its own evolving life with the Life of God.[25]

In Torrance's view Christ remains forever distinct from his church, but we are mystically united with Christ by faith, a gift of the Holy Spirit. Christ is supreme over the church, and yet by his Spirit makes himself available for the church. We are justified by his righteousness alone, yet we are engrafted into this righteousness by faith. Christ meets us in his Word and in the sacraments, but this is always his free decision and not a necessary outcome of ritual performance. Through the ministrations of the church we participate in the body of Christ, but this participation is always contingent on the free movement of the Spirit to help and to heal.

In this whole discussion it is important to bear in mind that a truly biblical ecclesiology will be one of the center rather than one of below or above. An ecclesiology from below begins with the church as an earthly institution and then tries to relate this to the mystical body of Christ. An ecclesiology from above begins with the mystical body of Christ and then tries to relate this to visible social forms and structures. The ecclesiology I espouse begins with the paradox of the church as a divine-human community in which the divinity is hidden in the humanity. Our point of departure is neither the heavenly nor the earthly but the heavenly in the earthly, the infinite in the finite. The church is the earthen vessel that receives the heavenly reality and carries it through the power of this reality. The church is essentially neither a sociological institution nor a divine organism but a divine-human fellowship animated by faith and love and sustained by hope. It is a paradoxical event with two sides—the human and the divine. These sides are never to be identified but always held together in creative tension. In this perspective the church is not "the coming together of regenerate individuals to form a system of mutual interaction and cooperation" (as in Schleiermacher)[26] but the descent of the heavenly into the earthly, transforming it from within.

We need to avoid both a docetic and an ebionitic way of viewing the church. In the first the church is reduced to a purely spiritual society in which we share a common spiritual vision. In the second the church is defined in terms of visible rites and ceremonies which sustain human relationships. In the evangelical perspective I uphold, the church is both inward and outward, spiritual and temporal, divine and earthly. But the spiritual or divine is hidden in the earthly and human. Like Jesus Christ, its Lord, the church has two natures, not one. Yet they are not loosely associated as in Nestorianism but inseparable and indissoluble.

The Kingdom in the Making

The church is an anticipatory sign of the kingdom that is coming, but it is something more—the springboard and vanguard of this kingdom. We should here understand the church as the community of all those who confess Jesus Christ as Savior and Lord and strive to live in obedience to his teachings. The kingdom is the creative and redeeming force of God's Word and Spirit giving birth to a new humanity. The kingdom is the essence of the church and the goal of the church. It is the power of moral regeneration that reorders human relationships, bringing everything into submission to Jesus Christ. The church is the worldly agency of the kingdom, the earthen vessel that carries the new wine of creative transformation. The kingdom creates the church just as the church prepares the way for the kingdom.

P. T. Forsyth is helpful here in the way he relates church and kingdom. In his perspective the kingdom is "wider than the Church. . . . Inside the Church it works as holy love, outside it as holy righteousness."[27] The church is "the Kingdom in the making," the place where the kingly rule of Christ is made visible.[28] We do not build the kingdom, but the kingdom builds us up in the faith. We do not create the kingdom, but it creates us anew as its heralds and ambassadors. "We do not contribute to the Kingdom, we only work out a Kingdom which is ours wholly because our God works it in. The central thing in the Kingdom is not a state, nor a feeling, nor an act of ours, but it is an act and gift of God."[29] In Forsyth's theology the kingdom is an accomplished reality of which the church is a reflection and anticipation. The kingdom has already been ushered in by the cross and resurrection victory of Christ: our task is to proclaim the good news that God is with us and for us in Jesus Christ and that he promises to dwell within us by his Spirit. "It must make a vast difference to the action of the Church whether it is creating a Kingdom of God as we go on, or introducing one finished and foregone, whether it is laying the track or uncovering it."[30]

The church could be described as the medium of the kingdom in that the power of the new life in Christ is communicated through the preaching and ministrations of the church. In this sense the church is a veritable means of grace, a visible sign that God has acted and continues to act through the preaching of the Word and the celebration of the sacraments. The church is the kingdom in inchoate form (Forsyth). It furnishes the raw material that the Spirit uses to demonstrate the reality of new life and power in Jesus Christ. The kingdom of God is the power of moral regeneration that creates a new social order anchored in the transcendent. The church becomes the conduit of this power as it holds up Jesus Christ before the world.

As the community in which both the human and the divine are active, the church mirrors the new reality of the inbreaking kingdom of God. There are many whose lives are changed by the impact of this reality who for various reasons have not aligned themselves with any particular denomination. Their lives bear witness to the transforming power of the kingdom, but they have not yet joined the fellowship of the church. Avery Dulles wisely observes:

> It is not necessary that the Church, during the time of its historical existence, should physically include all those men who live by the grace of Christ and are saved by it. Rather, the Church is called to be a representative sign—one that includes a sufficient diversity of men so that Christianity cannot be mistaken for the religion of any particular segment of the human race.[31]

The real church is a church of sinners who are accounted righteous through faith in the merits of Jesus Christ. They are sinners, however, who are on their way to being made righteous through the purifying work of the indwelling Spirit. The kingdom of God is already inaugurated in the life, death and resurrection of Christ, but it is carried forward through history as the church lives out its mission of being a witness and sign of the new reality of the conquering Christ whose Spirit transfigures and purifies all that it touches. The church participates in both the ambiguity of the world of sin and the unambiguity of the new world of righteousness. The new order of restored human community is not yet visible for all to see, but it is an effective force within world history as it moves to bring this history to a climactic conclusion in the new heaven and the new earth testified to in biblical prophecy.

The Kingdom and World History

The kingdom of God is both realized and futuristic. It has been realized through Christ's death and resurrection. It is being realized now through the gift of the Holy Spirit. It will be realized when Christ comes again in power and glory to bring in the new heaven and the new earth.

The kingdom is not only announced but is also present (Lk 11:20). Believers have already been transferred from the realm of darkness and death to the realm of light (Col 1:13; 2 Pet 1:11). The kingdom was already being born in the midst of Jesus' disciples (Lk 17:21), but it is still to be revealed to the unbelieving world.

History is the arena in which the kingdom is carried forward by the Spirit. But there is no progressive evolution of history into the kingdom. As Michael Horton phrases it, "It comes as a decisive event, not as a gradual process, for it is not the church that carries the world into the Promised Land on her shoulders, but the church herself that is carried in the train of the rider of the white horse."[32]

Christian theology is primarily a theology of crisis rather than of process. The kingdom does not emerge out of history but breaks into history from the beyond. It signifies the rule of Christ over history rather than the gradual Christianizing of history. The kingdoms of the world have already been overcome by Christ's cross and resurrection victory, but this fact is still to be revealed to the nations. As Forsyth says, "Faith's greatest conquest of the world is to believe, on the strength of Christ's Cross, that the world has been overcome, and that the nations which rage so furiously are still in the leash of the redeeming God."[33]

In what Barth calls neo-Protestant theology, the kingdom was equated with the forward movement of civilization. For Albrecht Ritschl the kingdom is moral and social action inspired by love. It is not so much the subduing of the nations by the heavenly forces of righteousness as the civilizing of the nations by the power of love. Against this moralistic outlook Forsyth contended that "the Kingdom of God is not civilisation. It is not even spiritual culture."[34] Yet the Enlightenment idea of progress was not wholly absent even in Forsyth, who could describe "the coming of the Kingdom" as "the growing organization of spiritual Humanity under the Church's moral gospel and King of holy love."[35] This progress, however, does not have its source in the dynamics of history but in the power of the new aeon that breaks into history from the beyond. Ritschl often created the impression that Christ's coming is homogeneous with the texture of human events, that the kingdom of God is congruous with the rhythms of history, that its hallmark is the realization of a human ideal.[36] As I see it, Christ enters into history as an alien and at the same time transforming force turning history in a radically new direction. For Ritschl there is no rent in history that history cannot heal, whereas I contend that history itself needs to be redeemed by the power of Christ's cross and resurrection. Christ establishes his church within history, though its ground and origin is eternity.

Church tradition is adamant that the scope of the kingdom is universal, that the kingdom is destined to include the whole of humanity, though there will always be some mortals who will deny and oppose this all-encompassing reality. According to Forsyth, every person is born for the church, for the society of redemption.[37] The kingdom goes out to all, but it will not be received by all. History is not humanity's ascent to perfection but God's descent to human imperfection. It is not a mere process of moving forward morally or spiritually, but a grand drama in which people are regenerated through ever new outpourings of the Holy Spirit.

Like Forsyth and Hegel, Reinhold Niebuhr discerned the footprints of God in the sands of history. Yet while God directs history, his kingdom is never absorbed into history. The kingdom does not arise out of history but makes an ongoing and resounding impact on history. The kingdom is essentially "beyond history," though it leaves its imprint on history. Niebuhr could sometimes describe it as "the eternal dimension in which history moves." For him the kingdom remains a moral ideal that impinges on history but doesn't really take root within history. "It is always coming, but it is never here." Yet it is reflected in the partial triumphs of the human spirit within history over injustice and tyranny.[38]

Dietrich Bonhoeffer also resisted any utopian schemes of realizing the kingdom within history, though he held out the hope of attaining a higher degree of social righteousness through concerted moral action. A just social order is not the kingdom of God, but it can point beyond itself to the coming kingdom.

> This action of the church is indispensable, but the new order, society, community is not the order of the kingdom. All orders and all communities of the world will have to perish when God creates his world anew and the Lord Christ comes again to judge the old world and build the new. In this world there is peace only in the struggle for truth and right, but there the love of God will give eternal peace.[39]

In line with the witness of holy Scripture and holy tradition one can postulate three modes of the kingdom: nature, grace and glory. All of humanity belongs to the kingdom of nature, for we are all created by God and for the service of God. The kingdom of grace is the new order of social relationships inaugurated by Jesus Christ in his cross and resurrection victory. It is an ever-widening reality hidden in the old structures of human existence corrupted by sin and death. The kingdom of nature does not invariably lead to the kingdom of grace, because the former has been seized by the principalities and powers which defy God's reign, though God continues to reign in the midst of their defiance. The kingdom of glory is the final stage of the plan of salvation in which the kingdoms of the old order will be transformed into the kingdom of everlasting righteousness and peace. The millennial kingdom, the rule of Christ over the nations, will be replaced by the eternal kingdom in which God will be all in all. To use Barthian terminology, creation will be superseded by reconciliation, and both will be fulfilled in redemption. Or to build upon the vision of Joachim of Flora, the kingdom of the Father will be followed by the kingdom of the Son, and finally both will be brought into the service of the kingdom of the Spirit. Yet we must not see the eschatological fulfillment occurring within human history (as did the Joachimists), for history will come to an end when all things are taken up into Christ. At the same time it is important to bear in mind that the eschatological kingdom of God is not a state of timelessness but a synthesis of temporality and eternity in which duration will continue on a new level, though now without decay and death.

The kingdom of God is better envisaged as the goal of history than as a later state in history. It stands over history as the judgment of God on human perfidy, but it holds out hope for history as the domain in which the promises of God will be partially realized. Every eschatology should include the millennial hope in which some of God's purposes will be realized on earth as well as in heaven. Yet we should always remember that the millennial kingdom is not the eternal kingdom, that sin and death do not cease until Christ comes again to set up the kingdom that shall have no end. The millennial kingdom is the church militant moving forward in history, reclaiming a world that has lost its way in its insatiable craving for power and fame. The eternal kingdom is the church triumphant in which sin, death and the devil are done away with. Yet it is important to understand that the church militant and the church triumphant refer finally to one church—the holy catholic church—which triumphs even in its continuing battles with the forces of unrighteousness. Even in its eternal rest the church triumphant continues to be the church militant until history itself is transformed into the eternal kingdom of God.[40]

We as Christians cannot bring in the kingdom, nor can we build the kingdom, but we can testify to its invincible presence and its irrefragable imminence. We need to acknowledge that the coming of the kingdom rests not on the refinements of human culture nor on "the potentialities and powers of the world religions" (as in Moltmann)[41] but on the Word and Spirit of the living God, on the evangelical proclamation communicated in the power of the Spirit.

·FIVE·

AUTHORITY IN THE CHURCH

I will give you the keys of the kingdom of heaven,
and whatever you bind on earth shall be bound in heaven,
and whatever you loose on earth shall be loosed in heaven.

MATTHEW 16:19

A Christian assembly or congregation has the right
and power to judge all teaching
and to call, appoint and remove teachers.

MARTIN LUTHER

There is no church unless
it is obedient to the Word of God and is guided by it.

JOHN CALVIN

The Gospel of God's historic act of grace
is the infallible power and authority over both Church and Bible.

PETER T. FORSYTH

The debate over authority in the church has taken multifarious forms. On the one hand there are those (namely Roman Catholics) who vigorously defend papal authority, contending that the pope, while not the creator of doctrine, is its supreme guardian and interpreter. On the other hand, there are those (Eastern Orthodox, Anglo-Catholics and some Roman Catholics) who appeal to the authority of the councils over that of the pope, especially the ecumenical councils of the first five centuries. Then there are those (mainly but not exclusively evangelical Protestants) who uphold the authority of the holy Bible over that of the universal church. A contrary position (advanced chiefly by Catholics and Orthodox) is that the Bible derives its authority from the church and that the church gives the right interpretation of the Bible. A closely related polarity is that between restorationism and developmentalism. The former encourages a return to the pristine church of the apostolic era. The latter avers that the right doctrinal understanding develops or unfolds through the ages under the guidance of the Holy Spirit. It is said that right doctrine has its basis in Scripture but receives its definitive articulation in the theological commentary on Scripture in the history of the church. Finally, there are those (mystics, enthusiasts, pietists) who champion religious experience over the authority of both Scripture and sacred tradition. Experience is also not surprisingly given more credence than conscience or reason.

Papalism versus Conciliarism

One of the sources of the festering division between Eastern and Western churches has been the uncertain relationship between the popes and the councils. Eastern Christians were for a time willing to accept the western pope as titular head of the church but never as the definer and final interpreter of doctrine. This uneasy tension between papalists and conciliarists persisted in the Roman Catholic communion through the middle ages. The Council of Constance in 1415 made clear that its authority was derived directly from the Holy Spirit and that it took precedence over that of the pope.

> This synod, legitimately assembled in the Holy Spirit, which forms an ecumenical council and represents the Catholic Church in dispute, has its authority directly from Christ; everyone, of whatever estate or dignity, even if this be papal, is bound to obey it in matters relating to the faith, the eradication of the said schism and the universal reformation of this church of God, head and members.[1]

The decree goes on to affirm that anyone "of whatever condition, estate and dignity, even if this be papal, who stubbornly refuses obedience to the commands, resolutions, ordinances or precepts of this holy synod and any other general council legitimately assembled" shall "be subject to the appropriate punishment and be duly punished, by other legal means should this be necessary."[2]

While the Council of Constance was unequivocal in affirming conciliar over papal authority, there was a revival of papal absolutism in the years following. At the Fifth Lateran Council (1516) Pope Leo X declared, "The Roman pontifex now existing . . . has authority over all the councils."[3] Papal hegemony was further asserted at the First Vatican Council of 1870, though the Second Vatican Council (1962-1965) "powerfully reinstated the conciliar idea and in its constitution on the church magisterially laid down the collegiality of bishops and Popes."[4] Catholic theologian Hans Küng speculates that in the providence of God the ecumenical council might come to have a kind of "controlling authority" over the Pope, beyond "the emergency of the time."[5]

Evangelical theology in the tradition of the Reformation acknowledges the relative authority of the councils of the undivided church in the first several centuries after Christ, but it resists the notion that either popes or councils can give definitive formulations of doctrine that are absolutely binding upon all Christians in every age and culture. Even the creeds of the Reformation were held to be under the authority of sacred Scripture. Sacred tradition is not nullified by Scripture, but one must recognize that tradition contains many erroneous declarations, and this is why the church should always be open to continual reformation in the light of the guidance of the Holy Spirit speaking through Scripture. While it is regrettably true that some of the orthodox followers of the Reformation practically enthroned their own creeds and confessions, the more biblically astute theologians recognized that the creeds contain chaff as well as wheat and that a rigid adherence to creeds must never be made a condition for fellowship among Christians.

From my theological perspective the creeds of the church may have an irrevocably binding character in certain situations where the church is struggling against heresy, but they must never be seen as eternal or irreformable statements that have equal authority with the Scriptures or the gospel.[6] In the confession we may hear the living Word of God speaking to us giving guidance and commands. Our conscience is indeed subject to the divine commandment, but this commandment must not be identified with a creedal pronouncement, not even with a biblical declaration when it is taken out of its historical and theological context.

In evangelical theology the authority of the pope is not ruled out a priori, but it is considerably qualified and modified. The pope has authority when he submits himself unreservedly to Scripture, when he places the gospel of God over his own wisdom and insights. The pope may earn the right to be listened to when he ceases to think of himself as a supreme authority in the church and is willing to view himself as simply a servant of the Word.[7] He can only speak for the universal church when he acknowledges, not just outwardly but inwardly, that Jesus Christ alone is the head of the church. Papal declarations can only be a dim reflection of the truth of the gospel, and while they may contain much scriptural wisdom, they stand in need of purification and reinterpretation by the Holy Spirit speaking through the Scriptures to the people of God in every age. The Spirit may indeed also speak through popes and councils, but what he truly says must be clearly differentiated from the cultural idiom and historical matrix in which the decree is given. An evangelical catholic will recognize that both popes and councils can err, that the final decision concerning the truth or falsehood of any papal or conciliar pronouncements must be left to the individual conscience, though this is a conscience bound to the Word of God and illumined by the Holy Spirit. If we would acknowledge in Christian humility the relativity and transient character of our ideas and formulations, we would then be more open to guidance and correction by the Spirit of the living Christ.

In the last analysis theological authority is circular rather than perpendicular. It proceeds from Scripture to church to experience and then back to Scripture. It is not from the top down nor from the bottom up but from the intermeshing of what is above and what is below. It does not begin with an absolute principle and then draw conclusions from this principle deductively. Nor does it rise inductively from an investigation of the claims of the church through the ages and how these correspond to biblical tenets. Instead, its basis lies in the Absolute making himself known in and through relative or finite means and instruments. We never have the Absolute directly, but we receive glimpses of the Absolute through pondering the Scriptures, hearing the evangelical proclamation, listening to the ecumenical councils, learning from the lives of the saints. The Word of God authenticates himself as we allow ourselves to be taught by the Spirit of God and corrected by the church of God, that is, the church illumined and judged by its Lord and Master, Jesus Christ. The living Word of God is always over the empirical church, but we have access to this Word through the mediation of the Spirit who is always at work in the historical church—one that stands in continuity with the apostolic confession of faith as found in the New Testament.

In Reformed perspective, tradition is not an echo of the truth of faith but a response to this truth. It is not a definitive expression of the faith but a continuous search for a fuller and truer expression. Tradition is not the mouthpiece of Christ but the servant of Christ. Its precepts and witness must not be confused with God's self-witness in the Bible, but they can be appreciated as faithful attestations to the message of Christ insofar as they are related to and grounded in holy Scripture.

Biblicism versus Ecclesiasticism
The perduring dividing line between evangelical Protestantism on the one hand and Roman Catholicism and Eastern Orthodoxy on the other is the enigmatic relation between holy Scripture and holy tradition. The Catholic churches assign tradition a role virtually equivalent to that of Scripture. The final norm for faith is held to reside in Scripture,

but tradition communicates and interprets this norm to all generations after Christ. Protestants who adhere to the tenets of the Reformation insist that Scripture interprets itself by the power of the Holy Spirit, and the role of the church is to be obedient to this interpretation. The Reformers upheld *sola scriptura*. Catholics and Orthodox generally affirm Scripture plus tradition as the ultimate authority for faith.

In the perspective of Orthodox theologian John Meyendorff, the essence of the kerygma is indeed contained in the books of the New Testament, but "this *kerygma* would be mere human words if it is not delivered in the full context of the living tradition, particularly the sacraments and the liturgy of the church."[8] The Bible arose out of the living tradition and would be mere letter unless animated by the Spirit working through the church. Sacred tradition is "the initial and fundamental source of Christian theology—not in competition with Scripture, but as Scripture's spiritual context."[9]

John Henry Newman (d. 1890), who moved from evangelical Anglicanism to Anglo-Catholicism and then to Roman Catholicism, contended that dogma has its ground in the revelation in Scripture, but its implications are unfolded in the history of the church as the Spirit guides the church into deeper understanding. This developmental process takes place in the mind of the whole church, laity included. We cannot simply repeat the New Testament message but must draw upon the wisdom of the saints and scholars of Catholic tradition, who relate this message to the concrete situation of their time.

The Lutheran Pietist Johann Albrecht Bengel insisted that the teachings of the church be grounded in Scripture, though Scripture itself could be vibrant only in the bosom of the church.

> Scripture is the life of the Church: the Church is the guardian of Scripture. When the Church is strong, Scripture shines abroad; when the Church is sick, Scripture is imprisoned. Thus Scripture and the Church exhibit together the appearance of health, or else of sickness; so that the treatment of Scripture corresponds with the state of the Church.[10]

A similar outlook can be detected in the Protestant church historian

Philip Schaff who vigorously adhered to the Reformation doctrine of scriptural primacy, yet regarded Scripture and church as inseparable in the communication of the gospel: "The Bible lives and has power as God's word, only in and by the church, the Body of Christ."[11] Schaff was committed to a church based on biblical authority. At the same time he opposed a narrow biblicism that denied the sustaining and redeeming role of the Spirit in the life history of the church.

P. T. Forsyth was adamant that the church is subordinate to Scripture, yet Scripture conveys its truth to us through the preaching and teaching of the church. The church did not produce Scripture but received it from the Holy Spirit, the ultimate author of Scripture. "The books of the Bible were given *to* the Church, more than *by* it, and they descended on it rather than rose from it."[12] The church is under the Bible, but both church and Bible are under the gospel, the divinely given message that shines through the Bible.

According to Forsyth the church is not a mediator alongside of Christ but a herald of the good news that Christ alone atones for sin and procures our redemption.

> Our mediatorial Christ leaves no room for a mediatorial Church. He is so much the direct presence of God that no Church could take the part Rome assumes without sharing Christ's relation to God; without prolonging (rather than answering) the Incarnation, in a way to obscure Christ rather than reveal Him.[13]

At the same time, Forsyth perceived that Christ reaches out to us through the church and its sacraments, which therefore in some way partake of Christ's authority: "If the final authority is God in [the] Gospel, the Church shares in that authority as the expert of the Gospel and the soul."[14] One should note that when Forsyth spoke of the church in this context, he had in mind not any particular denomination or institution but the company of the committed in all ages who are united with Christ through faith in his name. "When I speak of the Church, I mean, of course, the true Catholic Church, the Church of Christ, the Church in all the Churches, the community of the faithful."[15]

Protestant theology through the ages has been willing to affirm the infallibility of the church, but it generally takes exception to the traditional Catholic view that the church possesses an infallible teaching office that by itself determines what is true and false in the church's reflection.[16] The infallibility of the church resides in the divine teacher, the Holy Spirit, who guides the church into all truth (Jn 16:13). The church is kept by the Spirit from substantial error, but it nevertheless time and again lapses into error through the pride and arrogance of its leaders and theologians. The church is not always faithful to its Lord, but its Lord sustains it in its folly and disobedience. When the church becomes faithless, it ceases to be the church. According to Karl Barth, "The Church as a whole cannot err in its fundamental faith," and "the people of God, as such, whatever may be said by or of individuals, cannot mistake its goal."[17] This position is congruous with that taken by some Catholic theologians. Yves Congar declares, "The Church has, in its pastoral magisterium, approached truth in different ways. It has made mistakes. It has fallen short and has been forgetful of its task. . . . The Holy Spirit helps the Church . . . so that error will not ultimately prevail."[18]

Both Catholics and Protestants of a latitudinarian bent have been attracted to Vincent of Lérins (fifth century), who seemed to make the consensus of Christian tradition rather than popes or councils the final criterion for faith and practice. What takes precedence over all theological speculation and creedal formulation is what has been believed "everywhere, always, by all."[19] What is troubling is that Vincent was a semi-Pelagian.[20] It should also be noted that despite his appeal to a universal consensus he explicitly affirmed the abiding normativeness of Scripture. The church is to be invoked only to insure the right interpretation of Scripture. In his celebrated statement on the authority of Christian consensus, Vincent undoubtedly had his finger on one side of the truth. The universality of Christian faith can surely be a way by which we evaluate innovations in theology. At the same time, we must not unduly elevate the consensus of church tradition because this consensus was itself a source for new error in the church. One example is the concept of grace, which was lamentably misunderstood by a sizable portion of the church fathers and was only later rediscovered in its New Testament meaning as the favor of God to undeserving sinners.[21] Another example is the teaching concerning love. The majority of church fathers and medieval theologians understood love in terms of eros, the search for perfecting union with God, rather than of agape, the sacrificial love of the cross, which was powerfully reaffirmed by Luther.[22] Luther's view involved a decisive break with a widespread consensus in church tradition and theology. If we hold too closely to the criterion offered by Vincent of Lérins, we foreclose the possibility of church tradition being corrected by a fresh discovery and application of God's holy Word by prophets raised up by the Spirit of God for the reformation of the church. To be sure, God has spoken with power and clarity in the past, but he continues to bring forth new light from his holy Word, light that confirms and fulfills yet never negates the affirmations and teachings of holy Scripture.

In Catholic tradition papal authority in the church is supported by Matthew 16:13-19, where Jesus tells Peter, "Upon this rock I will build my church; and the gates of hell shall not prevail against it" (verse 18, KJV). In the following verse he says to Peter, "I will give you the keys of the kingdom of heaven, and whatever you bind on earth shall be bound in heaven, and whatever you loose on earth shall be loosed in heaven." The pivotal question is whether rock *(petros)* in verse 18 refers to Peter, the man, or to his confession of faith, as found in verse 16: "You are the Christ, the Son of the living God." Lutheran theologian Oscar Cullmann mounts a persuasive argument that the reference is to Peter, but there is nothing that implies that this power is passed on to successive bishops or popes.[23] Interestingly the young Joseph Ratzinger, in his dissertation on Augustine's ecclesiology, concluded that "if the church is founded on Peter, it is not founded on his person but on his faith. . . . The foundation of the church is Christ."[24]

Eduard Schweizer makes a convincing case that, while Peter is the subject of Christ's remarks, the authority to bind and loose is not restricted to Peter but is given to the whole company of the disciples (cf. Mt 18:18; Jn 20:23). Peter nonetheless has a preeminent position among the apostles not because of his confession as such but because of his election to a special task. According to Schweizer, Matthew "imputes no merit to Peter for his strength of faith, since faith comes not from the will or from actions but from God. As the first apostle to experience the miracle of faith, he remains the 'rock,' even when he turns into a 'stone of offense.' "[25] Jesus is not establishing a permanent teaching office in the church, however, but is assigning to Peter a jurisdictional authority that is nevertheless shared by the other disciples.

In the wider context of Scripture the keys of the kingdom are in the hands of all Christians, since we are all priests and kings in Christ (1 Pet 2:5; Rev 1:6; 5:10), and we are all assigned an evangelical mandate to preach the gospel to all nations. We all have a common vocation—to bear witness to what God has done for us in Christ in our words and actions. Jesus Christ himself is the chief cornerstone, the eternal foundation (1 Cor 3:11; Eph 2:20), but he calls all of us who believe to a missionary vocation. He speaks through his representatives and heralds (Lk 10:16; Mk 13:11). In the deepest sense Jesus' successor is not any one apostle nor bishops who stand in apostolic succession, but the community as a whole. Yet

> there is room for discussion whether a single leader would be useful to this total community in the performance of its ministry: a pastor or supervisor in the local church, a bishop in a larger region, a Pope in the universal church. But this must be clearly understood to be one form of organization among many, i.e. as something which may be retained at certain times and in certain places, but which should be replaced by other forms elsewhere.[26]

In rabbinical tradition "to bind and loose" means to declare certain actions forbidden or permitted. Later Christian tradition extends this principle to include the power to forgive or retain sins (Mt 18:18; Jn 20:23). Postapostolic Christianity ascribes to the apostles the prerogatives of Jesus (Mt 10:40; Lk 10:16); yet this presupposes not an infallible magisterium but the repeated condescension of the Spirit of God who deigns to use many instruments in the service of Christ.

Scripture is clear that Jesus alone is the foundation and final criterion for faith (1 Cor 3:11; Eph 2:20). He alone possesses "the key of David" (Rev 3:7) and "the keys of Death and Hades" (Rev 1:18). Yet he assigns to his disciples the role of disciplining and consoling the little flock of the fainthearted (Lk 12:32-48). It is noteworthy that the act of forgiving in John 20:23 is in the perfect tense. One possible translation is "those whose sins you forgive have been forgiven; those whose sins you do not forgive have not been forgiven." In the strict sense Christ alone forgives and retains sin, but his ambassadors and heralds can declare and announce this forgiveness.[27] They can also withhold the declaration of forgiveness if individuals do not repent of their sins and strive to obey Christ's teachings. Bonhoeffer rightly points out that the forgiveness of sin which is communicated by the apostles is not unconditional—"sometimes sin must be retained. It is the will of the Lord himself that the gospel should not be given to the dogs."[28] The representatives and heralds of Christ are commissioned not only to proclaim the gospel but also to maintain ecclesiastical discipline. "Sanctification means driving out the world from the Church as well as separating the Church from the world."[29]

In short, we as members of Christ's body can pronounce God's judgment as well as his mercy. We can withhold God's word of consolation as well as absolve from sin in the sense of granting assurance that sins are indeed forgiven through the sacrifice and resurrection of Christ. We can be priests to one another, intercessors and counselors, but only because the Spirit chooses to make use of our witness in order to bring greater glory to God in Christ. We are not co-redeemers with Christ, but we are witnesses to his once-for-all redemption on the cross. Through our witness, that is, through the witness of the church, the impact and fruits of Christ's sacrifice are communicated and bestowed to those who repent and believe in the gospel.

The church must avoid claiming too much for its pronouncements and ministrations. It should take care never to present itself as the mediator of Christ's redemption. On the other hand, the church must not abdicate its responsibility to teach, correct and reprove. Karl Barth shares these words of wisdom:

> The church will not let itself be diverted from its promise or its task by its loneliness and impotence, by the indifference and opposition that is shown it by the rest of the world. All this will constantly remind it of its own worldliness, but also of its call to continual return to its starting point in the free grace of God. The same humility in which it constitutes itself will prevent it both from flight into inwardness or invisibility, i.e., from abandoning itself as a concrete and visible order, and equally from claiming or seeking any abstract fullness of the truth and power of the community or its offices, i.e., from abandoning its foundation in the free divine act of grace. As the bride of Christ it is also his handmaiden, and therefore it must do its work aright, yet it must do it within its limits as service, not with any confusion or presumption. As the earthly body of its heavenly Lord, it will take its *earthly* existence quite seriously, fully affirming, willing, and practicing it as such.[30]

Experientialism versus Rationalism

From earliest times many Christians have sought for a viable alternative to heteronomy, submission to an external standard, and they have generally found this in an appeal to either rational or experiential corroboration. In both cases authority is located in the self (autonomy), and revelation is equated with the inner light. Paul Tillich has proposed another option—theonomy, in which authority is anchored not in the self as such but in the self upheld by God.[31] The criterion for faith and practice nevertheless continues to be located within the human subject, though it is one now united with its theonomous ground.

Rationalism can take the form of biblicism or ecclesiasticism.[32] The truth of faith in both instances is reduced to a set of beliefs that are available either in the Bible or in the creeds and pronouncements of the church. Revelation is no longer a divine-human encounter but the communication of propositional truth. Reason becomes the point of contact with divine revelation. The truths of faith become public truths capable of being established or confirmed by rational investigation.

Experientialism can take the form of either mysticism or an empiricist naturalism. In the first the truth of faith is located outside the parameters of discursive reason. In the second rational probings are united with the data of religious or simply human experience. The appeal is no longer to a priori general principles but to rational evidences. We see this approach in both later Protestant evangelicalism and process theism.

In a theology of Word and Spirit the final authority is situated outside the self in God's self-revelation in Jesus Christ. The datum of revelation is not accessible to natural reason, and it also transcends the compass of human experience. Yet it makes contact with reason and experience through the work of the Holy Spirit as he brings the biblical text to life in the event of preaching and hearing. To rest the case for Christianity on the inner word is to fall into the crevice of either rationalism or experientialism. To appeal exclusively to the written word is to end either in a narrow biblicism or in credalism. Yet we must not discount the role of both the written word and the inner word to lead us to truth, but they do this only when they are united with the revealed word—the living Christ who confronts us in the decision of faith. The biblical alternative to both autonomy and heteronomy is Christonomy, in which we are lifted out of ourselves, out of our experiences into the promises of God that can never deceive (Luther). Revelation is not the discovery of the ground of the self (as in Tillich's theonomy) nor the inner persuasion of the validity of biblical claims (as in rationalistic autonomy) but being known and addressed by the living God, which will involve both reason and experience as vital components in the drama of salvation. Reformation Protestantism does not rest its claims on either conscience or experience but on a conscience bound to the Word of God (Luther) and an experience of being grasped by the Spirit of God as we are confronted by the significance of what God has done for us in Jesus Christ. Neo-Protestantism, which arose out of the Enlightenment, has been much more inclined to celebrate the sufficiency of the individual conscience than the authority of either church or Bible.

In our battle against experientialism and mysticism we must not succumb to the danger of emptying the faith of its experiential content. While revelation cannot be reduced to religious experience, it nonetheless contains a vital experiential element. Otherwise it would consist simply in the communication of information. Martin Luther, who was constantly alert to the vagaries of religious enthusiasm, still valued the reality of personal religious experience: "This I have not only from the Scriptures but also from experience, for the name of Christ often helped me when nobody else could. So I've had words and deeds in my favor, Scriptures and experience, and God gave me both in abundance."[33]

P. T. Forsyth is especially helpful in the way in which he relates experience to the gospel of God, the transcendent criterion of faith. Experience itself is not the authority for faith, but the truth of faith is appropriated in experience. "Christian experience is the experience of the authority of the Gospel; it is not an experience which becomes the authority for the Gospel."[34] "Experience is the fruit of faith, or its medium, more than its ground."[35] Forsyth perceived the need to avoid both the Scylla of rationalism and biblicism and the Charybdis of experientialism and mysticism.

In radical Pietism and mysticism the direct experience of God in the depths of the soul is valued above the hearing of the Word or the celebration of the sacraments. The experience of rebirth becomes the basis of the church's life and ministry rather than being a fruit of this ministry. According to the radical Pietist Gottfried Arnold, "The Christian is related directly to God because the church does not mediate rebirth, but rather is first formed by the reborn."[36]

A theology of Word and Spirit is especially evident in Dietrich Bonhoeffer, who tried to hold together both a high view of the church and the Bible and a recognition that faith must have an experiential dimension if it is to be a vital force in the life of the Christian. Our experiences of God and Christ may attest the genuineness of our faith, but the object of faith is the living Christ who remains hidden in our experiences and who remains veiled to our reason even in the event of revelation. For Bonhoeffer, grace is always much more than our experience of it. Grace is something that has to be believed.[37]

A theology of Word and Spirit will be a theology of paradox rather than either affirmation (cataphatic theology) or negation (apophatic theology). Truth is arrived at neither through building upon glimpses and signs of the divine presence in experience nor through a radical negation of concepts and images. Truth confronts us through the paradox that God became man in Jesus Christ, a paradox that can be grasped only by faith. Søren Kierkegaard should be our mentor in this area of theology, not Hegel, who sought to resolve the paradoxes of faith and life in a rational system. Most contemporary theologians (including Pannenberg and Moltmann) are much closer to Hegel than to Kierkegaard, though theologians in an earlier period (including Reinhold Niebuhr, Karl Barth and Emil Brunner) were much more supportive of Kierkegaard than Hegel. One can discern both influences in Tillich, though Hegel's is certainly the greater.

The Church Militant and Triumphant

In Christian tradition the distinction is often made between the church militant and the church triumphant. The first refers to the struggling church in history; the second refers to the church in heaven—composed of the glorified saints and angels. As the hymn writer expresses it, "we feebly struggle, they in glory shine."[38] Yet there is also the complementary truth that the saints on the other side pray for us and thereby assist us in our struggle. Moreover, in our sojourn on earth we do not simply struggle but also overcome. We do not merely suffer but also triumph through suffering. The church militant and the church triumphant are not two separate churches but two dimensions of the life history of the one holy catholic church, which bears the bruises and wounds of its Lord but also experiences the power of his resurrection glory. This intermeshing of the pilgrim church and the church at rest is presupposed in the hymn of S. Ralph Harlow:

> O Church of God, triumphant
>> Above the world's dark fears,
> Wherein our souls find refuge
>> Through all these earthly years!
> Christ's steadfast holy purpose,
>> Illumined by the cross,
> Guards her from evil's power
>> Revealing it but dross.[39]

The kingdom of glory is already present in the pains and travails of the earthly church. The kingdom is born in the church, and the church is born for the kingdom. Eberhard Arnold, founder of the Bruderhof, puts it this way: "In the Church, the beginning of the coming kingdom is present in its full power and challenging clarity."[40] "The mystery of the Church is Christ shining in her. He reveals His presence in the pure fire of the Holy Spirit. The clarity of His light tolerates no defilement. The mystery of the Church is the pure expectation of the coming of God's majesty in glory."[41]

While the kingdom is inseparable from the church, it cannot be reduced to the empirical church.[42] The kingdom is wider and deeper than the church, but the kingdom includes the church as it surges forward in history toward the final consummation when Christ will be in and through all things. The church is the sign of the advancing kingdom and also the means (though not the only means) by which the kingdom extends its power and influence in human history.

The church is able to engage and overcome the principalities and powers because it is imbued with the hope of the coming triumph of the kingdom, which is assured through Christ's resurrection from the grave, the outpouring of the Holy Spirit at Pentecost and his glorious second advent. This vision of coming triumph is graphically captured by Isaac Watts:

> They go from strength to strength
> > Through this dark vale of tears,
> Till each arrives at length,
> > Till each in heaven appears;
> O glorious seat,
> > When God our King
> Shall thither bring
> > Our willing feet![43]

·SIX·

MARKS OF THE CHURCH

Where Jesus Christ is, there also is the Catholic Church.

IGNATIUS OF ANTIOCH

There should be only one Church, but this unity can come only from a powerful renewal
of faith, a new Reformation created out of the depths of the Gospel.

EMIL BRUNNER

The New Testament knows nothing of institutional sanctity, of a sacred "it"; it does not
speak of a Church which invests as many of its institutions, places, times and implements
as possible with the attribute "holy."

HANS KÜNG

The church is present wherever "the manifestation of the Spirit" takes place.

JÜRGEN MOLTMANN

T he tensions between logocentric and pneumatocentric theology are especially noticeable in the ongoing discussion on the marks of the church. When the church is defined primarily or exclusively in terms of its fidelity to the Word, we find ourselves in the camp of logocentrism. On the other hand, when the church is described as the domain where the Spirit rules (as in Irenaeus and Moltmann) we may be verging on pneumatocentrism. The Reformers of the sixteenth century tried to hold together the dimensions of Word and Spirit, but by subordinating the Spirit altogether to the Word, they sometimes tilted in the direction of a biblicistic rationalism, and this was even more apparent in their orthodox followers.

The Catholic Consensus

The so-called classical marks of the church have their basis in the Niceno-Constantinopolitan Creed, which affirms "one holy, catholic and apostolic church." These marks—unity, holiness, catholicity and apostolicity—are sometimes described as the attributes of the church, since they are inseparable from the church's very being. Hans Küng calls them "dimensions" of the church, for they tell us what the true church is.[1]

The oneness of the church signifies its inherent unity. There can be only one true church—that which was founded by the Lord Jesus Christ and made viable and visible by the outpouring of the Holy Spirit. Catholics and Orthodox are right in affirming the existence of only one church, but they are wrong when they identify this one church with a particular empirical or historical institution. The unity of the church is to be found not in its rites or creeds but in its obedience to Jesus Christ, its one head and Lord. While perceiving the need for institutional structure, Avery Dulles astutely recognizes that the unity of the church is deeper than any external apparatus. The unity favored by a biblically oriented theology "is not the external unity of an organized society but rather the interior unity of mutual charity leading to a communion of friends."[2] P. T. Forsyth contended that the unity of the church lies "not in itself but in its message, in the unity of the Gospel that made the Church."[3]

The one church exists in its relationship to the one Lord, and this relationship is present to a degree in all the churches that appeal to holy Scripture as their infallible guide and criterion. While there is only one church, we can speak of remnants of this church in the diversity of churches. No one church can claim for itself the fullness of the mystical life of Christ, but every church that confesses Christ as its Lord partakes of this mystical life.

Holiness too has been universally acknowledged among Christians as belonging to the essence of the church. The church is holy because it is marked off from the world by the interior illumination and cleansing work of the Holy Spirit. Its holiness is anchored in its Lord, but it is reflected, sometimes only dimly, in the members of his mystical body. Luther considered the church holy "even where fantastical spirits do reign, if only they deny not the Word and Sacraments. For if these be denied, there cannot be the Church."[4] Calvin perceived holiness as a dynamic interplay between Christ and his people, who are led by his Spirit toward a deeper measure of holiness. "The church is holy . . . in the sense that it is daily advancing and is not yet perfect: it makes progress from day to day but has not yet reached its goal of holiness."[5] Paul Tillich reveals his Protestant lineage by conceiving of the holiness of the church as lying outside of itself in its transcendent source and foundation, the New Being in Jesus Christ:

> The churches are holy because of the holiness of their foundation, the New Being, which is present in them. Their holiness cannot be derived from the holiness of their institutions, doctrines, ritual and devotional activities, or ethical principles; all these are among the ambiguities of religion.[6]

Hans Küng reflects the catholic balance between objective and subjective when he declares, "The Church is holy by being called by God in Christ to be the communion of the faithful, by accepting the call to his service, by being separated from the world and at the same time embraced and supported by his grace."[7] For Küng holiness is not wholly extrinsic to human activity and striving but includes this activity even while going beyond it.

The catholicity of the church refers to its universality and inclusivity. It also contains the idea of continuity with the ancient traditions of the church. In Küng's words, "The catholicity of the Church . . . consists in a notion of entirety, based on identity and resulting in universality. From this it is clear that unity and catholicity go together; if the Church is one, it must be universal, if it is universal it must be one. Unity and catholicity are two interwoven dimensions of one and the same

Church."[8] Küng goes on to assert that the responsibility for the recovery of catholicity lies in both the "mother church" and the "daughter churches":

> The so-called "Catholic Church" will never achieve the necessary unity or catholicity of the Church without sorting out its relationship to the Churches which directly or indirectly have sprung from her, and on her side making peace with them. All the movements towards reform and renewal within the Church, which we must all welcome, will remain incomplete if the connections . . . with the other Churches are ignored. If on the other hand these connections are examined sympathetically and taken up positively, then these movements of reform will assume new breadth and depth.[9]

Evangelicals can learn from contemporary Catholic scholars on how to realize a fuller catholic expression of the faith. Too often evangelicals see the word *catholic* as standing in antithesis to the gospel, whereas it should be understood as belonging to the essence of the gospel. We should be willing to affirm with Avery Dulles that catholicity "is not the accomplished fact of having many members or a wide geographical distribution, but rather the dynamic catholicity of a love reaching out to all and excluding none."[10]

When we confess the apostolicity of the church we acknowledge that the true church is founded on the apostles. The faith of the church must stand in continuity with their enduring witness. I again concur with Küng, who here sounds very Protestant:

> As direct witnesses and messengers of the risen Lord, the apostles can have no successors. No further apostles were called. Apostleship in the sense of the original and fundamental ministry of the first witnesses and messengers died out with the death of the last apostle. Apostleship in this sense of witness and mission cannot be repeated or continued. What remains is a task and a commission. The apostolic commission is not finished, but will remain to the end of time. The apostolic task is not completed; it embraces all peoples to the ends of the earth.[11]

Apostolic succession in Reformed perspective does not lie in physical linkage with the original apostles through a sacramental laying on of hands, though the Catholic doctrine is not wholly bereft of historical support. The real apostolic succession consists in a reaffirmation of the teaching and doctrine of the apostles in the history of the catholic church. I here fully agree with Moltmann: "The apostolic succession is, in fact and in truth, the evangelical succession, the continuing and unadulterated proclamation of the gospel of the risen Christ."[12] What I must add is that the proclamation of the church in every age should involve not a repristination or repetition of apostolic words but a fresh appropriation of apostolic truth that is directed to a new situation.

It is necessary to maintain that these attributes or marks of the church are not simply gifts bestowed on the church but tasks that the church is to realize in ever new ways.[13] The church is already one, but it must become more visibly one through the efforts of church people across denominational lines to draw closer together—in faith and in practice. The church is already holy in its source and foundation, but it must strive to produce fruits of holiness in its sojourn in the world. The church is already catholic, but it must seek a fuller measure of catholicity by assimilating the valid protests against church abuse and obfuscation into its own life. The church is already apostolic, but it must become more consciously apostolic by allowing the gospel to reform and sometimes even overturn its time-honored rites and interpretations.

Practical Marks

In addition to the attributes that define the nature of the true church, theologians have postulated marks that render the catholic and apostolic church visible to the world. These are marks that have to do with the activity of the church, the way it demonstrates its faith and witness in the wider society. These marks may also be regarded as confirmations of the truth and identity of the catholic and apostolic church.

What is important to recognize is that these so-called practical marks of the church are not proofs of its reality but indicators of its authenticity, which are fully grasped only with the eyes of faith. Hans Küng trenchantly observes:

> There are signs by which the Church can be recognized, signs that can be perceived by everyone. Even the non-believer is aware of them, but as a non-believer he will ultimately misinterpret them; he will recognize them and yet mistake their true significance. For him their deeper reality is veiled, not clear.[14]

Among the signs that attest the reality of the presence of Christ in the midst of the faithful is the pure preaching of the Word of God. The evangelical theology that has its source in the Protestant Reformation was very determined that this sign be recognized above all others. By the Word of God the Reformers did not have in mind a verbal formula or a theological interpretation but the truth of the gospel illumined and communicated by the Holy Spirit. As Luther phrased it, "Where there are the Word of God and the Holy Spirit, there is the church."[15]

The second pivotal sign held up by the Reformers was the right administration of the sacraments. In addition to the proclaimed and written word of God was the visible word—the water of baptism and the bread and the cup in Holy Communion. John Calvin put it very succinctly: "Wherever we find the word of God purely preached and heard, and the sacraments administered according to the institution of Christ, there, it is not to be doubted, is a Church of God."[16] In Reformation theology the sacraments were clearly subordinated to the preaching of the Word and in fact derived their validity and efficacy from their authorization by the Word. Ultimately for Luther, "there is but one Sacrament, the Word, by which God 'lays hold of' and 'puts on' 'the creatures' of water, bread and wine."[17]

Church discipline was also designated by various Reformers as a hallmark of the church. Luther on occasion referred to the "power of the keys," the power to absolve from sin and to withhold absolution from sin. John Calvin strongly advocated the practice of church discipline but declined to name it as a sign of the true church.[18] Martin Bucer went beyond Calvin in including discipline with the Word and sacraments as a prime indicator of the church. The disappearance of discipline in Protestant modernity is very much to be deplored, for a church that lacks the capacity to reprove and admonish its wayward members is in danger of losing continuity with the New Testament *ecclesia*.[19]

In Pietism the fellowship of love (the *koinonia*) was often cited as a mark of the church. This tradition is reflected in Schleiermacher's dictum: "The essence of the church is fellowship."[20] The strength of Pietism lay in the fact that it gave the laity a role in determining the validity of the church's witness and rites. It is not simply the message we profess but the fruits we produce by living a Christian life that attest the apostolic reality of the church (cf. Mt 7:16-20; 12:33; Gal 5:22).

Pietism also added the urgency of mission as a mark of the true church, though this was not always explicitly stated. The church does not fulfill its mandate until it acts to share the good news of Christ's redemption with the world outside its fellowship. John Chrysostom manifested this evangelical concern already in the fifth century: "There is nothing colder than a Christian who is unconcerned about the salvation of others. . . . Do not say 'I am unable to help them,' for if you are truly a Christian it is impossible for you to make such an admission."[21] This same sentiment is echoed in P. T. Forsyth, whose spirituality has its roots in both Pietism and Puritanism: "A Church cold to missions is a Church dead to the Cross."[22]

Good Samaritan service is still another contribution of the spiritual movements of purification after the Reformation. For General William Booth, founder of the Salvation Army, a church that is not passionately involved in ministering to the material needs of people falls drastically short of its commission to bring the gospel to all peoples. Yet he did not confuse faith in the gospel with love for our neighbor. The demonstration of Christian love prepares the way for commitment to the truth of the gospel as well as follows this commitment. His motto was "soup, soap and salvation," but he was adamant that our mission remains unfulfilled if we are concerned only with the first two and not with the last.

Right teaching reflected in creeds and confessions is also a mark of the true church, and here we need to thank confessional orthodoxy for reminding us of this fact. Adherence to the true faith expressed in creeds and confessions is itself a sign that we stand in continuity with the holy catholic church founded by Jesus Christ. The true church will not only be involved in the ministry of service and evangelism but will also be committed to education for this ministry. Catechesis is as important as revival in making the church a viable arm of the kingdom of God.

The Anabaptist tradition has also made a signal contribution to this discussion. For Anabaptists the prime marks of the church include peace, suffering, spiritually faithful ministers and shepherds and separation from sin. The mark of suffering or persecution is especially significant in Anabaptist spirituality, though this mark has also been acknowledged by other streams of spiritual life in the church including Roman Catholic and Lutheran. J. Heinrich Arnold of the Bruderhof gives cogent expression to this motif: "Part of the experience of true conversion is the willingness to suffer with Christ, the suffering One. I do not believe that true conversion is possible without this."[23]

Part of the genius of Dietrich Bonhoeffer was his discernment that community belongs to the salient marks of the church. Here we see an affinity to the Pietist emphasis on fellowship, except that Bonhoeffer means much more than living in a relationship of love. He has in mind the readiness to share both goods and time with people in need, especially those who belong to the household of faith. Christianity is evidenced by the willingness to live in solidarity with both our fellow believer and our neighbor and to celebrate this solidarity through living a common life involving mutual confession of sins, intercessory prayer and the sacramental rites of baptism and the eucharist.

The Pentecostal revolution has focused attention on still another mark of the church—signs and wonders. The witness of the New Testament makes clear that signs and wonders will accompany the proclamation of the gospel to the heathen, and these signs will include deliverance from demons, healings and other miracles (Mk 16:17-18; Acts 5:12; 19:11-12; Rom 15:18-19; Heb 2:4). Signs and wonders do not prove the truth of the gospel, but they demonstrate the reality of the faith of those who follow the gospel. Yet even here we must be cautious, since Scripture tells us that false prophets too can produce signs and miracles (Mk 13:22) and that in the last analysis faith relies not on external signs but on the promises of Christ in the Gospels to protect and empower all those who confess his name before the world.

Liberation theology has also shed light on this issue of signs and marks of the true church. Among these signs are solidarity with the poor, sensitivity to oppression, the search for justice and peace. Liberation theologians generally agree that wherever there is a passion for social justice one can discern the inbreaking of the kingdom, which is wider and deeper than the empirical church and may even contradict the stance of the church on occasion. Whenever the church tries to ensure its survival in the world it contradicts its mission to be a revolutionary force for justice and peace in the world. It then reveals its infidelity to its Lord, who commands the church to make itself vulnerable for the sake of the poor and disinherited wherever they might be. I contend that the church also abrogates its responsibility to carry the cross of Christ into the depths of the world's misery when it capitulates to a social ideology that is more interested in political correctness than in fidelity to truth and justice.

Finally, we need to give attention to prayer as a mark of the church. I am thinking here not of ritual prayer in which we simply repeat time-worn phrases but of the cry to God out of the depths of one's being, the pouring out of the soul before God.[24] When prayer is uttered in the name and for the sake of Jesus Christ it becomes Christian prayer. Only a church fortified by prayer can be assured that its witness will bear fruit. The Holy Spirit must pray within us with sighs too deep for words (Rom 8:26) if our prayer is to reach the most high God who upholds and empowers us even while he is hidden from us. The indispensable role of prayer in the life of the church is fully affirmed by Catholic,

Orthodox and Protestant theologians of whatever stripe.

In this whole discussion it is wise to make a distinction between marks that belong to the being (*esse*) of the church and those that belong to its well-being (*bene esse*). In my opinion the marks that define the essence of the church include the classical marks of oneness, catholicity, apostolicity and holiness together with the preaching and hearing of the Word, the fellowship of love and the practice of prayer. The sacraments are highly important and indeed necessary for the well-being of the church, but we cannot deny the reality of the church where sacraments are not present. Otherwise we must question the validity of the Salvation Army and the evangelical Quakers as bona fide churches of Jesus Christ. Likewise, creeds and confessions certainly attest the authenticity of the church, but they do not belong to the essence of the church, as do the fellowship of love and the practice of prayer. Certainly suffering for the sake of Christ belongs to the fullness of the church's mission, but we cannot say that the absence of persecution implies the absence of the mystical body of Christ, though it may very well indicate that the church is in ill health spiritually and morally. The church exists wherever the gospel is preached and people repent and believe. The Holy Spirit is present wherever people live in holiness and truth as these are defined in the Bible. Yet we must be careful not to make the parameters of the church too narrow, excluding those whom God includes even though their witness to the faith and their style of life fall short of the demands of the law and gospel. In my view prisoners who may not have access to Holy Communion and yet who confess the name of Christ and pray to God for deliverance, and children who hear and believe the gospel but are not yet baptized or confirmed, are still included in the mystical body of Christ. The church is present among them, but they do not yet experience the fullness of the church's presence and outreach.

What is crucial is whether those who profess to be disciples of Christ continue to believe in his mercy, even though they abysmally fail to measure up to the requirements of his law. So long as they genuinely acknowledge their sin and strive to overcome it, they still belong to the family of God and have the assurance of Christ's salvation. If they come to take God's grace for granted, however, they can no longer count on the help of Christ in times of trial.

Marks of the False Church

Just as the true church is distinguished by various signs, so the same can be said for the false church. Among these is insularism, the desire to enjoy the benefits the church confers without reaching out in sacrificial love to a world groping in darkness. Insularism often takes the form of exclusivism, in which the grace of God is confined to the rites and pronouncements of the church, and the message of God is limited to those who share common values and social allegiances. It may also take the form of credalism or confessionalism, in which subscription to a statement of faith takes precedence over personal faith in the living Christ. Insularism is most often associated with an arid orthodoxy that sees its role as conserving the treasures of church tradition. Presbyterians are sometimes described—not always fairly—as God's "frozen chosen," since the doctrine of election if not rightly interpreted can contribute to a false sense of assurance that resists any innovation, even if biblically grounded. A church may have correct doctrine and biblically based rites and still be devoid of power and enthusiasm. A church can be a regenerating force in society only when it is both imbued by the Spirit of God and committed to the Word of God.

The church, to be sure, is given the task of handing on the truths of sacred tradition, but truths that the church can master and dissect are not to be identified with *the* truth, which God alone reveals in his own way and time. Our creeds and rites point to and may even correspond to the truth of divine revelation, but they cannot encapsulate this truth. Hans Küng wisely observes, "Truth must be rediscovered, reconquered anew in every age. Truths cannot be handed on like bricks, preferably undisturbed. Truth is not like stone, it is a thing of the spirit which is lost if it is allowed to petrify."[25]

An opposite danger is inclusivism, which characterizes a church without perduring standards and goals. In the inclusivist mentality all are welcomed into membership whatever their creed or style of life. To insist on a moral code as a requirement for membership is considered a throwback to legalism. We tend to forget that Christians are called to curb the passions of the flesh and live lives dedicated to the glory of God (Rom 12:1; 13:12-14; Gal 5:16-24). We are not justified by our works, but our works attest a justification already won for us by Jesus Christ on the cross. The true church is a church of sinners, as antinomians never tire of reminding us, but it is also a church of the righteous, that is, of those who strive for righteousness. We must uphold both the message of free grace that goes out to all and the demands of costly grace, which are designed to keep us on the narrow road to salvation. Today inclusivism is very much in fashion in the mainline churches, which regrettably have little apprehension of either the gospel or the law. As a result we have churches that equate the gospel with social engineering; sin with inflexibility and stubbornness; salvation with self-realization; and absolution with therapy. No wonder that people within the churches are confused regarding the mandate of the church and powerless to implement this mandate. Sometimes in order to discover the true church we must separate from the false church, but only as a last resort. The better way is to work for reform within the structures of the empirical church, although if this task seems too monumental we must explore other avenues. In all things we should go to the Lord in prayer and be directed by his word before embarking on any particular strategy.

Another closely related manifestation of the false church is latitudinarianism, the subordination of doctrinal allegiance to life and character. This deformation often takes the form of a false irenicism, in which we extend the hand of fellowship indiscriminately without demanding acceptance of the gospel tenets and submission to the Bible as the Word of God. The latitudinarian mentality is prominent in unionism, the desire to bring denominations together without agreeing beforehand on what is essential and nonessential in our doctrine. A latitudinarian church is not a church without principle but a church that is willing to bend principle in order to remain at peace—with other churches and with the world. The whole ecumenical movement has been placed in jeopardy because of the reluctance of various churches to demand a normative understanding of the revealed mysteries of the faith. A latitudinarian church invariably elevates ethics over doctrine, life over theology, cultural accommodation over cultural confrontation. This kind of church is neither cold nor hot and will most assuredly be spewed out of the mouth of a God whose holiness cannot tolerate sin and whose truth cannot coexist with error (Rev 3:16).

Still another mark of the false church is heterodoxism, which in this context means open heresy. A latitudinarian church will not commit itself on divisive issues; a heretical church will blatantly champion stances that contradict the norms of both sacred Scripture and sacred tradition. A latitudinarian church will recognize that there *may* be other ways to salvation besides faith in Christ. A heretical church will contend that there are indeed other ways to salvation and will more than likely find these in other religions or in a syncretistic hodgepodge of religions. A latitudinarian church will be agnostic concerning the plan of salvation; a heretical church will openly promote its own plan of salvation, which patently contradicts the biblical model. A latitudinarian church will celebrate Jesus as teacher and example; a heretical church will acknowledge other teachers and saviors who may well supplant Jesus as the object of devotion. A latitudinarian church will likely be henotheistic—allowing for the possibility of other gods in the divine pantheon; a heretical church will be irremediably idolatrous, upholding a god other than the God of the Bible.

Dietrich Bonhoeffer has asserted that the challenge to the church today is to rediscover heresy.[26] The hope of orthodoxy is to recognize the virus of heresy within its midst and then seek to exterminate it. In combating heresy, however, we must take care not to vilify heretics, for heresy may embody a legitimate protest against an exaggerated orthodoxy. Heresy may well win the support of sensitive and pious souls who are truly seeking the reform of the church. We must not routinely read heretics out of the kingdom, for true faith can still exist in persons whose theology is out of balance. The church should move against heretical teachers only when they pose a dire threat to the integrity of its message. Moreover, the defenders of church doctrine must be motivated by love for both the heretics and the truth they deny. The best way to overcome heresy is through open dialogue with our opponents. The truth will defend itself if it is allowed a place in the open forum. On the other hand, when the truth is openly and shamelessly defamed and resisted without any sign of a change of heart or willingness to listen, then the adversary of truth must finally be disciplined, and this may entail excommunication—the breaking of fellowship with the recalcitrant sinner, no longer recognizing that person as a bona fide member of the church. The ban of excommunication is an indictment not only of the heretic but also of the church for failing to present its case in such a way that people are not only convinced of the truth of its message but also converted by the love and zeal of its messengers. The goal of excommunication is not the isolation and damnation of heretics but their restoration to the fellowship of the church through admission of error, repentance for sin and resolution to reaffirm the faith of the church.[27]

Finally, we need to deal with still another mark of the false church—experimentalism. Here we discern a penchant for novelty, a desire for change—not in the message of faith but in the forms by which faith is communicated. The search for new forms, however, often involves an alteration in the content of faith, for form and content belong together in every faith tradition. I am not recommending that we remain closed to all innovation, since the new wine of the gospel will often call for new wineskins (Mt 9:17; Lk 5:37-39). Yet the new wineskin that Scripture speaks of has already been provided in the church of the Lord Jesus Christ, and we cannot remain within the parameters of the community of faith unless we respect the forms and language in which this faith comes to us. So-called contemporary worship prides itself on its free adaptation of the gospel to current fashions in music and drama, but what too often results is a spirituality that mirrors the uncertainties and idolatries of the times rather than one that glories in the cross of Christ (Gal 6:14).[28] We must be open to the new wind of the Spirit, yet fully cognizant that other winds are blowing. We must pray energetically for the gift of discernment so that we will be able to distinguish what is true from what is false. A church that rushes to embrace the fads and fashions of the age and eagerly lets go of the liturgical richness of the past under the cover of a quest for relevance is one that clearly reveals itself to be a false church. This does not imply that it no longer contains any remnant of the truth; it indicates only that the truth is being compromised by an unwholesome desire to exhibit our own piety and sagacity before both church and world. What is required today is not an innovative church but a faithful church, one that gives priority to the truth of the gospel over church growth, one that is willing to embrace a servant role in which the apologetic motif is subsidiary to the evangelical proclamation.

Word and Spirit

Part of the legacy of the Enlightenment was the sundering of the paradoxical unity of Word and Spirit. On the rationalistic side the Word was transmuted into moral instruction, and the Spirit became the inner light or the illuminator of conscience. The sacramental nature of the sermon was lost sight of, and the cerebral came to dominate over the mystical.

As a backlash against the ascent of rationalism in both liberal and conservative Protestantism, catholic movements of renewal have emerged that seek to reclaim the centrality of the eucharist in worship. The sermon is seen as a preparatory stage in the service for the eucharistic celebration. Wolfhart Pannenberg reflects this catholic emphasis when he affirms that "the Eucharist, not the sermon, is in the center of the church's life. . . . The sermon should serve, not dominate, in the church. It should serve the presence of Christ which we celebrate in the Eucharist."[29]

Reflecting similar sentiments, Christof Gestrich argues that the sermon is not integral in worship and that a full service of worship does not require a sermon.[30]

> Pastors should be put in a position of enjoying an inner freedom that gives them permission time and again not to preach in the worship services they conduct. Less would often be more. With its rich liturgical possibilities the worship service is also able to lend expression to that adoration of God which always both edifies the worshipers and elevates them to a position of dignity.[31]

Acknowledging his indebtedness to the later Barth, Gestrich further affirms that preaching should be regarded as a testimony to grace rather than a means of grace. The sermon does not bring redemption but points to a redemption already procured by Jesus Christ. "The fact God is and can be our deliverer from death and sin does not at all depend on whether there is preaching, or 'preaching that is done properly.' God *is* this Deliverer."[32]

With the Reformers and the early Barth, I contend that both sermon and sacraments are means of grace—not through any quality of their own but through the redeeming action of the Spirit, who uses visible signs to impart spiritual truth. The preaching of the Word of God is not simply preaching about the Word but the very Word of God itself, as the Second Helvetic Confession duly recognizes.[33] The sacraments have no power in themselves to produce faith, but in union with the Word of God they can be channels of grace as they are laid hold of by the Holy Spirit.

Preaching and sacraments in and of themselves are not marks of the true church, but only in their unity with the Spirit do they make visible the integrity and validity of the church's witness. Dietrich Bonhoeffer phrases it well:

> *Where is the true church?* Where preaching stands and falls by the pure Gos-

pel of the gracious God against all human self-righteousness. Where the sacraments depend on the word of Christ without any magic. Where the community of the spirit stands in service and not in domination.[34]

The devout study of the Bible as the Word of God could also be considered a mark of the true church. Yet the essence of the church is to be found not in the Bible as such nor in the sermon and sacraments as such but in the descent of the Spirit into our midst, opening our inward eyes to the eternal significance of the external forms and rites of the church. The so-called marks of the church do not convince anyone unless that person has been grasped by the reality that the marks signify and proclaim. The marks of the church must not remain external to us but must enter into the deeper recesses of our being and profoundly alter our life vision and lifestyle. This mystical side of the signs and marks of the church is astutely perceived by J. Heinrich Arnold: "As regards the Word, it does not matter what we feel or think, nor what we memorize—even if we know all the words of Jesus as written in the New Testament—but that his words are burned into our hearts by God himself. That is the Gospel."[35]

In summary, it is not enough to have sound preaching of the word. This preaching must be animated by the Spirit if it is to convey the water of life. Nor is it sufficient to have the right observance of the sacraments. Baptism with water accomplishes nothing unless it is joined to baptism into the death of Christ (Rom 6:3-4). The Lord's Supper is not a holy communion unless we eat and drink in the power of faith. The church cannot be recognized as the mystical body of Christ unless people are brought into mystical union with Christ through faith and repentance.

·SEVEN·

WORSHIP IN SPIRIT AND TRUTH

Worship the LORD in all his holy splendor. Let all the earth tremble before him.
1 CHRONICLES 16:29-30 NLT

God is spirit, and those who worship him must worship in spirit and truth.
JOHN 4:24

The greatest product of the Church is not brotherly love but divine worship.
And we shall never worship right nor serve right
till we are more engrossed with our God than even with our worship,
with His reality than our piety, with His Cross than our service.
PETER T. FORSYTH

The whole common life of the Christian fellowship oscillates between
Word and Sacrament, it begins and ends in worship.
It looks forward in expectation to the final banquet in the
kingdom of God.
DIETRICH BONHOEFFER

A local church exists to do corporately what each Christian
believer should be doing individually—and that is to worship God.
A. W. TOZER

I f there is anything that characterizes modern worship it is the loss of the sacred. Whether the service of worship is low church or liturgical the sense of the Holy too often appears to be missing. Edward Farley trenchantly observes that

---

the discourse (invocation, praises, hymns, confessions, sacred texts) indicates that the event celebrates a sacred presence. But this discourse is neutralized by the prevailing mood, which is casual, comfortable, chatty, busy, humorous, pleasant and at times even cute. This mood is a sign not of a sacred reality but of various congregational self-preoccupations. The sacred is not so much a presence as a theme and content of the ritual activity. Lacking is a sense of the terrible mystery of God, which sets language atremble and silences facile chattiness.[1]

Farley goes on to note that the brightness of the sanctuary

resembles the illuminated rooms of malls or banks. The sounds of chatter bracket the worship service. The mood is easy and casual, friends (and some strangers) gathering to enjoy a common experience. Humor, laughter and occasionally even applause are part of the experience. Cuteness marks the children's sermon. Classic instrumental music suggests the concert hall. The written sermon . . . occasionally humorous, centers the experience.[2]

P. T. Forsyth, who wrote long before the emergence of so-called contemporary worship, astutely perceived that something was wrong at the very heart of the worship experience:

The poverty of our worship amid its very refinements, its lack of solemnity, poorly compensated by an excess of tenderness and taste, is the fatal index of the peril. We do need more reverence in our prayer, more beauty in our praise, less dread of tried and consecrated form.[3]

Eastern Orthodox theologian Georges Florovsky (d. 1979) reminds us of the priority of worship in the life of the church: "Christianity is a liturgical religion. The Church is first of all a worshipping community. Worship comes first, doctrine and discipline second."[4] I agree with this sentiment so long as we do not reduce worship to a formal liturgy. The praise of God has a certain priority over doctrine and discipline. *Doxa* (worship) is muted unless it is united with dogma and praxis. Dogma and praxis, on the other hand, become lifeless unless they are rooted in *doxa*. Theology is both dogmatic and doxological. Study and prayer belong together.

Karl Barth too assigned a preeminent place to worship in the life of the Christian. It is worship that enlivens the church on its pilgrimage of faith and keeps the church centered in the gospel. He could even claim that "the church service is the most important, momentous and majestic thing which can possibly take place on earth, because its primary content is not the work of man but the work of the Holy Spirit and consequently the work of faith."[5] Worship is not efficacious in molding the Christian life, however, unless it is united with a passion to help people in need, which becomes a parable of our love for God.[6]

Worship in Biblical Perspective

Biblical religion endorses not any kind of worship but only that which is done "in spirit and in truth" (Jn 4:23-24 REB). True worship is directed not to the finite but to the infinite, who nevertheless meets us in the finite—in the spoken word and in the sacramental ritual. Worship that glorifies God is animated by his Spirit and informed by the truth of his revelation in Jesus Christ. True worship is grounded in the paradoxical unity of logos and pneuma.

The worship of the community will always involve outward forms or rituals, but it is never to be reduced to these forms. What is acceptable to God is not "ritual sacrifices" and "burnt offerings" but the sacrifice of broken and contrite hearts (Ps 51:17; cf. 1 Sam 15:22-23; Amos 5:21-24; Mic 6:7-8; Hos 6:6; Rom 12:1). The apostle warns in 2 Timothy 3:5 against embracing the forms of godliness without the power. This same note is found in Isaiah:

> These people come near to me with their mouth
> and honor me with their lips,
> but their hearts are far from me.
> Their worship of me
> is made up only of rules taught by men (Is 29:13 NIV).

True worship is characterized not by the observance of holy days but by holy obedience (Gal 4:10). True repentance consists not in the rending of garments but in the rending of hearts (Joel 2:13). True spirituality directs people not to holy places but to the holy God, who is always available by the indwelling of his Spirit (Jn 4:20-24).

Worship that is done in spirit and in truth will entail an encounter with the Holy, who includes and transcends moral goodness (R. Otto).[7] A true encounter with the Holy precipitates a sense of awe in which we experience our helplessness and littleness before an almighty God. The apostolic writer summons us to "worship God as he would be worshipped, with reverence and awe; for our God is a devouring fire" (Heb 12:28-29 REB). We should praise both the loving deeds of God and "the splendor of his holiness" (2 Chron 20:21 REB). True worship does not, however, reduce the human subject to nothingness; instead it elevates and edifies us in the knowledge that God is not only our Master but also our Friend. Yet God is Master before he is Friend,[8] and it is only as we experience the chasm that separates us from God that we come to appreciate the irrevocable fact that God has bridged this chasm in Jesus Christ and that he is therefore *with* us as well as *over* and *against* us.

In the fuller biblical perspective worship is a creative response to God's gracious act of condescension in Jesus Christ, a response that takes the form of praise, proclamation, recollection and prayer. Worship is not a methodical attempt to discover the God within us or unite ourselves to God by rites of purification. Its goal is not even to satisfy the human need for God. The focus of acceptable worship is not God as he is in himself but God *for* us and *with* us in the revelation of the Torah and in Jesus Christ. The believer does not seek to delve into the hidden abyss of God but to celebrate what God has done for us and the whole world in his saving work in the history of Israel culminating in Jesus Christ. It is not the spiritual fulfillment of the self but the gracious condescension of the living God that should be our chief concern. Worship celebrates the story of salvation that is unfolded in events in the history of a particular people, but whose benefits are applied to the whole of humanity.

Worship that is done in spirit and truth will be unabashedly theocentric. Its purpose is to glorify God, not celebrate human ingenuity and wisdom. It is inspired not by a love that seeks God as its highest possession (eros), but by a love that offers itself as a sacrifice to God through service to the world for which Christ died (agape). In worship, love is united with faith so that God is magnified and his deeds are commemorated. Regrettably in much modern worship sentimental love reigns over adoring love, and the act of worship is made to serve the feeling of being confirmed in our manner of life.

As has already been noted, true worship does not obliterate the human subject but elevates that person to the status of a son or daughter of God. As Irenaeus put it, "The glory of God is humanity fully alive." Those who worship the true God are not cast down into depression, for they are sustained in the knowledge that their sins are forgiven and that they have received power from God's Holy Spirit. The worship of the living God brings dividends: peace, faith, hope, love, wisdom, humility, fortitude. Yet our worship is done not to achieve these blessings but only to glorify God and magnify the name of Jesus Christ. Such blessings are a consequence and fruit of our worship, not its motivation and focus. We do not worship in order to realize the potentialities of the self, but self-realization will invariably accompany worship that is done in spirit and truth.

Worship that is based on Christian faith involves not the repetition of Christ's atoning sacrifice but the proclamation and celebration of this sacrifice. In true worship we offer sacrifices of praise and thanksgiving to the living God, not sacrifices of reparation or propitiation. Jesus has already atoned for the sins of the world through his self-sacrifice on the cross, which is sufficient for the salvation of all peoples. Our task is to thank God for the mercies bestowed on us in Christ and proclaim this good news to a lost and dying world.

The motivation for worship should be joy for what God has done for us in Christ, faith that his Spirit will see us through every trial, hope that his promises will be realized in our lives. Proper self concern is not excluded from the worship experience, but it is always subordinated to the glory of God and the wonder of his love. We worship not in order to make ourselves holy but to give thanks to God for his holiness revealed to us in Jesus Christ and assured to us through the outpouring of the Spirit at Pentecost.

Worship and service belong together in the Christian life, but worship must never be reduced to service. Worship is not simply an attitude that permeates all things Christians do, but an engagement with the sacred in acts of praise and thanksgiving. Service to our neighbor proceeds from worship, but worship is something much more than service. It involves an encounter with the Holy that brings us interior peace and salvation. Yet God is not pleased if in our worship of him we neglect the dire needs of our neighbor, both spiritual and material. The service of God's glory involves the service of humanity's deepest hopes and aspirations, both earthly and heavenly. The worship of God takes us out of ourselves into the crying needs of the world that remains lost and condemned apart from faith in the Lord Jesus Christ.

Christian theology has always taught that there are duties we owe to God as well as to our neighbor. What we owe to God are works of piety: prayer, meditation, baptism, participation in the Lord's Supper, corporate worship, fasting, witnessing, sabbath observance and so on. What we owe to our neighbor are works of mercy: charitable giving, hospitality, visiting the sick, helping the incapacitated, feeding the hungry, comforting the afflicted and so on. We are also enjoined to do works of justice: alleviating the distress of our neighbor through social pressure and legislation. What we owe to God takes precedence over what we owe to our neighbor, but the former without the latter becomes a purely external observance devoid of inner power.

Although we are justified by faith alone, faith does not remain alone but takes the form of obedience to God and his law as well as service to our neighbor. We must avoid the traps of both cheap grace and works-righteousness. We are lifeless apart from the gift of God's Spirit, but through his Spirit we become energized to do works of charity and works of piety. Our worship is directed to God and God alone, but the evidence of the genuineness of our worship lies in our service to the needy and downtrodden of the world.

The person of piety will strenuously avoid any temptation to idolatry, the cardinal sin of Judeo-Christian religion. We are to "shun the worship of idols" (1 Cor 10:14; cf. Rev 14:9-10), but we are also summoned to shun the practice of immorality (Rom 6:12-14; 1 Cor 6:7-11; Gal 5:16-21; Eph 4:17-32; 1 Pet 1:14-17). Being indifferent to the plight of our neighbor in our selfish pursuit of pleasure and power can be as subversive of life in the Spirit as the yearning after other gods. Theocentric worship involves compassion for a hurting humanity. The celebration of free grace entails bearing the cross as a disciple of Christ for the glory of God and the good of our neighbor. Worship in biblical perspective is correlative with service to the lowly and the maltreated. Service to the lowly on the other hand will always be rooted in a living faith in the holy God who upholds us in our trials and empowers us in our weakness and indecision.

What is important to understand is that in true worship God's grace precedes human effort, God's love gives rise to human faith. Michael Horton puts it well: "The worship service is not primarily our offering to God, but his offering to us. It is his coming again and again into our lives, judging, justifying; condemning, delivering; crushing, restoring. Our response must accommodate all of these divine actions."[10] Worship in the biblical sense is theocentric not only because its goal is the glory of God, but also because its origin lies in the Spirit of God. Its central content, moreover, is God's gift of salvation to us and the whole world in the person of Jesus Christ, in his sacrificial life and death. The culmination of Christian worship lies in an acknowledgment of the mystery of the incarnation of Christ and of the paradox of his glorious triumph through the powerlessness of the cross.

God Transcendent
To worship God in spirit and truth presupposes a God who both towers

above us in his being and relates to us by his Spirit. He is a God who finds us rather than a God who is found by us. This is the God who is known only in his self-revelation in biblical history culminating in Jesus Christ. He is not a God who is known by the exploration of nature or by the examination of the self. All persons are inescapably related to God, but none of us can find God on our own. Because of our sin we cannot gain valid knowledge of God apart from God's revelation, though we can attain a rudimentary knowledge that is sufficient, however, only to lead us astray.

I take the side of Pascal over Tillich: the God of Abraham, Isaac and Jacob is not the god of the philosophers.[11] The personal-infinite God of biblical faith cannot be reconciled with the impersonal-infinite god of classical philosophy and religion. Nor can the biblical God be harmonized with the impersonal-finite god of modern philosophy and spirituality. The God of the Bible is neither the abstract, distant god of classical thought nor the ineffable, incommunicable god of mysticism. Nor can this God be identified with the creative process or *élan vital* of modern naturalism. The God we worship is the God of historical revelation, the God who communicates to us through the historical events testified to in the Bible. He is the God who confronts us as another subject so that we can enter into an I-Thou relationship with him.

The God of the Bible is not anonymous. He has a name and therefore can be described in language that mirrors his self-revelation and not merely by metaphors drawn from human experience. In the Old Testament God's proper name is Yahweh or LORD. In the New Testament he has the trinitarian name: Father, Son and Holy Spirit. He also confronts us by the name of Jesus, the name that is above every name (Eph 1:21). Certainly in our references to God in the worship celebration we are obliged to call God by his proper name, though we assuredly may use metaphors and similes for God that have a solid biblical basis. Because God is personal, because he addresses us as both a loving Father and a caring Son, it is incumbent on us to use pronominal language in our depictions of God. This language, however, will be confined to the use of the masculine pronoun and pronominal adjective, since this is how the Bible consistently refers to God. God is like a Mother in many of his activities, but he addresses us as Father, Son and Spirit, and this is also how we must address him, especially in public worship.

The God of sacred Scripture is not a transcendental ideal that is outside the ebb and flow of history, but a personal Spiritual Presence who enters into our time and space in order to have real relations with us. He is the living God who takes the initiative in approaching us and communing with us. He is both radically transcendent and ineradicably immanent, though he is transcendent before he is immanent. He is the God who makes himself immanent even though he does not need the human or cosmic creation, since he has perfect fellowship within himself as a triune being. He is transcendent, moreover, even when he is immanent. He relates to us but never becomes part of us, nor are we ever absorbed into his nature, though we are allowed to participate in his life-giving energy through faith. He is both the Wholly Other and the Infinitely Near at the same time.

As a living God he allows himself to be affected by the thoughts and actions of his people. He is not impervious to pain nor immune to suffering but enters into our pain and suffering. He is the One who not merely decrees but who acts and speaks. He is not an all-pervasive Spirit who transcends the subject-object cleavage but the Absolute Subject who makes himself an object of our perception and understanding. He is both the concrete universal and the absolutely singular. He is the definitive person who is absolutely related to all that exists, though this is because he wills to be so related.

The God of the Scriptures is both infinitely loving and irrevocably holy. He cannot tolerate sin, but he embraces the sinner. He loves us even while judging us, and he judges us because he loves us. His love is not the sentimental love that overlooks our failings, but a searing holy love that equips us to deal with our failings. His is the love that does not let us alone but pursues us even into the darkness (Nahum

1:8) so that we will finally return to the tried and true paths (Jer 6:16).

It is also important to bear in mind that this God is sovereign—over life and history. A God who is simply a "fellow-sufferer who understands" (Whitehead) can be admired but not worshiped.[12] The human spirit can only adore a God who has "the whole world in his hands." We can empathize with a god who is struggling, as we are, to realize inner potentialities, but we cannot worship this kind of god. One reason why so much modern worship is bereft of awe and wonder is that too many clergy have succumbed to the beguilements of process philosophy and theology.

We need to emphasize that God's power and holiness are subordinate to his love. Because God is holy as well as loving, his love is ipso facto a holy love. Because God is all-powerful as well, his love is ipso facto an efficacious love. It goes forth from his being and does not return to him empty (Is 55:11).

As a God of holy love, God is both *nomos* (law) and *agape*. If he were agape alone he would not have to satisfy the demands of his holiness and could therefore forgive without judging. Agape does not overthrow but fulfills God's law (Mt 5:17). This is why in the service of corporate worship there can be a place for the reading of the Decalogue as well as for the confession of the Apostles' Creed. God is *nomos* and *agape*, but he is not *eros*.[13] He does not aspire to self-fulfillment, for he is already fulfilled. But he descends to the plane of humanity even in its sin and dereliction because he wills to share the bounty of his goodness and mercy. He is pleased when we respond to his initiatives in repentance and faith. The God of Scripture is not absorbed in himself (as is Aristotle's Unmoved Mover), but he goes out of himself in seeking and embracing love for the sake of his creation.[14] God demonstrates his caring concern by calling us to participate in the interior life of his triune being and raising us by his grace to the level where this is possible. He is not content that we remain merely his servants. He welcomes and embraces us as his sons and daughters and rejoices when we return to him seeking his mercy and forgiveness (Lk 15:11-32).

In imitation of God who reaches out to us, we should reach out to our neighbor in self-giving love. We should also reach up to God in adoring love—out of gratitude and joy for what God has done for us in Jesus Christ. To adore God is to delight in God, yet not in order to embellish the self or satisfy the spiritual hunger of the self, but to show him our love and thankfulness for his mercy.

I will not join Ritschl in outrightly rejecting the mystical heritage of the church revived in Pietism, since our love for God must include the hope of seeing his face and delighting in his presence.[15] But our primary motivation in seeking God is not to find personal peace and contentment (though this will certainly occur) but to give thanks to God for creating us and redeeming us in Jesus Christ. Our task as Christians is to serve God and advance the cause of his kingdom through our words and actions. But we are also summoned to delight in God, not only in his service but also in his presence. We are called to be not only his heralds and ambassadors but also his worshipers. In the worship of God our spiritual longings and yearnings reach fulfillment, but this is a consequence of our mandate to give him all the glory and honor. The realization of heartfelt desire is not the goal of the Christian life but a felicitous byproduct.

Word and Image

Christian faith is founded on God's self-revelation in his Word, but Scripture warns us not to make a graven image of the divine because of the omnipresent danger that the image itself may become an object of worship (cf. Ex 20:4-6; Deut 5:8-10; Ps 78:58; Is 40:18). In addition there is the incontrovertible fact that an image invariably gives a false picture of God because it is necessarily limited in what it can denote. Calvin declared that "only those things are to be sculptured or painted which the eyes are capable of seeing: let not God's majesty, which is far above the perception of the eyes, be debased through unseemly representations."[16] James I. Packer forcefully argues that images "inevitably conceal most, if not all, of the truth about the personal nature and character of the divine Being whom they represent."[17] According to Packer even a symbol like the crucifix obscures the glory of Christ, for it "hides the fact of His deity, His victory on the cross, and His present kingdom. It displays His human weakness, but it conceals His divine strength; it depicts the reality of his pain, but keeps out of our sight the reality of His joy and His power."[18]

Reformed worship will always contain an iconoclastic element because of its astute perception that images and paintings open the door to idolatry. Aaron's golden calf was intended as a visible symbol of Jehovah, but it came to supplant Jehovah in the minds of the worshipers.[19] I would not go as far as Packer in prohibiting all symbols in the act of worship, for most of them do not purport to embody the sacred reality they are meant to represent. Yet even symbols that have been acceptable in the Reformed tradition, like the empty cross, can become the object of our veneration. We need to remember that only Jesus Christ is the image or icon of the invisible God (Col 1:15). This is an image, moreover, that is known only through proclamation, not through artistic representation.

The argument against images for God is rooted in both the biblical prohibition of image worship (Ex 20; Deut 5) and the biblical claim that God is transcendent and invisible. Our Lord declared, "No one has ever seen God; the only Son, who is in the bosom of the Father, he has made him known" (Jn 1:18). We can know the living God by faith but not by sight. We can know the reality of the transcendent, but we cannot see this reality. And when we attempt to portray it through painting and sculpture we invariably distort it.

The God of Scripture is both hidden and manifest, but he is manifest only to the inward eye. Even in his self-revelation he remains hidden *(deus absconditus)*. He remains out of the reach of our senses and imagination even when we are in communion with him. To try to see God reveals an unwholesome desire to control God, for over what we see we gain a measure of power.[20] Faith comes by hearing and hearing comes by the preaching of the gospel (Rom 10:17). To see is to possess, to hear is to wait and then to act. Luther wisely perceived that the point of contact with God is the ear, not the eye. "In order to see God we must learn to put our eyes into our ears. . . . Christ's kingdom is a kingdom of hearing, not a kingdom of seeing. For the eyes lead and guide us not thither where we find Christ and get to know Him, but the ears must do this."[21] Similarly in a sacramental hymn Thomas Aquinas declares:

> Sight, feeling, taste delude themselves
>> about thee.
> By hearing alone is sure faith
>> given.
> Only what God's Son has said
>> do I believe.
> The Word is truth, and what can
>> be more true?[22]

While by no means ruling out artistic depictions of the historical characters and events in the Bible, I have serious reservations about pictorial representations of God. The commandment against graven images seems to disallow even representations of things on earth because of the propensity of the human imagination to confuse the heavenly and the earthly. From a Reformed standpoint the attempt to embellish worship by banners, paintings and statues is bound to result in worship whose object is to exhilarate the senses rather than give glory to God. Protestant tradition does make a place for the visible word, the sacrament of Holy Communion, but it insists that the visible word must always be united with the audible word and indeed serves the audible word. My Lutheran background prevents me from being a complete iconoclast. Symbols in worship can point beyond themselves to the invisible God. But my Puritan allegiance makes me extremely wary of incorporating artistic depictions in the service of worship, aware as I am that symbols as well as images are likely to distort the human perception of God more than guide the imagination toward a true understanding of God.

We must not discount the fact that words too can become an obstacle to spiritual worship. The word that comes forth from the preacher's mouth is not necessarily the word of the gospel, and it may well be a false interpretation of the gospel. Words that signify the projection of the personal experiences of the preacher rather than the truth of the scriptural text must be deemed chatter rather than wisdom. Even when the words of the preacher appear to correspond to the biblical text, if the Holy Spirit is not acting, the words will be devoid of power to convict and transform.

In worship that is done in spirit and truth the word of the Bible must be united with the life-giving energy of the Spirit. The gospel is both wisdom and power, and it is not one without the other. Karl Barth referred to the impossibility of preaching the real Word of God because the human mind can never comprehend the mysteries that God imparts through his witnesses in holy Scripture.[23] Yet he also perceived that though our words can never capture or contain the reality of God's self-revelation in Christ, God through his Spirit can use our words to reveal the magnitude of his mercy and power in Christ. The finite cannot comprehend the infinite, but the infinite can penetrate the finite and thereby convert the finite into a veritable means of grace.

I fully endorse James Packer's keen observation that the commandment against images extends to mental as well as molten images.[24] Whenever we conjure in our mind what God really is in himself, we are in danger of confusing human conceptions with sacred realities. One cannot engage in the theological task without having some idea of who God is, but we need always to recognize that God infinitely transcends the highest reaches of human conception and imagination (Is 55:8-9; Rom 11:33-36). The specter of idolatry emerges when we rename God in order to bring God into conformity with cultural expectations. The reimagining conferences organized by feminists in the mainline denominations prove to be unwitting ventures in idolatry, since the new depictions of God stand in sharp contrast to God's self-designation in Jesus Christ. Adherence to traditional depictions of God does not guarantee that we have escaped the snare of idolatry, for we may attribute to God characteristics that are meant to be taken only figuratively or metaphorically, not literally or univocally. God is not a man (Hos 11:9), but he relates to us primarily in the masculine mode. We cannot know the biblical God apart from the earthen vessel of the biblical language, but even when we use biblical language we are not really in contact with God until we have received the illumination of his Spirit.

The Crisis in Spirituality

The crisis in worship today signifies a crisis in spirituality—the way we live out our faith. Traditional worship has become formalistic; contemporary worship is gnostic and secular. The first clings to the past, the second seeks the approbation of the present. The first makes worship an obligation; the second converts worship into therapy. The first is intent on preserving continuity with the tradition; the second severs the ties to tradition in the search for novelty.

It is an indisputable fact that for a growing number of people the old forms no longer seem to have the power to instill conviction and to deepen faith. In reaction to the reduction of worship to prescribed formulas, the new spirituality seeks to cultivate an experience with God that bypasses the forms and rituals of church tradition. Ecstasy rather than doctrinal purity or biblical fidelity is the primary concern in contemporary worship. We would do well to heed this warning of P. T. Forsyth:

> Spiritual life is not exuberance. The Church is not a company of soul-adventurers. It is not made by moral experimenters or imaginative explorers. It is not for treasure-seeking; it has found the pearl of all pearls. It does not answer the call of the wild in the soul's unexplored interior, but the call of the Grace that finds it. It is committed not to a quest but to a faith.[25]

The reconception of God is a sign of the crisis in spirituality today. God is no longer the personal-infinite God but the finite god who struggles as we do for self-fulfillment. He is not the creator of nature but the creative power or organizing force in nature. He does not transcend nature but is himself the divinization of nature. This is a god who meets us in the depths rather than a God who addresses us from the heights. He has been described by his devotees as the "Pool of Unlimited Power" and "Unlimited Possibility."

Similarly, faith has been reconceived as a power force that can be used for good or bad. No longer an empty vessel that simply receives God's grace, faith is now a catalyst that energizes the self and works miracles. Its power lies in the tongue—the spoken confession. If we claim it we will gain it. Faith is the mechanism that even God uses to create and heal.[26]

Biblical spirituality is now in eclipse, and this is especially evident both in services of worship and in private prayer. We no longer hear from the pulpit the clarion call to repentance but an invitation to discover the spirit of the divine within us. Mysticism prevails over prophetism, naturalism over supernaturalism, gnosticism over biblical personalism. Worship is now a means to tap into the creative powers within us rather than an occasion to bring before God our sacrifices of praise and thanksgiving. Hymns that retell the story of salvation as delineated in the Bible are being supplanted by praise choruses that are designed to transport the soul into a higher dimension of reality. Fellowship with God is based not on the incarnation of God in materiality but on the capacity of the soul to rise above materiality into the realm of pure spirit. No wonder that Harold Bloom calls gnosticism the real religion of America.[27]

True Spirituality

Worship in spirit and truth lies in a recovery of true spirituality—the living out of our vocation to be witnesses and ambassadors of the Lord Jesus Christ. In order to worship rightly we must be sealed with the Spirit and rooted in the truth. We must both believe in the message of the cross and bear the cross as a token of our gratitude for God's inestimable mercy revealed and fulfilled in Jesus Christ.

Spirituality in the biblical panorama signifies not the ascent to divinity (as in the old mysticism) nor the ascent to a superhumanity (as in the new mysticism) but the descent of divinity to a sinful humanity. Through faith in Christ we are lifted into the presence of God, but this is an undeserved blessing from God rather than a mystical work of self-purification.

Prayer in the biblical perspective is not opening ourselves to the creative surge within us (as in much current naturalism and vitalism) nor is it the contemplation of the infinite abyss of being (as in classical mysticism). Instead it is the outpouring of the soul before a gracious and holy God. Biblical prayer is not immersion in the being of God, but the conversation of the heart with God. It will include thanksgiving and adoration as well as petition, but its essence is petition. The goal is not wordless or mindless prayer, but prayer in which we make known our needs and concerns to a holy and merciful God. Paul urges his hearers to "persevere in prayer, with minds alert and with thankful hearts" (Col 4:2 REB).[28]

Worship in the context of a biblical or prophetic spirituality is not an adventure into novelty (Whitehead) nor the contemplation of eternity, but the celebration of a divine intervention into a particular history—that is mirrored in holy Scripture. Worship involves not a quest for meaning or rapture but an acknowledgement that meaning and salvation for our lives has been provided by God's incomparable act of redemption in Jesus Christ.

The focus of true spirituality is not on the creative advance in history (as in Henry Nelson Wieman and Bernard Loomer)[29] but on the crisis of history, the point in history where God became man in Jesus Christ. What should command our attention is not our breakthrough into self-understanding but God's breakthrough into the world of sin and death.

Renewal in worship lies not in resymbolization nor in technique that enables us to unfold our divine potential. Instead it lies in repentance and faith in the living God. True spirituality is to give glory to God through worship of the Trinity, the proclamation of the gospel and service to the world in the name of Jesus Christ.

The role of silence in worship and devotion has long been a subject of debate among theologians. Those on the mystical side see silence as indispensable in bringing us closer to God or in making us more aware of his presence. Those on the orthodox side, who tend to equate revelation with the communication of propositional truth, generally regard the call to silence with reservations, sometimes even with suspicion. Yet Scripture tells us because "the LORD is in his holy temple" all the earth should "keep silence before him" (Hab 2:20; cf. Zeph 1:7; Zech 2:13). In the biblical view silence has a salutary role in preparing us to hear the Word of God. It does not take us beyond the Word but helps us to be open to the Word. Rudolf Otto proposed a sacrament of silence as the culmination of worship.[30] In contrast to Otto, the culmination of evangelical worship is not silence but the preaching and hearing of God's Word and prayer on the basis of God's Word. I would argue against Pannenberg and the mainstream of Catholic tradition that the high point in the worship celebration is not even the sacrament of the eucharist, but the biblical, evangelical proclamation. The eucharist is nonetheless a high point in the worship celebration. At the same time, as Reformed or evangelical theologians we must insist that the sacrament receives its content and power from the Word.

The act of worship is not a flight from reason but the offering up of our reason to the glory of God. It is rational as well as volitional and affectional, but it also takes us beyond the rational. In worship that is done in spirit and truth we meet the wisdom of God as well as experience his power and holiness.

We need always to guard against two opposite dangers: rationalism and mysticism.[31] In rationalism we have an emphasis on the Word but to the neglect of the Spirit. In a rationalistic milieu the worship service is cerebral rather than affectional, didactic rather than kerygmatic. Sermons are reduced to lectures thereby losing their character as announcements of good tidings. In rationalistic orthodoxy philosophers are sometimes quoted nearly as much as prophets and apostles, thus lending the sermon the air of worldly sagacity. Sermons in this tradition frequently have a polemical or apologetic ring and are intended to persuade more than to convert. In Unitarian-Universalist churches sermons often take the form of discourses on moral themes rather than celebrations of God's act of self-sacrifice in Jesus Christ.

In mysticism the worship service is designed to lead us into the presence of God but without providing a rational grasp of who or what this presence is. The sermon offers illumination on progressing in the Christian life but not on clarifying the mysteries that constitute the foundation of faith. Pneuma and praxis take priority over logos in a radical or consistent mysticism.

I fully agree with Berkouwer when he says, "It is a serious misconception to believe that the value of faith and obedience increases to the degree that the object of faith becomes more inconceivable and more enigmatic."[32] Faith acknowledges paradox in the divine revelation, but it does not glory in paradox. It takes us beyond the parameters of human reason, but it does not necessarily go against reason. Faith is not irrational, but neither is it exhaustively rational. God is truly revealed in Jesus Christ and in holy Scripture, but he is hidden even in his revelation, and this is why faith is necessary.

Evangelical worship involves interpretation as well as celebration. It may lead us into experiences of rapture or ecstasy, but it does not allow us to remain in these rapturous heights. Instead it draws us down into recollection—not of our divine origin but of God's mighty acts in history. In worship in spirit and in truth we will delight in being in the presence of God but also declare our readiness to do the will of God in the daily tasks of life.

The recovery of worship in spirit and in truth lies in a rediscovery of the God of the Bible—of the purity of his holiness and the generosity of his love. True spirituality will acclaim Jesus Christ as "the radiance of God's glory, the stamp of God's very being" (Heb 1:3 REB). It will remind us that the Son of God in conjunction with the Father and the Spirit "sustains the universe by his word of power" and that he has "brought about purification from sins." It will call us to the confession and proclamation of the message of the cross: "not that we loved God but that he loved us and sent his Son to be the expiation for our sins" (1 Jn 4:10). It will direct our attention away from our own strategies and preoccupations to God's incomparable act of reconciliation and redemption in Jesus Christ (2 Cor 5:18-19). True spirituality is glorifying God by the confession of the name of Jesus and by sacrificial service to our fellow human beings for whom Christ died and rose again for the salvation of us all.

Appendix A: Contemporary Worship

A new style of worship has taken hold in many churches, both conservative and liberal. The Willow Creek Community Church in Barrington, Illinois, with its user-friendly services, is only one example of a growing trend in worship.[33] Lyle Schaller hails the new mood for its elevation of the "spontaneous and visual" and its "freeing the preacher from the pulpit." He also commends it for replacing "worship" with "celebration."[34] There is some evidence that the new style is attracting suburban families in particular, but how lasting its impact will be is another question. The principal issue we must deal with is whether so-called contemporary worship is unwittingly compromising the truth of the gospel.

Methodist pastor Craig Rice of Hamilton, Ohio, voices this complaint:

> What is so often missing from much of contemporary worship is a sense of the beauty, the blessing, and the being of God. . . . As long as the church continues to confuse the hunger for God, extant in every human heart, with the same yearnings that drive a market culture and a consumerist society, its worship will remain irrelevant at best, and an outright impediment at worst. As long as the church insists on serving up "Twinkies," even new and improved ones, many of those once-churched-now-unchurched will continue to seek their bread in the world at large.[35]

Michael Horton sees in contemporary worship a desire to control the movement of the Spirit, and in this respect it reproduces the failings of a hypertraditionalism.

> Proponents of contemporary worship are remarkably like their critics. The difference is that they think they have God in their control by negating everything the traditionalist holds dear. They too seem to believe that their novel forms are the keys that unlock the Holy Spirit's gilded imprisonment in classical idioms. They believe that by not uttering specific words, by not using classic hymns or choral arrangements, by not following any particular structure or pattern, their spontaneity and honesty will be rewarded by the Spirit. They have made themselves "open" and "available" by getting rid of written prayers, learned sermons, richly biblical hymns and formal opportunities for public confession, Scripture reading, and the declaration of forgiveness.[36]

My attitude toward contemporary worship is decidedly more reserved than supportive, though I see some redeeming qualities. I am perturbed by suggestions that "pulpits, altars, and even crosses be removed" as "barriers to seekers' faith."[37] The specter of heterodoxy arises when cultural appeal takes precedence over biblical fidelity, when the desire for novelty in worship is accompanied by a disdain for tradition. Form and spontaneity must both be present in a worship that seeks to be biblically faithful as well as culturally relevant. But when the accent is on the latter, the danger arises that the new wineskins will be holding the new wine of the culture rather than the new wine of the gospel. The Holy Spirit may be working in the new styles of worship, but we must not close our eyes to the possibility that evil spirits may also be at work turning people from a passion for the gospel to a passion to be accepted by the surrounding society.

Salient Marks

While contemporary worship is marked by considerable diversity, there are features that give it a semblance of commonality. Among these is eros spirituality, the desire to possess the highest good. This is especially evident in so-called contemporary music in which love is portrayed in terms of passion and longing for God.[38] Whereas the great hymns of the church were characterized by adoring love, the new emphasis is on sentimental or passionate love. This is why we are encouraged in some of these songs to "fall in love" with God. Even though much attention is given to the praise of God, the motivation tends to be egocentric—the satisfaction of the heart's desire. This is strikingly apparent in the praise song "As the Deer":

> I want You more than gold or silver,
>   only You can satisfy.
> You alone are the real joy giver
>   and the apple of my eye.[39]

Again contemporary worship is marred by an excessive individualism. The paradigm is the solitary individual in union with God. New style worship is concerned not with the people of God who unite their voices in a tribute of gratitude and adoration to God, but with the seeker after God who aspires to rise above the pressures and trials of living in the world in order to be lost in wonder, love and praise.

The focus of contemporary worship is not on content but on method. The aim is to create the right mood rather than to teach revealed truth. The praise choruses often take the form of mantras in which there is extended repetition of certain phrases (such as "Lord We Praise You" or "Our God Reigns"), which are designed to calm the soul rather than to enlighten the mind.[40]

The sermons for the most part are practical rather than theological or doctrinal. Scriptural texts may be used, but they prove to be only points of departure for discourses on themes that pertain to daily living. Typical sermon topics are "What the Bible Says About Friendship" and "Ways to Draw Near to God."

A common description of the worship service is that it is "user-friendly," meaning that it is easy to learn. It makes few demands on the celebrants other than rising and sitting. It is designed not so much for those who already believe as for those who are seeking. It neglects the biblical truth that we can seek only through the power that comes by hearing the gospel. To try to correlate the Christian faith with the seeking of the natural person is bound to result in a compromised gospel.

The music that enlivens the services does not readily lend itself to congregational singing. It often takes the form of solos and ensembles. In short it is an elitist music. The congregants for the most part remain spectators even though they may join in singing the praise choruses. New style worship is essentially a performance; the congregation is generally passive, assuming the role of onlookers who add to the air of theatricality by providing applause.[41]

In contrast to much traditional worship, the emphasis is not on the story of salvation but on cultivating intimacy with God. It is not on obedience to God's will but on the experience of God's presence. The search for ecstasy takes precedence over the cost of discipleship. When discipleship is talked about, the reference is usually not to the model of the suffering servant but to that of the possibility thinker. Being a disciple is how one finds happiness and fulfillment.

Modern Protestantism is faced with a paradigm shift of immense proportions. The key sacrament is no longer the Word or even the eucharist but the inward experience. The important thing is what goes on in the depths of the soul, not what is unfolded from the biblical text. Feeling takes priority over hearing. In many cases, particularly when special music is presented, one has difficulty in hearing the words because of the raucous beat of the drums and tambourines. But the words are not that significant; it is the mood that is the crucial element in the new worship paradigm.

While contemporary worship has the appearance of spontaneity, the forms that it spawns soon become inflexible and sacrosanct. The dances that are performed by selected persons are carefully rehearsed. This is in contrast to the dances in mainstream Pentecostal services, which are genuinely spontaneous and thereby seem to reflect the free movement of the Spirit.

In short, contemporary worship represents a marked deviation from traditional worship. It is a difference not only in form and method but also in content. Worship is no longer a celebration of what God has done for us in Christ but a mechanism by which the celebrants raise themselves above the clamor and dissonance of the world. Worship brings us into tune with the infinite rather than convicts us of sin and drives us to the cross of Christ in repentance. In the more avant-garde churches, worship has been reduced to entertainment, whereas in biblical perspective worship is confession, adoration and intercession.

How to Rectify the Situation

It is too easy simply to recommend that we return to traditional forms of worship. We need a theology of worship that instructs us on what is genuine and what is spurious, what is abiding and what is ephemeral. One of the cardinal axioms of an evangelical theology that draws upon the Protestant Reformation is that the kingdom of God take precedence over the satisfaction of spiritual and emotional needs. Our chief concern should be not the enhancement and preservation of the self but the glory of God that dims the claims of the self, yet does not abrogate the quest of the self for meaning and well-being.

People in the pews need to be both intellectually challenged and morally and spiritually stirred. It is important that sermons be theological as well as practical. As pastors it behooves us to feed our people on the first principles of the gospel, but if we are to help keep them in the faith we must go on to explore the ramifications of the word of God for doctrine and for life (cf. 1 Cor 3:2).

Finally, our seminaries ought to include courses on hymnody in which the instructors are informed theologically as well as musically. The music in a church service should be in the hands of the pastor or theologically trained elders, not of inexperienced laypersons or youth. The aim of church music is not to impress the worshipers with the talents of its members but to thank and praise God for his many blessings, particularly the gift of the Lord Jesus Christ for the salvation of the world.

Does contemporary worship and contemporary music contain only peril and not promise? We need to be open to the new wind of the Spirit, and this means that we should not routinely eschew all experimentation. There may be a place for bands or orchestras in the church, but these should never be substitutes for the organ, which through the power of the Spirit seems to convey at least some intimation of the grandeur of God. The organ and piano may well be played in unison on various occasions. The important thing is that we must not abandon the great hymns of the church for musical medleys that are designed to raise our consciousness to a higher spiritual level. The goal is worship services that are vibrant and alive, but the key is not new techniques but the gift of the Spirit. In the last analysis only the Spirit can liven up the service of worship, and the Spirit works primarily through the word—written and proclaimed. We will not begin to sing in the joy of the Spirit until we hear preaching of the word that is done in the power of the Spirit. But this kind of preaching will generally not take place unless it is fortified by people who pray in the Spirit.

The gulf between the transcendent God of biblical faith and the strivings and yearnings of a despairing humanity cannot be bridged by spiritual techniques nor by mystical ladders. It can be bridged only by the living God himself, and he has already done this in the person and work of Jesus Christ and in the outpouring of his Spirit on the church. Our goal is not to try to create the proper atmosphere for facilitating the spiritual quest but to acknowledge that God has decisively acted on our behalf in unconditional love in Jesus Christ. Our task is to respond to this fact in our worship of God and in our service to our neighbor for whom God in Christ died. We are called to exercise faith not as a power force that releases divine potential within us, but as an expression of our gratitude for what God has done for us in Christ and as a pledge to live no longer unto ourselves but now unto him who died for us and rose again for our salvation.

Appendix B: An Evangelical Order of Worship

Prelude

*Call to Worship

*Invocation

*Hymn of praise

Confession of sin

Assurance of pardon

*Gloria Patri

Hymn of redemption

Announcements

Testimony in song (anthem or special music)

Scripture readings

   Old Testament & New Testament

     or

   Gospel & Epistle

Hymn of preparation (sermon hymn)

Sermon

Sermon prayer & Lord's Prayer

Offertory

*Doxology & Offertory Prayer

Prayers of intercession

*Hymn of consecration

*Benediction

*Postlude

*Indicates standing

Commentary

1. This order of worship is not offered as a rule but as a model. It is low church but only slightly so. It is designed to maintain a balance between form and spontaneity.

2. The confession of faith (the Apostles' Creed) can be inserted in the service on occasion—preferably after the Scripture reading.

3. The confession of sin and assurance of pardon may take the form

of responsive prayers.

4. A worship service may on occasion include three readings from Scripture: Old Testament, Gospel and Epistle.

5. The service should generally last one hour, and the sermon should be around twenty minutes. The attention span of modern listeners will not tolerate sermons that are much longer.

6. The Communion service should follow the sermon and the offertory. It should then reach a climax in the prayers of intercession. Communion should be celebrated about once a month, thereby giving time for the necessary inward preparation.

7. Children's sermons have no place in a worship service that celebrates the glory of God. In such sermons God is often reduced to a Santa Claus doling out gifts. No one feels judged. Children should be encouraged to participate in the whole service. Special children's services are questionable.

8. Hymns should be drawn from a variety of traditions. The words must be faithful to the scriptural message, and the melodies must be singable by an ordinary congregation.

9. There should probably be at least four hymns in a church service in the evangelical tradition. The trend today is to substitute solos and praise choruses for hymns, and this practice should be resisted.

10. It is important that the prayer of intercession be a free prayer, but it should address itself to world and national events as well as to personal needs in the local congregation. I would urge that the sermon prayer also be offered in the freedom of the Spirit.

11. If lay people are asked to participate in the leadership of the service, such as the reading of Scripture, they should be chosen partly on the basis of their capacity to speak loudly and clearly. The church should be ready to provide such persons with instruction in voice projection and articulation.

12. Unison prayer and responsive readings have a place in the church's liturgy but not as a rule that must be followed every Lord's Day. We must resist both formalism and formlessness, allowing for the free movement of

the Spirit without abandoning structured worship altogether.

Appendix C: A Reformed Worship Center

A church that stands in the tradition of the Protestant Reformation will be Word-centered rather than altar-centered. A pulpit should be centrally located in the frontal or chancel area of the sanctuary with a table below the pulpit. This shows the subordination of sacrament to Word. The sacrament is highly important but is dependent on the proclaimed Word for its efficacy. A baptismal font should also be in the front fully visible to the congregation. It should preferably be on one side allowing the pulpit to remain central. The Communion table may include a chalice.

The pulpit is a powerful symbol especially if it holds an open Bible. To remain behind the pulpit in our preaching shows that our thinking is presumably controlled by Scripture. Yet the preacher should not feel irremediably confined to the pulpit. The pulpit should be roomy, allowing for walking back and forth, if this is how the Spirit guides the preacher. In some charismatic churches the pulpit is reduced to a lectern, and the sermon is given "on the floor" rather than from behind the pulpit. But this indicates a possible separation of Spirit and Word.

What is vitally important is for the minister to maintain eye and ear contact with the people. The pulpit should not be so removed from the congregation that this is no longer possible. The pulpit should be neither too high nor too set apart, for this makes the pastor distant from the people.

Reformed worship is Word-centered but not preacher-centered. It is not the preacher who should be magnified but the Lord Jesus Christ. Worship is not a performance but a confession. By tying the preacher to the pulpit we bind the preacher to the Word. Similarly, the preacher should dress with decorum, not with fancy robes but with a plain black robe or teacher's gown, or a suit that does not draw attention to itself.

There is a place for symbols in a Reformed worship center but not icons, which may become objects of veneration. Symbols always point beyond themselves whereas icons supposedly carry divine power in themselves. Art has a place in the worship center, but art does not mediate revelation. Its role is to witness to revelation. Art is important in fashioning a worship center, but art should always be subordinate to the Word. Our people need to be both aesthetically elevated and intellectually challenged. Worship is both affectional and cerebral. The visible Word is in the service of the proclaimed word. The proclaimed word in turn is dependent on the interaction of the Spirit and the written Word.

The sanctuary should be beautiful, but its beauty is not necessarily enhanced by decorations and paintings (it may even be undercut by these things). Stained glass windows may be appropriate, but windows transparent to the outside can call attention to the integral connection between creation and redemption. The chapel at New Melleray Abbey outside of Dubuque has been widely praised for its beauty; yet it is virtually bereft of symbols and images, and the windows are transparent to the outside. This is consonant with Cistercian spirituality. What makes the chapel more medieval than Reformed is that the congregational area is separated from the worship area by a screen or partition wall, thereby conveying the notion that the people are observers rather than participants in the act of worship.

It is important that a Reformed sanctuary be acoustically sound. Faith comes by hearing and hearing by preaching (Rom 10:17; 1 Cor 1:21; Gal 3:2, 5), but if the words are not distinct and clear people will not fully grasp what is being said. I recommend relatively low ceilings and a circular sanctuary as opposed to a long narrow nave, which makes both the reading and expounding of Scripture too removed from where the congregants are sitting.

A choir may occupy the space behind the pulpit, or it may be in the back of the sanctuary behind the congregation. The symbolism in the first instance is that the choir anthem is a testimony to the Word received by the people in the pew. In the second instance the primary role of the choir is to assist people in the singing of the hymns. In addition, by staying in the back the choir members do not draw attention to themselves but only to the words that they utter in song. An organ and piano may be situated either at the side or back of the sanctuary. Reformed theology will surely allow freedom in these matters. My own preference is for the choir to be in the front, since this reinforces the Reformed focus of worship on the proclaimed Word.

In summary, a Reformed worship center will not be barren, yet it will be simple, not ornate. The proclamation of the Word of God is central in the service of worship, and this centrality is symbolized by subordinating altar or table to the pulpit. Paintings and images are generally not recommended because they tend to give a distorted portrayal of who God really is. There may be a place for candles and other symbols, but these can give the appearance of a cluttered sanctuary rather than one that is open to the wind of the Spirit.

I do not claim that this kind of worship center is the only one that is truly Christian or biblical. Other worship centers will reflect other traditions within the church, and such traditions should be respected so long as they do not lead to idolatry. A worship center in all Christian traditions should be luminous and cheery, not dark and somber. It should be congruous with the message that the light shines in the darkness and the darkness has not vanquished it (Jn 1:5). We should be of good cheer, for Christ has overcome the world (Jn 16:33).

The worship center should not be patterned after a theater or orchestra hall, nor should it necessarily conform to the early synagogues in the time of Jesus and the apostles. It should be in accordance with the basic vision of New Testament faith, and I believe that this vision was faithfully articulated by the Protestant Reformers. Yet this does not mean that we should simply imitate Reformation churches or strive to reproduce them. Their pulpits were generally too high and their preachers too removed from the people. We need constantly to explore new ways of being faithful to our Reformed heritage without capitulating to cultural pressures that can only result in the secularizing or profaning of worship.

While holding to the centrality of preaching, we must not ignore the pivotal role of the sacraments in worship. We can see the effect of sacramental erosion in many new church buildings.

> The ecclesiastical furniture of sacrament—the tables, the baptistries—are less and less noticeable, if visible at all. New churches are designed as spaces for communication, not sacrament or ceremony. We have moved persuasion—with rhetorical flourish, the pastor presents a "message" to the people—to the center of our worship.[42]

Worship that is truly Reformed and catholic will focus on both Word and sacrament, with the latter subordinate to the former. The service of Holy Communion should not be separate from the service of the Word but integrally included in it. The same can be said for the celebration of holy baptism. Special services of baptism on Sunday afternoons or during the course of the week reduce baptism to a moral obligation, whereas it should be seen as a rite of initiation into the holy catholic church. At the same time, we should always keep in mind that there can be a complete service of worship apart from sacraments. The fullness of worship is contingent not on sacramental rites but on God's decision to send forth his Spirit wherever the gospel of Jesus Christ is proclaimed and praises and sacrifices are offered unto him in a spirit of faith and repentance. Sacraments do not so much add to the fullness of worship as manifest this fullness in a striking way and confirm the real presence of Christ in the congregation of the faithful.

·EIGHT·

RETHINKING SACRAMENTS

He saved us through the water of rebirth and the
renewing power of the Holy Spirit.

TITUS 3:5 REB

The sacrament takes away sin not because the sacrament is done
but because one believes the sacrament.

AUGUSTINE

The grand and new testament was not a Sacrament,
but the Gospel. For a Sacrament does not save;
it only edifies those saved by the Gospel.

PETER T. FORSYTH

Neither word nor sacrament works automatically;
where there is no faith, they are not operative.

HANS KÜNG

I t can be shown that the sacraments have been sources of division in the church more than of unity. This does not abrogate their significance, since they could not be a serious cause for division unless they were essential to the well-being of the church. The principal controversy surrounding the sacraments is whether they are only symbolic of the realities they describe or whether they actually transmit these realities through the power of the Holy Spirit.

Sacrament is an extrabiblical word going back to the Latin *sacramentum*—a sacred pledge of fidelity publicly symbolized by a visible sign. It often carried the meaning of a military oath of obedience.[1] The Greek original *mysterion* referred to hidden realities or sacred rites such as those found in the ancient mystery religions. Tertullian (c. 160-c. 220) was one of the first Christian authors to speak of the baptismal ritual as a *sacramentum*. As the church developed, many of its rites and ceremonies were called sacraments or believed to have a sacramental significance. Peter Lombard, in the early and mid-twelfth century, postulated seven sacraments: baptism, confirmation, penance, the eucharist, ordination, marriage and unction. This came to be the official position and was declared so at the Council of Florence (1439) and the Council of Trent (1545-1563). Reformation theology limited the sacraments to two—baptism and the Lord's Supper—since only these had explicit biblical sanction.

Sacramental Understanding in Christian History

Whereas originally in the church the sacraments were viewed as testimonies of the good news of redemption through Jesus Christ, they soon came to be seen as having sacred power in themselves. The priest was no longer first of all a herald or emissary but now a miracle worker. Baptism came to be regarded as a bath of regeneration—one that "effects it rather than the one which preaches and conveys it."[2] The eucharist came to be celebrated not primarily as a meal of commemoration but as a sacrifice of propitiation. The sacraments fell more and more under the control of the clerics who presented themselves as channels by which the head of the mystical body of Christ is linked to the various members of the body. Sacramentalism and sacerdotalism go hand in hand, and the deleterious result is a stifling clericalism that tries to regulate rather than submit to the redeeming action of the Holy Spirit.

Among the church fathers and mystics the sacraments were never separated from faith, but faith was definitely subordinated to the right performance of the sacramental ritual. The Spirit was believed to work automatically through the sacramental action *(ex opere operato)*, bringing purification and regeneration. Diadochus of Photica (fifth century) declared, "Through the medium of water, under the action of the Spirit who is holy and who gives life, we have in consequence become regenerate; we have been purified both in body and soul."[3]

Augustine's theology of the sacraments has special significance in the development of the life and thought of the church. It was Augustine who defined a sacrament as "a visible sign of an invisible grace." A sacrament has two sides—the inner reality and the outward sign; these two come together through the power of the Holy Spirit. The sacrament has no efficacy in and of itself, but it must be linked to the word and to faith. "Take away the word and the water is nothing but water."[4] For "where does the water get its lofty power to bathe the body and cleanse the soul if it is not through the action of the word? And not because it is spoken, but because it is believed?"[5] Augustine's emphasis was not on the sacrament as a magical cure-all but on "the inner acceptance of the grace offered in the sacrament."[6] His basic understanding of the sacrament was symbolic. He frequently described the bread as only a sign or *figura* (image) of the body of Christ. At the same time he could make this claim: "Once the bread that you see on the altar is sanctified by the word of God, it is the body of Christ. And once the chalice is sanctified by the word of God, what the chalice contains is the blood of Christ."[7] Augustine was basically a Christian Platonist, who believed that external signs in themselves can never confer on us spiritual gifts, since these signs are lower in the hierarchy of being. "Augustine does not look for God or grace in external things, but rather urges us to turn inward."[8]

In the thirteenth century Thomas Aquinas reaffirmed many of Augustine's insights but added some of his own. Aquinas saw the sacrament as a commemorative sign of a past event, a sign of the working of grace in us and a prognostic sign of future glory.[9] The sacrament is an instrumental cause of salvation, but the efficient cause is Jesus Christ himself working by the Holy Spirit. Joseph Martos observes that for Aquinas "God's purpose in giving the eucharist to the church was not to make bread and wine an object of worship . . . but to give Christians a means of spiritual nourishment. The reality of the sacrament was therefore a grace, the grace of union with Christ experienced in the reception of communion."[10] Aquinas declared that "the reality of this sacrament is love, and not just the power to love but the activity of love, which is kindled in [the reception of] the sacrament."[11] Some of the canonists after Aquinas stressed the sacrament not simply as an instrumental cause of grace but as an effective cause. The emphasis shifted from the atoning death of Christ and his glorious resurrection to the proper performance of the ritual.[12] It is interesting to note that Aquinas substituted the Aristotelian "matter" and "form" for the earlier distinction between "element" and "Word."[13]

The late medieval church was the scene of a conflict between realists and symbolists. The former contended for the real objective presence of Christ in the elements of bread and wine; the latter held that the elements are symbolic of the spiritual presence of Christ. Peter Lombard reflected the ascendant view when he maintained that the sacraments not only contain grace but mediate grace. The way was open for the doctrine of transubstantiation, which affirmed that by the words of consecration in the sacramental rite the substance of the bread and wine is changed into the very reality of the body and blood of Christ. This doctrine was defined as *de fide* at the Lateran Council of 1215 and further affirmed at the Council of Trent.

The church has always been uncomfortable with the physicalistic view that suggests that the bread and wine become directly the body and blood of Christ so that the materiality of the bread and wine cease. The bread and wine remain accidents, but the inner metaphysical reality changes. At the same time, the Catholic Church encourages the adoration of the host, the consecrated bread, and thereby tends to confound the infinite and the finite.[14]

Reformation theology uttered a resounding "no" to the magical understanding of sacrament, which depicted it as working automatically so long as the right words are said and the right actions performed *(ex opere operato).* Both Luther and Calvin were quite firm that there is no sacrament apart from faith,[15] but the practice of infant baptism presented a problem for them. Luther tried to solve it by positing an implicit faith that even infants can possess. A more biblical way of casting light on the sacramental mystery was Luther's insistence that the spiritual reality signified by the sign of water baptism is a process of inward purification that lasts throughout life. The outward sign points to this reality and inaugurates it when it is joined to the Word in the congregation of faith. For Calvin, who is here very close to Augustine, the sign becomes an instrument or means of grace when united with the preaching of the Word and the decision of faith.

Both Calvin and Luther affirmed the real presence of Christ in the eucharist and the objective reality of the gift of the Holy Spirit in baptism.[16] The bread and wine remain signs and are not changed into the spiritual reality they signify, but they communicate this reality to people of faith and repentance. This realistic sacramental understanding is also evident in Martin Bucer: "In this sacrament we receive not only bread and wine but at the same time his body and blood, and indeed not these only but with them the whole Christ, both God and man."[17] Ulrich Zwingli, on the other hand, thought within the framework of a radical dualism that separated the spiritual and the material so that the only efficacious baptism is the baptism of the Spirit. The outward sign becomes not a means of grace but a testimony to grace. In the radical Zwinglian view the sacraments become signs of faith and commitment.

In more recent times Congregationalist theologian P. T. Forsyth advocated a rediscovery of the sacramental understanding of baptism and the Lord's Supper without slipping into the morass of ritualism and sacerdotalism. In his view, "sacraments, and not socialities, make the center of our Church life and social unity."[18] "The Sacraments are the acted Word—variants of the preached Word. They are signs, but they are more than signs. They are the Word, the Gospel itself, visible, as in preaching the Word is audible."[19] At the same time, Forsyth made clear that the external symbol must never be confused with the inward or transcendent reality. The goal of the sacrament is not the elevation of the host but the transformation of the human heart. "The real intimate means of grace are sacramental souls and not sacramentarian elements. Conversion, regeneration, is the true Transubstantiation."[20] To baptize without calling for faith is to lapse into magic or, even worse, idolatry. "We may not give Baptism unless we also bring the Gospel, and promise to keep bringing it, to the young life till it can assume responsibility in confirmation or in taking up membership."[21] "The Church should not give Baptism where there is no prospect of Christian discipline and nurture in its own interior. Baptism, apart from that, easily becomes a mere salving rite, instead of a saving grace, indulging the superstition of the parents."[22] Against the Anabaptists, Forsyth was insistent that baptism *unto* faith is as sound as baptism *upon* faith. "In infant Baptism the grace is impropriated; in believer's Baptism it is appropriated. But there is no regeneration except as the man becomes spiritually active for himself, and the appropriation takes place."[23]

Advocating a quite different position was Karl Barth, whose theology was strikingly similar to Forsyth's in many other areas. The early Barth was still somewhat of a neo-Calvinist and defended the idea of sacraments so long as they were not divorced from the preaching and hearing of the Word of God, the chief sacramental reality. Barth could declare, "How the Reformed Church has been misunderstood—by herself too as well as by others—when later the impression prevailed that she was a church without sacraments, even a church hostile to the sacraments!"[24] In his later theology Barth hailed Jesus Christ himself as the only sacrament and viewed the sacramental rites of baptism and the Lord's Supper as witnesses to the event of God becoming man in Jesus Christ. Barth sagaciously perceived the danger of people placing their trust in rituals they could perform and control rather than in the living God himself, who is never at the disposal of human work and belief. "To believe in Jesus Christ *and* in water consecrated by His presence is a dangerous thing and is not confirmed by any necessary relationship between the two."[25] Barth did not repudiate the sacramental understanding, but he now applied it to Jesus, not to the ceremonies of the church. His new position revealed a significant departure from the catholic understanding:

> Baptism and the Lord's Supper are not events, institutions, mediations, or revelations of salvation. They are not representations and actualizations, emanations, repetitions, or extensions, nor indeed guarantees and seals of the work and word of God; nor are they instruments, vehicles, channels, or means of God's reconciling grace. They are not what they have been called since the second century, namely, mysteries or sacraments.[26]

If the so-called sacraments do not communicate saving grace, what is their proper role? Barth showed an affinity to both Zwingli and the Anabaptists by viewing baptism and the Lord's Supper as occasions for obedience and consecration to Jesus Christ. Barth did not hesitate to follow through the logic of his position by affirming only believers' baptism, since baptism is the sign by which the person of faith pledges to live out a vocation of discipleship under the cross of Christ. Barth thus built a bridge between the Reformed faith and the Anabaptist tradition, but it seems he was much closer in his final thoughts to the latter than the former. The ordinances of baptism and the Lord's Supper are still necessary to the faith of the church, but their promise lies in what they proclaim and testify to, namely, the living Christ and his atoning work on the cross. The rites of the church do not confer God's grace but are the human answer to God's grace, who works in his own way and time—sometimes in conjunction with the word of preaching and the rites of initiation and sometimes over and against these things. God's grace never falls under the control of the church, but it is the hand of God himself directing the church and calling the Christian to follow the one Lord of the church—Jesus Christ.

Baptist churches have been shaped more by Zwinglian and Anabaptist modes of thinking than by the teachings of Calvin and Luther. Not surprisingly, many contemporary Baptists find support in Karl Barth, a staunch defender of believers' baptism. Some Baptist theologians, however, motivated by an ecumenical concern, have been open to a more sacramental outlook. One of these is the erudite Old Testament scholar H. Wheeler Robinson, who was principal for many years at Regent's Park College in London and then at Oxford. Robinson makes a direct connection between what he calls prophetic signs and sacramental practices. He argues on the basis of Scripture that prophetic signs do more than point to or suggest another reality: they assist in enacting it.[27] Regarding baptism in the New Testament he says, "There can be no question of 'mere symbolism,' for the act is the partial and fragmentary, but very real accomplishment of a divine work, the work of the Holy Spirit."[28]

Holy Baptism

Holy baptism is the pivotal sacrament for incorporation into the mystical body of Christ. It does not in and of itself insure membership in Christ's church, but it ratifies and certifies what faith achieves through the power of the Spirit. It symbolizes the spiritual baptism into the death and resurrection of Christ. This symbol is not an empty one, for it is used by the Spirit to prepare for and confirm the union with Christ realized in faith.

Baptism is not a ritual that automatically effects regeneration, but neither is it a barren symbol that simply points to regeneration. It is a sacramental sign that when joined to the Word of God and the outpouring of the Spirit effects what it symbolizes. It does so, however, as an instrumental cause. The efficient or effectual cause is the Holy Spirit, who breathes new life into the convert through the rite of baptism.

We practice baptism because it is the explicit command of Christ (Mt 28:18-20; Mk 16:15-16) and also because it seals the new life in Christ within us when it is united with faith. Baptism is our response to Christ's baptism into death, but it also links us with this spiritual baptism through the action of the Spirit. We are baptized only once because the entrance into the kingdom of Christ occurs only once. Paul declares that there is "one faith" and "one baptism" (Eph 4:5). I heartily agree with Michael Green: "'Rebaptism' is wrong because it cannot be done! . . . Baptism means beginning. And it cannot be done again. . . . Baptism is ever to be remembered but never to be repeated."[29]

Many texts in the New Testament appear to support a sacramentalist understanding of baptism, but a close examination of these texts reveals that water baptism is only the sign, though an essential one, and that Spirit baptism alone is equivalent to the new birth. Paul avers, "By one Spirit we were all baptized into one body . . . and all were made to drink of one Spirit" (1 Cor 12:13). I concur with W. Harold Mare that Paul here has spiritual baptism in mind.[30] It is this spiritual baptism that engrafts us into Christ's body, and this liberating act is attested by water baptism. Similarly "the water of rebirth" in Titus 3:5 (REB) probably refers to the living water of life that is synonymous with rather than preparatory to "the renewing power of the Holy Spirit." First Peter 3:21 declares, "Baptism . . . brings salvation through the resurrection of Jesus Christ" (REB). Here the reference is very likely to the sacrament of baptism, but again it is not water as such but the resurrection power of Jesus Christ that effects salvation. In John 3:5 we are told that we must be baptized with water and the Spirit in order to enter the kingdom of God. I here agree with Calvin that John is describing a spiritual reality and is probably not thinking of the sacramental water of baptism.

Another passage that sacramentalists often appeal to is Colossians 2:11-12:

> When you came to Christ, you were "circumcised," but not by a physical procedure. It was a spiritual procedure—the cutting away of your sinful nature. For you were buried with Christ when you were baptized. And with him you were raised to a new life because you trusted the mighty power of God, who raised Christ from the dead. (NLT)

Francis W. Beare aptly comments: "Not baptism itself, but the spiritual experience represented in baptism is the 'spiritual circumcision.'

Paul is not glorifying one external rite in order to depreciate another."[31] A comparable passage is Romans 6:1-4. The apostle here declares that we were buried with Christ through baptism into death, but this is a spiritual baptism effected by faith, yet graphically symbolized by the rite of water baptism.

Virtually all the biblical passages that speak of baptism into Christ's death have sacramental allusions and were used by the early church to argue for the importance of the rite of baptism. The danger arose when this rite was divorced from a living faith in Christ and was believed to impart sacred power simply through the act of being performed.

Against evangelical sectarians and latter day Barthians I hold that the rite of baptism is salvific and not merely ethical. It sets us on the path to salvation when it is united with the Word of God and the decision of faith. Against the sacramentalists I contend that baptism in and of itself is only a symbol and does not effect anything. But as a vehicle of the Spirit it receives power to confirm and ratify our salvation procured by Christ's death and resurrection.

One of the enduring controversies in the church is the perplexing relation between baptism as a rite and the spiritual reality of regeneration. The sacramentalist view espoused by Catholics, Orthodox and some Lutherans and Anglicans is that baptism as a rite of the church necessarily brings about the regeneration of the human soul. This position is aptly described as a sacramental objectivism in which regeneration takes place outside of and prior to human decision. It elevates the sacrament of baptism but at the price of diminishing faith. Catholic theologian Paul Quay gives voice to this mentality: "Baptism constitutes a true remission and cleansing away of all sin by a rebirth into the divine life and can do this without the knowledge or consent of the recipient."[32] A similar note is found in Pannenberg: "Faith in the gospel without baptism is not yet Christian saving faith in the full sense. It is still something that we exercise under our own control, whereas by the act of baptism we become new subjects."[33]

A second position is what might be called decisional regeneration in which regeneration is thought to be realized through the decision of faith. The danger here is synergism in which the human subject is portrayed as contributing something of his or her own to the unfolding of salvation. God does part of it, and we also do our part. This position loses sight of the miracle of divine election whereby God reaches out to us before we are able to respond. And when we do respond it is through the power of the Holy Spirit working within us. The truth in this position, which is pervasive in evangelical Protestantism, is that regeneration entails a decision of faith, that there is no initiation into the body of Christ without personal appropriation of the truth of Christ.

Still another position is covenantal objectivism, which creates the impression that we are regenerated through procreation.[34] In the orthodox Reformed understanding children of believers too belong to the covenant community. They are baptized toward faith, but their faith is already assured through divine election. Calvin often spoke this way, though he also tried to hold this insight together with a sacramental view of baptism.

Finally, we are obliged to treat seriously Karl Barth's Christological objectivism in which our regeneration and sanctification are definitively accomplished in Christ's death and resurrection. Both faith and the ordinances of faith point to Christ's prior work of salvation on the cross. Baptism testifies to a salvation already achieved, rather than realizes a salvation that is yet to be completed.

Revealing an affinity to evangelical Pietism, I confess that I am closer to decisional regeneration, since the Bible does not teach regeneration apart from personal faith. Yet when we speak of decision we must have in mind not just our decision for Christ but his decision for us, and we must emphasize the priority of the latter, especially when speaking of regeneration. What secures our salvation is not our baptism with water but his baptism with blood. Yet the fruits of the salvation won for us by Christ take effect in us as we respond in faith and repentance and seal our response in a public act of baptism. This public act represents our obedience to Christ, but it also testifies to Christ's election of us. Moreover, it is used by the Spirit to confirm Christ's gracious election in our lives and thereby to seal us in his body.

Yet another controversy associated with baptism focuses on the age of reception. Should baptism be given to children (pedobaptism), or should it be limited to adults who publicly profess their faith in Christ? Those who argue for infant baptism point to the household baptisms in the apostolic church and also build on the parallels with circumcision.[35] Those who defend believers' baptism see an analogy to Jewish proselyte baptism and thereby regard personal faith as necessary for the completion of baptism. Pedobaptism can create a false sense of security, that everything is taken care of by the church. Believers' baptism on the other hand can promote self-righteousness. The advantage in pedobaptism is that the child is placed under the sign of redemption. The disadvantage is that it fosters the illusion that one is already and automatically in the family of God. It often constitutes an inoculation against real Christianity. Pedobaptism is a more credible symbolism for the mystery that God's election is prior to human decision. Believers' baptism calls our attention to the biblical truth that God's election is realized through human decision. My recommendation is that both sides in this dispute respect the integrity of the other side and also accept the baptism of the other side, so long as it is performed in the name of the Father, the Son and the Holy Spirit and in the context of the community of faith. Against those who defend pedobaptism, I contend that baptism is ineffectual apart from personal faith and that it is not complete until the dawning of faith. Against those who champion believers' baptism, I am firmly convinced that there should be no rebaptism. I also believe that baptism should be seen as sacramental and should take place in a service of worship where the Word of God is read and proclaimed.[36]

Regarding the mode of baptism, I support *pouring* over both *immersion* and *sprinkling*, simply because the symbolism of baptism as the pouring out of the Spirit is more fully preserved. Yet I fully accept the legitimacy of the other modes of baptism. When baptism is applied to children, a strong rite of confirmation is necessitated in order to under-line the importance of personal decision for salvation.[37] Confirmation presupposes conversion and does not itself create conversion, as in a fully sacramentalist view.

Because pedobaptism today has virtually become a means of cheap grace, I personally favor the rite of believers' baptism but always inter-preted in a sacramental way, as a means of grace. When baptism is given to believers, it does not impart salvation but confirms and ratifies a salvation already set in motion by the experience of conversion. Con-gregationalist theologian Daniel Jenkins has voiced the complaint that infant baptism has become in too many circles a celebration of natural birth rather than of the new birth.[38] This need not be if confirmation would again be elevated—not as a sacrament but as a sacramental ordinance in which the laity are ordained into active service in Christ's kingdom.[39] Baptism itself becomes a rite of the ordination of the laity when it is applied to believers.

It should be made clear that baptized infants do not have a privi-leged position over other children raised in Christian homes and exposed to the means of grace but who are not yet baptized. The important point is that all children of believers are elected and adopted into the family of God through the universal atonement of the Lord Jesus Christ. Our assurance of hope is grounded not in our own faith nor in a sacramental rite, whether this be baptism or confirmation, but in the atoning death and glorious resurrection of Jesus Christ, who claims the entire world for obedience and service in his name. Yet God's decision does not reach us until we hear the Word of God pro-claimed and see the fruits of this Word demonstrated in a Christian life. God's decision in order to be effectual for our salvation must take root within us. We are saved by the electing grace of the Father, the redeeming grace of the Son and the empowering grace of the Holy Spirit. Baptism is a sign that all of these dimensions of grace are extended to us so long as we repent and believe and take up the cross of discipleship, following Christ as our Lord and Savior until the end of our days. Baptism itself does not redeem, but it is an effectual sign of Christ's redemption when accompanied by the hearing of the Word and the obedience of faith. I desire to retain baptism as a bona fide sacrament of the church but resist embracing a sacramentalism that promotes the illusion that we are already Christian simply through the act of being baptized.

Holy Communion

Just as baptism incorporates us into the community of faith, so the Lord's Supper sustains us in this community. We observe this holy supper because it was commanded by Jesus to be the abiding memorial of his sacrificial death on the cross (cf. Mt 26:26-29; Mk 14:22-25; Lk 22:14-20; 1 Cor 10:16; 11:23-26). The sign of the sacrament is bread and wine; the spiritual reality is Christ dying for us and rising again to vanquish death and sin.

The blessed sacrament has various dimensions and must not be reduced to any one of these. First of all, it is a commemorative meal, recalling to mind the final drama of the events of salvation in the life and ministry of Jesus. Second, it is an eschatological banquet, an anticipation of the glory that is yet to be revealed to us (cf. Mt 26:29; Mk 14:25; Lk 22:18; 1 Cor 11:26). Third, it is a manifestation of the mystical bond of fellowship that we have with Christ and with our fellow believers. Finally, it is an occasion in which we present our sacrifices of praise and thanksgiving as a sign of our gratitude for what God has done for us in Jesus Christ.

The Lord's Supper is not a repetition or even a re-presentation of the sacrifice of Christ on Calvary but a proclamation and symbolic reenactment of this sacrifice.[40] It is not a propitiatory sacrifice but a eucharistic sacrifice—a sacrifice of praise and thanksgiving. It is not a perpetuation of the sacrifice on Calvary but a remembrance of this sacrifice. It is also a means by which we appropriate the fruits of this sacrifice in our lives.[41]

The church through the ages has been sorely divided on the meaning of the real presence of Christ in the blessed sacrament of the eucharist. Roman Catholic tradition supports the doctrine of transubstantiation, by which the elements of bread and wine are substantially changed into the body and blood of Christ. Some Lutherans have advanced the view of consubstantiation, in which the body and blood are given in union with the sacramental elements, but these elements are not materially altered. Some Catholic scholars today subscribe to transignification, in which the significance of the elements is changed after the consecration. Another option proffered by forward-looking Catholic scholars is transfinalization, in which the *telos* or goal of the sacramental elements is altered.

From my perspective we should affirm the real presence of Christ but refrain from engaging in abstruse metaphysical speculation. Moreover, we should acknowledge his presence not simply in the elements but in the whole eucharistic celebration. An ontological change occurs, but it is in the hearts of those who believe, not in the elements. In this sacred meal the Spirit of God descends into our midst. Grasped by the Spirit, we are elevated into the presence of Christ as we repent of our sins and join our fellow believers in an act of praise and thanksgiving. We do not adore the host, the consecrated bread, but we adore the living Christ who dwells with us and in us and who relates himself to us in an intimate way as we eat of the bread and drink from the cup. We feed upon Christ spiritually as we eat and drink of the material elements that become signs of his real presence in our midst. Calvin contended that in the eucharistic meal Christ is more vividly present than in any other rite or ceremony of the church.[42]

In the eucharistic celebration the table becomes an altar on which we present our sacrifices of praise and thanksgiving. It is also an altar in the sense that the sacramental ritual represents or depicts the atoning sacrifice of Christ on the cross. In this holy meal we make contact with this sacrifice through the action of the Holy Spirit. Yet his sacrifice is not repeated or perpetuated (as in the Tridentine view) but proclaimed and celebrated.

Catholic theology in recent times has sought an ecumenical consensus on the nature of the eucharist. More and more it is being said that the sacrament does not work automatically or mechanically but is effectual only when true faith is present. Balthasar declares, "Sacramental reception of the Eucharist is vain, unless it is accompanied with living faith and love."[43] Edward Schillebeeckx asserts, "The physical reality does not change, otherwise there would no longer be a eucharistic sign."[44] According to Hans Küng, "The elements by themselves have no significance . . . it is in the light of the word that we should understand the Lord's Supper. The word here has not primarily the function of consecrating and transforming, but of proclaiming and testifying."[45] One of the remaining stumbling blocks is whether Christ offers his sacrifice to the Father in the eucharist or whether we appeal to his sacrifice once offered for the assurance of being in communion with him. Those who share the Reformation vision stress the all-sufficiency of the one sacrifice of Christ that does not need to be repeated or perpetuated. At the same time, they endorse the view that the eucharist becomes the wellspring of new life and hope for the people of God as they celebrate it in faith.

In Anabaptist circles it is sometimes said that the most potent symbol of the body of Christ is not the bread and wine as such but the breaking of bread.[46] The eucharist would then be comparable to the rite of footwashing, which calls us to follow Christ in obedience under the cross. The sacrifice we offer is not the eucharist but lives of praise and thanksgiving. By taking up the cross and following Christ we play a modest role in making his cross efficacious in the world. In my opinion we have much to learn from this spiritual tradition, but I believe the pertinent texts point to the bread and the cup as themselves being symbolic of Christ's sacrifice and victory over sin.

Yet it would be a mistake to limit the presence of Christ to the elements. John Polkinghorne here states a growing ecumenical consensus:

> Modern Eucharistic thought places emphasis not solely on the elements, but rather upon the whole Eucharistic action, taking place in the gathered com-

munity of believers. There is a recovered recognition of the work of the Spirit, who may indeed be thought immanently to act within the openness of the Christian community.[47]

The holy communion that takes place in the Lord's Supper should be conceived not in terms of mystical assimilation into Christ but of confrontation with the living Jesus Christ, crucified and risen. I propose a biblical personalistic view of the eucharist, as opposed to a mystical view, on the one hand, in which we inwardly commune with the all-encompassing Spiritual Presence, and a rationalistic view, on the other hand, in which we rethink what has happened in the past.[48] What takes place is not simply a remembrance of a past occurrence in history but the experience of the impact of this event in the present. What occurs is a divine-human encounter in which we are given both a realistic intimation of Christ's suffering and death and a foretaste of his coming glory.

The Lord's Supper should not be offered indiscriminately to any who desire it: it should be reserved for the company of the committed. Justin Martyr here reflects the position of the ancient church: "We call this food 'Eucharist,' which no one is allowed to share unless he or she believes that the things which we teach are true, and has been washed with the washing that is for the remission of sins and unto a second birth, and is living as Christ commanded."[49] The holy supper is indeed open to all who are baptized and profess faith in Jesus Christ, but if we show that our faith is inauthentic by continuing in the practice of some mortal sin the eucharistic host and cup should then be withheld from us until we repent and believe anew. If we eat and drink without examining ourselves and pledging to forsake all sin we will be bringing divine judgment upon ourselves (1 Cor 11:27-30).[50]

At the same time I am supportive of intercommunion—Communion across denominational lines. Where formidable doctrinal barriers still remain between Christian bodies (as in the case of Protestants and Roman Catholics), we should agree to wait for the common celebration of Communion, for this would then be a fitting climax of ecumenical endeavor.[51] On the other hand we must not insist on overall doctrinal or theological conformity as a precondition for Communion. John Wesley even advocated that the table be open to all who genuinely seek for the salvation of Jesus Christ. This would make Communion a converting ordinance and thereby not restricted to the community of faith. I recommend that Communion be limited to all those who have been baptized and publicly profess faith in Christ, but that those who live in mortal sin be exhorted to forsake their sin before taking Holy Communion. I also contend that theological uniformity must not be made a condition for Communion, but any one who believes that Christ is truly present by his Spirit in the eucharistic meal and in the service of celebration should be warmly invited to partake of this meal.

Because of the Pauline admonition to examine oneself carefully before partaking of Holy Communion, my recommendation is that Communion be celebrated at least but ordinarily not more than once a month. If this sacred meal becomes too familiar, we begin to lose sight of the fact that it is a special occasion in the life of the church, and it is likely that we will ignore the injunction to examine ourselves and repent of all sin before communing with Christ in the eucharist.[52] Communion is a high point of the worship service, but it is not essential for a worship celebration. While the ideal is weekly Communion, the pressures of modern life argue for a less frequent observance of the supper. The Sunday or Wednesday preceding the observance could be devoted to self-examination and confession.

Finally, we must say some words concerning the agape meal, which was often practiced in conjunction with the eucharistic rite. The agape meal must not be confused with the eucharist, but it is an exemplary byproduct of the whole worship celebration. After the formal worship has ended we can then share the fruits of our labors with others in a wider fellowship meal. This fellowship meal can also be a means of grace so long as faith and love are present, but it must not be called a communion of the body and blood of Jesus Christ.[53]

Confession

Although the churches of the Reformation generally held to two sacraments—baptism and the Lord's Supper—one side of the Reformation
also entertained penance or confession as a sacrament. The sacramental status of confession was clearly affirmed in the Augsburg Confession.[54] Confession was listed as a sacrament in the Ten Articles of
religion of the Church of England in 1536. In the 1552 Book of Common Prayer, however, auricular confession had disappeared and was
replaced by a general confession of sins. While recommending that we
should generally go to God alone with the burden of our sins, the Second Helvetic Confession (1566) allowed for confessing sin before a
pastor or godly Christian brother when the burden persists.[55]

In the early church penance ordinarily took the form of a public confession of sins followed by acts of contrition and absolution from the
priest. As penance developed, it came to denote an exchange between
priest and sinner in the confessional and was performed in secret. It
also increasingly came to be seen as a second plank in salvation that
one could cling to if the security of baptism were taken away.[56] Catholic theologians were adamant that original sin is forgiven in baptism,
but sins after baptism are remitted through the sacrament of penance,
consisting of confession of sin, priestly absolution and acts of penitence, which supposedly reduce time spent in purgatory after death.
Absolution remits the eternal punishment due to sin, but temporal
punishments persist until they are mitigated through acts of reparation
and expiation, which testify to the genuineness of our repentance.
Penance received its charter at the Fourth Lateran Council (1215) and
was reaffirmed at the Council of Trent.

Penance also came to be associated with indulgences—remissions
of the temporal penalty that accompanies sins. These are conferred by
the church on penitent sinners on the condition that they perform acts
of contrition and reparation prescribed by the priest or bishop. The
practice of indulgences became an occasion for abuse, especially in
the later middle ages, when unscrupulous clerics began to grant indul-

gences in exchange for money or other material gifts. Johann Tetzel, Dominican friar and seller of indulgences at the time of Luther, declared:

> As soon as the coin in the coffer rings
> The soul from purgatory springs.[57]

No wonder that Luther protested against the practice of indulgences as a descent into the worst kind of works-righteousness.

The Reformers opposed the sacrament of penance as it was defined in the Catholic Church on the grounds that it patently contradicted the gospel message of justification by faith alone. They also objected that it tended to foster a rigoristic spirituality by insisting that the penitent confess *every* sin to the priest. In short it made confession into a law rather than a glorious opportunity to get rid of burdens by hearing the good news of God's free forgiveness from the mouth of a priest or Christian brother or sister.[58]

While the Reformers rightly contended that every Christian may go to God directly with the burden of sin, some of them perceived the value of confiding in a fellow believer and receiving the assurance of forgiveness from that person. Martin Luther, who had benefited greatly from the counsel of his own confessor in the monastery, John Staupitz, manifested a desire to retain an evangelical form of confession:

> As for secret confession as practiced today, though it cannot be proved from Scripture, yet it seems a highly satisfactory practice to me; it is useful and even necessary. I would not wish it to cease; rather I rejoice that it exists in the church of Christ, for it is a singular medicine for afflicted consciences. If we lay bare to a brother what lies on our conscience, and in confidence unveil that which we have kept hidden, we receive, through the mouth of a brother, a comfort which God has spoken.[59]

And again:

> I refuse to go to confession simply because the Pope has commanded it and insists upon it. For I wish him to keep his hands off confession and not make of it a compulsion or command, which he has not the power to do. Never-

theless, I will allow no man to take private confession away from me, and I would not give it up for all the treasures in the world, since I know what comfort and strength it has given me. No one knows what it can do for him except one who has struggled often and long with the devil.[60]

Luther sharply called into question the spiritual foundations of the Catholic sacrament of penance when he averred that the whole life of the Christian must be one of repentance. We gain our assurance of God's pardon, moreover, not from the acts of contrition we perform nor from the absolution that the priest pronounces but from the gospel message that Christ has died for our sins and that his righteousness is imputed to all who believe. Luther nevertheless discerned that the assurance of salvation can be confirmed through candid confession of sins to one another and receiving the promise of forgiveness from the mouth of a fellow Christian.

Pannenberg points to the crucial difference between Catholic and Evangelical understandings of the remission of sin in the life of the Christian:

> The difference of this Reformation view of penitence from the usual act of sacramental penance in the medieval church of the West consists above all of the fact that the promise of Jesus Christ himself, or the promise of the gospel, replaces the priestly formula of absolution. The Protestant pastor no longer exercises the power of the keys as an independent judicial power but simply proclaims the forgiveness that is grounded in Christ's own promise and that forms the content of the gospel.[61]

Auricular confession as a formal rite of the church virtually disappeared in the churches of the Reformation, but the practice of confession in the presence of a Christian brother or sister has been a recurring reality in the history of these churches. One can think of the class meetings of John Wesley, the mourner's bench in the revivals of Charles Finney and the open confession of sins in the house parties of the Oxford Group movement.[62] Some high church movements in Lutheranism and Anglicanism have sought to reinstate the sacrament of auricular confession, but their efforts have not had a noticeable impact on Protestant church life.

Catholic theologians have tried to give a more personal interpretation of penance by seeing it in terms of an emotional or spiritual reinforcement that the counselor gives one who is seeking spiritual help.[63] Penance becomes a rite of reconciliation whereby the sinner through a frank admission of personal shortcomings finds peace with both God and neighbor. Yet the idea that the penitent must also do something to gain confidence of God's mercy persists in the Roman Catholic communion. Von Balthasar asserts: "God forgives through free grace and not on the basis of acts of penance, but . . . forgiveness cannot become effective unless there is an expiatory conversion of the person."[64] In the words of the *Catholic Catechism,* "Absolution takes away sin, but it does not remedy all the disorders sin has caused. Raised up from sin, the sinner must still recover his full spiritual health by doing something more to make amends for the sin: he must 'make satisfaction for' or 'expiate' his sins."[65] As an evangelical theologian I prefer to say that Christ by his sacrifice on the cross has made adequate reparation for all sin and that our task is to proclaim this fact and live according to it.[66]

The wholesale rejection of the Catholic sacrament of penance on the part of the Reformation churches has been a mixed blessing because it has sundered the idea of the solidarity of the communion of saints. We are urged to confess our sins to one another (Jas 5:16) and declare the good news of God's forgiveness to our fellow believers (Jn 20:22-23), especially those who seek from us a word of consolation and encouragement. Confession should not be regarded as a sacrament because it is doubtful that the rite was formally instituted by Christ, and moreover it lacks visible signs. Yet it certainly has a sacramental dimension in that the words of assurance of pardon both in the worship service of the church and in the one-to-one relationship between Christians can be veritable means of grace to tormented souls living with unconfessed sin.

What has taken the place of confession in many churches is pastoral counseling, which for the most part is anchored in the therapeutic sciences rather than in holy Scripture and the wisdom of the saints of the church.[67] We can learn positively from secular psychotherapy, but we must not confuse catharsis and rehabilitation (the goals in therapeutic counseling) with the remission of guilt and regeneration.[68] *Seelsorge* (the cure of souls) is not client-centered therapy. Therapy can sometimes deal with problems on the purely emotional level, though many of these problems have their source in unconfessed sin and hostility. Some theologians have tried to draw upon the insights of therapeutic counseling in dealing with the problem of guilt.[69] What happens too often is that with the help of psychotherapy the troubled person is able to overcome feelings of guilt but at the price of failing to come to terms with the fact of guilt, the broken relationship between the sinner and the holy God that is only dealt with adequately through confession of sin and hearing the words of absolution. The goal of *Seelsorge* is not the denial of sin or guilt but open acknowledgement of sin on the basis of being assured of God's unconditional love and forgiveness.

As I see it, there are four ways of dealing with the problem of sin and guilt in the modern context. First is a penitential piety in which we try to bring the troubled person to a conviction of sin by pointing him or her to the law of God. After hearing the confession of sin we then assure that person of God's forgiveness. This approach is anchored in Catholic mysticism and Protestant Pietism. Second, there is a eudaemonistic spirituality associated with the modern pastoral care movement, which sees the hope of the tormented soul in drawing upon one's innate recuperative powers. We gain release from guilt and dread by discovering the law of our own being. Third, there is the new spirituality, a neo-gnosticism, which aims to lead people to a discovery of the divinity of the self. We escape the tension caused by our finiteness and the sorrow caused by our sin through a denial of both our finitude and our sin. Finally, there is an evangelical or eucharistic spirituality based on the gospel of God's unconditional forgiveness. Yet there is also a place for the law of God in this kind of piety, since once convinced of the truth of the gospel we are then motivated to bring our sins before God in repentance. Out of gratitude for what God has done for us in Christ we are now open to receiving a word of admonition to forsake sin and live according to the commandments of God. Repentance involves forsaking the life of sin, not making reparation for sin. It entails taking up the cross and following Christ—not to gain spiritual merits but to help our neighbor in need. The goal of evangelical confession is not self-understanding, as in classical humanism and eudaemonism, but reconciliation—with God and our neighbor. The counselor becomes a spiritual director who points the penitent to Jesus Christ, to the gospel and to the law.

Forgiveness in the Christian sense is not the same as forgiveness in the therapeutic sense.[70] Christian forgiveness is being pardoned of sin by gratuitous love. Forgiveness in the therapeutic sense is being accepted even in our weakness and folly. In therapeutic forgiveness we forgive in order to be healed. In Christian forgiveness we forgive out of gratitude for God's forgiveness of us. Forgiveness in the biblical sense does not cancel the judgment upon sin but brings one through judgment.[71] There is no forgiveness without judgment, and judgment is indeed the first step in gaining assurance of forgiveness. Forgiveness is unconditional, but it is not indiscriminate. It is demanding as well as absolving. Forgiveness is not the benign overlooking of human foibles but the victorious assault on entrenched evil.[72] It is not the pardoning of what is excusable but the overcoming of what is inexcusable. Forgiveness does not give permission for sin, but reveals the hideousness of sin and may well be accompanied by an admonition to cease living in sin.[73] Forgiveness is not a technique to achieve inner healing, but healing will certainly follow the assurance that our sins are forgiven through faith in Jesus Christ. The goal of forgiveness is not to enable those of us who receive it to accept ourselves or forgive ourselves but to empower us to change ourselves.

I concur with Dietrich Bonhoeffer that our life together as Christians should involve confession of sins to one another (cf. Jas 5:16). The public confession of sin in the service of worship can meet some of our spiritual needs, yet too often it becomes an empty form, though this can also be true of the confessional. We may be helped by a spiritual director, one who is godly and sensitive to spiritual need and hunger, but having such a confidant should not be seen as necessary for a Christian life. What must be insisted on is that the confession of sins in the presence of a pastor or another believer be held in strict confidence. The Catholic confessional was right in holding that these things should be kept secret. The exception is when a brother or sister spurns our attempt at reconciliation; we should then go to that person with representatives of the church and ask that he or she listen to the church (Mt 18:15-17). According to Bonhoeffer, it is imperative that we recover "sacramental confession, wherein the Christian seeks and finds assurance that his sins are forgiven. Confession is the God-given remedy for self-deception and self-indulgence."[74] Indeed, "It is . . . only by rediscovering the divine office of confession that the Protestant Church can find its way back to a concrete ethic such as it possessed at the time of the Reformation."[75] In this anxiety-driven age in which we live, we need to be given the opportunity to unburden ourselves to a Christian brother or sister and then hear the words of comfort that the paralytic heard from the mouth of Jesus: "Take heart, my son; your sins are forgiven" (Mt 9:2).[76]

Yet we must be alert to another side of confession—that it can become a law that stifles the free movement of the Spirit, a snare rather than a balm. We would do well to keep in mind that some sins should be confessed only to God because of the disruption that an open confession might cause in the community. Some sins should be hidden even from those closest and dearest to us—for their sake, not necessarily for ours. We do not confess in order to add burdens to another but to receive renewed confidence that God is with us and for us. Confession of sins to another believer or body of believers must be a divine commandment, never a general or universal principle.[77] It is for freedom that Christ has made us free (Gal 5:1). We must be free to go to another

Christian who can exercise his or her priestly prerogative to bring us assurance of God's forgiveness, but we are always free to go to God alone with any problem or heartache. This should certainly be the course of action when any person or persons might be seriously hurt if the knowledge of our transgression came to public view. God is there for us always: his Son is our intercessor and his Spirit is our comforter. Yet God wills on occasion to speak his word of consolation through people of faith, sometimes even through people bereft of faith. Christ himself is the sure antidote for sin, but earthly counselors can direct those in need to this antidote and can thereby become veritable means of grace.

Word and Sacrament

Evangelical and Catholic traditions are united in affirming the centrality of Word and sacrament in the life of the church. Thomas à Kempis, beloved by Protestant Pietists as well as Catholic and non-Catholic mystics, astutely perceived that what holds the church together are the two tables—one containing the Word of God and the other the Bread of God.

> You have therefore given me in my weakness Your sacred Body to be the refreshment of my soul and body, and have set Your Word as a lamp to my feet. Without these two, I cannot rightly live; for the Word of God is the light of my soul, and Your Sacrament is the bread of my life.[78]

Jesus Christ himself is the *Ursacrament* of the church, the visible sign of invisible grace, but he has chosen to act through the instruments of preaching and the sacraments. A church grounded in Christ will have sacraments but not magic. It will have rituals but not ritualism. No sacrament or ritual has within itself the power to redeem, but when united with the Word of God, proclaimed and written, it may play a salutary role in making Christ's salvation concrete and efficacious.

We are engrafted into Christ through conversion.[79] Baptism is an outward sign, though not an empty sign. When conjoined with the Word of God, baptism can either prepare the way for conversion or confirm and seal the gift of conversion in all those who seek in the power of the Spirit. Baptism with water and baptism with the Spirit constitute the two sides of the reality of regeneration. Both are important—the outward sign and the inner experience—but only the latter is indispensable for salvation. The sign and the thing signified become organically related through the action of the Spirit. In the case of infant baptism, our regeneration is begun in the sense that we are baptized toward regeneration. The infant is embraced by the Holy Spirit but not yet purified and reconstituted as a new creation. In the case of believers' baptism the person of faith receives a deepening and confirmation of being elected and adopted into the family of Christ. With Mercersburg theologians John Nevin and Philip Schaff, I affirm baptismal grace but not baptismal regeneration.[80]

The eucharist is central in the life and worship of the church, but it is not a sacrifice for sin. It is a rite in which we proclaim and make manifest our oneness in the fellowship of Christ's love and the reality of our baptism into Christ's death and resurrection. I here agree wholeheartedly with Father Hugh Behan, editor of the *Catholic Missourian,* whose remarks hold ecumenical promise:

> The Eucharist is at the heart of how we express our faith, but the heart of our Faith is what the Eucharist proclaims, namely, that Jesus died, rose again, has gone back to heaven, and still intercedes for us. His dying meant that all sins are forgiven, there is no further need for sacrifice, and we as Christians can claim his power to offer that forgiveness and to experience it and the power and the grace to be challenged by his Good News. "Grace" means that God in Christ has done the work by his own free choice, it means that we cannot win, or earn or pay for or do anything about it.[81]

Philip Schaff, an ecumenical pioneer in his time, was alert to the twin perils of rationalism and pietism. Both underrated the symbols of the church and elevated the individual conscience and personal experience into supreme authorities. He rightly observed, "The undervaluation of the church and her symbols led gradually to the undervaluation of the apostles and their writings, and terminated finally in a denial of the divinity of Christ himself."[82]

From a similar perspective, Reformed theologian M. Eugene Osterhaven warns against denigrating the sacraments even while subordinating them to the Word:

> Those Christians who depreciate the sacraments through disuse or by giving
> them minimum meaning because of their material nature, if consistent,
> might seek a word from God beyond the paper and ink of Scripture or adopt
> a docetic Christology in which the humanity of Christ, an earthy reality, is
> denied. In denigrating the sacraments, they reject a gift that God has given
> to God's people for the enrichment of their spiritual life and the strengthen-
> ing of their faith.[83]

It is important to keep in mind that the goal of both the preaching of
the Word and the celebration of the sacraments is to direct attention
away from ourselves, away from the elements to the living Jesus
Christ, crucified and risen, and the promises of his gospel. Michael Horton offers these words of wisdom: "The whole purpose of sacraments
is to drive us further *out* of ourselves, not *into* ourselves! They take our
focus off of our own experience, performance and imagination, guiding us to Christ's Cross."[84] Again with Horton we need to affirm that "a
sacrament not only reveals; it confers. Through Word and sacrament,
God actually gives that which he promises in his gospel—forgiveness
of sins, freedom from the tyranny of sin, and eternal life."[85]

In upholding the need for sacraments in the life of the church, we
must at the same time resist a pansacramentalism which sees every
phenomenon in nature and history as a potential means of grace. Paul
Tillich mirrors this mentality: "Any object or event is sacramental in
which the transcendent is perceived to be present. Sacramental
objects are holy objects, laden with divine power."[86] From my perspective, only God himself is divine, only his Word and Spirit are filled with
divine power. Even the preaching and hearing of the gospel does not
automatically convey sacramental reality and power. The preached
word and sacraments are signs and tokens of divine action in history,
but they are not vessels that hold divine energy. God reaches out
through them to kindle the flame of faith in the hearts of his elect peo-

ple, but in and of themselves they have no capacity to convert or redeem. Holy objects and holy places belong to primitive and ritualistic religion but not to the prophetic religion of biblical faith.[87] A pansacramentalism closes the distance between God and humanity by postulating a universal Spiritual Presence in all of nature and history. A ritualistic sacramentalism binds God to ceremonial acts performed by the clerics of the church. A theology of Word and sacrament affirms that God is free to reveal himself or hide himself in the rites that he has commanded to be celebrated in his holy Word. Because God has promised to speak wherever people call on his name and because he has promised to impart his truth and power through the preaching of the gospel, the water of baptism and the sacramental meal, we can go to these means of grace confident that we will meet the living Christ and experience the fruits of his sacrifice so long as we forsake our sins and cling to the promises of Christ in faith.

At the same time, we cannot presume that God will act whenever the church acts, that God will listen if we come to him with unconfessed sin. We cannot presume on the kindness of God, but we can hope that God will hear our cry for mercy and send his Spirit upon those who are baptized into his death and who eat and drink of the eucharistic elements in faith and repentance. Sacraments announce that Jesus is present; faith receives and acclaims this presence; faith working through love demonstrates and manifests this presence to the world.

Appendix D: An Ecumenical Consensus?

One of the most important documents on the subject of sacraments is that issued by the Commission on Faith and Order in the World Council of Churches in 1982: *Baptism, Eucharist and Ministry* (BEM).[88] This report is remarkable in the way it brings together tenets and insights from the various Christian traditions in the hope of attaining an ecumenical consensus. Without in any way diminishing its undeniable ecumenical significance, I wish to raise questions concerning the direction of some of its theses.

Regarding baptism BEM tends to endorse baptismal regeneration, yet recognizing that to be complete baptism must include both repentance for sin and confession of faith. It tries to hold together the traditional practice of infant baptism and the biblical and apostolic legacy that baptism includes human response. It declares that salvation is "embodied and set forth" in baptism, thereby finding the objective basis for baptism in the ritual act itself.[89] I deem it more evangelical to contend that the fruits of Christ's salvation are communicated through baptism and faith. BEM asserts that we are engrafted into the body of Christ in baptism. A more biblical articulation is that we are engrafted into Christ through personal conversion with baptism as the visible or public sign of both God's electing grace and the believers' commitment to obedience.

On the Lord's Supper BEM hails this sacrament as "the central act of the Church's worship."[90] It is a high point in the worship celebration, but surely the central act is God's self-revelation in Jesus Christ through both Word and sacrament, the former including prayers and hymns as well as sermonic proclamation.[91] The pivotal climax of worship is not simply our offering of praise and thanksgiving but Christ's sending forth of his Spirit to convict us of sin and assure us of God's mercy. The vital role of the Spirit is duly recognized in this document.

BEM asserts that there is only one sacrifice for sin but that this sacrifice is "made actual" in the eucharist.[92] It is theologically more sound to contend that his sacrifice was made actual in past history, that recorded in the Bible; yet its impact is brought home to us by the Spirit in the whole worship celebration. We do not make his sacrifice present, but Christ makes himself present as his word is proclaimed and believed. BEM implies that Christ continually offers his sacrifice to the Father in the eucharist. It is more evangelical to hold that in this rite we appeal to his one unique sacrifice for sin as the ground for our pardon and deliverance.[93]

BEM also claims that the acceptance of episcopal succession is necessary for full Christian unity. The evangelical contention—that the real apostolic succession is fidelity to the gospel proclaimed by the apostles—appears to be compromised or called into question by the authors.

In this whole discussion it is important to affirm the role of the sacraments in the church's thought and worship without falling into sacramentalism, in which the performance of ritual actions effectively takes the place of personal decision and commitment. As I see it, there are three dangers in sacramental observance that BEM does appear to be aware of, though perhaps not sufficiently. The first is *localizing* the presence of Christ in the bread and wine. BEM rightly affirms the real presence of Christ in the eucharist, but it needs to warn against focusing on the outward signs rather than on the transcendent reality to which the signs point. A second danger is *mechanizing* the action of God's grace in Christ through the sacrament. The sacrament is then regarded as automatically effecting what it is designed to achieve. To its credit BEM appears to be alert to this pitfall by calling for inward contrition and personal faith. Finally, there is the danger of *monopolizing* the sacrament by connecting it with the idea of ministerial order in apostolic succession. Where this succession is not deemed to be present, doubt is cast on the full reality and efficacy of the sacrament. I have difficulty with the claim that the sign of apostolic succession (the laying on of hands for ordination) both ensures historical continuity and manifests "an actual spiritual reality."[94] There is biblical precedent for a ministerial laying on of hands for Christian service including service as a pastor of a congregation, but that this rite can be considered a special means of grace is debatable.

In summary, BEM deserves the wide recognition and study that have attended it, and it is my hope that it will be used by the Spirit to reopen questions that evangelicals in particular have generally ignored. Perhaps in reexamining these issues in the context of a genuinely ecumenical encounter involving traditions as dissimilar as Anabaptist, Calvinist, Roman Catholic and Orthodox, we will all receive new light from the Holy Spirit regarding both the practice and the theology of baptism, the Lord's Supper and ministry. If this happens the document will have then achieved its purpose.

·NINE·

THE DEMISE OF BIBLICAL PREACHING

The time is coming, says the Lord God,
when I shall send famine on the land,
not hunger for bread or thirst for water,
but for hearing the word of the LORD.

AMOS 8:11 REB

Cursed are all preachers that in the church aim at high and hard things, and neglecting the saving health of the poor, unlearned people, seek their own honor and praise.

MARTIN LUTHER

It is not sermons we need, but a Gospel, which sermons are killing.

PETER T. FORSYTH

Preaching must be done in the power of the Word of Christ. A man or woman may be ever so brilliant and eloquent . . . but it does not become preaching until one is taken captive by God's Word and has no other desire except to let the Word itself speak.

BO GIERTZ (SWEDISH LUTHERAN BISHOP, BORN 1905)

The church must reclaim the pastoral office as the preaching office of Biblical exposition, and free it from its captivity to managerial and psychological stereotypes.

JAMES R. EDWARDS

A ccording to the prophet Amos, the worst famine that could devastate a land is a famine of the Word of God (Amos 8:11-12). The right words may still be uttered, but if the Spirit of

God is not animating these words they remain lifeless, incapable of communicating regenerating power. A disobedient church shares much of the blame for vitiating the message of faith, but in the last analysis the disarray in the church is brought about by the living God himself who withdraws his grace as a judgment upon the church. The word of preaching without the gift of the Holy Spirit cannot speak to humanity's spiritual hunger. The frantic resort to gimmicks to make worship more palatable to an increasingly secularized culture is a sign not of spiritual sagacity but of spiritual rebellion. What finally communicates the treasure of salvation is not our ability to find points of contact with our listeners but our reliance upon the efficacy of the gospel to deliver from sin and death, and such reliance is born out of faith in the living God and in his incomparable revelation in Jesus Christ.

A Legacy in Peril

Not long ago a friend of mine reported that a church he had previously pastored in New Zealand removed the large, central pulpit (its only pulpit) and substituted a screen, which is used for praise songs and choruses and also to relay graphically illustrated biblical stories and sermonic messages. What is surprising and disconcerting is that this church is related to the Church of Scotland, a branch of Christianity that has prided itself on biblical, expositional preaching. Yet what happened in this church is not unusual: throughout the Protestant world today there is an unmistakable movement from the audible to the visual, from word to image. Worship is fast becoming entertainment; the goal is no longer the glory of God and the service of his kingdom but the well-being and fulfillment of the human creature. Besides preaching, other casualties in this megashift include the prayer of intercession and corporate confession of sin followed by the assurance of pardon. Extended Scripture reading as a preparation for the sermon is also becoming less frequent. Solos or musical renditions by some special ensemble are increasingly taking the place of congregational singing.

The evangelical legacy that goes back to the Protestant Reformation and the renewal movements of Puritanism and Pietism sought to hold Word and sacrament together in dialectical tension, but the emphasis was on the preached Word of God. Karl Barth rightly observed that preaching virtually becomes a third sacrament in Reformation theology.[1] In the words of the Second Helvetic Confession, "The preaching of the Word of God is the Word of God."[2] The Word proceeds from the mouth of God and is delivered to the church and the world through the testimony of his ambassadors and heralds.

The Reformers regarded the truth of divine revelation as something both objective and subjective. Its basis and content are objective, for it concerns God's very utterance in conjunction with the events of sacred history mirrored in the Bible and celebrated in church tradition. Its communication is both objective and subjective, since this truth is given by the Spirit in the evangelical experience of an awakened heart.

Aberrations After the Reformation

The Reformation rediscovered the revitalizing power of biblical preaching, but within one generation an anthropocentric orientation began to supplant the theocentrism of the Reformers. The emphasis was no longer on justification by free grace received through faith and demonstrated in a life of obedience but rather on justification by belief in right doctrine (as in orthodoxy) or on human preparations and confirmations of justification (as in Pietism). A biblical sermon will indeed entail a call to decision, but our decision constitutes a response to the gospel rather than the content of the gospel. It is a response, moreover, induced by the outpouring of the Holy Spirit rather than an accomplishment of human free will, which would then make justification a matter of works as well as of grace.

In both conservative and liberal Protestantism that followed the Reformation, preaching often degenerated into *moralism* in which God's acceptance of us was made contingent on human effort. Moralism is preaching the law without the gospel so that our hearers are told what to do in order to ensure for themselves a place in God's kingdom rather than what God has already done for us and the whole world in Jesus Christ. Sometimes the gospel is made into a new law: it is no longer the divine promise but the divine commandment. Here Protestantism comes dangerously close to the style of preaching prevalent in Catholic churches in which a moral homily, usually brief and to the point, takes the place of the kerygmatic proclamation.

Gnosticism is another temptation that we need to take seriously if we are to remain faithful to the biblical and Reformation mandate of preaching the gospel to the whole creation. In gnosticism preaching is designed to awaken powers latent within the human psyche. The task of the preacher is to enable us to discover our own divinity or to realize untapped human possibilities. This heresy also involves the claim to a secret knowledge of the future based on the right interpretation of biblical prophecy. The mystery of revelation is no longer the knowledge of the mighty acts of God open to all people of faith but a secret wisdom available only to those who submit themselves to the discipline of deciphering the apocalyptic code language in which a portion of the Bible is written.

Another aberration is what some in the Wesleyan Holiness movement call *easy believism* and Dietrich Bonhoeffer termed *cheap grace.*[3] Here we are confronted with a truncated form of orthodoxy in which the message of justification is fully affirmed, but the call to personal holiness—our response to God's act of mercy—is muted or downplayed. In this kind of preaching we discern the gospel but not the law, whereas the whole gospel involves the preaching of the law as well as the good news of Christ's victory over sin. A fully biblical sermon will sound the call to costly discipleship as well as celebrate the gift of costly grace—grace that cost God the life of his Son. Our mandate is to proclaim not only the message of the cross but also the command to take up our own crosses and follow Christ—not to gain salvation but to demonstrate a salvation already accomplished by God's reconciling work in Jesus Christ.

In what I choose to call *orthodoxism,* teaching takes precedence over preaching, and the sermon is reduced to Bible study, which can be edifying and instructive, but it is not the power of God unto salvation. The expansion of the human mind is a worthy goal, but what the sinner needs most is the regeneration of the human heart. Preaching will certainly entail a didactic as well as a kerygmatic dimension, but if it remains merely didactic it will have little efficacy in convicting people of sin or instilling faith. Jesus was not simply a great teacher but the Savior of the world, and until we duly recognize this fact we will lack the power to make a genuine decision of faith. It is possible to preach from the Bible and yet not preach Jesus Christ or the gospel, and this is what both Protestant conservatives and liberals need to keep in mind in preparing men and women for the ministry.

Exhibitionism also lures many Protestants away from biblical and Reformation moorings. Here the aim of preaching is to make an impression on our audience rather than to give a faithful rendition of the scriptural message. Preaching becomes a performance rather than an act of obedience. The worship service is centered no longer on the Word but on the preacher—on the personality and talents that he or she brings. Preachers are expected to be masters in the art of communication more than diligent students of the Word. Their success is determined by the numbers who attend their services or give to church programs rather than by the work of the Holy Spirit in convicting people of sin and turning them to the cross in repentance and faith.

Religious enthusiasm is still another deviation from faith in the gospel. Enthusiasm, which involves constantly seeking new experiences of God, was roundly censured by both Luther and Wesley. Here the Spirit is elevated above the Word, and religious experience is prized more highly than fidelity to the gospel and the law. Sharing experiences often takes the place of expounding a biblical text. Faith, to be sure, is an experience as well as an act of commitment, but it is an experience that transports us beyond all experiences into communion with the living Christ. In faith we are taken out of our subjectivity into the service of the kingdom of Christ, which involves ministering to others. Luther said, "our theology is certain" because "it snatches us away from ourselves and places us outside ourselves, so that we do not depend on our own strength, conscience, experience, person, or works but depend on that which is outside ourselves, that is, on the promise and truth of God, which cannot deceive."[4] There may be occasions when personal experience has a place in our preaching; yet we must never remain with the experience but always point to Christ's experience of our sin, guilt and death, which alone procured our salvation.

Finally, we come to the heresy of *politicizing* the gospel: here the church is reduced to an ethical culture society or a political lobby. The politicization of the gospel is often associated with liberal Christianity rather than evangelical Christianity, but today we see an ideological agenda intruding into the proclamation of the conservative church as well. Avoiding an ideological gospel does not mean that we should refrain from pointing our people to the political implications of the biblical gospel. Nor are we released from the obligation to preach against social evils, for this is included in the preaching of the law. At the same time, we should never confound the kingdom of God with a social program, or divine justification with social justice. Politicizing the gospel is a form of moralism, for it makes law rather than gospel the theme of our message.

What has brought about this abysmal state of affairs? Surely one determinative factor is the desire to make the gospel palatable to its cultured despisers and thus take away the scandal of the cross (1 Cor 1:23). In the process the gospel has been redefined to include the celebration of human potential and freedom. Or we succumb to the temptation to interpret the gospel in light of the religio-cultural ethos that has shaped our identity (such as "the American way of life"), thereby blunting the rough edges of the gospel. Even in conservative circles the gospel as divine revelation is often confounded with the cultural baggage of various faith traditions. On one occasion a friend in theological academia gave a quiz to his class, asking them to define the gospel. He received as many definitions as there were students in the class, and many of these answers could not be reconciled. The gospel, of course, cannot be encapsulated in a simple definition, for this would convert the simple gospel into a simplified gospel. The doctrine of justification by faith belongs to the essence of the gospel, but it is not the whole of the gospel. The gospel also includes sanctification through the outpouring of the Spirit. The gospel is not only the message of salvation but also the power of salvation (Rom 1:16), though this power is not within our control or possession.

Toward the Recovery of Biblical Preaching

The contemporary church—Protestant, Catholic, Orthodox—sorely needs the recovery of biblical, evangelical preaching. Protestantism in the tradition of the Reformation has been known for its stress on the cruciality of preaching, but now it is part of the problem rather than the solution.

We must learn again to preach the whole counsel of God—the full gospel—and this includes the law as well as the gospel.[5] We preach the law in order to convict people of sin and also to guide them in the paths of righteousness. We preach the gospel in order to console and also to instill the motivation to do works of faith and love. We must never confuse the law and the gospel, but at the same time it is imperative that we affirm their inseparable unity. The gospel must never be converted into a new law, nor should the law ever be a substitute for the gospel.

Preaching plays a pivotal role in the service of worship, but it does not exhaust worship. It should take place in the context of worship, but worship entails much more than preaching. Worship is the corporate response—in prayer, singing, and reflection—to God's self-revelation and reconciling work in Jesus Christ. Worship is not a performance designed to induce faith but a celebration of God's mighty deeds, including the gift of faith by the power of his Spirit. Worship, like preaching itself, is centered in the audible, not the visual. We respond to what we hear from the reading of Scripture and from the mouth of the preacher. The visual is not excluded, for we worship God through the celebration of the sacraments as well as through prayer and hearing. Yet the visual is subordinated to the audible, for the sacrament gains its power only in its unity with the proclaimed and written Word of God.

Ideally the sermon is an interpretation of the scriptural text, not an exhibition of superior knowledge or the demonstration of communication skills. Preaching, indeed the whole of worship, has for its object the glory of God and the regeneration of sinful humanity. It is also designed to equip the saints for service in the kingdom of God.

Sermons that are biblical will be, ipso facto, theological as well. What is disturbing is that so many sermons from evangelical pulpits today are palpably nontheological. Pragmatic concerns overshadow doctrinal concerns, a point well made by Os Guinness, Mark Noll, David Wells and many other keen observers of the evangelical scene.[6] The focus is on solving problems rather than interpreting God's Word correctly. We urgently need to overcome our fear of theology if we are to be good expositors of God's Word and thereby agents of God's grace.

A few decades ago biblical preaching was high on the agenda of the mainline Protestant denominations. Under the influence of the biblical theology movement and neo-orthodoxy, theological seminaries were engaged in the challenging task of making the Bible central again in the church's worship and mission. The emphasis, however, was on gaining release from personal doubt and inward anxiety rather than on deliverance from sin, death and hell. God's reconciling work in Christ was duly celebrated, but it was often made to serve a social agenda—the reconciliation of classes and races. While preaching was still seen as a vital element in the church's life and worship, the shift from preaching to doing, from dogma to praxis was already apparent. With the rise of theologies of revolution, liberation and multiculturalism, preaching has increasingly been relegated to the background. It has also taken new forms, such as sharing stories of personal struggle and triumph. The Bible is no longer the infallible guide and norm for faith and practice but now a resource for spiritual growth and fulfillment. Scripture is interpreted through the lens of a hermeneutics of suspicion rather than through the lens of faith in the crucified and risen Savior.

I do not deny that there are still many faithful pastors who wrestle with Scripture and who know what the gospel is. Yet we seldom hear of them because they expend their energies in self-giving service to their congregations rather than seeking positions of affluence and power within their conferences and denominations. There is still a remnant (including some conference ministers and bishops) who confess the name of Christ and whose witness is used by the Spirit of God to preserve the church from capitulation to demoralizing forces within the culture. But it is not enough that the church should be preserved. The church is called to advance under the banner of the gospel and bring the whole world into submission to Jesus Christ. The symbols of the church will take on new vitality and power when the gospel is rediscovered by both clergy and laity. When people again hear the gospel and the law proclaimed from the pulpits, they will be motivated to confess their sins and become light and salt in a society that sorely needs regeneration.

Every sermon should include the gospel of God's work of reconciliation and redemption in Jesus Christ, even though it may not explicitly focus on this theme. Even when we preach from the Old Testament, we should preach Jesus Christ and him crucified (cf. 1 Cor 1:23; 2:2). Too many sermons merely repeat the stories of biblical heroes rather than show how these heroes point to Jesus as the sole source of our redemption. Samson, for example, can be celebrated for the way in which he liberated the people of Israel from the Philistines, but we are not yet preaching the gospel unless we show how Samson witnesses to Jesus Christ. Just as Samson pulled down the pillar of the temple and destroyed both himself and the Philistines so Jesus gave his life not only for the believing community but for the whole world. While Samson was motivated, it seems, primarily by the desire for vengeance,

Jesus was motivated by vicarious love. Jesus, moreover, rose from the dead on the third day. He came to bring eternal life and not simply extended life on earth.

What the church needs today is not a return to scholastic orthodoxy with its emphasis on assent to right doctrine or even to neo-orthodoxy with its vision of the utter transcendence of God over history. Nor should we try to restore the pristine theology of the Reformation, which was born out of the polemical struggles with the Catholic Church, resulting in a preoccupation with free grace to the exclusion of all works-righteousness. We must by no means sever the bond that ties us to the glorious heritage of the Reformation and to the orthodoxy that flowed from it, for it was the Reformation that rediscovered the gospel in all of its stark simplicity and profundity. At the same time, we should not simply remain with the Reformation, but look behind and beyond it to the testimony of the fathers, mystics and saints of the universal church and to the Bible as the living Word of God, which has primacy over all ecclesiastical tradition and creedal formulation. In the spirit of the Reformers we should return to the Bible as hearers and learners, waiting for God to speak in a fresh way through his Spirit. We should see ourselves not as masters of a secret wisdom but as servants of the Word. We are not co-redeemers nor co-creators in forging the kingdom of God; instead, we are ambassadors of the Lord Jesus Christ with a message to proclaim and a commission to fulfill. If we take this task seriously Jesus' words will come to fruition: "He who hears you hears me" (Lk 10:16). We will then, and only then, be a means of grace to a lost and ailing world.

Postscript

The church has a host of articulate preachers who are well-versed in so many areas, but the problem is that it lacks preachers who see their mission as the presentation of the very Word of God and who thereby subordinate their own ideas and plans for the church to the dictates of the living Christ.[7] It also lacks congregations who flock to its services of worship primarily in order to hear the word of God from the mouths of their ministers. When the laity seek from their shepherds confirmations in their own opinions or lifestyle or a periodic spiritual uplift rather than the Word that both kills and makes alive (Deut 32:30; 1 Sam 2:6), it is no wonder that the result is too often a compromised message from the pulpit. We must not blame the laity for this dismal state of affairs, however, for pastors, teachers and elders have for the most part abdicated their task of nurturing people on the Word of God.

If the people who occupy the pews had the proper teaching, their expectations in the services of worship would very likely be considerably different. Sound teachers produce good learners, and both produce strong leaders and preachers. Yet no individual Christian or company of Christians simply by fulfilling their tasks can produce revival. Revival comes only by the free decision of God to send forth his Spirit. But God often ties his decision to the persevering prayers of the faithful and the diligent study of his Word. If the church begins to reform itself in light of God's Word, the strong possibility is that revival will not be far away.

As theologians of the Word of God we must always keep in mind that the truth of the gospel never becomes a possession of the church. The church does not hand out the gospel, but it bears witness to the gospel through the power of the Holy Spirit. Despite his sacramental predilection at one stage in his faith pilgrimage, Barth never lost sight of the discontinuity between God's word and the words of the church and its leaders: "However clearly and precisely the Gospel is preached, the divine incognito still remains. The pure, non-ecclesiastical Gospel is proclaimed by no human mouth."[8] At the same time, God may speak in conjunction with our speaking, and herein lies the hope of the church and of the world. We can really hear and know the Word of God, not through our own efforts and programs, but through the free condescension of a God of mercy and love. We can know and believe because God has spoken in the Bible and most of all in his only begotten Son—Jesus Christ, apart from whom no one can be saved.

·TEN·

A SOCIO-
THEOLOGICAL
TYPOLOGY

Solitary religion is directly opposite to the Gospel of Christ. "Holy solitaries"
is a phrase no more consistent with the Gospel than "holy adulterers."

JOHN WESLEY

The once-born are the chief spiritual peril in the Church, the religious-minded
without the religious experience, with a taste for religion, but no taste of it.

PETER T. FORSYTH

Salvation is neither doctrine nor conviction concerning a doctrine,
but the Word of God in Christ as it speaks to us in the heart.

EMIL BRUNNER

What has brought confusion into the American religious scene is that the sects
have become churches (without knowing it) and that the churches
have become sects (without being willing to admit it).

REINHOLD NIEBUHR

The world-wide church needs the examples of . . . groups committed to consistent
discipleship, which demonstrate the liberty of Christ more unhesitatingly than
church leaders and more radically than the masses.

JÜRGEN MOLTMANN

J ust as the Chalcedonian formula views Jesus Christ as having
two natures—the divine and the human—so it furnishes the
rationale for viewing the church in the same manner. The
church has an ontological foundation that is invisible. But it also has a

sociological matrix that is visible. In this chapter I intend to explore the social ramifications of the church, showing that they have profound theological significance.

A Typology of Religious Association

With the rise of the sociology of knowledge and the history of religions it has become increasingly evident that the dogmas of theology cannot be separated from their social and historical nexus. Ernst Troeltsch, Max Weber, H. Richard Niebuhr and James Luther Adams are among those who have ascertained the close connection between dogma and historical context.[1] In my judgment we can learn from their astute analyses, both positively and negatively. A doctrine of the church must be sociologically informed as well as theologically and biblically grounded.

Ernst Troeltsch (d. 1923) in particular has pioneered in the whole area of the interrelationship between creed and social status. In his celebrated *Social Teaching,* he proposes a typology of church, sect and mystical society.[2] It roughly corresponds to Max Weber's typology of authority: traditional, rational-legal and charismatic. The church is an institution endowed with grace and salvation, which are imparted through its self-designated representatives and its self-created sacramental rites. It seeks to be coterminous with the secular community and thereby accommodates itself to the reigning social ethos. One is born into a church as spiritual life shapes natural life. The sect, by contrast, is a voluntary society comprised of people who have made a definite commitment of faith and who testify to an experience of rebirth. The adherents of sects are painfully aware of the gulf between their religious values and the values of the secular community. Their emphasis is on law more than on grace, on the visible manifestation of religion in daily life rather than on the preservation of inherited forms of worship and piety. The Christ of the church is the Redeemer who has objectively achieved redemption once for all and imparts to individuals the benefits of his saving work through the ministry of Word and sacraments. The Christ of the sect is the Lord, "the example and lawgiver of Divine authority and dignity, who allows His elect to pass through contempt and misery on their earthly pilgrimage, but who will complete the real work of Redemption at His Return, when He will establish the Kingdom of God."[3] The concern of the sect is not the development of a comprehensive systematic theology, but the living out of a strict ethic and the cultivation of "a passionate hope for the future."[4]

As opposed to both of these types, the mystical society seeks to rise above outward forms and rites in its search for an immediate or direct experience of God. It does not repudiate formal worship and doctrine, but its focus is on "a purely personal and inward experience," which "leads to the formation of groups on a purely personal basis, with no permanent form."[5] This tends to "weaken the significance of forms of worship, doctrine, and the historical element."[6] The Christ of mysticism is "an inward spiritual principle, felt in every stirring of religious feeling, present in every influence of the Divine 'Seed' and the Divine 'Spark.'"[7] While the church tends to absorb the secular order and to dominate the masses, and the sect seeks to withdraw from or even challenge the secular order, the mystical society is intent on making contact with the eternal by turning its gaze inward.

Troeltsch sees the church type exemplified in Roman Catholicism, Eastern Orthodoxy and original Protestantism, especially Lutheranism. He discerns the sect type in the radical Baptists, the Anabaptists, the Quakers, the Methodists, the Levellers and many other such groups. Sectarian and mystical ideals were blended among groups like the Quakers and the Moravians. Calvinism and Puritanism signified an attempt to bring together the opposing visions of church and sect. Pietism sought to make a place for the sectarian impulse within the church by its cultivation of "*ecclesiola* in *ecclesia*."

Another category that Troeltsch acknowledges but does not develop is that of the denomination, which presupposes a pluralistic society. Here we see an attempt to preserve the concern of the church to embrace the whole of society and the sectarian emphasis on personal decision and commitment. A denomination demonstrates a relativistic mood and spawns bureaucracy in its desire to centralize power. A denomination necessarily has an unstable character, for it tends to gravitate toward either a sect or a church. H. Richard Niebuhr makes a cogent case that just as a sect is a phenomenon of the lower class so a denomination draws its main allegiance from the middle class.[8] This allegation has been disputed by sociologists of religion, but it contains the element of truth that the disinherited and dispossessed find their solace in sects more than in established religious institutions that are socially respectable.

One form of religious association that Troeltsch fails to consider is that of the cult, where there is an emphasis on charismatic leadership and conscious commitment to syncretism. The cult is an excursus religion that is not interested in restoring pristine forms of piety and organization (as we find in the sect) but in creating an entirely new spiritual ethos. The cult combines elements of the sect and the mystical society. It challenges the religious establishment not by calling for reform but by presenting a new vision for both the church and society. It is not indifferent to rites and ceremonies (as is the pure mystical society) but frequently creates new rites for a new kind of religious and world order. The cult is a seedbed of a new religion rather than an effort to purify existing forms of religion.

Some other forms of religious association also merit our attention. The religious order tries to hold together the reformist impulse with express loyalty to the church or denomination that it seeks to revivify. Conventicles and paraparochial fellowships of renewal aim to instill new life in the church by drawing upon the spiritual resources of religious tradition.

Troeltsch makes it unmistakably clear that he is referring to ideal types that are only approximated and not fully imbedded in any particular social group or movement. With Max Weber he tends to regard the ideal type as a tool for analysis rather than a guide for behavior. Its role is descriptive, not normative. The ideal type is a synthetic construct that throws light upon complex social forces, but does not claim to be a precise and definitive expression of the way things really are.

At the same time Troeltsch does make normative judgments in his development of his religious typology. He views a sectarian movement as narrowing and restrictive yet at the same time preserving the intimacy of Christian fellowship. He sees merit in the role of mysticism and spiritual religion in fostering religious tolerance. Yet he recognizes that mysticism is prone to sacrifice fellowship altogether and easily falls into a rampant individualism. He is keenly aware of the way in which a church gives permanence and identity to a social ethos, but he is profoundly alert to the way in which a church is used by the ruling powers to justify their favored position in society and to silence all dissent. Troeltsch is unwilling to dismiss any particular type of religious association, but his ultimate allegiance seems to be to a spiritual idealism that subordinates the practice of religion to the spiritual ideal of the kingdom of God found within all seekers after truth.

A Theological Interpretation

In his *Social Teachings* Troeltsch sought to explain church dogmas by the sociological factors that shape the life of the church. He contended, for example, that the dogma of the divinity of Christ arose out of the growing practice of the worship of Christ.[9] This historicist thrust became more prominent as Troeltsch developed his theology. Although he tried to find a transcultural criterion in the religious a priori, the yearning for God in human nature, he basically surrendered the unique Christian claims to the relativism of a theology of religious history.[10]

Against Troeltsch I maintain that while sociological factors cast light on the dogmas of faith they do not render an exhaustive explanation of these dogmas. Surely the source and goal of faith's affirmations lie in a transcendent criterion, divine revelation, which enters into and directs the course of human history. A theology divorced from sociology becomes necessarily abstract and lifeless. A sociology that is not anchored in theology becomes blind and purposeless. Troeltsch avers that Christian thought is dependent on sociological factors.[11] I, on the contrary, believe that while the development of Christian thought is shaped by sociological factors it is *not determined* by them. We must allow for the incontrovertible fact of human freedom and the mysterious superintendence of the Spirit of God in the progression of Christian thought and doctrine.

Instead of beginning with the concrete or empirical church as a social institution, I think it wiser to begin with the holy catholic church, the invisible fellowship of faith, and assess the social manifestations of religion in the light of this transcultural and transindividual criterion. Whereas sociology is mainly descriptive, theology is necessarily and primarily normative. The paramount question is not the impact of the church on society or vice versa but the truth of the church in a sea of untruth and misconception. We should seek not a blend of church, sect and mystical society but a theological critique of all three forms of religious association. Troeltsch is right that forms of religious association are closely linked with doctrinal and theological interpretations. This fact neither supports nor subverts the validity of these interpretations. To determine the validity of any particular truth claim or doctrine we must go first of all to the revelation unfolded in holy Scripture and brought home to us by the Holy Spirit. We should then try to assess the bearing of theological ideas on the place of the church in society.

We as Christians affirm one holy and apostolic church, and this church is indeed present in the variegated ways in which it organizes itself in society. The gospel is both unveiled and concealed in the various forms of religious association. The challenge that the theologian finds in the church type is to overcome the formalism and ritualism that reduce grace and salvation to powers controlled and dispensed by the clerics of the church. The challenge that the sect poses to evangelical theology is its transforming of gospel into law and its triumphalist claim to be a genuine restoration of the apostolic church. The error in the mystical society is to conceive of Christ as an indwelling spiritual principle rather than the incarnation of the Son of God in human history. Not all mystics succumb to this error (as Troeltsch would acknowledge), but mysticism as a movement tends to separate truth from history and elevate the direct experience of God into a final criterion for truth.

In short, all social expressions of Christian faith involve compromises with cultural ideology as well as creative attempts to bring the gospel ideal to bear on the social situation. A church that is not a living and transforming force in society has no real future either as a social institution or as an arm of the kingdom of God. Yet because every church or religious group is composed of sinners, it becomes a battleground in the struggle for power, the essence of human sin. The task of an evangelical theology is to teach all Christians, whether they are traditionalist, sectarian or mystical, a certain humility regarding their positions on social and moral questions, and to remind them that the final truth is not their unique possession but only their future hope. The true church of God will endeavor to combat the sacerdotalism and sacramentalism of the state (or folk) churches;[12] the arrogance, legalism and separatism of the sects; and the syncretism and eclecticism of the mystics. In this endeavor the abiding truth in all these forms of religious organization will be laid hold of and preserved.

Learning from the Sects

Churches, institutions firmly established in society and standing in continuity with Christian tradition, need to incorporate the sectarian impulse if they are to maintain their religious identity and remain true to their mission of bringing hope and meaning to a lost and despairing world. P. T. Forsyth was one who recognized the positive role of the sects in restoring balance to the church:

> The sects arose as gifts of God to the Church. They rose for a churchly need and purpose. They were appointed to recall the Church to this or that neglected point in the fulness of the Gospel. They were parts and servants of the Church, and should from the first have been so regarded.[13]

Emil Brunner, too, was fully aware of the fact that the sects addressed a deep-felt need in the church for fellowship and community: "The never-ending fissure of new sects from the Church springs ever afresh from the impulse to approximate more closely to the *Ecclesia* of the New Testament, indeed to become completely identical with it in every particular."[14] In Brunner's view the bane of the church is its elevation of form and ritual over community. The sect furnishes an antidote to formalism, though it generally ends by creating a formalism of its own.

While the sects provide personal fellowship and experiential contact with the living God, they also pose a threat to the faith because of their manifest imbalances in both thought and devotion. The church must endeavor to answer sectarian claims if it is to justify its existence as the earthen vessel of the Word of God. Johann Arndt, sometimes called the father of Pietism, underlined the need of the church to forge a credible defense of the historic doctrines of the faith against deviant forms of Christianity: "The pure teaching and truth of the Holy Christian faith must necessarily answer sects and heretics and defend itself according to the example of the holy prophets who preached firmly against . . . false and idolatrous prophets."[15]

First let us consider how the churches can learn from the sects. "Sects" in this context refers to any reformist or restorationist movement that arises out of the churches in order to give substance and life to the model of a pure church. Among the hallmarks of the sect is the urgency of mission. Whereas both folk churches and denominations have experienced a debilitating loss in missionary personnel, the sects display pronounced missionary fervor as they sedulously seek to bring the message of redemption to all peoples. This accounts for the startling rise in numbers that we see in the Jehovah's Witnesses, the Pentecostals, the independent Baptists, the Seventh-day Adventists, the Mormons, etc.[16] Again, the sects provide for their adherents a fellowship of love, a life-support system that ministers to their emotional and physical as well as spiritual needs. The sect also makes a prominent place for the lay ministry and thereby gives substance to the apostolic affirmation that we are all priests, prophets and kings. Finally, the sect provides certainty in an age of uncertainty. It does not embark on a mystical quest but heralds a definite message. In order to live purposeful lives people need to be anchored in some credible and sustaining authority. The sect at its best points people to the unsurpassable authority of the living God. At its worst the sect holds up a heteronomous authority, submission to an external standard that is in the possession or control of the religious group.

It is also incumbent on the churches to show how the sects can lead people astray. While most of the mainstream sects have a high view of the Bible, they are prone to be biblical literalists and obscurantists, championing the young earth theory, for example, and giving precise predictions for the inauguration of the millennial kingdom. They also tend to be restorationists and thereby blithely disregard the ongoing commentary on the Bible through the ages. They regrettably believe that the original church can be restored in its pristine purity simply by sloughing the many centuries of sacred tradition, which has served as the enduring nexus of the gospel. More often than not the sects fall into legalism, in which salvation is made to hinge on fulfilling the requirements of law. A corollary of legalism is separatism, in which believers are encouraged to separate or detach themselves from the wider secular society. Finally, we need to warn against the omnipresent danger of idolatry: the sect leaders are elevated into mouthpieces of the living God, and their interpretations are put on the same level as the inspired Word of God. Membership in a sect can foster a blatant self-righteousness stemming from the claim that one possesses final or ultimate truth and therefore does not need the correction of either holy Writ or holy tradition.

A sect is necessarily countercultural in that it sees the life of the Christian in terms of an antithesis to the wider cultural or secular ethos. Its vision of the kingdom of God tends to be apocalyptic rather than world transforming (as Troeltsch keenly observed). The Christian community is obliged to hear the call to separate and come out from among them (2 Cor 6:17), but we must also heed the call to bring all of creation under the domain of the Lord Jesus Christ (Mt 28:19-20; Lk 24:47). The Christ-against-culture motif must be made to serve Christ-transforming-culture if the church is to maintain both its social relevance and catholic vision.[17] William Penn, an early Quaker leader, wisely observed: "True godliness does not turn men out of the world but enables them to live better in it and excites their endeavors to mend it."[18] We must resist the gnostic call to "fly away" to some higher spiritual realm and instead apply our efforts to bringing the wider society into conformity with the ideal of social righteousness as this was articulated by the biblical prophets.

Epilogue

It is interesting to compare Troeltsch's typology of church, sect and mystical society with a typology that I have sometimes employed—orthodoxy, heresy and apostasy.[19] This typology is more thoroughly theological, but it also has sociological implications. It would be a mistake, however, to view these two typologies as correlative. Some churches have embraced heterodoxical if not heretical stances at some time in their history.[20] A group may be a sect sociologically speaking, and still be fairly orthodox in its teaching.[21] Many mystical societies tend to be cults and thereby embody new faith orientations that sharply conflict with traditional church teaching. Examples of cultic aberrations in Christian history are the Brethren of the Free Spirit, the Theosophical Society, Spiritualism, Swedenborgianism and the New Age movement. Other mystical societies seek to work within the established forms of religious life as a transforming leaven. Here we might think of groups like the Friends of God, the Brethren of the Common Life, Camps Farthest Out, the Disciplined Order of Christ and the Oxford Group movement.

One might say that true orthodoxy is achieved only when the church incorporates in its own life the valid concerns of both the sect and the mystical society. The true church will be both exclusive and inclusive. It will herald an inclusive gospel—directed to all people—but seek to include in its membership only those who openly confess the name of Christ and are ready to follow Christ as an example for living. It will be both a sacramental church having visible means of grace and a believers' church.[22]

The strength of Pietism lay in its strategy to work within the established churches, bringing new life to these churches by an emphasis on personal religion and voluntary association. Emil Brunner found in Pietism a concerted effort to rediscover the ideal of the *ecclesia*—the closely-knit fellowship of true believers—without abandoning the structures of church life. While Brunner faulted Pietism for sliding into subjectivism and thereby sundering the dialectical relationship between Word and Spirit, he paid tribute to this movement for rekindling the flame of the gospel within the churches: "Quite apart from its rejuvenation of the dried-up Protestant Church, what Pietism accomplished in the sphere of social amelioration and foreign missions is at least the token of that Spirit which is promised in the Bible to those who truly believe, and is among the most splendid records of achievement to be found in church history."[23] Pietism rediscovered the church as *Gemeinde* (community) but sometimes, especially in its radical forms, lost sight of the need for structure and order in the life of the church.

Søren Kierkegaard, who like Brunner had his spiritual roots in Pietism, also sounded the call for the reform of the church through the recovery of the personal dimension in faith.[24] For a time he believed that renewal might come through a return to the monastery, but he then came to see that all Christians must embody the spirit of exclusive or single-minded commitment to Christ if the church is to be revitalized according to the principles of the gospel. His impassioned commitment to reform is evidenced in this somber appraisal of the religious scene: "Christendom has done away with Christianity, without being quite aware of it. The consequence is that, if anything is to be done, one must try again to introduce Christianity into Christendom."[25]

Troeltsch proposed a spiritual religion that would infuse the inherited forms of church life with the spirit of the gospel. I propose a theology of Word and Spirit that applies the truth of divine revelation, attested in the Scriptures, to the concerns of daily life in the modern world. It is not spiritual idealism that we need, but an evangelical catholicity that draws upon the treasures of the historical church in the power of the Spirit and through the lens of faith in the biblical gospel.

The two dangers, as Brunner acutely perceived, are objectivism and subjectivism.[26] The former, which we find in both the church and the sect, absolutizes the outward forms of faith. The latter internalizes the claims of faith so that faith is reduced to a religious experience (as in mysticism, spiritualism and radical Pietism). Brunner regarded subjectivism as the greater danger: "As objectivism leads to torpidity, so subjectivism to dissolution. What is torpid can be awakened again to life; but what is dissolved is no longer in existence."[27]

In contrast to Catholic and high Lutheran ecclesiology, Brunner perceived the true church, the church founded by Jesus Christ, as a movement of renewal with only rudimentary form and structure rather than a social institution with sacraments and a monarchial episcopate:

> The church *has* offices, it *uses* sacraments; it therefore *has* institutions—if one wishes to place offices and sacraments into this category—but it *is* no institution. The church also has its rules and needs them; but the church *is* no set of rules, and the rules of the church do not constitute the church. In the New Testament the church is never anything else than the community of those who belong to Christ through faith, whom through His Word and Spirit he has constituted the community.[28]

Brunner can be justly criticized for underplaying the institutional dimension of the apostolic church, but he is nonetheless right that the church of the New Testament was much more than a social institution: it was a revolutionary movement of spiritual renewal that was both empowered by the Spirit of God and informed by the Word of God.

The alternative to objectivism on the right and subjectivism on the left is a theology of Word and Spirit, which bases itself on the proclamation of the gospel, as found in Scripture, and the outpouring of the Holy Spirit in the Christian community. If we have orthodoxy or right doctrine alone we will then be unable to avoid the ossification or petrification of faith that frequently follows the initial commitment and burst of enthusiasm. If we have experience alone we will then witness the probable dissolution or evaporation of faith. We need a faith that is both rational and spiritual, one that is founded on the Word of God and animated by the Spirit of God. We shall then have a church that stands in continuity with the historic creeds and confessions (orthodoxy) and also one that seeks to live out the claims of Christian faith in daily life (the concern of the sects). In addition we will have a church that is constantly revivified by the free movement of the Spirit working through the proclamation of the Word and the observance of the sacraments. The reform of the church in light of the Word and the revival of the church in the power of the Spirit should be the aim of every theology that seeks to be faithful to the teachings and the vision of the apostolic community.

Appendix E: Further Thoughts on Sects and Cults

A number of scholars in the areas of theology and church history have questioned whether the terms *sect* and *cult* because of their pejorative connotations have any place in the contemporary discussion.[29] It is my contention that in view of the fact that these designations have a long and celebrated history they can still be profitably employed in the reigning discourse. To be sure, in recent years both sects and cults have been associated with undue adulation of the group leader and unwarranted attempts to control and manipulate people, sometimes with grievous consequences. It should be borne in mind that the drive for power is manifest in established churches and denominations as well as in sects and cults and that this drive is sometimes curbed and even overcome in the sectarian and cultic milieu.

While in this chapter I have been using the typology of church, sect and cult mainly in a sociological sense, I have made clear on numerous occasions that this typology also has far-reaching theological implications. It is not only theologically permissible but also theologically mandatory to make distinctions between religious bodies on the basis of divine revelation. All religions are not the same with regard to either truth claims or moral values. Only some groups in Christian history have been faithful to the tradition of apostolic faith. Only some groups mirror and serve the true church—holy, catholic and apostolic. To call sects and cults "minority religions" or "countercultural religions" is acceptable so long as we do not allow sociological categorization to be the last word. We need also to engage in a theological or doctrinal critique, which will sometimes involve derogatory judgments, though these judgments will be tempered by the realization that no one church or system of theology can encompass the totality of truth.

We are living in an age of latitudinarianism and syncretism in which it is erroneously believed that all roads lead to God. We are allowed to say that Christianity is true for us, but we cannot proclaim that Christianity is true for all people without being labeled a dogmatist or religious imperialist. The reigning virtue today is tolerance, and the overriding sin is intolerance or rigidity. Interestingly this tolerance does not extend to those who hold to the precepts of biblical tradition. In this sometimes intimidating ideological climate it is salutary for Christians to use terms like *sect* and *cult,* since this terminology rests on the sound premise that there are real, even irresolvable differences between religions. It is incumbent on Christians to distinguish between religious claims if they still believe in objective truth given in divine revelation.

Granted that in recent years the sect-cult terminology has taken on nuances of meaning that are mainly negative, it does not follow that we should therefore abandon this kind of typology. We are obliged to reinterpret the typology, to use these terms with more care and diligence. To abandon terms like *sect* and *cult* also betrays a readiness to discard such designations as *heresy, heterodoxy* and *apostasy.* Dietrich

Bonhoeffer urged the church in his time to rediscover the meaning of heresy, since without a lively perception of heresy we lose the ability to affirm and defend orthodoxy. Similarly without a keen grasp of what is sectarian and cultic (these are not the same), we are unable to affirm the reality of the one true church of God. A church in the theological sense is known primarily in its differences from sects, which often presumptuously claim to be the true church. The Bible calls us to test the prophets, for not all prophets are from God (Mt 7:15; 24:11, 24; Mk 13:22; Lk 6:26; 2 Pet 2:1; 1 Jn 4:1).

Sociologically we can make a place for various forms of religious association, for there is no one social formation that is intrinsically closer to the kingdom of God than any other. Perhaps it can be said that a sect or separatistic group is nearer to the biblical vision of the true church than is a state church or folk church in which religion is fully assimilated into a cultural ethos. Yet the Word of God can be proclaimed and heard in a folk church as well as in a sect. Even in a mystical society one may hear and know the veritable Word of God and thereby come to a saving faith in the Lord Jesus Christ. The New Testament ideal is a believers' church, which one enters through a personal decision of faith and commitment. When religion becomes habitual and perfunctory, as in most folk churches and denominations, it loses its salt and vitality. It no longer poses a challenge to the culture but instead becomes a reflection of the values that the culture holds dear.

Let us continue to make distinctions between religious groups, both Christian and non-Christian, but let us always keep in mind that the Word of God can be served even in the most outlandish sect, and the Word can be blocked and distorted even in the most dogmatically pure church. May we learn from both sects and cults, but may we always be wary of claims that lack biblical and apostolic sanction. May we continue to strive for the ideal of the true church while keeping in mind that this ideal is eschatological. It can be realized in this life only in part; its full realization is in the future when the church becomes identical with the kingdom of God.

·ELEVEN·

THE DIVERSITY
OF MINISTRIES

And his gifts were that some should be apostles, some prophets, some evangelists,
some pastors and teachers, to equip the saints for the work of ministry.
EPHESIANS 4:11-12

The ministry is a prophetic and sacramental office; it is not a secretarial, it is not
merely presidential. It is sacramental and not merely functional.
PETER T. FORSYTH

All members of the Church have their charism,
their special call and their personal ministry. . . . Pastoral ministries
are not the only ones in the Church.
HANS KÜNG

Our mission is to teach people to pray and bring people to Jesus.
MOTHER TERESA

Any in-depth examination of what the New Testament says about ministry will yield the conclusion that the original Christian communities contained a diversity of ministries, though in the later apostolic period, reflected in some New Testament books including the pastoral epistles, there was a discernible shift toward centralization. Beginning toward the end of the first century a threefold ministry of bishops, presbyters and deacons developed. It seems that judicial and spiritual power was now invested in bishops who ultimately determined who was qualified for ministry. In the pastoral epistles the idea of a monarchial episcopate was definitely in

place. At the same time, the lines between bishop and elder or presby-
ter were often blurred, even in the later New Testament writings. In
Titus 1:5-7 the qualifications for an elder and a bishop appear to over-
lap. The writer of 1 Peter, who claims apostolic rank (1:1), addresses
the elders as a "fellow elder" (5:1). It seems that all bishops were
elders, but not vice versa. In the earlier period the presbyters of Ephe-
sus were also called overseers or bishops (Acts 20:28).

In the original or Pauline communities of the church, ministry and
charism were closely related; there were indeed as many ministries as
charisms. Paul writes that the gifts of the Spirit were distributed in
such a way that a variety of ministries were created: "His gifts were
that some should be apostles, some prophets, some evangelists, some
pastors and teachers, to equip the saints for the work of ministry" (Eph
4:11-12; cf. 1 Cor 12-14; Rom 12:4-8). The earliest Christian churches
appeared to be loosely connected, and the apostles or overseers had a
moral or spiritual more than an administrative authority. Already in
the early second century the monarchial episcopate was in force. In
the letters of Ignatius (not later than A.D. 117) it is contended that "no
gathering of his church for baptism, Eucharist, or Agape was valid
without his presence or authorization."[1] The idea of a special priesthood arose in the third century and was connected with the priesthood
of the Old Testament, which focused on the offering of sacrifices to
God. In the Christian context the priest now offers the one sacrifice of
Christ to the Father through the ritual of the mass. Bishops were given
the sole right to confirm—the laying on of hands for the reception of
the Holy Spirit.

If we restrict ourselves to the New Testament witness, no definitive
form or pattern of ministry appears to be endorsed. I here agree with
the biblical scholar Walter Brueggemann: "There is no one single or
normative model of church life. It is dangerous and distorting for the
church to opt for an absolutist model that it insists upon in every cir-
cumstance."[2] The Faith and Order Commission of the World Council of
Churches came to a similar conclusion: "The New Testament does not

describe a single pattern of ministry which might serve as a blueprint or continuing norm for all future ministry in the Church."[3]

The transition from loosely knit communities to hierarchy was already in progress in the first two centuries of the church. Catholic theologian Hans Küng regards this movement as an impoverishment, for it signaled the subverting of burgeoning lay ministries and the investing in the ministries of elders and bishops special powers that belong only to God. Commissioned and appointed ministries tended to bind and quench the free movement of the Spirit and resulted in clerical control. Küng's observation on the narrowing of authority in the church is both accurate and cogent:

> The fellowship of believers, the collegiality of all believers, of all those who had charisms and fulfilled their own ministries, the collegiality of the whole Church, in short, gave place to the *collegiality of a special ministry* within the community: the collegiality of the leaders of the community, the *episkopoi* or elders, who increasingly began to see themselves as distinct from the community, from the "people"; this is where the division between "clergy" and "laity" begins.[4]

While no polity or order in the apostolic church can claim universal sanction, we can learn much about how ministry is to be realized by reflecting on the New Testament witness. Küng again is helpful when he declares, "The Church must be seen first and foremost as a fellowship of faith, and only in this light can ecclesiastical office be properly understood."[5] Every Christian is called to ministry, and every Christian has been endowed with charismatic gifts to equip the believer for ministry. "Anyone who is qualified for a particular ministry—as prophet, teacher, helper, superior, bishop or deacon, etc.—and who performs it properly, has received the call of God and the charism of the Spirit."[6]

If we take the ministry of Jesus as our paradigm we can see that ministry does not mean elevation over others but service to others—both spiritual and material. Jesus was sent by the Father in order to serve those in need. "I am among you as one who serves" (Lk 22:27; cf. Jn 13:13-15). "Greatness in . . . ministry is accounted, not in outward rank, but in proportion to service" (Mt 20:25-28; Mk 10:42-45; Lk 22:24-27).[7] Jesus called his followers to preach the coming of the kingdom of God. After his resurrection this message was made more concrete as the church focused on the person and work of Jesus as signifying the embodiment of the kingdom. Apostolic ministry means proclaiming the gospel of the cross in the power of the Spirit as members of the body of Christ. It also involves baptizing people in the name of the Father, Son and Holy Spirit and celebrating the sacrament of the Lord's Supper as a memorial to what God has done for us in Christ. Christ abolished a special priestly caste, for he himself offered the one sacrifice that avails for redemption from sin (Heb 9:11-28; 10:14-18). At the same time he calls all believers to share in the universal priesthood of interceding for the saints and for the world.

While all Christians are involved in a priestly ministry (1 Pet 2:5; Rev 1:6; 5:10), while all are given an apostolic vocation, only some are equipped for pastoral ministry. Not all have the gifts of speaking and leadership, not all are required to undergo arduous training for preaching and teaching. As Christians we all share in Christ's prophetic office as well as his priestly office, but we are not all recipients of the gifts for pastoral leadership in the assembly of faith. Küng again is on target:

> All Christians have authority to preach the word, to witness to their faith in the Church and in the world, to "missionize." But only pastors with a special calling, or those commissioned by them, have the particular authority to preach in the meetings of the community.[8]

Pastors differ from other Christians primarily in their function, but also in the charismatic gifts that enable them to fulfill their special task as ministers of the Word. If the Reformers were right that the preaching of the gospel is a sacramental act, then those who preach the gospel publicly are involved in a sacramental ministry. P. T. Forsyth puts it well: "The ministry is a prophetic and sacramental office; it is not a secretarial, it is not merely presidential. It is sacramental and not merely functional. It is the outward and visible agent of the inward gospel of

Grace. . . . It is the trustee of the one sacrament of the Word, the Word of New Creation."[9] This position does not imply, however, that ordination is itself a sacrament or that only pastors are invested with the priestly authority to speak the truth of the gospel, to hear confessions, to baptize and distribute Communion, to intercede for the faithful and pray for the lost. It means that those who are called to the public ministry of preaching the Word and leading the congregation of faith have a special responsibility—not only to convey the treasure of the gospel through public preaching but also to equip the saints for ministry and thereby counsel them and guide them as they struggle to realize their vocation under the cross.

In addition to pastors there are prophets, who speak the word of the Lord to a particular situation, often giving us a glimpse of the future; counselors, who are endowed with words of wisdom and knowledge that enable them to help people in distress; teachers, who unveil the mysteries of faith to those who seek deeper grounding in the faith; healers, who communicate the balm of the Spirit to those who suffer either physically or spiritually; administrators, who oversee either churches or other educational and charitable religious institutions; helpers, who engage in errands of mercy; speakers in tongues, whose prophecies when interpreted give guidance to the assembly or to particular persons in the assembly; prayer warriors, whose gift of wonder-working faith enables them to rescue people in otherwise hopeless situations; seers and exorcists, who through the gift of discerning of spirits help to free people from demonic oppression and possession; deacons and deaconesses, who engage in a public ministry of service; and full-time evangelists, who travel from place to place bringing the message of revival to the despairing and the lost. In the history of the church we can surely acknowledge that new charisms have been distributed, new ministries have been created by the Spirit. Among these is the monastic vocation, where brothers and sisters in the spirit live together in community; service as medical missionaries, which may involve the gift of healing and will necessitate a long period of training; hospital, prison and military chaplaincies; and Christian writing, which may take the form of fiction or nonfiction. Many other ministries could be mentioned! The important thing to remember is that every Christian has an apostolic vocation, for we are all called to bear witness to the faith even in our secular tasks—by word and example. Brother Lawrence, a Carmelite lay brother in seventeenth-century France, had a ministry of prayer that was realized in the menial tasks that he performed, washing pots and pans, sweeping the kitchen floor and so on. In this ministry he experienced the joy of being in the constant presence of the living God.[10]

Every Christian is called to full-time service in the name and for the sake of Christ. Yet some ministries may indeed be deemed more important than others in certain periods of the history of the church. The apostles made this clear when they told the assembly that it was not right that they should give up preaching the Word to serve at tables. As a result certain persons were chosen from the community to devote themselves to the work of service so the apostles could be free to engage full-time in prayer and the ministry of the Word (Acts 6:1-5). What is interesting to note is that some of those chosen to be deacons also came to include in their ministry the work of evangelism and mission. The significant fact is that any one Christian may engage in a number of different ministries depending on the charisms given by the Spirit.

The church fundamentally is a community of charisms. This is not to deny that every church needs form and structure as well, but the church is essentially a fellowship, not an institution.[11] Truth is imparted not from the top down nor from the bottom up but from the risen Christ in whom we live and move and have our being. Christ speaks to us in his Word and also in our conscience. He is above us, within us and in the midst of us. The authority for faith is neither heteronomous, centered in an external standard or ministerial office, nor autonomous, centered in our own conscience and experience. Instead it is theonomous—centered in the living God whose voice can never be identified with the clerics of the church, though it may truly be heard in elected or appointed leaders. Those who are deacons and presbyters need to be guided by bishops, but bishops in turn may be challenged and corrected by prophets. Every prophet must be tested by church authorities to make sure that the message that is being uttered is anchored in the wisdom of Scripture and sacred tradition. But when prophets are examined by the church in this way we run the risk of quenching and grieving the Spirit. The true church of God needs to be brought into obedience to the Word and at the same time animated by the Spirit.

The New Testament does not prescribe any particular polity, though at various points in the history of the church one of the polities has proved to be more conducive to Christian renewal than others. Each of the principal polities—congregational, presbyterian, episcopal—has some promise, and each can present roadblocks to the gospel. We do not guarantee the prospering of the church by the kind of polity we embrace, even one that claims apostolic succession. It is not polity but lifestyle that reveals the genuineness of our faith and mission. If we are truly obedient to the commission of our Lord to preach the gospel to the whole creation and teach them to observe everything that Christ commands (Mt 28:19-20), we will then be blessed by the living God, and our ministry and church will flourish. On the other hand, if we engage in ministry in order to advance ourselves, in order to gain positions of influence within the church out of a desire for prestige, our ministry will then be bereft of power and purpose.

The church will always need guardians and overseers, but these should be in the service of the whole family of God and not exclusively of a special priestly caste within the church. Would the evangelical church ever support papal hegemony as a pathway to Christian unity? The answer can only be a resounding *no,* for such implies papal control and domination. On the other hand, if the papacy could be reinstituted as basically a moral or spiritual office and the pope could be seen no longer as the vicar of Christ but now as "the servant of the servants of God," the motto of Gregory the Great, evangelical Christians might be more open to this possibility. At the same time, the deadly enemy of charismatic ministry in the church has always been centralization of power and the substitution of ecclesiastical authority for the authority of Word and Spirit.

Genuine progress toward real Christian unity can come only when the various churches admit that they have been on the wrong side in some of the debates in the past and are open to correction and reform by the Spirit of God who seeks to apply the Word of God to the religious situation in every period of the life of the church. What biblical Christians want is a church under the Word of God but also one that courageously bears witness to this Word in every new crisis in the life of the church. A pope or bishop who preaches the gospel of salvation by grace alone to be received only by faith is much to be preferred to an evangelical minister who testifies only to the marvels of his or her own religious experience and whose trust is basically in a church growth program rather than in the free movement of the Spirit in bringing the written Word of God to bear on the problems at hand. Sacred tradition can be helpful in determining the course of action that a church should pursue, but church tradition is never to be put on the same level as holy Scripture. What is disturbing is that the evangelical community tends to absolutize its own traditions (such as the seven dispensations and scriptural inerrancy) and to read Scripture through the lens of these traditions. The way to reform and renewal is to cease defending our own theological turf and seek to be taught by the Holy Spirit, even if this involves reinterpreting and sometimes even abandoning cherished notions and practices that constitute an impediment to true faith rather than a force for spiritual liberation.

Protestant Religious Orders

In its protest against works-righteousness the Protestant Reformation subjected the monastic orders of the Catholic Church to careful scrutiny and found them wanting. Although allowing for free forms of community life, the magisterial Reformers did not explore this possibility in any depth or with any degree of enthusiasm. The position of the Catholic Church is that in addition to the general ministry of Christian service, in which all believers share, there is the special ministry of the religious life, in which one lives apart from family, property and secular duties in exclusive devotion to Christ. The Reformers stoutly contended that all Christians are called to full-time work for the kingdom and that the elevation of the monastic life is elitist and pharisaical. They also convincingly challenged the claim that the monastic life is more meritorious than ordinary life in society and that it thereby contributes to securing our justification before God.

Despite their strictures against the monastic vocation, the churches of the Reformation witnessed various attempts to recover this kind of witness in the service of evangelical faith. The Möllenbeck monastery near Rinteln in northwest Germany was one of the first communities to appear within Protestantism. Originally Augustinian, it transferred its allegiance to Protestantism in 1558. It actually began to prosper as an evangelical community, though it could not survive the bitter controversies associated with the Thirty Years War. Other survivals of Catholic monasticism within Lutheranism included the cloister at Loccum, which had originally been a Cistercian monastery; and the convent of Marienberg in Helmstedt, formerly an Augustinian cloister for nuns.[12]

With the rise of evangelical Pietism in the seventeenth and eighteenth centuries new ventures in community life appeared, sometimes including married couples with families as well as single persons. Among the new centers of mission and prayer were the Community of Little Gidding in England; the Pilgrims' Cottage of Gerhard Tersteegen, a German Reformed mystic and devotional writer; the Trevecka Community, associated with the evangelical revivals in Britain; the Ephrata cloister near Lancaster, Pennsylvania, founded by Johann Conrad Beissel, a German Pietist; the Shaker communities of Mother Ann Lee; and the Herrnhut community of Count Nicholas von Zinzendorf. In the nineteenth and early twentieth centuries mention should be made of the Harmony Society of "Father" George Rapp, north of Pittsburgh; the Amana communities in southeastern Iowa; and the Society of Separatists at Zoar in Ohio.[13]

In addition we should consider the Protestant missionary societies that began flourishing in the nineteenth century, including the China Inland Mission, which later became the Overseas Missionary Fellowship; the Sudan Interior Mission; the Basel Mission; the St. Chrischona Pilgrim Mission; and the Barmen Mission (several of which had a communal base). The Dohnavur Fellowship in south India, founded by Amy Carmichael, who was originally sponsored by the Church of England Zenana Missionary Society and the Keswick Mission Committee, came to function as a faith mission in which members had virtually all things in common.

Paraparochial fellowships that specialize in campus ministries are also worthy of note: Young Life, Campus Crusade for Christ, InterVarsity Christian Fellowship and the Navigators. Are all of these mission-oriented fellowships the Protestant equivalent of religious orders? Perhaps they more roughly correspond to third orders in Catholicism, which make a place for married and singles working together under a common discipline.

Community life became much more of a live option for Protestants after the Second World War, when experiments of many different kinds began to flourish.[14] Among these are the Taizé community in southeastern France, originally founded by Reformed churchmen and now an ecumenical monastic community; the Evangelical Sisterhood of Mary in Darmstadt, Germany, whose roots are in Protestant Pietism; the Brotherhood of Christ in Selbitz, Germany, founded by a Lutheran pastor and his wife; the Casteller Ring, an evangelical sisterhood near Würzburg, Germany; the Iona community in Scotland; Lee Abbey and St. Julian's community in England; Operation Mobilization, drawing support from the Moody Bible Institute and the Plymouth Brethren; Koinonia Farm in Americus, Georgia, now defunct, which was in the front lines in the battle for civil rights for the black community; the

Community of Jesus on Cape Cod, Massachusetts, which includes single brothers and sisters as well as married persons; the Jesus Army in the British Isles;[15] the Torchbearers, associated with the Keswick higher life movement; Jesus Abbey in South Korea; the Moral Re-Armament community in Caux, Switzerland; Bethany Fellowship in Minneapolis, Minnesota; and Francis Schaeffer's L'Abri Fellowship near Montreux, Switzerland, aimed at reaching secularized youth for the gospel. Some of these new ventures have their source of inspiration in the charismatic movement within both Protestantism and Catholicism. The Jesus movement of the 1960s and 1970s is reappearing in new guises at the turn of the century.

The paramount question is whether these new forms of church life are compatible with evangelical theology. Those of us whose allegiance is to the Reformation can certainly perceive the value of communities as centers of evangelism and world mission. But can there be communities devoted primarily to prayer and meditation? Also, can there be in an evangelical context vows of celibacy, poverty and obedience that seem to bind people to a new law? In Protestant tradition celibacy has been welcomed as a special gift, but it has been questioned as a law that binds the conscience. I shall say more about this in the concluding section of this chapter.

As one who has made a study of religious community life, I have been impressed by the spiritual fervor and vigor of some of these communities, but I have also been chagrined to discover how many of these ventures have only a brief life span and how many fail to make a lasting impact on the churches.[16] I have detected snares in community life including pharisaism and legalism, in which law supplants gospel as the motivating force and criterion for Christian living. Yet a religious community can rise above these temptations when it places all of its confidence in the God of free grace.

I sincerely welcome the new surge in community life, but I wish to enumerate some guiding principles for those contemplating this kind of vocation. First, the paradigm for evangelical community life should be the natural family. The almost total separation of the sexes that we find in some Catholic religious orders seems to conflict with the biblical axiom that man and woman are created to be in fellowship with one another. Woman was given to man as a helpmate and thereby crowns God's creation of humanity (cf. Gen 2:18-25). The early Moravians exemplified the evangelical ideal when they made a place for single brothers and sisters, each group living in its own houses, and married couples with families, all united in the work of mission to the lost. This recommendation does not denigrate those who feel called to make their witness in separate sisterhoods and brotherhoods, but these ventures should not be isolated from each other or from the wider church and should indeed exist in creative interaction. They should be open, moreover, to receiving guests of both sexes and of all denominations. An evangelical community will try to combine the first, second and third orders of Catholic tradition so that married and single work together to prepare the way for the coming kingdom of God. The Orthodox monastic experiment on Mount Athos, Greece, has much to commend it as a haven of rest for weary souls, but evangelical churches would find great difficulty in throwing support to a venture that barred women, even female animals, from its premises.

Second, an evangelical community will be based solidly on the biblical message of justification by the free grace of God. The monastic life is not a means by which we earn justification for ourselves, but a sign that justification has already been accomplished through the atoning death and glorious resurrection of our Lord Jesus Christ. An evangelical community will be constantly alert to the dangers of legalism and self-righteousness that elevate community life to a higher level spiritually than ordinary life in the world. In evangelical theology all Christians are under the gospel imperative of wholehearted consecration to Christ, but they will realize their vocation in different ways. Having done all, they will continue to confess that they are only sinners saved by grace, that faith alone secures their salvation and that Christ alone is to be given all the glory in the procuring of their salvation.

Third, a community in the evangelical sense will be a center for evangelism and world mission. It will be both a training center for mission and a locus of mission. A concerted attempt will be made to draw those who come for retreats into personal faith in Jesus Christ. The spiritual center of the community will be its chapel, where the Word of God is being read and proclaimed, for faith comes by hearing (Rom 10:17). The certification of a community as evangelical will be based not on how well it keeps the canonical hours but on the significance it attaches to the proclamation of faith in the main service of worship.[17] Such a community will also be measured by the depth of its prayers for the church and the world, its fidelity to the Bible in its preaching and teaching ministry and its generosity in offering hospitality.

Fourth, the community will be solidly grounded in private and corporate prayer including adoration, confession, thanksgiving and petition. Evangelicals find difficulty with the Catholic monastic ideal of contemplation understood as the transcendence of reason in an ecstatic vision of the ground and source of our being. This ideal has roots more in Neoplatonic mysticism than in biblical evangelicalism. The evangelical communalist will be devoted to intercession for the world rather than to the perfection and transfiguration of the seeking soul. We enter this kind of vocation not to find God (he has already found us) but to witness to the mighty acts of God as declared in holy Scripture. The longings of our hearts will indeed be satisfied if we find our solace in God's gracious act of condescension in Jesus Christ rather than in spiritual techniques designed to elevate us into the presence of God.

Again, an evangelical community will not claim to be an embodiment of the kingdom of God, nor will it set out to build the kingdom of God on earth (as in utopian communities). Instead, it will endeavor to be a sign and witness of the kingdom, whose coming is in the hands of the living God. The community will see itself standing under the judgment of the kingdom and therefore will be open to continual reform and purification by the Spirit of God.

Finally, the evangelical community will be intimately related to the evangelical church. It will include on its board of directors or advisors active church people who identify with its purpose and mission. A community must be accountable to the wider church, and this means being willing at times to relinquish some of its power. The problem with interconfessional communities like Taizé is that their connections with the churches can be weakened by a commitment to a broad ecumenicity. When communities become interfaith, as in Moral Re-Armament, this danger is exacerbated.

In evangelical parlance it is more appropriate to speak of interdenominational fellowships of renewal rather than of monastic orders, since the accent is not on separation and withdrawal but on the penetration of society with the values and goals of Christian faith. The purpose is not to sunder the lines of communication with the wider church but to make an impact on the church through word and life and thereby contribute to its revitalization. The community must sound the call to periodic withdrawal from the tempests of the world but withdrawal only for the sake of return, this time on a deeper level.

Ernst Troeltsch reflects the influence of Schleiermacher and the Pietist tradition in general when he perceived the need for new ventures in spiritual life that would penetrate the bastions of secularism and materialism: "It is germ-cells of a new spiritual freshness, power, concentration, and discipline, which have everywhere to be formed against the crudity, shallowness, and vulgarity of a trivialized, . . . increasingly disintegrated and desolate civilization."[18] Out of these germ-cells will emerge spiritual forces of righteousness that will shape and direct public life.[19]

Standing in this same general tradition, Christoph Blumhardt declared,

> God always wants to have a place, a community, which belongs to Him really and truly, so that God's being can dwell there. God needs such a place from where He can work for the rest of the world. There must be a place on the earth from where the sun of God's kingdom shines forth.[20]

This place or community ideally should be the local church, but when the church succumbs to the values of the secular culture we then need to turn toward paraparochial fellowships where the witness to the gospel is clearer and purer.

D. Elton Trueblood, the eminent Quaker theologian who was for many years involved in the renewal movement within Protestantism, gives this timely admonition: "We can be wonderfully thankful for the new life springing up in the general deadness of our day, but we must plead with its representatives to seek to remain firmly within the church and revolutionize it *from the inside.*"[21] The ever-present danger is that the renewal movement will become a sect and thereby see itself as God's exclusive mouthpiece and the church as an encumbrance to the gospel. We need to be reminded that both the fellowship of renewal and the institutional church must serve the kingdom of God, a kingdom that already encompasses the whole of humanity, but only partially and rudimentarily. God's kingdom is now advancing in the world, and our task is to equip people to bear witness to what God has done by the demonstration of a life of obedience and the proclamation of God's act of grace in Jesus Christ.

Not every Christian is called to discipleship in a religious order or community. Those who are called in this way should not set themselves up as superior to Christians who choose to make their witness within the structures of ordinary society. At the same time, they should not be intimidated by church authorities to withdraw from a commitment that may indeed come from God, but should go forward in the confidence that God's will shall be done and also perceived when we submit to God's Spirit, who directs us always to God's incarnate Word, Jesus Christ, and to his written Word, holy Scripture.

Women in Ministry

One of the divisive issues in the church today, both Catholic and Protestant, is the role of women in ministry. In order to address this issue with any degree of competence, we must first explore the biblical understanding of the relationship between the sexes. Although mirroring a decidedly patriarchal society, the Old Testament frequently elevates woman to a position equal to that of man. Both man and woman are created in the image of God (Gen 1:27), and though the destiny of woman is to be ruled by man, this is a consequence of the Fall rather than an order of creation (Gen 3:16). When the prophetic writer describes woman as "a helper fit for man" (Gen 2:18), this could just as well be translated as a helper "matching him."[22] Such a depiction involves "the notion of similarity as well as supplementation."[23] In the Old Testament, women as well as men had profound religious experiences. They participated in worship led by Ezra after the return from the exile (Neh 8:2). They offered sacrifices to God (Judg 13:23) and were allowed to take the Nazirite vows of spiritual consecration (cf. Num 6:2). While barred from the Levitical priesthood, they were free to engage in a prophetic ministry. Among women prophets were Miriam (Ex 15:20), Deborah (Judg 4:4; 5:7, 12), Huldah (2 Kings 22:14) and Noadiah (Neh 6:14). Deborah became one of the judges of Israel, a position of spiritual as well as legal leadership. Esther was a queen whose spiritual authority was fully acknowledged by her subjects. The apocryphal Judith, through her political sagacity and daring, delivered her people from the Assyrians and became for a time the recognized spiritual leader of her people. The wise woman of Tekoa (2 Sam 14:1-20) and of Abel (2 Sam 20:14-22) gave political as well as spiritual counsel. The book of Proverbs holds up the woman who manages her household and also a thriving business (Prov 31:10-31). In addition, she reaches out her hands to the poor and needy (Prov 31:20). It is no wonder that she is called blessed by both her husband and her children.

At the same time, the Old Testament incontrovertibly reflects the mores of a patriarchal culture, and this includes the subtle and sometimes not so subtle devaluation of woman. Biblical teaching transcends and challenges patriarchalism, but the culture in which the Bible was written bears the imprint of this mindset. The purpose of marriage in patriarchalism is to secure children to carry on the family name and to inherit family wealth. The wife is to serve her husband in docility and reverence. The woman has no claims to inherit and no right to divorce. She is the property of the husband, not a collaborator with the husband in determining the spiritual direction of the household. While the early Old Testament writings were characterized by the free association of woman and man, in a patriarchal climate woman is isolated and separated from the wider community and is virtually restricted to household duties. In the developing rabbinic Judaism, patriarchalism became more pronounced. The Jewish writer Josephus wrote that the woman is "in all things inferior to the man."[24] In the words of Ecclesiasticus, "If she does not accept your control, bring the marriage to an end" (Sir 25:26 REB). One of the rabbis said, "Happy is the man who has male children, woe to him who has female children."[25]

In the New Testament, women are held in surprisingly high esteem. Jesus sought out the company of women and had enduring spiritual friendships with some of them. Mary, the mother of our Lord, was given the highest gift that God ever bestowed on humanity—to be the bearer of the Incarnate Word. All generations will call her "blessed" because of this great honor (Lk 1:48). While women were not numbered among the disciples, probably because women engaging in itinerant evangelism would not be adequately protected, they did have a pivotal role in ministry. In the original Pauline communities women freely uttered prophecies, sometimes in other tongues, thus fulfilling the prophecy of Joel that in the last days the daughters of Israel as well as the sons will prophesy (Joel 2:28-29). Priscilla and Aquila were engaged in a team ministry, and Paul lists the wife first. It appears that both of them gave spiritual direction to Apollos (Acts 18:26). Phoebe is referred to as a deaconess, and we know that deacons were sometimes engaged in preaching (Rom 16:1; Acts 8:4-6). In Romans 16:7 (KJV) Paul sends greetings to Junia, whom many scholars regard as an apostle in the wider sense, one sent forth to preach.

In the later New Testament period, church leaders sought to curb women teaching in the public assembly, probably because of Gnostic prophetesses who were leading women astray (1 Tim 2:8-15).[26] Yet even the Pauline writer of 1 Timothy acknowledges women in the office of deacons. The requirement is that they be "sober, and trustworthy in every way" (1 Tim 3:11 REB). When he writes that "salvation for the woman will be in the bearing of children" (1 Tim 2:15 REB), he seeks to counter the Gnostic claim that childbearing is unworthy of those whose goal is to be spiritual. But the apostle is surely not suggesting that childbearing exhausts the vocation of woman, for in the wider New Testament witness it is clear that women too engage in ministry (Acts 2:17-18). The magna charta for women in ministry is Paul's declaration in Galatians: "There is no longer Jew or Gentile, slave or free, male or female. For you are all Christians—you are one in Christ Jesus" (Gal 3:28 NLT). Paul was not addressing only men when he exhorted the church in Colossae to "let the words of Christ . . . live in your hearts and make you wise. Use his words to teach and counsel each other. Sing psalms and hymns and spiritual songs to God with thankful hearts. And whatever you do or say, let it be as a representative of the Lord Jesus, all the while giving thanks through him to God the Father" (Col 3:16-17 NLT).

The case for women in ministry does not hinge on specific illustrations of women engaged in apostolic work (though there are some in the New Testament), but it does depend on the underlying biblical claim that all members of the family of God have a common vocation: to be witnesses and ambassadors of the Lord Jesus Christ. All believers share in the prophetic and priestly offices of our Lord. While Jesus chose only men for the discipleship of itinerant evangelism, it should be noted that he revealed himself in his risen glory first to women, and these women were then the bearers of good news to the wider apostolic community. It is no wonder that they have been called in church tradition "apostles to the apostles." Significantly Mary and some other women were present on the day of Pentecost when the Spirit was poured out among the whole company of believers (Acts 1:14). Among the prophets of the burgeoning New Testament church were the four unmarried daughters of Philip the evangelist (Acts 21:9), and prophecy in the biblical context is a charismatic ministry. It is interesting to note that the apostles took their wives with them on their missionary journeys (1 Cor 9:5), though we do not know whether these women shared in the preaching mission of their husbands.

The New Testament clearly teaches the subordination of woman to man, and this is often seized upon by those who would bar women from ministry. Yet this subordination is not the servile subordination that has its roots in patriarchalism; it is a free, loving subordination that is not absolute, but relative. It is a subordination *sui generis,* connoting an opportunity for liberation, not domination and acquiescence.[27] Man is the "head" *(kephale)* of the woman, though not as a governing authority but as an inspirer, protector and enabler. Man does not have authority *over* woman but *for* woman. In the marital relationship the woman is called to submit to the man, but the man is obliged to sacrifice for the woman. Subordination in the Pauline sense involves yielding to the love of the other, responding in love to the one who reaches out in loving embrace. Just as Jesus radically reinterpreted the role of "lordship" so that it becomes transforming servanthood (Mt 20:26-28; 23:10-11; Jn 13:13-15), so Paul revised the concept of headship so that it becomes guidance in living out a vocation under the cross. I concur with R. Paul Stevens's contention that headship is *"priority* within a relationship of equals—not the hierarchical rule of the male, but a loving sacrificial leadership."[28] In the biblical view man is prior to the woman but not master of the woman. The one master is Jesus Christ, and all members of the household are subject to his authority.[29] The husband mediates this authority but only insofar as he embodies Christ's spirit of sacrificial service. The subordination that the woman owes her husband is one of helping or supporting. She assists her spouse to be the spiritual leader he is intended to be in the Christian family. If he reneges on his responsibility, she is then free to assume full leadership.

The Christian family is not a hierarchy in which the husband is *over* wife and children, nor a democracy in which the husband simply stands *alongside* wife and children and decisions are made on the basis of consensus; instead, it is a confraternity with levels of responsibility—the husband going *before* and *behind,* as one who leads and assists but does not dictate or try to control. The husband is representative head but not lord or master. He carries out his mandate under the direction of Christ (who alone is Lord) and exercises his leadership as an empowerer and facilitator rather than arbitrary ruler. He is a guide, not a tyrant; a shepherd, not a commanding officer.

Similarly to the Christian family, a relationship of superordination and subordination is present to a degree in the ministry. Women in ministry are prayerfully to seek counsel and guidance not from their male counterparts only but from the whole congregation of God. As deacons and elders they submit to pastors and bishops (who are more often men than women). They are not autonomous agents in the service of the kingdom but persons who collaborate with their male counterparts in bearing witness to the gospel. Men and women in ministry engage in partnership for kingdom service, but the order of relationship between man and woman still remains. Women, too, are called to be pastors and spiritual leaders, but they should exercise this calling as women, not in imitation of men. I oppose a gender egalitarianism that erases the very real differences between men and women, but I hold to the full equality of both sexes under God and to women in ministry.

I would underline the fact that in the order of redemption the roles assigned to man and woman in creation are sometimes transcended, even reversed, so that women become leaders of men, even spiritual leaders, as we see in the cases of Deborah; St. Margaret of Scotland; Catherine of Siena, who admonished even popes;[30] Joan of Arc; Catherine Booth, cofounder of the Salvation Army; her daughter Evangeline Booth, who became the top commanding officer in the same organization; Aimee Semple McPherson, founder of the Foursquare Gospel Church; Dora Rappard, mother of the St. Chrischona Pilgrim Mission; and many others.

The subordination that woman is called to make is first of all to Jesus Christ and then to her husband as the representative of Christ in the family. Karl Barth maintains that the subordination is first of all to the order or procession in which woman is created, not to the man as such, either as father or husband.[31] My position is close to that of Barth, though whether he would fully endorse women as leaders of congregations is not entirely clear.

Wayne Boulton throws light on some of the difficult biblical passages that depict the subordination of woman to man within the ordinance of marriage:

> The Ephesians and I Peter passages [cf. Eph 5:21-33; 1 Pet 3:1-7] commending the subordination of Christian wives are of particular interest, because with appropriate gravity and directness, they both *appeal to the wife as a person*. This appeal was without parallel in first-century Greek and Jewish literature. Christian wives are not being told to follow their husband's orders; they are being asked to decide for themselves.[32]

What Boulton is suggesting is that the subordination of wife to husband is not an imposition but an invitation. This would indeed mirror the voluntary subordination of the Son to the Father in the Trinity and the Spirit to the Father and the Son for the purpose of the creation and redemption of the world.

As I see it, there are three contrasting positions on the relation of man and woman, particularly with regard to marriage. The first is hierarchicalism, which depicts man as ruling over woman. Woman belongs to man as his property. The second is egalitarianism, in which man and woman work alongside each other but each pursuing a separate career. The third is covenantalism, in which man and woman agree to submit to one another in the Lord and to become one flesh, though allowing for a relative autonomy in the recognition of real differences.[33] The symbol that best portrays the first option is the *march*. Here man leads and the woman obediently follows. The feminist or egalitarian model is the *race*. Here man and woman both aspire to realize their particular aims and dreams in the framework of mutual support. The danger is that they may soon become competitors, and this is especially acute when both are ministers. The covenantal model is best symbolized by the *dance*. Here one partner (the man) leads and the other (the woman) dutifully though freely follows, and the result is an underlying harmony and beauty. What we see in covenantal marriage is complementarity in unity, not complementarianism in the sense that each partner is restricted to fulfilling certain roles, such as fatherhood or motherhood. On some occasions the man will permit the woman to lead, but this highlights rather than diminishes his role as leader and protector. Such a typology reveals an attempt to transcend the cleavage between patriarchalism and feminism. I affirm the full equality of the sexes but accompanied by a frank recognition of enduring differences.

This typology is especially pertinent to the ordinance of marriage, but it has bearing upon ministry as well. Man and woman in ministry are not to see themselves as rivals who compete with one another in winning the affection and support of the congregation. This often happens when both partners are in ministry and both are involved with the same congregation, evident in the disturbingly high divorce rate for clergy couples. Nor are man and woman to envisage their relationship in terms of master-servant, in which the woman is completely subordinate to the man. Instead, the relationship should be viewed as covenantal, in which man and woman work together as a team respecting their real differences but acknowledging the leadership role of the man in decision making. This does not imply, however, that man should necessarily make decisions on his own. In a co-ministry, man and woman make decisions together but always acknowledging the priority of man in a fellowship of equals, a priority that remains even when the woman holds a higher office in the ministerial hierarchy than the man.

Paul declared that Christ is the head of the man and man is the head of the woman, but woman is the glory of man (1 Cor 11:3, 7). Man is incomplete without woman; woman is vulnerable without man. Man is

children

dependent on woman for the realization of his God-appointed goals; woman is dependent on man for her security and earthly happiness. This does not imply that every person is called to marriage, but it does imply that even in the single state man and woman need one another as coworkers in the cause of the kingdom, as cobelligerents in the battle against evil. Even those who retire into monasteries depend on the prayer support of nuns and vice versa. Man should never engage in a flight from woman, nor should woman ever try to realize an ideal existence apart from man. Such strategies can only lead to the tragedy of sexual truncation and perversion. In both a covenantal marriage and a covenantal ministry man should always be there *for* woman, as provider and guide, and woman should always be there *for* man as consoler and energizer. The woman is there to hold up the man in the trials of life, and the man is there to protect the woman, even to sacrifice for the woman (Eph 5:25). Christian faith (unlike gnosticism) does not denigrate sexual differences, but it also does not use sexual differences as a cloak for oppression and abuse.

The complete human being is man and woman together existing in mutual and loving relationship. As Jacques Ellul put it, "The masculine alone is never the image of God, nor the feminine—only love as union. The basic responsibility of both men and women is that the image of God should be present on earth."[34] The Christian ideal is neither the autonomy of the sexes nor the heteronomy implied in patriarchalism; it is the theonomy that affirms the cooperative unity of the sexes in fulfilling the commission to which humanity is called. I do not uphold each sex in its own, nor one sex over the other, but both sexes making their distinctive contribution to realize a common destiny to glorify God.

I think it is a profound mistake to downplay or deny the biblical teaching of voluntary subordination of woman to man and children to parents as we see in an acculturized Christianity. But it is also necessary to uphold the reciprocal subordination that grows out of a relationship of sacrificial headship and supportive collaboration, characteristic of a Christian marriage. Every Christian should lovingly submit to every other (Eph 5:21) so long as Christ's glory and honor are being served and the message of the gospel is being proclaimed. There is no authoritarian chain of command in a Christian marriage or family or in a Christian ministry, but there is a synergy—man and woman working together to render service to a despairing humanity for whom Christ died. Man may ordinarily be in the driver's seat, yet woman is not in the back seat but in the front as the navigator, and on occasion she too is the driver. Her faithful obedience to Christ makes possible man's servant leadership in marriage and in the wider social realm.

One of the things that impressed Tertullian after his conversion was the equality and caring in man-woman relationships in the church.

> They pray together, they worship together, they fast together; instructing one another, encouraging one another, strengthening one another. Side by side they visit God's church and partake of God's Banquet; side by side they face difficulties and persecution, share their consolations. They have no secrets from one another; they never shun each other's company; they never bring sorrow to each other's hearts.[35]

This cooperative spirit was overshadowed by a creeping hierarchicalism and patriarchalism that came to dominate in the later patristic and medieval periods.

Against those who would bar women from ministry in the church, I affirm on the basis of the biblical witness that women, too, may be called to full-time church service in the role of deacons, presbyters, evangelists, healers, teachers, etc. I again fully agree with R. Paul Stevens: "Men and women are joint heirs of the spiritual gifts and coleaders of God's people under the New Covenant" (cf. Acts 2:17-18; Rom 12:3-8; 1 Cor 12:1-31; Eph 4:11-16).[36] Women, too, receive charismatic endowment for ministry, and this fact should be acknowledged by all parties. We should not close our eyes, however, to the implacable reality that women are more vulnerable than men in the office of minister or pastor, especially if they are unmarried and do not have the full support of a husband and family. In a time when many women are seeking the pastoral ministry to advance the cause of feminism, the church must be careful in its selection of women candidates for ordination. In the case of a married woman, her husband's involvement in another vocation may present problems if either has to move because of job demands. If both parents are working, the children may be left without adequate parental care. Women's liberation was right to protest the devaluation of women in a patriarchal society, but it has not succeeded in bringing women the happiness and security that the extended family with its patriarchal base once provided.

Marriage and Celibacy

In the Old Testament dispensation marriage was understood as being in the order of necessity. God's commandment was "Be fruitful and multiply" (Gen 1:28; 9:1, 7); the purpose was to ensure the continuation of both the human race and the elect people of God.[37] To remain in the single state as Jeremiah did was deemed a great trial and definitely an exception. Yet there were hints of blessings also for those in the single or childless state who hold fast to the covenant: they shall be given "an everlasting name which shall not be cut off" (Is 56:3-5).

The New Testament is palpably more positive concerning celibacy—lifelong commitment to the service of God in the state of singleness. Jesus gave his benediction to both lifelong partnership in marriage and celibacy for the sake of the kingdom (Mt 19:3-12).[38] Paul recommended celibacy over marriage partly in the expectation that the end of the world was imminent; yet he also perceived in celibacy a practical advantage in that believers free from the distraction of worldly cares could be devoted exclusively to the service of the kingdom (1 Cor 7:32-35). Paul did not, however, elevate celibacy on the basis that it was a higher spiritual station in life than marriage. There was nothing of the later ascetic depreciation of marriage in either Paul or the other writers of the New Testament. It should be noted that the brothers of Jesus and most of the apostles were married and were accompanied by their wives on their missionary journeys (1 Cor 9:5; cf. Acts 21:5).

Among the patristic fathers John Chrysostom of the Eastern Church (d. 407) held Christian marriage in high esteem. Although he himself chose the way of celibacy, he believed that marriage can also be a training ground for Christian caring and service. It too can be a symbol of heavenly reality. Chrysostom challenged the patriarchal assumption that the main goal of marriage is the perpetuation of the race:

> There are two reasons for which marriage was instituted . . . to bring man to be content with one woman and to have children, but it is the first reason that is the most important. As for procreation, it is not required absolutely by marriage. . . . The proof of this lies in the numerous marriages that cannot have children. This is why the first reason of marriage is to order sexual life, especially now that the human race has filled the entire earth.[39]

An otherworldly asceticism having its source in Gnosticism and Manichaeism nevertheless penetrated both Eastern and Western churches and resulted in a devaluation of marriage and an elevation of virginity and celibacy. Holiness came more and more to be associated with sexual abstinence and withdrawal from secular life. It was taught that only man is created directly in the image of God; woman reflects this image by virtue of being created out of man. Augustine acknowledged that woman can be a helpmate to man, but she fulfills this role by bearing children. Jerome believed that a virgin was superior to a married woman and that, in view of the purity of the body of Christ, "all sexual intercourse is unclean." At the same time both the Catholic and Orthodox churches as they developed recognized that women can attain measures of holiness comparable to men. In both churches various women have been acclaimed as saints to be imitated and solicited in prayer, and saints are higher than priests, even popes. Most of those who have been canonized as saints, however, are single or celibate, though they may have been married in an earlier stage in their lives.

The Reformers sharply protested against the elevation of celibacy over marriage and saw marriage as a veritable pathway to holiness.[40] Nevertheless they refused to acknowledge the sacramental dimension of marriage and relegated it to the order of nature rather than of grace. For Luther "the life of sex and erotic love are precisely not gifts of God with their own beauty to be freely used and shaped, but they are simply a tribute paid to Nature, which the Christian can and ought to make a means for the exercise of the love of one's neighbor."[41] Yet we need also to consider Luther's frank admission that his wife greatly aided him in fulfilling his vocation and his grateful acknowledgment of the mutual love and fidelity that marriage brings.[42] While their teachings in this area were often cast in a patriarchal mold, the Reformers stressed the fact that the husband is bound to care for and protect his wife in all circumstances. The patriarchal idea of the servile subjection of wife to husband was countered by a stress on loving collaboration, though this was mainly centered on running the household. Luther even referred to his wife on occasion as "my lord Katie," who made their home into a virtual house of hospitality.

The idea of companionate marriage or marriage as a life partnership in kingdom service is associated with Puritanism, later Pietism and Quakerism.[43] Marriage in this sense becomes a form of ministry in which the love of Jesus Christ is reflected in the daily sacrifices that the married person makes for the sake of the partner in marriage and the wider Christian community. In this perspective marriage has redemptive power only when it is based on faith, when it is marriage "in the Lord" (1 Cor 7:39). To a male recruit J. Hudson Taylor wrote, "Unless you intend your wife to be a true missionary, not merely a wife, homemaker, and friend, do not join us."[44]

More recently, Karl Barth has pioneered in exploring the relationship between marriage and celibacy.[45] According to Barth, marriage is a life-partnership whose primary purpose is the enhancement of a relationship of intimacy between man and woman as a parable of Christ's love for his church. Barth does not see marriage as simply a means to a higher end, even a Christian end, but an end in itself—giving the two partners a spiritual and emotional anchor in a world of chaos. This anchor will most certainly include a commitment of faith, for faith as well as love binds the partners together in their common vocation. "It must be said that faith and unity in faith not only may not be missing but are necessary as a critically and positively decisive element if there is to be true love and therefore a basis for marriage between man and woman."[46] Barth also sees children as enhancing the marital relationship, but he does not view children as the goal of marriage. "Marriage is not subordinate to the family, but the family . . . to marriage."[47] Barth is firm that marriage

> as a life-partnership cannot be made to subserve the mere purpose of satisfying sexual needs, or of easing the burden of man's professional work, or of meeting the instinctive need of woman to build a nest, to create a home and maintain a household, or especially of fulfilling the impulse for procreation and training of children and therefore the ends of the family.[48]

According to Barth, marriage in the New Testament no longer belongs simply to the order of nature, but it now is seen in the service of grace. Marriage and celibacy become alternatives in the living out of a life consecrated to Christ. "The Christian enters into marriage, not on the basis of a natural necessity, but on that of a special spiritual gift and vocation within his life history and the history of salvation."[49] Likewise the Christian may choose the way of celibacy in order to be free for a single-minded service that excludes the distracting cares of family life.

Max Thurian, formerly a theologian of the Taizé community, was close to Barth in this area.[50] As one who embraced celibacy as a vocation, Thurian acknowledged the special burdens that celibacy involves including loneliness and loss of intimacy, but he also pointed to its many blessings, including spiritual progeny. Thurian appealed not only to Barth but also to Calvin in his apologia for celibacy. He saw celibacy as an eschatological sign of the coming kingdom of God:

> In the Church celibacy is thus a reminder of the new order of the Gospel, whereas marriage is still a witness to the old order. In the kingdom of God the fulness of love will be such that no need for a limited intimacy will be felt. On

the contrary, it will appear as a diminution of love. Thus Christian celibates are signs of that fulness of love which will be experienced in the kingdom.[51]

In sharp contrast to the Reformation tradition, Thurian believed that the Bible lends support to promises of lifelong celibacy for the sake of the kingdom.

While Thurian has written a helpful book on this subject, I fault him for associating the call to full-time service to Christ only with celibacy and for not doing justice to the New Testament claim that marriage in the Lord, too, can be an eschatological sign of the kingdom. The Christian family can be a church in miniature and thereby a parable of the kingdom. Thurian interprets the New Testament call to let go of family for service to Christ as a call to celibacy (cf. Lk 18:29-30).[52] But I think the better interpretation is that Christ is urging us to give a new priority to our relationships in the context of a new order of life, which the New Testament calls the kingdom of God. I here agree with T. Ralph Morton of the Iona community: "Was Jesus not saying that his disciples, married and unmarried, had to find a new way of life, which was so diametrically different from contemporary attitudes to property, parents, children and wife that its emotion could even be called hate rather than love?"[53] When Paul admonishes those who have wives to "live as though they had none" (1 Cor 7:29) he is not advocating that Christians leave their wives or practice celibacy within marriage. Instead he is insisting that familial obligations be subordinated to Christ and his kingdom.[54]

Kierkegaard was surely right in his contention that what discipleship entails is an inward renunciation. The "knight of faith" does not withdraw from society but lives the life of inward denial and renunciation in the very midst of society. Only God knows for certain the depth of the sacrifice that the disciple of Christ may have to experience, for this sacrifice generally remains hidden in the daily tasks of life.[55]

With Barth I see the basis for both marriage and celibacy in the divine command. This means that marriage is not a universal but a particular calling. It can be a vocation to Christian service only if it is a free choice, and the same can be said for celibacy. The immediate purpose of marriage is the union between a man and a woman; the ultimate purpose is to give tangible expression to the claims and promises of the gospel. I do not believe that Scripture prohibits lifelong vows of celibacy, but I think the witness of celibacy should be treated primarily as a gift, not as a law (cf. Mt 19:11-12). The commitment to celibacy is not necessarily strengthened when it entails binding vows. Certainly in the cultural situation today to demand vows for celibacy does not guarantee that people will remain in the celibate life; witness the surprising number of petitions in celibate orders for release from monastic vows. The Protestant church in particular needs to encourage theological study on this problem, especially because of its far-reaching ecumenical implications.

Protestantism has erred by viewing marriage and family as superior to celibacy and the monastic life. Paul Althaus reflects this imbalance when he declares, "Marriage is the supreme task of personal fellowship—no one has the right to evade it."[56] Neither does Protestantism strengthen the family when it absolutizes family ties and obligations, for this places upon the family a burden it cannot bear. Nor does it help matters to romanticize marriage and family, to see these things as the key to happiness and security. Marriage is a praiseworthy earthly good but not the supreme good, a blessing from God but not the preeminent blessing. We should not expect too much from marriage and family, even though we should gratefully receive the joys and comforts that married life brings. Orthodox theologian Alexander Schmemann has some wise words on this subject:

> The real sin of marriage today is not adultery or lack of "adjustment" or "mental cruelty.". . . It is not the lack of respect for the family, it is the idolization of the family that breaks the modern family so easily, makes divorce its almost natural shadow. It is the identification of marriage with happiness and the refusal to accept the Cross in it.[57]

Christ calls us not to give up any hope for earthly happiness, only to place the kingdom of God and his righteousness first in our order of priorities. If we seek first the kingdom and his righteousness, our earthly securities and needs will be provided for as well (Lk 12:31). To be sure, sometimes it is God's will that we forego the joys of marital or family life for the sake of the kingdom; yet in most cases God allows us to experience these joys—never as ends in themselves but as a witness to his love and salvation. Even those whom he calls to celibacy are required not to separate themselves from the ordinary structures of human life but to live and work within these structures. God does not want "holy solitaries" but missionaries (Wesley). He does not call us out of the world but into the world as a leaven in the lump (Jn 17:15; Mt 13:33), a vanguard of the forces of righteousness in enemy-occupied territory (Jn 17:15-18). In this missionary vocation we should let our light shine so that outsiders will see our good works and give praise to the Father in heaven (Mt 5:16).

·TWELVE·

THE GOSPEL IN A SYNCRETISTIC AGE

Anything done that is not done for God is in vain. If you believe in Jesus,
but only in the sense of what you will gain, you will never overcome the world.

CHRISTOPH BLUMHARDT

Religion which has been reconciled to culture is for the most part nothing
but bad science and superficial morality; the saving salt of faith is gone.

ERNST TROELTSCH

A Gospel which is not exclusive will never include the world,
for it will never master it. No religion will include devotees
which does not exclude rivals.

PETER T. FORSYTH

The debate over the mission of the church has been with us since the Enlightenment of the late seventeenth and eighteenth centuries.[1] The traditional emphasis on the historicity of divine revelation as recorded in the Bible was supplanted by a focus on the universality of moral law. Jesus was no longer the Savior from sin but now a moral teacher and example. Kerygmatic proclamation was replaced by moral exhortation. The goal was to reconcile the claims of Christian faith with the wisdom of culture and philosophy.

With the rise of Romanticism in the nineteenth century, the emphasis shifted from upholding universal moral norms to the appreciation of cultural values. Moral absolutism was superseded by cultural relativism. An inclusivistic mentality gave way to a pluralistic vision in which the aim was no longer to arrive at a synthesis of the various cultures and religions but to celebrate the unique contributions of each culture and religion. Modernity was slowly being eclipsed by postmodernity. Foundationalism was overturned by historical relativism.

Friedrich Schleiermacher illustrates the new mood when he casts doubt on the finality of the Christian religion: "The Deity finds ever new devices. By His power alone, ever more glorious revelations issue from the bosom of the old. He sets up ever more exalted mediators between Himself and men."[2] The mission of the priest is no longer to pontificate on universal principles but to share personal experiences that cannot be duplicated yet can be appreciated by all souls who are sensitive to the deeper realities of the spirit. The pastor is no longer "a shepherd for a definite flock" but now an inspirational speaker who encourages his listeners to find the truth that can meet their particular needs.[3]

The rise of religious syncretism is especially evident in the History of Religions school (Weiss, Gunkel, Troeltsch), which saw the great world religions, à la Hegel, as products of the evolution of the divine Spirit in history. Hermann Gunkel could describe Christianity as "a syncretistic religion."[4] In the words of Johannes Weiss, "Modern study of religion shows that the whole circle of ideas and thought-forms—soteriological, Christological, sacramental, eschatological—as they crowd the pages of the New Testament, were already present in some form in the world of Jewish, Hellenistic, Oriental or syncretistic thought."[5] I shall deal with Ernst Troeltsch's signal contribution in the next section of this chapter.

Other influences contributing to religious relativism, pluralism and syncretism are the rise of the Theology of Religions movement (John Hick, Paul Knitter, Gordon D. Kaufman);[6] the Parliament of World Religions; the infiltration of Hinduism into the West; and the emergence of the New Age movement. Mahatma Gandhi articulated the new vision when he said, "The soul of religions is one, but it is encased in a multitude of forms. My position is that all the great religions are fundamentally equal."[7] A similar sentiment is found in the words of the Hindu philosopher Radhakrishnan: "That different people should profess different faiths is not unnatural. It is all a question of taste and temperament."[8] The post-Christian mystic Gerald Heard, who with his colleague Aldous Huxley helped to inaugurate the New Age movement, called for a frank admission that people can find salvation in their own religions. A syncretistic mentality is evident in his contention that the West has much to learn from Hinduism: "Since 'all roads lead to God' men have to find that road which suits best their nature. Catholicism helps some, hinders others; Vedanta likewise."[9]

This survey would not be complete without assessing the role of radical feminism in the evolving of the pluralistic vision. God in the gnostic-syncretistic milieu is reduced to a creative force in nature that lures us into new possibilities. Jesus is no longer the unique Son of God but a paradigm of human perfectibility. Carter Heyward alleges, "Jesus in reality was not God. . . . Jesus was human like us, and also, like us, he was infused with God, with sacred spirit, and in that sense was divine."[10] A critic of the ReImagining Conferences in Minneapolis warns against the heretical and pagan character of radical feminism:

> What I saw in Minnesota was a classic example of syncretism—the creative and intentional integration of Christian and non-Christian theology and worship. In a word, it was "another gospel.". . . I came away from the event with my mind reeling with images of carefully crafted but confusing rituals, the primal beat of well-orchestrated music, and the memory of women's faces filled with what appeared to be anger, pain and confusion.[11]

Rosemary Ruether, who tries to mediate between goddess religion and historical Christianity, cannot resist succumbing to the relativistic tide: "The idea that Christianity, or even the biblical faiths, have a monopoly on religious truth is an outrageous and absurd religious chauvinism."[12]

Princeton Seminary theologian Diogenes Allen makes a credible case that the upsurge of relativism has its source in the crisis of modern culture, which has been unable to hang on to metaphysical absolutes:

> Many have been driven to relativism by the collapse of the Enlightenment's confidence in the power of reason to provide foundations for our truth-claims and to achieve finality in our search for truth in the various disciplines. Much of the distress concerning pluralism and relativism which is voiced today springs from a crisis in the secular mentality of modern Western culture, not from a crisis within Christianity itself.[13]

Whereas the Enlightenment urged seekers after truth to turn inwards and discover the divine core that animates the spiritual quest, postmodernism bids us gaze into an uncertain and unknown future armed with the spiritual resources for human survival. A leading philosopher of postmodernism, Richard Rorty, gives voice to the relativistic worldview, which actually borders on nihilism: "There is nothing deep down inside us except what we have put there ourselves, no criterion that we have not created in the course of creating a practice, no standard of rationality that is not an appeal to such a criterion, no rigorous argumentation that is not obedience to our own conventions."[14]

Syncretism and relativism feed into one another. When it is alleged that many roads lead to God, this creates the undeniable impression that we can learn positively from those who have chosen other roads. It also holds out the possibility that the different roads may ultimately converge and even coalesce. If many roads lead to God, we should then respect other religions and philosophies and feel free to draw on them in constructing our own worldview. Christians no longer need to have compassion for the lost, since there are no spiritually lost. We should view outsiders as fellow travelers on the way to nirvana or interior peace. The primary sin is intolerance, since this prevents us from discerning the light in other religions and philosophies that can help us in our quest for truth.

The so-called theology of religions propounds that all religions share a common ethical perspective, which provides a point of contact between Christ and culture. Evangelical theologian Alister McGrath is sharply critical of the view that all religious traditions share a common outlook on justice and liberation: "This arrogant imposition of political correctness upon the world religions glosses over the patently obvious fact that the world religions have differed—and continue to differ—significantly over social and political matters, as much as over *religious* ideas."[15]

Some theologians of religions uphold a theocentric over a Christocentric approach. Our starting point should be our own experience of God rather than our understanding of Christ. From this experience we can embark on a quest for interfaith understanding. McGrath utters these needed words of admonition: "Pluralists have driven a wedge between God and Jesus Christ, as if Christians were obliged to choose between one or the other."[16]

To affirm the exclusive claims of Christian revelation does not imply that there is no wisdom or value whatever in other world religions. It means only that we must exercise discrimination in our treatment of truths outside the compass of Christian faith. H. R. Mackintosh has rightly said that "to be strict, syncretism is only present when elements derived from various religions are admitted on equal terms."[17] If we reach out to assimilate insights from non-Christian philosophy and culture into a Christian world vision we must be clear that these insights have be to torn from their original context. When brought into the service of divine revelation they are altered in their fundamental meaning and content. In syncretism the claims of faith are altered or muted.

As Christians we proclaim an exclusive message with an inclusive goal—to include the whole world in the church of Jesus Christ outside of which there can only be ruin, lostness and despair. I must voice vigorous disagreement with Clark Pinnock's claim that "the Bible does not teach that one must confess the name of Jesus to be saved."[18] The Christian world mission is founded on the thesis that there is no other name given by which we must be saved, namely, the Jesus Christ of biblical faith (Acts 4:12). Syncretism can only lead to religious obfuscation. Standing firm on the message of the gospel will lead to redemption and deliverance for all peoples.

Troeltsch's Theology of Religious History

A pivotal movement that has shaped modern theology is the History of Religions school associated with such illustrious names as Hermann Gunkel, Johannes Weiss and Ernst Troeltsch. The last in particular deserves serious attention, since it was he who endorsed historicism as a worldview, and historicism is the precursor of postmodernism with its critique of all absolutes and universals. Historicism is the consciousness that everything in history is conditioned by historical and cultural factors. Historicism sees "everything in the river of becoming, in endless and always new individualization, in determination by the past towards an unrecognizable future."[19] Historicism "regards truth, values, and institutions" as indissolubly related to "specific historical times and places."[20] To glean meaning in life we must try to see everything in its historical and cultural context. There can be no absolute in history, but there can be a high degree of coherence in historical inquiry, since history is "shot through by the progressively self-revealing thought of God."[21] What Troeltsch proposes is a theology of historical relatedness in which the pathway to meaning lies in perceiving the continuities that link events together. "All events are woven into the same web and are of the same general pattern, all are explicable by immanent forces."[22]

Troeltsch was profoundly indebted to the spiritual idealism that we see in Kant, Hegel, Schelling and Schleiermacher. He also acknowledged affinities with Bergson's philosophy of life. Hegel in particular was an important mentor, and yet Troeltsch was wary of Hegel's extreme rationalism. Against the Enlightenment idea that truth can be encapsulated in propositions, Troeltsch proposed the idea of "meta-logic" in which all values are seen under the rubric of fate, decision and individuality. Truth cannot be reduced to clear and distinct ideas (as in Descartes); yet it can be apprehended in historical probings that yield no comprehensive vision but an illuminating perception. In his later thought he introduced the idea of polymorphous truth, truth that is binding and valid in certain historical contexts but not in others.

Troeltsch was acutely aware of the peril of relativism and tried to guard against it, though in my opinion not successfully. He sought to combine Enlightenment universalism and Romantic particularism. In historicism, he said, the goal of historical study is to grasp the significance of the particularities of each culture rather than try to find universal laws. Yet the stress on uniqueness finally leads to a thoroughgoing relativism.

Like Hegel, Troeltsch believed in an Absolute Spirit *(Geist)* that was realizing itself through the ebb and flow of history. We can gain intimations of this evolving, self-actualizing God through the religious a priori, the sense of the Infinite that every human creature possesses. Yet as soon as we put this experience in words, we are faced with the fact that from the outset these words are culturally and historically conditioned. The Absolute eludes our cognitive grasp, but we can still know some things about it. Troeltsch would say with Tillich that we can have a "true awareness" of the infinite God but not a comprehensive understanding.[23] While he did affirm absolute values beyond history, they remain purely formal until they are made concrete in history.

Troeltsch wanted to uphold the historical uniqueness and abiding validity of the Christian religion, but the logic of his position led him to compromise the unique claims to truth of this religion. In *The Absoluteness of Christianity* he perceived Christianity as both "the culmination point" and "the convergence point of all the developmental tendencies that can be discerned in religion."[24] "Christianity remains *the* great revelation of God to men, though the other religions, with all the power they possess for lifting men above guilt, grief, and earthly life, are likewise revelations of God, and though no theory can rule out the abstract possibility of further revelations."[25] Later, however, he abandoned this inclusivistic vision for a pluralistic one in which every religion is treated as a possible way to salvation. "An absolutely universal advocacy of Christianity for all individuals is not possible, since there will always be some who are not capable of it; and there may also be peoples who are likewise incapable and hence will remain at lower levels."[26] Rather than finding universal laws that link the various religions together, Troeltsch now tried to discern the particular values that each religion has to offer to the shaping of a spiritual universe.

In this kind of theology, the mission of the church is no longer the conversion of the heathen to the true faith, but the cultural uplift that people experience when they are exposed to the treasures of European and Germanic civilization. The "mission of the present is something other than the ancient Christian mission. . . . Today's mission is the promulgation of the world of religious ideas of Europe and America in intimate association with the extension of the European sphere of influence."[27]

In his early writings Troeltsch depicted the kingdom of God as "something thoroughly objective, the community of men in complete peace and complete love."[28] But later he gave up the dream of a global spiritual community and focused his attention on the particularities of each expression of the religious spirit. His theology prepared the way for a multiculturalism that celebrates the diversity in religion and culture. At the same time, Troeltsch was a believing Christian and was wary of any attempt to merge the religions in a syncretistic manner.[29] It seemed that for him we can still claim that the truths of Christianity have validity, yet only for us who live in a particular historical community and culture—that of the West.

For Troeltsch, religion becomes the unfolding of inwardness on the screen of history. In history we see the footprints of God in the sands of time. What is missing in his thought is that eternity became incarnate in history in the person of Jesus Christ. It is Jesus Christ himself who constitutes the transcultural and transhistorical criterion for faith and meaning. This criterion is not relativized by history but shines into history from the beyond. It is a matter of perceiving what God is saying in his self-revelation in Jesus Christ. Troeltsch reminds us that Christianity is a historical religion, but fails to recognize that Christianity has its basis and goal in eternity. Revelatory truth is reflected in history but always points us beyond history to eternity. The God of Troeltsch is the self-evolving divine Spirit who is caught up in the relativities and ambiguities of history. The God of the Bible is sovereign over history, directing it toward a transhistorical goal. This God is not detached from history but decisively enters the historical panorama at one particular time and place—where the Word was made flesh in Jesus Christ. Jesus Christ as the light of the world shines everywhere in the darkness of the world's tribulation, but this light cannot be appreciated or understood apart from faith in the One who revealed himself fully and sufficiently in the sacred history mirrored in the Bible. Troeltsch believed in a transhistorical realm that "surrounds history." Yet in contrast to Karl Barth, he could not bring himself to affirm that the transhistorical God has incarnated himself in a particular historical personage and that the mission of the church is to herald this fact, which stands in palpable contradiction to the teachings and ethos of other world religions as well as the presuppositions of speculative idealism.

Troeltsch, who grounded the Christian religion in a particular cultural ethos, was unable to resist the nationalist fervor that gripped the German nation during and after the First World War.[30] Karl Barth, who contended that the Christian revelation constitutes the judgment and crisis of history, was able to see through the pretensions of militant German nationalists and racists and therefore can be considered the prophet of the true church for his time. For Troeltsch, Christianity becomes a religion alongside other religions. For Barth, the revelation that forms the basis of Christianity signifies the purification and abrogation of humanity's religious longings and searchings. Troeltsch reminds us that we find the absolute only in the relative. Barth helps us to see that the absolute remains absolute even as it is revealed through the relative.

Moltmann's Global Theology

In contrast to Troeltsch, Jürgen Moltmann tends to follow Hegel in constructing a faith-culture synthesis that will give purpose and animation to the churches. The particularities of the world religions are made to serve the universal or cosmic vision of the reconciliation of God with a torn creation. Moltmann believes that the animistic religions can help us in heralding the redemption of nature as well as of history. Striving for a synthesis of primitive and biblical religions, he looks forward to an emerging religion of the earth "which will save the world."[31]

According to Moltmann, theology is not merely a "function of the church." Nor can it restrict itself to a Christian "doctrine of faith" (Schleiermacher), a "grammar of faith" (Lindbeck) or a "church dogmatics" (Barth).[32] Theology is not primarily a transmission of religious traditions but the vision of a new world in which humanity joins with nature in singing "God's great song of creation."[33] Theology is the creative attempt to fathom the dawning of a new age in which the concerns of theology and ecology will be united. Moltmann seeks to transcend the polarity of fundamentalism and pluralism in a theology of the kingdom of God, which is worldwide in its outreach. He contrasts this approach with a church theology that restricts itself to preserving the truths of the Christian tradition.

The mission of the church in Moltmann's theology is to enhance and preserve life. "The religions and cultures of other peoples are not destroyed but rather are opened up to God's future and filled with the spirit of hope."[34] All religions are invited to become "guardians of life."[35] He advocates "the charismatic adoption of other religions" in which we engage "their life forms in the service of the kingdom of

God."[36] Anything in other religions and cultures that serves life is good and "must be appropriated into the 'culture of life.'"[37] In this new pluralistic theology of religions "people do not even need to become Christians at all if they have found the divine truth in their own religions."[38]

The old missiology called for separation from superstition and idolatry. The new missiology challenges us to assimilate insights and practices in other religions that enhance life. Premodernity must be respected as bearing the stamp of God's good creation. Modernity should be accepted as "a child of Jewish and Christian hope."[39] For Moltmann "the mission intrinsic to Christianity is not the mission of evangelizing for conversion but the 'mission of life.'"[40]

Moltmann believes that Christian theology should become public theology, but it can do so only when it is open to learning from other religious traditions. The theology faculties of public universities "are to remain faculties of *Christian* theology—on the condition that Christian theologians syncretistically absorb into their theology the contributions of other religions, insofar as those serve 'life.'"[41] Christian theology must seek to overcome its own insularism and provincialism in order to become a global theology that is in dialogue with all of the great world religions.

Moltmann proposes a hermeneutic of emancipation—from cultural and religious imperialism. He espouses a theology of nature over a theology of history. Faith means seeking "community with the human Christ in every situation in life, and in every situation experiencing his own history."[42] We need to be bold in order to forge a new vision that is both ecologically sensitive and spiritually inclusive. "We gain and fortify this power of soul when we begin to love ourselves. Self-love evokes strength of soul, and strength of soul gives us the power to move mountains."[43]

In contrast to a sacramental-hierarchical church, Moltmann proposes an "open dialogue church" that welcomes the insights and truths that other religions have to offer.[44] A church that is open to the world "seems to be best able to meet the interests of educated men and women in our society."[45] As an alternative to both kinds of churches, I uphold an evangelical, kerygmatic church that has as its mission the proclamation of the gospel to the whole of creation. Our posture with regard to the world religions should be the call to faith and repentance rather than an invitation to build a Christ-culture synthesis. This approach does not rule out dialogue, but it finds motivation for dialogue in bearing witness to Jesus Christ, who stands as the judge over both Christian and non-Christian forms of life and theology. Before the church can be a vessel of God in the transformation of culture it must be vigorous in upholding the Christ who brings an end to the vanity and pretension that rule over culture.

The Church's Apostolic Mission

In a climate of religious pluralism and syncretism it is incumbent on the church to emphasize the uniqueness and finality of Jesus Christ. He is not one truth among many, but *the* truth—about God, the world and ourselves. Yet this truth is not our property to be handed over to those who seek it, but it is the speech of the living God that can be heard and received only through the power of God's Spirit. The apostolic mission of the church is to proclaim the gospel to the whole creation, but we must always bear in mind that our words are only approximations of his Word, that we can point to the truth but cannot dispense the truth. For people really to hear the gospel, God himself must speak, and he does this with our words and through our words, sometimes over and against our words.

Evangelism is sharing the glorious gospel of redemption with the spiritually lost. We proclaim not our experiences but Christ and his salvation; yet our experience of Christ's saving work gives our proclamation credibility and power. Every Christian is obliged to bear witness to the truth of the gospel, though not all are commissioned to full-time evangelistic work.

Evangelism is not the whole of the church's mission. We are also summoned to a ministry of service *(diakonia)*, teaching *(didachē)* and prayer. Our mission is to make disciples of Christ, teaching them to observe all things that Christ has commanded (Mt 28:20). In addition, each Christian has a special mission depending on the charisms that are bestowed by the Spirit of God. All believers are called to speak of Christ and take up the cross and follow Christ, but not all are called to be full-time pastors, evangelists or professional theologians.

It is helpful to differentiate between the spiritual and cultural mandates of the church.[46] The spiritual mandate is to bring people into a right relationship with the living God. The cultural mandate is to bring the implications of the claims of faith to bear upon the moral and social issues of the time. These two mandates are interrelated, but they must not be confused, just as social justice must not be confounded with the righteousness of the kingdom. Christians armed with the sword of the Spirit must be involved in the ongoing task of reforming society in order to bring it more in accord with the law of love, which always remains, however, a transcendent ideal. The law of love is the measuring stick by which we advance toward a higher degree of justice in society, but it does not provide immediate solutions to the vexing problems that confront society.

In determining its strategy for penetrating the bastions of society the church must hold fast to its ultimate criterion—divine revelation. This revelation cannot be synchronized or harmonized with the religious searchings and strivings of a fallen humanity, but it can be a means by which these strivings are purified and redeemed. Divine revelation signifies both the negation and the fulfillment of human religious longings and endeavors. There can thus be a true religion—one that is open to the reforming and transforming power of the Spirit of Jesus Christ, one that allows itself to be reformed and transformed by the eternal gospel of redemption.

The gospel sires not only our other-worldly hope of being with God in heaven but also our this-worldly hopes for a more just society. The millennial hope in which the eschatological promises of God transfigure the earthly landscape must be sharply differentiated from the eternal hope, which ushers in a new heaven and a new earth. Yet the two dimensions of hope are related. The millennial dawn always points beyond itself to the eternal city of righteousness that brings an end to all earthly striving and conflict.

The immediate goal of evangelism is not a just social order but spiritual rebirth, which enables us to battle for a higher degree of justice in society. Social reformation has its genesis in personal transformation. In evangelical theology the latter always has priority, but it is never an end in itself.

The rebirth to which the church bears witness is a changed relationship between the holy God and the sinful human creature. It is definitely not a rebirth into a spirit of openness to other religions and cultures. We are liberated not from provincialism into cosmopolitanism or globalism, but from the dominion of darkness into the dominion of light (Col 1:13-14). We are liberated from both religious insularism and religious syncretism into an evangelical catholicity that is at the same time radically exclusivistic and remarkably inclusivistic. There is only one way to salvation, but this one way is intended to embrace the whole of humanity.

In the evangelistic task we do not try to find a point of identity between the gospel and the faith orientation of our hearers. Nor do we seek to correlate the answer of the gospel with the creative questions of our hearers. Instead we confront the religious claims of our hearers with the message of the gospel and call our hearers to break with their present commitments and embrace a message that is utterly new, disrupting and transforming.

The mission of the church is not the preservation of life (as Moltmann claims) nor the reform of society (as Walter Rauschenbusch held) but the spreading of faith. Life is to be protected, but life, even human life, is not an absolute value. From faith comes new life, the abundant life that can withstand even the trauma of death.

I heartily agree with James Edwards:

All efforts to produce a gospel compatible with society have been disastrous for the church's witness and credibility. The church cannot experience the renewal that is called for today without settling one account: confessing Christ as Lord means refusing that honor to anything else.[47]

Peter T. Forsyth scores the modern church for losing sight of the objective work of Christ in overthrowing the powers of sin, death and hell and for reducing salvation to a profound religious experience. As he phrases it, "We are failing to mission the world because of a failure in the only faith that overcomes the world, the failure of a real living faith that the world *had been* overcome."[48]

Karl Barth's diagnosis of the modern church is similar. The church must cease trying to ensure its own survival and begin to share the good news that Christ has come to redeem the whole world. According to Barth, "A Church which is not as such an evangelising Church is either not yet or no longer the Church, only a dead Church, itself standing in supreme need of renewal by evangelisation."[49] The church's ministry is given its form and shape by the historical gospel of redemption through the life and death and resurrection of Jesus Christ. "The ministry and therefore the witness of the community is also essentially and in all circumstances and forms the explanation or explication of the Gospel."[50] Loss of confidence and trust in the objective gospel of redemption and reconciliation can only result in the church's loss of identity as the herald of the good news of Jesus Christ.

The predominant stance today in both church and culture is syncretism and universalism. The renowned existentialist philosopher Karl Jaspers here speaks for many: "We believe that all roads will lead in the right direction if we are truthful, but that all is lost if we are not. Only a life that pursues truth without restrictions can have meaning."[51] What Jaspers overlooks is that in the sight of God all people are liars (Rom 3:4 KJV) and that the open search for truth is a chimera. The human quest for truth is always in the service of the preservation and enhancement of the self, and therefore truth that is absolute and universal is always outside our grasp. The paradox is that only when we acknowledge that the truth is not in us and that all humanly contrived roads to truth are deceptive, do we then begin to have an intimation of the One who is the way, the truth and the life (Jn 14:6); apart from him we dwell in falsehood. Truth is not an idea that enables us to understand ourselves and the world better, but a new relationship with the One who personifies truth—the living Lord Jesus Christ. To come to truth in this sense is not a human possibility but a divine gift—the outcome of divine predestination.

The church can pursue its mission only when it resolutely stands against both syncretism and radical historicism. Ernst Troeltsch defined history as "the realm of the contingent, the unpredictable, the uncalculated."[52] But this tends to make *chance* the key category in historical understanding rather than either *fate* or *providence*. Christian theology allows for a measure of contingency in history, but it perceives the hand of God directing all events toward a future consummation. It opposes the historicist view that history is constituted by random acts. Instead it acknowledges the guiding hand of God over history. It also finds the thread of unity in history—God's self-revelation in Jesus Christ which throws light upon history. History is not the product of human caprice but the product of divine superintendence. It is God who brings good out of evil and steers all things to their predetermined goal. God does not impose his will on history, however, but acts *with* us and *in* us directing us to the glorious end he has designated for us and for the whole of humanity—the transfigured heaven and earth, the interfusion of time and eternity.

Although keenly aware of the pluralistic milieu in which we live, evangelical theology does not recognize pluralism as a valid source for religious understanding. It opposes the postmodern dismissal of all absolutist claims and stoutly contends that while our witness will always partake of the relative it can nevertheless be a true witness that stands in correspondence with God's self-witness in Jesus Christ. Gordon Kaufman argues with a degree of plausibility that our religious reflection is *"our own* imaginative and intellectual activity," "not a direct expression of divine revelation."[53] He tries to make the case for a theology that is fully contextualized—incarnated in the culture. But this kind of theology would be manifestly incapable of speaking a prophetic word from the beyond to the culture.

Relativism and postmodernism finally prepare the way for nihilism, in which people are forced to create their own meanings in order to survive in what is basically a meaningless world. Christianity asserts that ultimate meaning has become incarnate in the world at one time and place but is accessible only to people of faith. While respecting those who hold other positions, we as Christians must be courageous enough to affirm that they are profoundly wrong. The answer to radical pluralism and postmodernism is the confession that God has spoken decisively and definitively in Jesus Christ and the sacred history mirrored in holy Scripture and that we can give a reliable and trustworthy account of this revelation by virtue of God's own Spirit working within us. Reason cannot build a viable foundation for religious truth, but foundational truth can break into our limited horizons, bringing us hope and confidence in what God will do for his people in the future.

·THIRTEEN·

T<u>O</u>WARD THE REUNI<u>O</u>N <u>O</u>F THE CHURCHES

May they be brought to complete unity to let the world know that you sent me
and have loved them even as you have loved me.

JOHN 17:23 NIV

The Churches in the World Alliance have no common recognition
of the truth. . . . We may not play with the truth, or else it will destroy us.

DIETRICH BONHOEFFER

Free justification, Scripture and faith are the essence of Protestant doctrine;
when properly understood there is no irreducible fundamental
contradiction between them and Catholic doctrine.

GEORGES TAVARD

The road to unity is not the return of one Church to join another,
but a common crossroads, the conversion of all Churches to Christ
and thus to one another.

HANS KÜNG

T he current ecumenical movement has its roots in the cooperation of the churches in world mission already evident in the
nineteenth century. The World Council of Churches, embracing mainline Protestant bodies and a significant number of Orthodox
churches, was formally organized in 1948. In 1961 at the assembly in
New Delhi, the International Missionary Council and the Russian

Orthodox Church joined the World Council, bringing the total number of participatory bodies to around 200. By 1998 the number had increased to 332.[1] It is important to note that the ecumenical movement is much wider than the World Council of Churches, since it embraces conversations and agreements between specific churches and between families of churches, such as the Lutheran World Federation and the World Alliance of Reformed Churches.

On the surface the ecumenical movement appears to be quite robust, but there are growing signs that the whole movement could begin unraveling. The Eastern Orthodox churches are increasingly uncomfortable with the ideological cast of modern Protestantism, especially its openness to feminist and homosexual concerns. Several decades ago Dietrich Bonhoeffer uttered these prescient words: "The concept of heresy has been lost today because there isn't any teaching authority. . . . The modern ecumenical councils are anything but councils, because the word 'heresy' has been stricken from their vocabulary."[2] One of the most promising ventures in ecumenicity is the Joint Declaration on the Doctrine of Justification issued in July 1998, a product of the efforts of Lutheran and Roman Catholic theologians. Yet in response to this Joint Declaration Rome declared that eternal life is "grace but rewards as well, given by God for good works and merits."[3] It remains to be seen whether this document will bridge the barriers that have separated the churches for so long.

The Trauma of the Reformation

The major divisions that continue to afflict the churches are those between Eastern and Western churches and those that separate the Church of Rome and the churches of the Reformation. It is this second division that will be the focus of this chapter, though the goal of ecumenicity is the eventual union of all churches in the kingdom of God.

The Reformation of the sixteenth century was a traumatic event in the life of the church, precipitating religious and ethnic conflict. Jaroslav Pelikan has rightly called the Reformation a "tragic necessity."[4] It was necessary because the church's witness to the gospel was being compromised by a theology of works-righteousness. It was tragic because it tore the church apart and subverted the common witness of the people of God. The Regensburg Conference (1541) was a last-ditch attempt to resolve the deep-seated doctrinal rift between the Catholic and Protestant churches. Doctrinal agreement was reached on most of the issues, including justification, but the subsequent hostility of Luther, together with political rivalries, prevented any reunion from being effected.[5]

Regrettably, the atmosphere of polemics can prevent truth from being heard, and churches that are in fact close on some issues increasingly find themselves far apart on most others. While Rome denounced the Reformation churches as apostate, the latter labeled the pope as the "anti-Christ." Luther declared, "There is no doubt among us today that the church of the pope is the church of Cain. We, however, are the true church. Just as Abel did no harm to Cain, so we, too, not only do no harm to them but allow ourselves to be harassed, condemned, and slain by the pope's church."[6] Calvin wanted to retain some bridges to Rome, but he repudiated Rome's position on salvation as woefully heretical. Yet Calvin was willing to concede that "remnants of the Church *remain* in the papacy," that "ruins of the broken Church still exist there."[7] "When we categorically deny to the papists the title of *the* church, we do not for this reason impugn the existence of churches among them."[8]

Although anti-Catholic bias persisted in the evangelical movement after the Reformation, there was a remarkable openness to Catholic devotional writers such as Thomas à Kempis and Brother Lawrence. With the rise of the Enlightenment and modern skepticism, Catholics and evangelicals increasingly realized that they had a common enemy. The emergence of anti-Christian movements such as Marxism and National Socialism frequently drove Christians together to present a united front for the gospel. Ecumenicity has been given a new lease on life in the climate of religious persecution. But it is also being undermined by a growing insularism and triumphalism in the churches.

The Retreat from Ecumenicity

Despite evidence of increasing cooperation among the churches, including the evangelical churches, signs are multiplying that all is not well in the ecumenical panorama. Even many of those who champion church unity have been caught up in a beguiling romanticism that adulates the traditions of the past, especially the so-called undivided church of the first several centuries. While having indubitably good intentions, some Protestant scholars are effectively endorsing the catholicizing of the rites and ceremonies and even the creedal formulations of their churches. I do not dispute the commitment to genuine ecumenicity of theologians like Carl Braaten and Robert Jenson, but I have problems with their assertion that "there can be no discipline of pastors and parishes without the Catholic ecclesial structure headed by the pope."[9] I am even more dismayed by those pastors and scholars who view the Roman Church as "theologically healthy" and "missiologically vital."[10] We need to draw upon the liturgical richness and theological perceptivity of the "great tradition," but we also must not hesitate to correct this tradition when it stands in contradiction to the gospel of free justification through faith in the living Christ. My major difficulty with the Mercersburg movement in the German Reformed Church in this country is that it tended to idealize the past in its quest for an evangelical catholicity, a quest that I share.[11]

A second misdirection in ecumenicity is triumphalism, in which we identify the holy catholic church, the mystical body of true believers in all denominations, with one particular historical institution or one particular family of churches. The goal of ecumenical endeavor becomes conversion to one particular church or theology rather than to the living Lord, Jesus Christ. In Roman Catholicism it is commonplace for theologians to hold that the Roman Catholic Church represents the fullness of the body of Christ. We find this same triumphalist note in Eastern Orthodoxy, although Thomas Hopko contends that "perfect fulness" and "divine catholicity" are "exactly what the Orthodox Church does not admit about itself in its claim to be the one, holy, catholic and apostolic Church of Christ."[12] P. T. Forsyth sounds a timely warning against this kind of triumphalism: "The correct name of the Church which limits the true Church to a particular community is not the Catholic, but the *Monopolist* Church. No Church has a right to [the] name Catholic if it insists on unchurching all others which are not episcopal or established by the State."[13] Triumphalism also appears in evangelicalism when adherence to the precepts of evangelical doctrine is confounded with faith in Jesus Christ.

Ever since the Enlightenment the church has been threatened by latitudinarianism, which dissolves the binding power of creeds as well as the infallibility and authority of holy Scripture. Latitudinarianism signifies a false irenicism in which truth is sacrificed to the need for fraternal relations in love. This pitfall was evident in the founding of the Church of the Prussian Union (1817) when King Frederick William III mandated the union of Reformed and Lutheran churches for the sake of religious harmony. A product of this union, the Evangelical Synod of North America (now part of the United Church of Christ), continued to manifest a strong biblical spirituality for a time. Yet its future was always in doubt because it was a church in which rationalists and pietists could live together, but only at the price of downplaying doctrinal and confessional allegiance. Friedrich Schleiermacher, who enthusiastically endorsed the union church, was indeed a latitudinarian, especially in his earlier writings. His vision of the church was not the catholic vision but a liberal one: "The visible religious society can only be brought nearer the universal freedom and majestic unity of the true church by becoming a mobile mass, having no distinct outlines, but each part being now here, now there, and all peacefully mingling together."[14]

Finally, we must be on guard against globalism, the drive to achieve a union in spiritual quest and purpose that transcends all religious and theological barriers. The ecumenical movement thus becomes an interfaith movement. The only tie linking the various religions together is the mystical experience of the One in the All, or the ethical quest for justice and peace. We see this aberration in the theology of religions movement and also in the syncretistic New Age movement. Truth is no longer a definitive message but a profound religious experience. The church is no longer a herald of divine revelation but a community of seekers after truth and righteousness.

Syncretistic and latitudinarian ideas have penetrated the ecumenical movement and have been a cause of the tensions that have developed in this movement, especially those that impinge on Protestant-Orthodox relations. Dietrich Bonhoeffer put his finger on the root of the problem: "The really disquieting problem of ecumenical work is not the relationship between organism and organization but that between truth and untruth in the preaching of the different churches."[15] According to Bonhoeffer, if we play with the truth, the truth will destroy us.

Evangelical-Catholic Unity

The goal of the ecumenical movement is the unity of the church and the conversion of the world. The question is whether this is a visible, structural unity or a spiritual unity that embraces altar and pulpit fellowship. Certainly the ecumenical imperative involves evangelical-Catholic unity, the coming together of all the major branches of Christendom.

In seeking to overcome the obstacles that separate Rome and Protestantism, we must candidly recognize that major issues still await resolution: justification, church authority, papal primacy and infallibility, purgatory, Marianism and the sacraments, among others. The battle cry of the Reformation was justification by faith alone *(sola fide)*, but Protestant scholars have rightly contended that this doctrine has its basis in Catholic tradition as well as in Scripture, and this point is increasingly recognized by both parties. The fundamental question is whether justification is exclusively a forensic declaration by Christ, or whether it also involves the gift of new life in Christ. Catholic biblical scholar Joseph Fitzmyer strikes a remarkably evangelical note in his elucidation of Paul's understanding of justification:

When, then, Paul in Romans says that Christ Jesus "justified" human beings "by his blood" ([Rom] 3:25; cf. 5:9), he means that by what Christ suffered in his passion and death he has brought it about that sinful human beings can stand before God's tribunal acquitted or innocent, with the judgment not based on observance of the Mosaic Law. . . . Paul insists on the utter gratuity of this justification because "all alike have sinned and fall short of the glory of God" ([Rom] 3:23). Consequently, this uprightness does not belong to human beings ([Rom] 10:3), and it is not something that they have produced or merited; it is an alien uprightness, one belonging rightly to another (to Christ) and attributed to them because of what that other has done for them. So Paul understands God "justifying the godless" ([Rom] 4:5) or "crediting uprightness" to human beings quite "apart from deeds."[16]

On the Protestant side, Wolfhart Pannenberg warns against the imbalance in a purely forensic view of justification, contending that justification must not be separated from mystical participation in Christ by faith.[17] In the fuller sense, justification is both extrinsic and intrinsic, objective and subjective.

The question remains, however, whether we are justified solely on the basis of Christ's alien righteousness or whether God's justification also takes into account our moral progress toward holiness. The doctrines of purgatory, penance and indulgences all hang on the inward purification that the Spirit works within sinners thereby giving their works meritorious value. The recently published *Catechism of the Catholic Church* is unequivocal in its defense of purgatory and indulgences.[18] It seems that while individual Catholic theologians are moving toward a more evangelical understanding of justification and salvation by affirming both *sola gratia* and *sola fide,* the official position of the church that justification involves meritorious works remains unchanged.

The Marian dogmas of the Catholic Church also seem to present an almost insuperable barrier in ecumenical relations. Even so, it is important to consider that Luther was remarkably open to some of the Marian doctrines, including Mary's assumption, perpetual virginity and immaculate conception. While his formulation of the immaculate conception varied from the more traditional formulation, he steadfastly affirmed Mary's complete purity. Both Ulrich Zwingli and Heinrich Bullinger also tried to hold onto the more traditional views of Mary in catholic tradition.[19]

As Protestantism developed, however, opposition mounted to any formulation regarding Mary that did not have explicit scriptural sanction. With Luther and Zwingli, Karl Barth affirmed the *theotokos,* Mary as the mother of God, but he had profound reservations regarding the later Marian dogmas. The Catholic conception of Mary as Mediatrix of all graces and Co-redemptrix meets with almost universal rejection by evangelical Protestants. These doctrines have not yet been codified in dogma, but they loom as a dire threat to ecumenical relations, since they seem to deny the biblical affirmation that Jesus Christ himself is the sole mediator between God and humanity, and that the merits of his sacrifice on the cross are sufficient to redeem the whole human race from the slavery of sin. Christ alone redeems from sin, but Mary and the whole company of the saints make his redeeming work known to a waiting and seeking world.

The deepest division between Protestantism on the one hand and the Catholic and Orthodox churches on the other is in the area of spirituality. While Catholic and Orthodox spiritual traditions make free use of Neoplatonic categories in delineating the believer's quest for the vision of God, the accent in evangelical spirituality is on God's condescension to a sinful humanity. Its focus is on agape, God's undeserved love for sinners, rather than on eros, the human desire for eternal happiness through union with God. Whereas Catholic and Orthodox churches generally hold to the superiority of celibacy over marriage in the life of discipleship, Protestantism has emphasized the living out of salvation in the structures of the common life. Luther roundly criticized the monastic orders for giving more attention to the observance of canonical hours than to preaching the Word of God to lost sinners. The monks, he wrote, find their solace in their cowls and vigils rather than in the substitutionary atonement of Christ on the cross.[20] The Reformers revealed their biblical commitment by envisaging prayer as casting ourselves on the mercy of God rather than rising to the heights of contemplation where we become one with God (as in Catholic mysticism).

With Barth and Bonhoeffer I hold that the evangelical church of the Reformation is the true church and that Catholicism signifies a truncation and deformation of the biblical vision. At the same time I wish to differentiate between the hope of the Reformers for a gospel-centered church and the historical expression of this hope, which fell drastically short of their expectations. In its protest against imbalances in Catholic thought and devotion, the Reformation generated imbalances of its own, such as justification as bare imputation and double predestination, which makes God the creator of evil. We will regain a biblical and catholic balance only when we are united in the fellowship of the Word of God.

Hans Küng has made this cogent observation: "Faith made absolute displaces the Church, that is the Protestant danger. The Church made absolute disenfranchises faith, that is the Catholic danger. The vital fact is that God's saving act precedes both faith and Church."[21] We need to recover the biblical, dynamic view that God's self-revelation in Christ is the final authority for faith, but this revelation is attested and reflected first of all in Scripture and then certified and confirmed by the church.

Paul Tillich has rendered a signal service to the ecumenical church in his distinction between the Protestant principle and catholic substance.[22] The first signifies the protest against absolutizing the relative and thereby insures the church against all forms of idolatry. The second connotes the inheritance of the faith tradition transmitted from one generation to another. Where Tillich errs is in his failure to see that Protestantism was basically a confession of scriptural truth rather than a repudiation of unscriptural practices. It is theologically more felicitous to speak of evangelical substance and catholic outreach. The one great church of the future will affirm the glorious gospel of redemption through Christ alone and received by faith alone as well as be animated by a holy zeal to communicate this gospel to the whole of the human creation.

The church needs always to be reformed in the light of the gospel, but it can be thus reformed only when the wind of the Holy Spirit blows upon it. I here agree with Emil Brunner: "There should be only one Church, but this unity can come only from a powerful renewal of faith, a new Reformation created out of the depths of the Gospel."[23] Reformation has its roots in revival, but revival has its goal in reformation. Dietrich Bonhoeffer has trenchantly observed that America has experienced many revivals but no reformation.[24] The revival movements have fallen short by not pressing for a reformation in dogma and practice that rests upon the new light of the truth of the Word of God disclosed by the Holy Spirit to the church. This new light is in complete conformity with the old light; the new words of the Spirit are simply echoes and reverberations of the one true word contained in holy Scripture. At the same time, the new light means that the church must hear a new word from the living God addressed to the particular situation in which the church finds itself in a new age. "Jesus is Victor!" is the message of faith in all ages, but how Jesus overcomes the powers of darkness will naturally be somewhat different, for these powers wear various masks and undergo ever new incarnations.

In the spirit of the Second Vatican Council many Catholic theologians have emphasized the priority of Scripture over the postapostolic traditions of the church. There are not two sources of revelation, as Trent seemed to espouse,[25] but one source—Jesus Christ speaking through Scripture and church tradition. Protestant scholars, on the other hand, have been more ready to acknowledge the subsidiary role of sacred tradition in shaping the doctrines of faith. Catholic theologian Richard P. McBrien makes this welcome and arresting statement:

> If something is not in scripture, neither is it in Tradition—even if it happens to be a legitimate tradition of the church. In other words, Tradition is not a fact factory. It cannot create biblical "evidence" out of whole cloth. If some-

thing is not in scripture . . . it is not part of the deposit of faith. An appeal to Tradition cannot make it so.[26]

There are promising signs that God is bringing his people into greater accord and harmony to the extent that the churches can present a common witness to the world. Yet many obstacles have to be overcome before the ecumenical journey can reach its consummation. When creeds and dogmas of the past stand in the way of Christian fellowship and unity we must reexamine these icons of tradition in the light of holy Scripture and through the power of the Spirit and be willing to articulate them in a new way.[27] Sometimes we need to let go of traditional perceptions in order to speak to the modern world with a unified voice. Old truths should not be abandoned but should be recast in new language, provided that this recasting has a credible basis in holy Scripture, which remains the infallible standard for faith and practice for the church in all ages.

The Ecumenical Imperative

Christ's call for the unity of his church is especially acute in our day when a sectarian thrust is surfacing in all major Christian communions. This ecumenical imperative was powerfully voiced by Pope John XXIII: "Responsibility is divided." So "let us come together, let us make an end of our divisions."[28] We need unity for the sake of mission, but we also need mission for the sake of unity. We will not come together unless we are united in bringing all peoples the knowledge of what God has done for us and the whole world in Jesus Christ.

Our goal is not one world church but altar and pulpit fellowship among the churches. The holy catholic church will never be coterminous with any particular religious institution, but it will be manifest in countless churches and paraparochial fellowships that hold up Christ before the world. Structural unity can be a means to spiritual unity, but it is the latter alone that is vital for the mission of the church. I heartily agree with that ecumenical pioneer Philip Schaff:

Union is no monotonous uniformity, but implies variety and full development of all the various types of Christian doctrine and discipline as far as they are founded on constitutional differences, made and intended by God himself, and as far as they are supplementary rather than contradictory. True union is essentially inward and spiritual. It does not require an external amalgamation of existing organizations into one, but may exist with their perfect independence in their own spheres of labor.[29]

Divisions in the church that have their basis in doctrine need to be respected, but they should certainly make us uncomfortable. Spiritual unity does not imply theological uniformity, but it does presuppose a certain theological commonality. Michael Horton rightly says, "We Protestants . . . violate the catholic unity of the church when we show disregard for unnecessary divisions in the visible Body of Christ."[30]

Our mandate is to give tangible expression to the unity we already have in Christ. This necessitates not the conversion of one church into another but the continued conversion of all churches to Jesus Christ and his gospel. In our ecumenical conversations we should not downplay real differences, but we should seek convergence wherever possible. We should be engaged in new formulations of old truths, formulations that might bring us closer to our brothers and sisters in other faith communions. Pope John XXIII rightly reminds us that we should not confuse the abiding truth of the church's proclamation with the cultural form or language in which this truth is conveyed. The meaning of words changes from one generation to another, and we must be alert to words that cause rancor and unnecessary division in the church. We must not, however, allow our vigilance in this area to compromise any essentials of the faith, including the fatherhood of God.

The unity of the church is to be found not in its polity nor its program but in its message, as Peter Forsyth reminds us.[31] It is not apostolic succession through the laying on of hands by certified bishops that secures the unity of the church but fidelity to the apostolic message, and this is something that has to be continually retrieved. The

Second Helvetic Confession here voices my own sentiments: "Unity consists not in outward rites and ceremonies, but rather in the truth and unity of the catholic faith."[32]

The future of ecumenism rests not on denominational consolidations nor on church growth strategies, but on waiting and praying for a new outpouring of the Holy Spirit. But such an outpouring will not happen apart from a deeper immersion in the Word of God. It will also not occur apart from tangible expressions of love toward our brothers and sisters in other communions that constitute the worldwide body of the Lord Jesus Christ.

There are two kinds of sin: idolatrous action and inaction. We must not divinize the church or its ministry and sacraments, but we must also not procrastinate when Christ calls us to unity with other Christians. Sloth can be as serious a sin as pride and unbelief,[33] and it is often sloth that is responsible for missed opportunities to demonstrate our solidarity with Christians of other persuasions and backgrounds. Churches must be willing to give up their vested interests in order not to impede the inbreaking of the kingdom of God. The churches can play a modest role in mediating the coming of the kingdom, but not until they themselves are transformed by this coming through the crisis of repentance and faith. The show of support given by some Catholic bishops to the Billy Graham crusades is a sign that the spirit of ecumenicity still lives on. The united prayer vigils of charismatic Christians in all three branches of the Christian faith constitute further compelling evidence that old barriers are crumbling and that the latter day rain is beginning to fall on churches that have appeared to be moribund and close to collapse. Despite the obstacles that still impede church unity, we should rejoice in the glorious fact that God still reigns, that his kingdom is here and is expanding—even in the most unlikely places.

•FOURTEEN•

A C^ONFESSING CHURCH

If he have faith, the believer cannot be restrained. . . .
He confesses and teaches this gospel to the people at the risk of life itself.
MARTIN LUTHER

A Church, as soon as it is a believing Church must above all
else be a confessing Church.
PETER T. FORSYTH

There can only be a church as a Confessing Church, i.e., as a church which
confesses itself to be for its Lord and against his enemies.
DIETRICH BONHOEFFER

A confession must not only be correct; it must also be important:
definitive for the Church's whole life, for her walking in the truth.
G. C. BERKOUWER

W hen the foundations of religion and culture are crumbling, it is incumbent on the church to raise the question whether Christ is again calling us to confess his name boldly before the world, even if this should bring upon us calumny and persecution. When theocentric worship is fast eroding, when dogmatism in its best sense is being eclipsed by syncretism and mysticism, it behooves the church to remind its people that their hope and sustenance is in the living Lord of the universe, Jesus Christ, not in strategies of spiritual uplift and personal transformation. When people are hankering after other gods, the church is impelled to declare anew the biblical truth that there is only one God and that he has revealed himself decisively and irrevocably in Jesus Christ, who is attested and exalted in holy Scripture.

Just as the Barmen Declaration spearheaded a confessing church movement in Germany during the 1930s and 1940s,[1] so I believe a case can be made that with the dissipation of biblical substance in our churches and the unnerving alliance of segments of Christendom with cultural ideologies both left and right, the church is hard pressed to recover its evangelical and catholic identity. It is obliged to bear witness to the faith in a new way in the face of the challenges of our age.

The Meaning of a Confessing Church

By a confessing church, I do not mean a merely creedal church that gives intellectual assent to the dogmatic statements of another age. Instead, I have in mind a church that courageously confesses that Jesus Christ is Lord and that the gospel is crucial in our own time and culture. Such a confessional stance will invariably lead to a restatement of the Christian faith that will sharpen what is distinctive in the faith in contrast to the values and ideology of the culture.

The role of a genuine confession of faith is doctrinal discipline and freedom of proclamation. Confessions ideally serve the proclamation of the gospel. A church's proclamation is not based on a confession of faith, but the latter may well be an expression of the church's faith and mission.

A confession of faith is one of the evidences of a confessing church. It is not the source of the life of any church, but it can be a powerful catalyst that gives the church its shape and momentum. The Confessing Church in Germany was born with the Barmen Declaration.[2]

One may well raise the question: Can there be a confessing church without a confession of faith? As I see it, there can be such a church, but it will not remain a confessing church without the theological ferment that gives rise to a confession of faith.

A confessing church will seek to define itself against heresy. The

Augsburg Confession (1530) sought to counter misunderstandings of the faith in the Catholic Church of that time. The Barmen Declaration was occasioned by the need to combat the errors of the German Christians who in their attempt to amalgamate the faith with National Socialism appealed to new revelations in nature and history that in effect relativized and subverted the one revelation of God in Jesus Christ as attested in the Bible.

In a confessing church, as opposed to a sectarian church, the confession is always subordinate to the Bible. It binds us not to itself but to holy Scripture or better, to Jesus Christ speaking to us in Scripture through the power of his Spirit.

Confessions should seldom if ever invoke the support of secular authority. A confession of faith is not a legal test of orthodoxy having a quasi-civic function. Obviously faith cannot be imposed, but the truths of faith can be safeguarded. Confessions are signposts that direct us to the critical center of faith—Jesus Christ.

While only the living Word of God, Jesus Christ, has unconditional infallibility, the church too can be infallible insofar as it is obedient to the commandment of its Lord. It, too, can speak with the authority of its Master if it speaks out of Scripture and in the power of the Spirit. John Thomson, an American Presbyterian of the early eighteenth century, argued that the "matter" in a genuine confession of faith is infallible even though the "words" are imperfect.[3]

The basic function of a confession of faith is not to close the kingdom of heaven to theological mavericks, but to maintain the identity of the church. It signifies a concerted attempt to preserve the essential affirmations of the gospel in the face of latitudinarianism, syncretism, racism, or some other theological or ideological aberration.

A true confession has its basis not in the sudden inspiration of a committee or a desire to express the faith in the language of the day, but in deep-felt yearnings and unrest in the church at large. A confession based on the gospel arises not out of a quest for relevance but out of fidelity to the divine commandment. It is born out of a growing sense that both the church and the age stand under the judgment of the Word of God. True confessions generally are the product of prophets crying in the wilderness rather than church councils preoccupied with the survival of the church as a social institution.

Types of Confession

I see three basic types of confessions of faith. First, there is the one that derives its overriding inspiration from Scripture and addresses itself to the concrete spiritual and moral issues of its time for the purpose of renewing and purifying the church. This type is exemplified in the Barmen Declaration but also in the leading confessional documents of the apostolic and Reformation churches. Then there is the confession that is designed to reconcile or pacify disparate factions in the church in order to present to the world a façade of church unity. It might be likened to an umbrella that in its inclusiveness hides the reality of the situation. It was said of the original statement of faith of the United Church of Christ that it was so broad that both unitarians and Trinitarians could feel comfortable with it.[4] Finally, there is the confession that aims to defend or maintain the traditions of a particular church or party within the church for the purpose of a new church alignment. We often see this in fundamentalist or hyperorthodox statements of faith that are intended more to insure a consolidation of the faithful remnant than to prepare the way for a renewal of the church.

The first kind of confession alone is genuinely biblical and evangelical. This is the faith affirmation associated with a confessing church. The second connotes a compromising church, one that sees the need for a unified Christian witness but refuses to take the risk of making such a witness. The third is separatistic or sectarian. Its concern is with doctrinal correctness or institutional survival more than the reform of the church. Its motivation is the defense of the church or the perpetuation of a particular tradition within the church rather than radical obedience to the imperatives of the gospel.[5]

It should be recognized that there can be no genuine confession and no confessing church without a lively concern for doctrinal loyalty and purity. According to Karl Barth, the bane of modern Protestantism is a concern for life over doctrine, praxis over dogma. He held that renewal can come "only if we are willing to go the way that Luther *and* Zwingli *and* Calvin went, the straight and rigorous way that leads from *thought* to action—and *no* other."[6] At the same time, doctrine should never be seen as an end in itself but rather as a means to a higher end—the obedience of faith.

A genuine confession arises out of a moral or cultural crisis. Its basis is the perception that the church is confronted by a dire threat—internal more than external. Arthur Cochrane rightly criticized the Presbyterian Confession of 1967 on the grounds that it appeared more concerned with cultural relevance and the updating of language than with the integrity of the church's message and mission in the face of heresy that had penetrated into the inner life of the church.[7]

To be sure, confessions may become mere creeds, and reciting creeds is not the same as confessing one's faith. In the words of the Chicago Call, "We deplore two opposite excesses: a creedal church that merely recites a faith inherited from the past, and a creedless church that languishes in a doctrinal vacuum."[8]

A Book of Confessions, such as that of the Presbyterian Church (U.S.A.), is not the answer. Such a compendium has less a normative than a historical value. It is, as one observer remarked, instructive for all but binding on none. It is in fact questionable whether the Presbyterian Church (U.S.A.) is still a confessional church, though admittedly it is determined to maintain its confessional roots.

In a genuine confession of faith the Word of God becomes concrete and relevant—not by our efforts to be relevant but by being faithful to the mandate of the Spirit. In a false confession the Word of God is removed from the moral and spiritual issues of the day, signifying a subtle accommodation to the spirit of the times rather than a sign of the judgment of God on them.

There can be provisional or preliminary confessions that prepare the way for a genuine confession of faith, sometimes called transitional or working confessions. In some cases a church will need to make its way toward the one confession that has the full sanction of God through such preparatory steps. These preliminary statements are not necessarily false, but they are incomplete.

Hallmarks of a True Confession

What are the hallmarks of a true confession of faith? Certainly it will be intent on maintaining continuity with the historic catholic faith. It will seek to be not innovative but interpretive of the tradition. It will have for its goal not a new church but a purified and reformed church.

A genuine confession of faith will strive to speak to the whole church. Its aim is to be a confession of the holy catholic church. The Synod of Barmen declared that "we are bound together by the confession of the one Lord of the one, holy, catholic, and apostolic Church."[9] Furthermore, it will address itself to the concrete issues, theological and moral, that are facing the church of its day. It will not try to evade or cover up the grim realities of the religious and cultural situation but instead will grapple with these realities, trying to discover what the Word of God says about them.

An authentic confession of faith will endeavor to redefine the faith against heresies presently challenging the church. We cannot say *Yes* to truth without uttering a profound *No* to untruth. What is lacking in many of the confessional statements of faith in mainline Protestantism is this crucial No *(damnatio)* to heresy. Heresy itself has become an anachronism in liberal Protestantism, and there are sociological as well as theological reasons for this. Yet it means that the hope for renewal will probably have to come from other quarters, since only a church that is alert to death within itself can rise from the dead. It could be said that the reaffirmation of orthodoxy in our time lies in the rediscovery of heresy.

A true confession will sedulously strive to be faithful to the Word of God, regarding itself as under the Word rather than a new word that fulfills or supersedes the biblical Word. It will be biblical without being biblicistic. That is to say, it will be rooted in the biblical witness but be willing to speak a new word as the Spirit gives us illumination in a new situation.

Ideally, the confession of faith will function as an instrument of the discipline of the church. It will exclude as well as include. Although it will hold that its primary function is to serve as a *testimony* of faith, it will also recognize the importance of serving as a *test* of faith. Indeed, it will likely bring about division in the church before it results in unity on a deeper level.

A vital confession of faith entails considerable risk. It perceives that the danger to the faith is real, not imaginary. Confessions are often born in blood, for to uphold a confession means to place one's life on the line, to invite certain persecution. The Confessing Church in Nazi Germany eventually had to go underground as the secular authorities began reacting to its show of resistance to their regime.

A confession in Reformed understanding purports to utter not the definitive word to the church for all times but a provisional word that nonetheless takes on a compelling and binding character. It is open-ended toward the future but in continuity with the church in the past. It does not claim to supersede the wisdom of the past, above all the biblical past, but seeks to draw on this wisdom in its articulation of the truth of God's word for our time. A confession of faith should be seen as a vision of the whole of the faith from a particular vantage point. Because it does not pose as the final or exhaustive word from God, it is therefore open to reformation in light of the abiding truth of the gospel.

A confession of faith may well involve a prophetic critique of both society and religion. It will seek not only to hear the Word of God in Scripture but also to discern the hand of God in the times. It will proceed from the Word to the world, refusing to derive its agenda from the world but rather endeavoring to apply God's agenda to the world.

A confession of faith will speak on ethics as well as dogmatics. The Barmen Declaration defined the state and its duties in Article V. On the basis of this Declaration the Confessing Church sent a memorandum to Hitler condemning his racism and militarism. While there were no specific ethical injunctions in the Barmen Declaration, there was a solid ethical core. It is interesting to note that Karl Barth later felt compelled to criticize the Confessing Church on the grounds that it was fighting only for itself, for the freedom and purity of its proclamation, but keeping silent about the treatment of Jews and the suppression of the press.

In Reformed understanding a genuine confession of faith will be a product of both prayer and study. It presupposes in-depth theological reflection. Arthur Cochrane has aptly observed, "No Confession of Faith has ever arisen that was not preceded by long, arduous, and intense theological activity."[10]

By no means will a true confession of faith be ambiguous in its statement of the truth of faith and of the crisis confronting the church. It will not be afraid to point out heresy as heresy even while acknowledging that perfect orthodoxy remains the possession of God. In this connection, it is important to distinguish between heterodoxy and heresy. Heterodoxy signifies a reinterpretation that calls into question certain doctrines or tenets of faith; it can be considered an unbalanced presentation of the faith. Heresy, by contrast, means an outright denial of what is essential to the faith itself. It is a direct challenge to the integrity of the faith; indeed, it heralds a new faith.[11]

The church can tolerate private but not public heresy. When a heretical doctrine begins receiving wide acceptance, especially in the educational institutions of the church, then the church must act. When an aberrant movement poses as the true faith and thereby fosters confusion in the church, the church cannot remain silent. Confessions, says Brian Gerrish, "take seriously the possibility that a group may falsely claim to be a 'church,' and raise the question: Where are God's People to be found?"[12]

Again, a confession of faith in the deepest sense will arouse certain opposition from the world and the world within the church. It will be roundly attacked by conservatives as well as liberals, by any person or party who hews to an ideological position. Cochrane expresses it well: "A genuine Confession of Faith invariably provokes opposition from the false Church and from the world precisely because in its witness to God's free grace for all peoples it constitutes a radical attack upon the false Church and the world. As a fighting action of the Church it runs against the stream."[13] A confession anchored in the gospel will be polarizing even while it seeks to be as inclusive as possible.

Finally, it is incumbent on us to recognize that a bona fide confession of faith will confess Jesus Christ and the gospel of redemption through his work and grace. It will uphold Jesus Christ as the only Lord and Savior against the pseudo lords and false saviors of the world.

> While the Church confesses certain doctrines and dogmas and supplies answers to specific questions, it does so only in order to bear witness to Christ. It confesses a living Person who is the Lord and thus calls for a personal relationship of trust and obedience to him—not to the Confession as such or to the doctrines contained in it.[14]

A Confessing Church versus a Cultural Church

The cleavage I see taking place today in the churches of the West is between evangelical Christianity and cultural Christianity. By the first I do not mean popular or ideological evangelicalism, which is as cultural as its liberal counterpart, but the Christianity that remains faithful to the gospel as attested in holy Scripture; this group clearly includes Roman Catholics and Eastern Orthodox as well as Protestants.

In the theological crisis of our time, I see three principal theological options. The first is *repristination,* a return to theological or creedal stances of the past, a route that has been taken in various forms of confessionalistic orthodoxy, fundamentalism and Anglo-Catholicism. The second is *revision,* the attempt to reconceptualize or resymbolize the faith in order to make it credible or palatable to the modern mind. This is the approach of modernism or liberalism, and has found expression in process theology, liberation theology, feminist theology and neo-Catholic theology. The third is *confession,* the valiant effort to confess the faith once delivered to the saints in the language of our times but in contradistinction to the spirit of the times, an effort born of the realization that the Word of God stands in judgment over all ideologies as well as all attempts by the church to insure its own survival or to gain respectability in the eyes of the culture.

Are we entering a confessional situation in this country? Some observers, such as Arthur Cochrane, Dennis Okholm, Carl Braaten and I, foresee a new church struggle *(Kirchenkampf)* looming in response to the twin threats of secular humanism on the left and rising nationalism on the right. A growing number of pastors and scholars hold that the Western church is already in a confessional situation *(status confessionis)* and what remains is the growing realization of this fact in all segments of the church.[15]

The key words in mainline cultural Protestantism are *pluralism* and *inclusivism.* The way these words are used betrays a creeping latitudinarianism; life and sincerity are coming to be valued more highly than doctrine. The church that moves in such a direction proves itself unfaithful to its divine mandate to proclaim a gospel that will forever remain a stumbling block to Jews and folly to Gentiles (see 1 Cor 1:22-24).

We can welcome pluralism in liturgy, in methods of evangelism, and even in theologies; yet there can be no pluralism in dogma if the church is to remain the church of Jesus Christ. There can even be a certain pluralism in lifestyles but not in gospels: the church should earnestly strive to include people of all races, ethnic backgrounds, and classes but surely not of all beliefs. There is only one Lord, one faith, one baptism (Eph 4:5).

Churches standing in the Reformed tradition often pride themselves on upholding the principle of *ecclesia reformata semper reformanda* ("the church reformed and always being reformed"), but this entails a return to scriptural foundations rather than a "search for the new."[16] Indeed, it was the Reformers' goal to purge the church of the unbiblical innovations that had crept into late medieval piety. Church reform should take place always under the Word of God.

In his provocative book *The Church Against the World,* H. Richard Niebuhr presented a credible case that the modern church is in bondage to capitalism.[17] In our day it would be appropriate to say that it is under the spell of the technological mentality. For many the technological virtues of utility, efficiency and productivity loom more significant than the traditional Christian values of fidelity, piety and love. Confessing Jesus Christ as Lord in our situation entails challenging the gods of technology. Such a confession will very probably arouse the opposition of the military-industrial complex. It will also repudiate what Jacques Ellul calls the violence against personal morality: attacks on the family and promotion of the homosexual lifestyle, abortion on demand, sexual freedom and pornography.[18]

To confess Jesus Christ as Lord in our time will lead us to expose the ideologies and mythologies that enthrall contemporary culture. By *ideology* I understand a sociopolitical commitment that serves the aspirations of a particular class or interest group in society.[19] Its goal is not rational solutions born out of dispassionate reflection but social restructuring. Among the ideological movements that claim the allegiance of one or more parts of the church are classical liberalism (now called conservatism), welfare liberalism, socialism, environmentalism, feminism and pacifism. This is not to deny that each of these ideologies may contain something of great importance, but it is to protest against any unwarranted identification of these truths with the message of faith. Nor is it to suggest that earnest Christians should refrain from working in ideological movements; rather, it is to argue that they should inwardly detach themselves from the patently secular motivations and goals of these movements. Reinhold Niebuhr reminded us that there is always an ideological taint to human reasoning, including theological reflection. At the same time, he rightly maintained that an ideology can be partially transcended through the obedience of faith and prayer.

Our task today is not only to deideologize the faith but also to demythologize the culture. The myth of the class struggle culminating in the third age of a classless society may tantalize the Third World, just as the myth of what Alvin Toffler has called "the third wave"—the inauguration of the "practopia" of the electronic-computer society which supposedly signals the recovery of individuality and diversity—tantalizes the industrialized West.[20] A cultural church is willing to accommodate itself to the myths of the age, whereas a confessing church will try to expose them in the light of the gospel.

Confessing Jesus Christ as Lord also entails challenging the bureaucracies of the church that are intent on consolidating institutional power rather than losing themselves in the service of the Great Commission to bring the gospel to all peoples. If renewal is to come to the church in our time, it will probably come from concerned laity who have rediscovered the astounding claims of the gospel through a diligent study of the Bible.

In contrast to a cultural church, a confessing church will not ignore or explain away the social evils that threaten to engulf society but instead endeavor to bring them under the searing scrutiny of God's Word. Any church alive to the imperatives of the gospel cannot fail to be passionately concerned about nuclear violence, the growing disparity between rich and poor, indiscriminate abortion, and the rape of the environment by technology, to mention only some of the grave social ills that currently confront us.

Nevertheless, the heart of a confessing church movement is not protest against social wrongs but the resolute affirmation of the truth of the gospel against serious theological misunderstandings that threaten the integrity of the church's proclamation. Today the critical theological issues are the resymbolizing of God, the relativizing of Christ, the erosion of biblical authority, and the reconceptualizing of salvation evident in the politicizing and psychologizing of the gospel. The resymbolizing of God signifies a move away from a trinitarian monotheism to a naturalistic or idealistic immanentalism. The relativizing of Christ implies that there are other ways to salvation. Biblical authority is subverted when the Bible is treated no longer as the written Word of God or even as the original and primary witness to God's self-revelation in Jesus Christ, but instead as the record of the religious experience of a particular people in history or as a compendium of inerrant propositions. The biblical view of salvation as God's reconciling act in Jesus Christ is obscured when salvation is confused with either political liberation or self-realization. Among the theological aberrations that must be addressed in any vital confession of faith are process unitarianism, romantic universalism, neo-gnosticism, eudaemonism, experientialism and syncretism.

Behind many of the doctrinal and ethical deviations today is the ideology of secular humanism, which might better be termed technological humanism or technological pragmatism. This is the humanism that does not simply dismiss God to the periphery of life (as did Enlightenment deism) but is openly hostile to the idea of a transcendent and sovereign God. In America this humanism takes the form of both a radical egalitarianism and a democratic centralism, both of which portend a democratic totalitarianism in which the general will is made sovereign. In Nazi Germany the secularist upsurge took the form of ethnocentrism and racism. In all cases the secularist mentality tends toward a postmodern nihilism that heralds the overthrow of all existing institutions and the creation of an entirely new order.

A confessing church cannot come into being until the dangers to the faith are clearly discerned by at least a growing number of the faithful within the various denominations. Today there is increasing unrest in the church, but by and large there is a conspicuous lack of unanimity about where the real peril lies. Pope John Paul II sees the modern world in flight from reason and the principal challenge as the recovery of transcendent, objective truth in morals and religion.[21] While his observations are not bereft of wisdom, I think the deeper problem is a flight from faith in the living God and a growing hostility to traditional values that masks the emergence of a new paganism.[22]

The mood today in both conservative and liberal theological circles is to stress both *doxa* (worship) and praxis over dogma. On this point we should heed this warning of one of the celebrated figures of liberal Protestantism, Adolf von Harnack: "The demand for an undogmatic Christianity is a mistake. . . . Upon the path of the old Creeds we must remain; satisfied with them we cannot be." The church's duty is to "add a new Creed to those which already exist."[23]

The Work of a Confession

In examining the landmark confessions of the past, we can see that they enabled the church to overcome the obstacles that stood in the way of the proclamation of the gospel. According to Brian Gerrish:

> The classic French, Belgic and Scots confessions in actual fact show the Church *confronting* the world and the civic power with their witness to the Gospel of Christ. In these confessions the Church recovered her integrity, not only against ecclesiastical abuses, but also against confusion with state and nation.[24]

On the basis of his lifelong study of the confessions of the church, Cochrane has these pertinent words on how they came into being:

> None of the early church creeds, none of the Lutheran and Reformed confessions of the 16th century, and none of the confessions of the Church under Hitler were born of the need "to express in words and deeds the meaning of the gospel in contemporary life." They were born of an absolute, dire need in which the very life of the Church was at stake, in which the Church was devastated by heresy and error, and in which confession was the only thing left to the Church to do. It is silly to think of the Council of Nicaea, the Diet of Augsburg, or the Synod of Barmen being called to define the faith in contemporary language or because they had something "of interest and value" for church members.[25]

A confessing church will claim to be the true church for the situation in which it finds itself. It will acknowledge that its truth lies not in itself but in its Lord, who by his Spirit calls it to confess the true faith in the face of error. Its truth is conveyed through the confession, but it is not exhausted by the confession. Nor is it a property of the confession. Its authority is spiritual, not legal, though it will always have a legal dimension. As Cochrane rightly says, "Its authority ... does not depend upon its being ratified by Church law."[26]

Basically, a confession of faith will signify a fresh proclamation of the gospel against misunderstandings in the church and culture, but it will also seek to be a rule of faith that can be used to discipline the shepherds of the flock. A confessing church will not try to separate wheat from chaff (this is the path of sectarianism), but it will try to insure that its shepherds are not leading the sheep astray. In a confessing church, the task of disciplining falls on the leadership of the church, especially its teaching authorities. Even then, however, the investigative church body should not presume to judge the eternal destiny or state of grace of its members in leadership positions but only the doctrine that is being taught.

At the same time, we need to remember that the true faith is a matter of salvation and not just of right understanding. Dietrich Bonhoeffer warned that "whoever knowingly separates himself from the Confessing Church in Germany separates himself from salvation."[27] A confession deals with matters of life and death, not simply with ideas.

We must embark on a confessional path only when all other possibilities are exhausted. Barth's words at Cardiff in 1925 come to mind: "There are things which one may and can do only when one *must* do them." Every confession has its *kairos*, its divinely appointed hour, its moment in time when a witness to the truth must be given.

In the final analysis, a confession is God's gift of grace to the church occasioned when faithful Christians acknowledge their helplessness and radical dependence on his saving power. It is paradoxically both a means by which God witnesses to himself and a very human and broken witness to God's revelation.

One cannot know how the church would respond to a new confession of faith. If this confession had its source in fidelity to the divine commandment, if its desire were to glorify God in every area of life, then it could be mightily used by the Spirit to purify and renew the church. On the other hand, if it had its source in human vanity and pretension, if its focus was on the act of confessing rather than on Jesus Christ and his gospel, then it would likely have little effect beyond possibly diverting the church from its apostolic mission.

The dire need today is for a faithful church rather than a successful church, a church under the cross rather than a church that has accommodated to the culture. Only a church that boldly confesses the truth of the gospel in the face of the principalities and powers of the age deserves to be blessed by the Spirit and thereby fortified in its mission to serve and to heal.

Appendix F: The Voice of Orthodoxy

The Cambridge Declaration merits serious examination as a possible step toward a confessing church in American Protestantism in our time.[28] The product of a historic meeting of 120 evangelical teachers and pastors in Cambridge, Massachusetts, on April 17-20, 1996, it calls the evangelical church to repentance and renewal. This confession of faith has many of the earmarks of a genuine confessional statement, including a timely warning against misunderstandings of the faith as well as a forthright affirmation of the truth of the gospel. It is directly related to the deep-seated problems in the church and culture of our time in which salvation is converted into self-esteem and self-fulfillment and worship is reduced to an often crass entertainment. The Cambridge Declaration is basically directed against the therapeutic worldview that is increasingly penetrating the evangelical church—its preaching, worship and evangelistic strategy. In my opinion this statement nevertheless falls short of a truly catholic and evangelical confession of faith that speaks to the whole church. I have these reservations:

1. The Cambridge Declaration manifests a sectarian bent when it aspires to speak for a faction within the church rather than the whole church. A bona fide confession of faith will seek to bring together true

believers in all Christian communions.[29] The Alliance of Confessing Evangelicals does not have a broad enough representation in either mainstream Protestantism or the evangelical world to speak credibly for all Christians. I acknowledge that in the concluding statement there is an attempt to reach out to the wider Christian community.

2. The denial that "personal spiritual experience can ever be a vehicle of revelation"[30] reflects an evangelical rationalism that reduces revelation to the communication of ideas. Yet the awakening to faith is itself an experience. To receive the risen Christ into our lives through the power of the Holy Spirit is indubitably an experiential as well as a rational event. Certainly Paul's conversion on the road to Damascus involved both a crisis experience of surrender to the living God and the dawning of a new perception of reality.

3. The denial that "evangelicals and Roman Catholics are one in Jesus Christ," particularly where assent is lacking for the biblical doctrine of justification, presents an unnecessary impediment to ecumenical dialogue.[31] The statement overlooks the fact that many Catholic theologians staunchly adhere to *sola fide, sola gratia* and *soli Deo gloria,* some even to scriptural primacy.[32] But even if this were not the case, our unity in Christ rests not on correct theology but on a common faith that Jesus Christ is Lord and Savior. Catholics who profess faith in the crucified and risen Lord and who have been baptized into this faith are surely not on the same level as non-Christians. Are not they virtual if not actual brothers and sisters in the faith? At the same time, misunderstandings of the faith coming from whatever source need to be corrected, and these corrections can indeed be incorporated in a statement of faith provided that the statement penetrates to the heart of the problem that bedevils the church in any particular age. Even those—especially those—who are our brothers and sisters in the faith need to be reproved and corrected when they go astray.

4. The credibility of the Cambridge Declaration would have been heightened had it issued a call to personal and social holiness as the

sign and witness of the truth of the gospel. Justification becomes cheap grace unless it is indissolubly related to sanctification. Calvin said "faith alone," but he added "not without works." Many of the authors who defend the Declaration in the book *Here We Stand* nevertheless recognize that holiness in life needs to follow God's forgiveness and faith in the gospel. The indictment of secular penetration into both theology and worship in the evangelical church today is one of the abiding strengths of the Declaration and of the book.

5. The Confession would have been strengthened had it displayed a concern not only to combat synergism in the gaining of salvation but also deterministic monergism. In my judgment biblical faith rejects both determinism and synergism in order to safeguard the mystery of double agency in salvation, that God does all, but in and through human effort and obedience. The Reformation achievement was not a determinism of grace that overrules the human will, but the celebration of grace that liberates the will for repentance, faith and service. The conference would have been immensely helped had it invited George Hunsinger, then of the Karl Barth Study Center at Princeton Seminary, to state the case for double agency in salvation as this is set forth in the theology of Karl Barth.[33]

6. It is somewhat surprising and disheartening that the Declaration does not address any of the pressing moral issues of our time—the proliferation of weapons of mass extermination; abortion on demand; the deleterious breakdown of the family manifested in the rising tide of divorce; the wanton pollution of the environment; racial and ethnic conflict; and the growing disparity between rich and poor. A vital confession of faith will speak on ethics as well as dogmatics, as is evident in a number of the confessions of the Reformation.[34] The Cambridge Declaration admittedly has some significant ethical implications, as noted by several of its authors.[35]

7. The Cambridge Declaration makes some important points in its warnings against the false gospels of self-esteem and health and wealth, and the substitution of psychological wholeness for holiness.

When the gospel is reduced to a commodity in the marketplace, we are verging on idolatry. It is puzzling, however, to note that nothing is said about the issues that are presently dividing the churches—inclusive gender language for God, homosexual ordination, same sex marriages and the killing of unborn children.[36]

8. In conclusion, while I basically share the faith articulated in the Declaration, I have difficulty in lending it my firm support because it falls short of being truly ecumenical. What is needed today is not a narrowly conservative or traditionalist evangelicalism but an evangelicalism with the breadth of a catholic vision that nevertheless draws sharp lines between faith and culture, truth and falsehood.[37] I urge the signers of the Declaration to reach out to gospel believers in all denominations, even in Catholic and Orthodox churches, to make a common witness to the faith once delivered to the saints. The Cambridge Declaration might possibly fill the role of a preliminary confession of faith that prepares the way for an evangelical ecumenical confession that declares the Word of God to our time and generation, a Word that reaffirms the truth of the gospel but also speaks to the problem of sin—both personal and social.

Appendix G: The Meaning of the Gospel

We might also turn with profit to the more recent statement of faith drawn up by a number of evangelical leaders in June 1999: "The Gospel of Jesus Christ: An Evangelical Celebration," subsequently published in *Christianity Today.*[38] Like the Cambridge Declaration, this statement manifests a deep and growing concern for Christian and particularly evangelical identity in an age of pluralism and postmodernism. Although not directly involved in its formulation, I lent it my initial support because I could heartily identify with its overall thrust. Yet I harbor reservations that are similar to some of those shared by Roger Olson and Gabriel Fackre,[39] though I do not endorse all of their criticisms (as I shall make clear in this excursus). I have these comments—mainly but not always positive:

1. Fully in accord with the biblical witness, this credo forthrightly proclaims that Jesus Christ is the only way to salvation in the face of a latitudinarianism and pluralism that are ready to acknowledge other possible ways to salvation. We need to be reminded of this biblical truth in the relativistic ethos in which we now live.

2. With the apostle Paul and the Protestant Reformers "Celebration" rightly affirms the justification of the ungodly, that we are accounted righteous by our faith in the crucified and risen Christ even while we are still in our sins.

3. "Celebration" admirably distinguishes between the *ground* of justification, the unmerited love of Christ manifested in his atoning sacrifice for sin, and the *consequences* of justification, conformity to the image of Christ by the sanctifying work of the Holy Spirit.

4. Works-righteousness is a perennial temptation in all the churches, and this statement powerfully warns against all encroaching legalism and moralism.

5. The statement rightly discerns that justification is fundamentally forensic. Yet it should be more fully recognized that justification is not exclusively forensic, since it involves the fruits of God's justifying and sanctifying grace being made manifest in our lives. The necessity for fruits of righteousness in daily life is duly acknowledged (no. 15), though there is a marked reluctance to view these fruits as belonging to the drama of justification itself.

6. Roger Olson makes a telling point when he argues that this credo sometimes confuses propositional statements about the gospel with the gospel itself. At the same time, I would argue that the church's interpretation of the gospel, if it is faithful to Scripture, becomes a part of the gospel itself. Commitment to the gospel is inseparable from assent to church doctrine, so long as this doctrine rests firmly on Scripture and sacred tradition. Yet we need to recognize that the truth of the gospel always transcends the language in which it is expressed, and therefore every formulation needs to be revised and expanded as the conditions in the church and world change. Roger Olson wants a gos-

pel that is "short and sweet," but I contend that the gospel cannot remain in a condensed version once it is applied to the pressing moral and theological issues of the time.

7. Like Gabriel Fackre I am uncomfortable with the affirmation that anyone who denies the humanity of Christ, his incarnation and sinlessness, cannot be saved (no. 7).[40] Here again we must not confuse faith in the gospel with assent to particular doctrines in the church, even assent to the doctrine of justification. At the same time a faith that does not foster true understanding might well lead one into apostasy and ipso facto perdition. But the point must here be made that we are saved not by our theological sophistication or maturity but only by faith in the crucified and risen Christ. There are countless Christians whose theology is woefully inadequate to their experience of redemption through the cross and resurrection of Christ.

8. I agree with Fackre that the doctrine of substitutionary atonement does not exhaust the richness and profundity of the gospel message. Jesus was not only sacrificial victim but also, in Fackre's words, "the prophet and conqueror over death." Moreover, the atoning sacrifice on Calvary must be viewed more deeply as God's self-sacrifice in the person of Jesus Christ and not simply as the offering up of the humanity of Jesus (as in Anselm). We cannot lightly dismiss the many biblical passages that allude to if not explicitly refer to substitution (cf. 2 Cor 5:21; Gal 3:13; Heb 9:11-14, 28). Substitution is the essence of the gospel but not the whole of the gospel. There are other aspects of the gospel that need to be developed, and the church fathers as well as the doctors of the medieval church should be listened to in this respect.

9. "Celebration" can also be faulted for not relating justification to justice, faith to ethics. The burning social issues of the day need to be addressed by any vital confession of faith if it is to be relevant to the age to which it speaks. The object of our confession must always be Jesus Christ himself—Lord, Savior and Master. But this must be the living Christ who calls us to obedience in the cultural and religious milieu in which we live. More fundamentally what is needed here is an affir-

mation of the indissoluble relationship of gospel and law, that we are saved by faith, yet not apart from an obligation to obey the commandments of God in every aspect of life.

10. Fackre complains of the "imperial tone" of the document manifested especially in its singling out of Jesus Christ as the only way to salvation. I contend that this affirmation is so integral to New Testament faith that a restatement of the gospel must invariably include it. This is not to gainsay that we can nevertheless hope for every person, even those without personal faith, since Jesus Christ died for all and by his Spirit reaches out to all, though this does not mean that all will eventually come to believe.[41]

* * * * * *

In conclusion, "Celebration" is an impressive and timely statement, since the very meaning of the gospel is in dispute in today's church. Yet the statement does not go far enough or deep enough to rise to the level of another Barmen Declaration. We will always need to hear the message that we are justified by faith alone and by grace alone, but we must also hear the admonition that we are called to holiness, including social holiness. Our mission is not simply to wait for the second advent of Christ but to set up signs and parables of the kingdom of God. The stance of the church should be not retrenchment in the face of mounting secularism and relativism but confrontation with the powers of the age. A full-orbed statement on the gospel must also include an indictment of present worship trends that convert the worship experience into an experience of self-realization and personal fulfillment. "Celebration" is a welcome preliminary step toward creating a climate in which the Holy Spirit may well speak with new power and urgency to the church and through the church to a lost and despairing world. As one who is basically sympathetic with this confessional statement, I urge my fellow evangelicals to ponder the mystery and also the paradoxical unity of the gospel and the law as these relate to the burning social and spiritual issues of our time. We must confess again the power and promise of the living Christ, who is working in new and unexpected ways through his Holy Spirit but always in continuity with the wisdom already revealed in the scriptural and apostolic witness. This wisdom is reflected in "Celebration," but it is not exhausted by this or any other credo. I believe that "Celebration" bears the imprint of this transcendent wisdom, but along with all creeds and confessions can also be validly critiqued by this wisdom.

In joining with other Christians in making a common confession of the truth of the gospel, we should be resolute in our ongoing witness but also humble enough to accept admonition and correction from other parties in the church. This stance might eventually lead to a united Christian witness embracing a great many believers from various church traditions, a witness that will glorify God and his supreme revelation in Jesus Christ as testified to in holy Scripture.

The mark of a true confession of faith is that it leads us to confess Jesus Christ, not to certify the veracity of its principal theses. Its power lies not in its internal unity and consistency but in its openness to Jesus Christ and his gospel. If it motivates us to bear witness to what God has done for us in Christ before the world, then it can be accepted as the voice of an obedient and faithful church. If on the contrary it divides Christians without uniting them on a deeper level, then it does not contribute to the health of the community of faith and had best be replaced by a new statement more solidly grounded in the biblical witness.

APPENDIX 1
The Cambridge Declaration

Evangelical churches today are increasingly dominated by the spirit of this age rather than by the Spirit of Christ. As evangelicals, we call ourselves to repent of this sin and to recover the historic Christian faith.[1]

In the course of history words change. In our day this has happened to the word *evangelical*. In the past it served as a bond of unity between Christians from a wide diversity of church traditions. Historic evangelicalism was confessional. It embraced the essential truths of Christianity as those were defined by the great ecumenical councils of the church. In addition, *evangelicals* also shared a common heritage in the *"sola's"* of the sixteenth-century Protestant Reformation.

Today the light of the Reformation has been significantly dimmed. The consequence is that the word *evangelical* has become so inclusive as to have lost its meaning. We face the peril of losing the unity it has taken centuries to achieve. Because of this crisis and because of our love of Christ, his gospel, and his church, we endeavor to assert anew our commitment to the central truths of the Reformation and of historic evangelicalism. These truths we affirm not because of their role in our traditions, but because we believe that they are central to the Bible.

Sola Scriptura: **The Erosion of Authority**

Scripture alone is the inerrant rule of the church's life, but the evangelical church today has separated Scripture from its authoritative function. In practice, the church is guided, far too often, by the culture. Therapeutic technique, marketing strategies, and the beat of the entertainment world often have far more to say about what the church wants, how it functions, and what it offers, than does the Word of God. Pastors have neglected their rightful oversight of worship, including the doctrinal content of the music. As biblical authority has been abandoned in practice, as its truths have faded from Christian consciousness, and as its doctrines have lost their saliency, the church has been increasingly emptied of its integrity, moral authority, and direction.

Rather than adapting Christian faith to satisfy the felt needs of consumers, we must proclaim the Law as the only measure of true righteousness and the gospel as the only announcement of saving truth. Biblical truth is indispensable to the church's understanding, nurture, and discipline.

Scripture must take us beyond our perceived needs to our real needs and liberate us from seeing ourselves through the seductive images, clichés, promises, and priorities of mass culture. It is only in the light of God's truth that we understand ourselves aright and see God's provision for our need. The Bible, therefore, must be taught and preached in the church. Sermons must be expositions of the Bible and its teachings, not expressions of the preacher's opinions or the ideas of the age. We must settle for nothing less than what God has given.

The work of the Holy Spirit in personal experience cannot be disengaged from Scripture. The Spirit does not speak in ways that are independent of Scripture. Apart from Scripture we would never have known of God's grace in Christ. The biblical Word, rather than spiritual experience, is the test of truth.

Thesis 1: Sola Scriptura. We reaffirm the inerrant Scripture to be the sole source of written divine revelation, which alone can bind the conscience. The Bible alone teaches all that is necessary for our salvation from sin and is the standard by which all Christian behavior must be measured. We *deny* that any creed, council, or individual may bind a Christian's conscience, that the Holy Spirit speaks independently of or contrary to what is set forth in the Bible, or that personal spiritual experience can ever be a vehicle of revelation.

Solus Christus: The Erosion of Christ-Centered Faith

As evangelical faith has become secularized, its interests have been blurred with those of the culture. The result is a loss of absolute values, permissive individualism, and a substitution of wholeness for holiness, recovery for repentance, intuition for truth, feeling for belief, chance for providence, and immediate gratification for enduring hope. Christ and his cross have moved from the center of our vision.

Thesis 2: Solus Christus. We reaffirm that our salvation is accomplished by the mediatorial work of the historical Christ alone. His sinless life and substitutionary atonement alone are sufficient for our justification and reconciliation to the Father.

We deny that the gospel is preached if Christ's substitutionary work is not declared and faith in Christ and his work is not solicited.

Sola Gratia: The Erosion of the Gospel

Unwarranted confidence in human ability is a product of fallen human nature. This false confidence now fills the evangelical world—from the self-esteem gospel to the health and wealth gospel, from those who have transformed the gospel into a product to be sold and sinners into consumers who want to buy, to others who treat Christian faith as being true simply because it works. This silences the doctrine of justification regardless of the official commitments of our churches.

God's grace in Christ is not merely necessary but is the sole efficient cause of salvation. We confess that human beings are born spiritually dead and are incapable even of cooperating with regenerating grace.

Thesis 3: Sola Gratia. *We reaffirm* that in salvation we are rescued from God's wrath by his grace alone. It is the supernatural work of the Holy Spirit that brings us to Christ by releasing us from our bondage to sin and raising us from spiritual death to spiritual life.

We deny that salvation is in any sense a human work. Human methods, techniques, or strategies by themselves cannot accomplish this transformation. Faith is not produced by our unregenerated human nature.

Sola Fide: The Erosion of the Chief Article

Justification is by grace alone through faith alone because of Christ alone. This is the article by which the church stands or falls. Today this article is often ignored, distorted, or sometimes even denied by leaders, scholars, and pastors who claim to be evangelical. Although fallen human nature has always recoiled from recognizing its need for Christ's imputed righteousness, modernity greatly fuels the fires of this discontent with the biblical gospel. We have allowed this discontent to dictate the nature of our ministry and what it is we are preaching.

Many in the church growth movement believe that sociological understanding of those in the pew is as important to the success of the gospel as is the biblical truth which is proclaimed. As a result, theological convictions are frequently divorced from the work of the ministry. The marketing orientation in many churches takes this even further, erasing the distinction between the biblical Word and the world, robbing Christ's cross of its offense, and reducing Christian faith to the principles and methods which bring success to secular corporations.

While the theology of the cross may be believed, these movements are actually emptying it of its meaning. There is no gospel except that of Christ's substitution in our place whereby God imputed to him our sin and imputed to us his righteousness. Because he bore our judgment, we now walk in his grace as those who are forever pardoned, accepted, and adopted as God's children. There is no basis for our acceptance before God except in Christ's saving work, not in our patriotism, churchly devotion, or moral decency. The gospel declares what God has done for us in Christ. It is not about what we can do to reach him.

Thesis 4: Sola Fide. We reaffirm that justification is by grace alone through faith alone because of Christ alone. In justification Christ's righteousness is imputed to us as the only possible satisfaction of God's perfect justice. *We deny* that justification rests on any merit to be found in us, or upon the grounds of an infusion of Christ's righteousness in us, or that an institution claiming to be a church that denies or condemns *sola fide* can be recognized as a legitimate church.

Soli Deo Gloria: The Erosion of God-Centered Worship

Wherever in the church biblical authority has been lost, Christ has been displaced, the gospel has been distorted, or faith has been perverted, it has always been for one reason: Our interests have displaced God's and we are doing his work in our way. The loss of God's centrality in the life of today's church is common and lamentable. It is this loss that allows us to transform worship into entertainment, gospel preaching into marketing, believing into technique, being good into feeling good about ourselves, and faithfulness into being successful. As a result, God, Christ, and the Bible have come to mean too little to us and rest too inconsequentially upon us.

God does not exist to satisfy human ambitions, cravings, the appetite for consumption, or our own private spiritual interests. We must focus on God in our worship, rather than the satisfaction of our personal needs. God is sovereign in worship; we are not. Our concern must be for God's kingdom, not our own empires, popularity, or success.

Thesis 5: Soli Deo Gloria. We reaffirm that because salvation is of God and has been accomplished by God, it is for God's glory and that we must glorify him always. We must live our entire lives before the face of God, under the authority of God, and for his glory alone.

We deny that we can properly glorify God if our worship is confused with entertainment, if we neglect either Law or Gospel in our preaching, or if self-improvement, self-esteem, or self-fulfillment are allowed to become alternatives to the gospel.

A Call to Repentance and Reformation

The faithfulness of the evangelical church in the past contrasts sharply with its unfaithfulness in the present. Earlier in this century, evangelical churches sustained a remarkable missionary endeavor and built many religious institutions to serve the cause of biblical truth and Christ's kingdom. That was a time when Christian behavior and expectations were markedly different from those in the culture. Today they often are not. The evangelical world today is losing its biblical fidelity, moral compass, and missionary zeal.

We repent of our worldliness. We have been influenced by the "gospels" of our secular culture, which are no gospels. We have weakened the church by our own lack of serious repentance, our blindness to the sins in ourselves which we see so clearly in others, and our inexcusable failure adequately to tell others about God's saving work in Jesus Christ.

We also earnestly call back erring professing evangelicals who have deviated from God's Word in the matters discussed in this declaration. This includes those who declare that there is hope of eternal life apart from explicit faith in Jesus Christ, who claim that those who reject Christ in this life will be annihilated rather than endure the just judgment of God through eternal suffering, or who claim that evangelicals and Roman Catholics are one in Jesus Christ even where the biblical doctrine of justification is not believed.

The Alliance of Confessing Evangelicals asks all Christians to give consideration to implementing this declaration in the church's worship, ministry, policies, life, and evangelism.

For Christ's sake. Amen.

Alliance of Confessing Evangelicals
Cambridge, Massachusetts
April 20, 1996

APPENDIX 2
The Gospel of Jesus Christ:
An Evangelical Celebration

For God so loved the world that he gave his one and only Son, that whoever believes in him shall not perish but have eternal life. John 3:16

Sing to the Lord, for he has done glorious things; let this be known to all the world. Isaiah 12:5

Preamble

The Gospel of Jesus Christ is news, good news: the best and most important news that any human being ever hears.

This Gospel declares the only way to know God in peace, love, and joy is through the reconciling death of Jesus Christ the risen Lord.

This Gospel is the central message of the Holy Scriptures, and is the true key to understanding them.

This Gospel identifies Jesus Christ, the Messiah of Israel, as the Son of God and God the Son, the second Person of the Holy Trinity, whose incarnation, ministry, death, resurrection, and ascension fulfilled the Father's saving will. His death for sins and his resurrection from the dead were promised beforehand by the prophets and attested by eye-witnesses. In God's own time and in God's own way, Jesus Christ shall return as glorious Lord and Judge of all (1 Thess. 4:13-18; Matt. 25:31-32). He is now giving the Holy Spirit from the Father to all those who are truly his. The three Persons of the Trinity thus combine in the work of saving sinners.

This Gospel sets forth Jesus Christ as the living Savior, Master, Life, and Hope of all who put their trust in him. It tells us that the eternal destiny of all people depends on whether they are savingly related to Jesus Christ.

This Gospel is the only Gospel: there is no other; and to change its substance is to pervert and indeed destroy it. This Gospel is so simple that small children can understand it, and it is so profound that studies by the wisest theologians will never exhaust its riches.

All Christians are called to unity in love and unity in truth. As evangelicals who derive our very name from the Gospel, we celebrate this great good news of God's saving work in Jesus Christ as the true bond of Christian unity, whether among organized churches and denominations or in the many transdenominational cooperative enterprises of Christians together.

The Bible declares that all who truly trust in Christ and his Gospel are sons and daughters of God through grace, and hence are our brothers and sisters in Christ.

All who are justified experience reconciliation with the Father, full remission of sins, transition from the kingdom of darkness to the kingdom of light, the reality of being a new creature in Christ, and the fellowship of the Holy Spirit. They enjoy access to the Father with all the peace and joy that this brings.

The Gospel requires of all believers worship, which means constant praise and giving of thanks to God, submission to all that he has revealed in his written word, prayerful dependence on him, and vigilance lest his truth be even inadvertently compromised or obscured.

To share the joy and hope of this Gospel is a supreme privilege. It is also an abiding obligation, for the Great Commission of Jesus Christ still stands: proclaim the Gospel everywhere, he said, teaching, baptizing, and making disciples.

By embracing the following declaration we affirm our commitment to this task, and with it our allegiance to Christ himself, to the Gospel itself, and to each other as fellow evangelical believers.

The Gospel

This Gospel of Jesus Christ which God sets forth in the infallible Scriptures combines Jesus' own declaration of the present reality of the kingdom of God with the apostles' account of the person, place, and work of Christ, and how sinful humans benefit from it. The Patristic Rule of Faith, the historic creeds, the Reformation confessions, and the doctrinal bases of later evangelical bodies all witness to the substance of this biblical message.

The heart of the Gospel is that our holy, loving Creator, confronted with human hostility and rebellion, has chosen in his own freedom and faithfulness to become our holy, loving Redeemer and Restorer. The Father has sent the Son to be the Savior of the world (1 John 4:14): it is through his one and only Son that God's one and only plan of salvation is implemented. So Peter announced: "Salvation is found in no one else, for there is no other name under heaven given to men by which we must be saved" (Acts 4:12). And Christ himself taught: "I am the way, the truth and the life. No one comes to the Father except through me" (John 14:6).

Through the Gospel we learn that we human beings, who were made for fellowship with God, are by nature—that is, "in Adam" (1 Cor. 15:22)—dead in sin, unresponsive to and separated from our Maker. We are constantly twisting his truth, breaking his law, belittling his goals and standards, and offending his holiness by our unholiness, so that we truly are "without hope and without God in the world" (Rom.

1:18-32, 3:9-20; Eph. 2:1-3, 12). Yet God in grace took the initiative to reconcile us to himself through the sinless life and vicarious death of his beloved Son (Eph. 2:4-10; Rom. 3:21-24).

The Father sent the Son to free us from the dominion of sin and Satan, and to make us God's children and friends. Jesus paid our penalty in our place on his cross, satisfying the retributive demands of divine justice by shedding his blood in sacrifice and so making possible justification for all who trust in him (Rom. 3:25-26). The Bible describes this mighty substitutionary transaction as the achieving of ransom, reconciliation, redemption, propitiation, and conquest of evil powers (Matt. 20:28; 2 Cor. 5:18-21; Rom. 3:23-25; John 12:31; Col. 2:15). It secures for us a restored relationship with God that brings pardon and peace, acceptance and access, and adoption into God's family (Col. 1:20, 2:13-14; Rom. 5:1-2; Gal. 4:4-7; 1 Pet. 3:18). The faith in God and in Christ to which the Gospel calls us is a trustful outgoing of our hearts to lay hold of these promised and proffered benefits.

This Gospel further proclaims the bodily resurrection, ascension, and enthronement of Jesus as evidence of the efficacy of his once-for-all sacrifice for us, of the reality of his present personal ministry to us, and of the certainty of his future return to glorify us (1 Cor. 15; Heb. 1:1-4, 2:1-18, 4:14-16, 7:1-10:25). In the life of faith as the Gospel presents it, believers are united with their risen Lord, communing with him, and looking to him in repentance and hope for empowering through the Holy Spirit, so that henceforth they may not sin but serve him truly.

God's justification of those who trust him, according to the Gospel, is a decisive transition, here and now, from a state of condemnation and wrath because of their sins to one of acceptance and favor by virtue of Jesus' flawless obedience culminating in his voluntary sin-bearing death. God "justifies the wicked" (ungodly: Rom. 4:5) by imputing (reckoning, crediting, counting, accounting) righteousness to them and ceasing to count their sins against them (Rom. 4:1-8). Sinners receive through faith in Christ alone "the gift of righteousness" (Rom.

1:17, 5:17; Phil. 3:9) and thus become "the righteousness of God" in him who was "made sin" for them (2 Cor. 5:21).

As our sins were reckoned to Christ, so Christ's righteousness is reckoned to us. This is justification by the imputation of Christ's righteousness. All we bring to the transaction is our need of it. Our faith in the God who bestows it, the Father, the Son, and the Holy Spirit, is itself the fruit of God's grace. Faith links us savingly to Jesus, but inasmuch as it involves an acknowledgment that we have no merit of our own, it is confessedly not a meritorious work.

The Gospel assures us that all who have entrusted their lives to Jesus Christ are born-again children of God (John 1:12), indwelt, empowered, and assured of their status and hope by the Holy Spirit (Rom. 7:6, 8:9-17). The moment we truly believe in Christ, the Father declares us righteous in him and begins conforming us to his likeness. Genuine faith acknowledges and depends upon Jesus as Lord and shows itself in growing obedience to the divine commands, though this contributes nothing to the ground of our justification (James 2:14-26; Heb. 6:1-12).

By his sanctifying grace, Christ works within us through faith, renewing our fallen nature and leading us to real maturity, that measure of development which is meant by "the fullness of Christ" (Eph. 4:13). The Gospel calls us to live as obedient servants of Christ and as his emissaries in the world, doing justice, loving mercy, and helping all in need, thus seeking to bear witness to the kingdom of Christ. At death, Christ takes the believer to himself (Phil. 1:21) for unimaginable joy in the ceaseless worship of God (Rev. 22:1-5).

Salvation in its full sense is from the guilt of sin in the past, the power of sin in the present, and the presence of sin in the future. Thus, while in foretaste believers enjoy salvation now, they still await its fullness (Mark 14:61-62; Heb. 9:28). Salvation is a Trinitarian reality, initiated by the Father, implemented by the Son, and applied by the Holy Spirit. It has a global dimension, for God's plan is to save believers out of every tribe and tongue (Rev. 5:9) to be his church, a new humanity, the people of god, the body and bride of Christ, and the community of the Holy Spirit. All the heirs of final salvation are called here and how to serve their Lord and each other in love, to share in the fellowship of Jesus' sufferings, and to work together to make Christ known to the whole world.

We learn from the Gospel that, as all have sinned, so all who do not receive Christ will be judged according to their just deserts as measured by God's holy law, and face eternal retributive punishment.

Unity in the Gospel

Christians are commanded to love each other despite differences of race, gender, privilege, and social, political and economic background (John 13:34-35; Gal. 3:28-29), and to be of one mind wherever possible (John 17:20-21; Phil. 2:2; Rom. 14:1—15:13). We know that divisions among Christians hinder our witness in the world, and we desire greater mutual understanding and truth-speaking in love. We know too that as trustees of God's revealed truth we cannot embrace any form of doctrinal indifferentism, or relativism, or pluralism by which God's truth is sacrificed for a false peace.

Doctrinal disagreements call for debate. Dialogue for mutual understanding and, if possible, narrowing of the differences is valuable, doubly so when the avowed goal is unity in primary things, with liberty in secondary things, and charity in all things.

In the foregoing paragraphs, an attempt has been made to state what is primary and essential in the Gospel as evangelicals understand it. Useful dialogue, however, requires not only charity in our attitudes, but also clarity in our utterances. Our extended analysis of justification by faith alone through Christ alone reflects our belief that Gospel truth is of crucial importance and is not always well understood and correctly affirmed. For added clarity, out of love for God's truth and Christ's church, we now cast the key points of what has been said into specific affirmations and denials regarding the Gospel and our unity in it and in Christ.

Affirmations and Denials:

1. We affirm that the Gospel entrusted to the church is, in the first instance, God's Gospel (Mark 1:14; Rom. 1:1). God is its author, and he reveals it to us in and by his Word. Its authority and truth rest on him alone.

We deny that the truth or authority of the Gospel derives from any human insight or invention (Gal. 1:1-11). We also deny that the truth or authority of the Gospel rests on the authority of any particular church or human institution.

2. We affirm that the Gospel is the saving power of God in that the Gospel effects salvation to everyone who believes, without distinction (Rom. 1:16). This efficacy of the Gospel is by the power of God himself (1 Cor. 1:18).

We deny that the power of the Gospel rests in the eloquence of the preacher, the technique of the evangelist, or the persuasion of rational argument (1 Cor. 1:21; 2:1-5).

3. We affirm that the Gospel diagnoses the universal human condition as one of sinful rebellion against God, which, if unchanged, will lead each person to eternal loss under God's condemnation.

We deny any rejection of the fallenness of human nature or any assertion of the natural goodness, or divinity, of the human race.

4. We affirm that Jesus Christ is the only way of salvation, the only mediator between God and humanity (John 14:6; 1 Tim. 2:5).

We deny that anyone is saved in any other way than by Jesus Christ and his Gospel. The Bible offers no hope that sincere worshipers of other religions will be saved without personal faith in Jesus Christ.

5. We affirm that the church is commanded by God and is therefore under divine obligation to preach the Gospel to every living person (Luke 24:47; Matt. 28:18-19).

We deny that any particular class or group of persons, whatever their ethnic or cultural identity, may be ignored or passed over in the preaching of the Gospel (1 Cor. 9:19-22). God purposes a global church made up from people of every tribe, language, and nation (Rev. 7:9).

6. We affirm that faith in Jesus Christ as the divine Word (or Logos, John 1:1), the second Person of the Trinity, co-eternal and co-essential with the Father and the Holy Spirit (Heb. 1:3), is foundational to faith in the Gospel.

We deny that any view of Jesus Christ which reduces or rejects his full deity is Gospel faith or will avail to salvation.

7. We affirm that Jesus Christ is God incarnate (John 1:14). The virgin-born descendant of David (Rom. 1:3), he had a true human nature, was subject to the Law of God (Gal. 4:5), and was like us at all points, except without sin (Heb. 2:17, 7:26-28). We affirm that faith in the true humanity of Christ is essential to faith in the Gospel.

We deny that anyone who rejects the humanity of Christ, his incarnation, or his sinlessness, or who maintains that these truths are not essential to the Gospel, will be saved (1 John 4:2-3).

8. We affirm that the atonement of Christ by which, in his obedience, he offered a perfect sacrifice, propitiating the Father by paying for our sins and satisfying divine justice on our behalf according to God's eternal plan, is an essential element of the Gospel.

We deny that any view of the Atonement that rejects the substitutionary satisfaction of divine justice, accomplished vicariously for believers, is compatible with the teaching of the Gospel.

9. We affirm that Christ's saving work included both his life and his death on our behalf (Gal. 3:13). We declare that faith in the perfect obedience of Christ by which he fulfilled all the demands of the Law of God in our behalf is essential to the Gospel.

We deny that our salvation was achieved merely or exclusively by the death of Christ without reference to his life of perfect righteousness.

10. We affirm that the bodily resurrection of Christ from the dead is essential to the biblical Gospel (1 Cor. 15:14).

We deny the validity of any so-called gospel that denies the historical reality of the bodily resurrection of Christ.

11. We affirm that the biblical doctrine of justification by faith alone

in Christ alone is essential to the Gospel (Rom. 3:28; 4:5; Gal. 2:16).

We deny that any person can believe the biblical Gospel and at the same time reject the apostolic teaching of justification by faith alone in Christ alone. We also deny that there is more than one true Gospel (Gal. 1:6-9).

12. We affirm that the doctrine of the imputation (reckoning or counting) both of our sins to Christ and of his righteousness to us, whereby our sins are fully forgiven and we are fully accepted, is essential to the biblical Gospel (2 Cor. 5:19-21).

We deny that we are justified by the righteousness of Christ infused into us or by any righteousness that is thought to inhere within us.

13. We affirm that the righteousness of Christ by which we are justified is properly his own, which he achieved apart from us, in and by his perfect obedience. This righteousness is counted, reckoned, or imputed to us by the forensic (that is, legal) declaration of God, as the sole ground of our justification.

We deny that any works we perform at any stage of our existence add to the merit of Christ or earn for us any merit that contributes in any way to the ground of our justification (Gal. 2:16; Eph. 2:8-9; Titus 3:5).

14. We affirm that, while all believers are indwelt by the Holy Spirit and are in the process of being made holy and conformed to the image of Christ, those consequences of justification are not its ground. God declares us just, remits our sins, and adopts us as his children, by his grace alone, and through faith alone, because of Christ alone, while we are still sinners (Rom. 4:5).

We deny that believers must be inherently righteous by virtue of their cooperation with God's life-transforming grace before God will declare them justified in Christ. We are justified while we are still sinners.

15. We affirm that saving faith results in sanctification, the transformation of life in growing conformity to Christ through the power of the Holy Spirit. Sanctification means ongoing repentance, a life of turning

from sin to serve Jesus Christ in grateful reliance on him as one's Lord and Master (Gal. 5:22-25; Rom. 8:4, 13-14).

We reject any view of justification which divorces it from our sanctifying union with Christ and our increasing conformity to his image through prayer, repentance, cross-bearing, and life in the Spirit.

16. We affirm that saving faith includes mental assent to the content of the Gospel, acknowledgment of our own sin and need, and personal trust and reliance upon Christ and his work.

We deny that saving faith includes only mental acceptance of the Gospel, and that justification is secured by a mere outward profession of faith. We further deny that any element of saving faith is a meritorious work or earns salvation for us.

17. We affirm that, although true doctrine is vital for spiritual health and well-being, we are not saved by doctrine. Doctrine is necessary to inform us how we may be saved by Christ, but it is Christ who saves.

We deny that the doctrines of the Gospel can be rejected without harm. Denial of the Gospel brings spiritual ruin and exposes us to God's judgment.

18. We affirm that Jesus Christ commands his followers to proclaim the Gospel to all living persons, evangelizing everyone everywhere, and discipling believers within the fellowship of the church. A full and faithful witness to Christ includes the witness of personal testimony, godly living, and acts of mercy and charity to our neighbor, without which the preaching of the Gospel appears barren.

We deny that the witness of personal testimony, godly living, and acts of mercy and charity to our neighbors constitutes evangelism apart from the proclamation of the Gospel.

Our Commitment

As evangelicals united in the Gospel, we promise to watch over and care for one another, to pray for and forgive one another, and to reach out in love and truth to God's people everywhere, for we are one family, one in the Holy Spirit, and one in Christ.

Centuries ago it was truly said that in things necessary there must be unity, in things less than necessary there must be liberty, and in all things there must be charity. We see all these Gospel truths as necessary.

Now to God, the Author of the truth and grace of this Gospel, through Jesus Christ, its subject and our Lord, be praise and glory for ever and ever. Amen.

"The Gospel of Jesus Christ: An Evangelical Celebration" is copyright ©1999 by the Committee on Evangelical Unity in the Gospel, P. O. Box 5551, Glendale Heights, IL 60139-5551.

The Drafting Committee
John N. Akers
John Ankerberg
John Armstrong
D. A. Carson
Keith Davy
Maxie Dunnam
Timothy George
Scott Hafemann
Erwin Lutzer
Harold Myra
David Neff
Thomas Oden
J. I. Packer
R. C. Sproul
John Woodbridge

Notes

Chapter 1: Introduction

[1]See Paul Tillich, *Perspectives on 19th and 20th Century Protestant Theology,* ed. Carl E. Braaten (New York: Harper & Row, 1967), pp. 15-17.

[2]See William Ames, *The Marrow of Theology,* trans. and ed. John Dykstra Eusden (Boston: Pilgrim, 1968), pp. 77-78. See also Simon Chan, *Spiritual Theology* (Downers Grove, Ill.: InterVarsity Press, 1998), pp. 16-17. It should be noted that Puritanism and Pietism were kindred movements and often built upon one another.

[3]Friedrich Schleiermacher, *On Religion: Speeches to its Cultured Despisers,* trans. John Oman (New York: Harper & Row, 1958), p. 39.

[4]Friedrich Schleiermacher, *The Christian Faith,* ed. H. R. Mackintosh and J. S. Stewart (New York: Harper & Row, 1963), 1:5.

[5]Karl Barth, "Schleiermacher," in *Theology and Church,* trans. Louise Pettibone Smith (New York: Harper & Row, 1962), pp. 162-63.

[6]C. W. Christian, *Friedrich Schleiermacher* (Waco, Tex.: Word, 1979), p. 65.

[7]Schleiermacher, *Christian Faith,* 1:69.

[8]H. R. Mackintosh, *Types of Modern Theology* (1937; reprint, London: Nisbet & Co., 1949), p. 61.

[9]Schleiermacher, *Christian Faith,* 1:76.

[10]Ibid., 1:68.

[11]Mackintosh, *Types of Modern Theology,* p. 67.

[12]Cf. Barth: "Dogmatics must always be undertaken as an act of penitence and obedience. But this is possible only as it trusts in the uncontrollable presence of its ontic and noetic basis, in the revelation of God promised to the Church, and in the power of faith apprehending the promise." *Church Dogmatics,* ed. G. W. Bromiley and T. F. Torrance, trans. G. W. Bromiley (Edinburgh: T. & T. Clark, 1975), 1(1):22.

[13]Ibid., p. 17.

[14]Ibid., p. 20.

[15]John Weborg, in *Evangelical Theology in Transition: Theologians in Dialogue with Donald Bloesch,* ed. Elmer Colyer (Downers Grove, Ill.: InterVarsity Press, 1999), pp. 149-68.

[16]On *theologia prima* and *theologia secunda* in Catholic theology see Aidan Kavanagh, *On Liturgical Theology* (New York: Pueblo Publishing Co., 1984), pp. 73-95; and Herman Schmidt and David Power, eds., *Liturgical Experience of Faith* (New York: Herder & Herder, 1973), pp. 19-20.

[17]Weborg, in Colyer, ed., *Evangelical Theology in Transition,* p. 158.

¹⁸Ibid., pp. 158-59.

¹⁹Ibid., p. 159.

²⁰Ibid., p. 158.

²¹Torrance rightly reminds us that the datum of divine revelation remains God's own act and does not pass over into the self-consciousness and control of the Christian or of the church. T. F. Torrance, *Theological Science* (London: Oxford University Press, 1969), p. 351. See my further discussion in chap. four of this volume, pp. 74-75.

²²Schmidt and Power, *Liturgical Experience of Faith,* p. 101.

²³Cf. Barth: "Nor can it ever be the real concern of dogmatics merely to assemble, repeat and define the teaching of the Bible." *Church Dogmatics,* 1(1):16.

²⁴The following is a more comprehensive definition: Theology is the systematic reflection on God's incomparable self-disclosure in Jesus Christ, the meaning and impact of which are conveyed to us by the Spirit as we wrestle with Scripture and the church commentary on Scripture through the ages. All of these redefinitions comport with a theology of Word and Spirit and represent a deepening of the earlier definition given in volume one of the Christian Foundations series. See Bloesch, *A Theology of Word and Spirit* (Downers Grove, Ill.: InterVarsity Press, 1992), pp. 114-19.

²⁵P. T. Forsyth, *Positive Preaching and the Modern Mind* (1907; reprint, London: Independent Press, 1953), p. 45.

²⁶P. T. Forsyth, *The Church and the Sacraments* (1917; 2nd ed., London: Independent Press, 1947), p. 16.

²⁷The theme of a period of darkness in the Christian life is pervasive in both Martin Luther and John of the Cross.

²⁸Dietrich Bonhoeffer, *A Testament to Freedom,* ed. Geffrey B. Kelly and F. Burton Nelson (San Francisco: Harper Collins, 1990), p. 191.

²⁹*Luther's Works,* trans. and ed. Theodore G. Tappert (Philadelphia: Fortress, 1967), 54:94.

Chapter 2: Continuing Issues in Ecclesiology

¹See Avery Dulles, *Models of the Church* (New York: Doubleday, 1974), pp. 31-42.

²Elisabeth Schüssler Fiorenza, *Discipleship of Equals: A Critical Feminist Ekklēsialogy of Liberation* (New York: Crossroad, 1993), p. 34.

³Henri de Lubac, *Catholicism* (London: Burns, Oates & Washbourne, 1950), p. 29.

⁴Kevin Offner, "Mere Christianity & the Mere Christian," *Touchstone* 10, no. 4 (Fall 1997): 8.

⁵Wolfhart Pannenberg, *Systematic Theology,* trans. Geoffrey W. Bromiley (Grand Rapids, Mich.: Eerdmans, 1998), 3:32.

⁶Clark H. Pinnock, *Flame of Love* (Downers Grove, Ill.: InterVarsity Press, 1996), pp. 113-47.

⁷See Thomas O'Meara, *Romantic Idealism and Roman Catholicism* (Notre Dame, Ind.: University of Notre Dame Press, 1982), pp. 138-60. In his book *Loose in*

the World (New York: Paulist, 1974), O'Meara suggests that God is incarnate in universal history. See esp. pp. 62, 66, 76, 84, 113.

[8]See Kevin Orlin Johnson, *Expressions of the Catholic Faith* (New York: Ballantine, 1994), p. 58.

[9]Hans Küng, *The Church,* trans. Ray and Rosaleen Ockenden (New York: Sheed & Ward, 1967), p. 174.

[10]Jürgen Moltmann, *The Church in the Power of the Spirit,* trans. Margaret Kohl (New York: Harper & Row, 1977), p. 163.

[11]See Karl Barth, *Theology and Church,* trans. Louise Pettibone Smith (New York: Harper & Row, 1962), p. 344.

[12]All of these magazines seek to combine an ecumenical spirit with a biblical and catholic base. Some succeed in this task more than others.

[13]See Offner, "Mere Christianity & the Mere Christian," pp. 8-9; also see D. H. Williams, *Retrieving the Tradition and Renewing Evangelicalism* (Grand Rapids, Mich.: Eerdmans, 1999).

[14]See George A. Lindbeck, *The Nature of Doctrine* (Philadelphia: Westminster Press, 1984).

[15]Miroslav Volf, *After Our Likeness* (Grand Rapids, Mich.: Eerdmans, 1998), p. 244.

[16]Cf. Hans Küng, *Infallible? An Inquiry,* trans. Edward Quinn (New York: Doubleday, 1971), pp. 181-208; Yves Congar, *I Believe in the Holy Spirit,* trans. David Smith (New York: Seabury, 1983), 2:46.

[17]Barth, *Theology and Church,* p. 283.

[18]Eugene Bianchi, *Reconciliation: The Function of the Church* (New York: Sheed & Ward, 1969).

[19]Harvey Cox, *The Secular City* (New York: Macmillan, 1965), p. 134.

[20]Others who hold to pluralism include John Hick, Raimundo Panikkar and Paul Knitter.

[21]Peter C. Hodgson, *Revisioning the Church: Ecclesial Freedom in the New Paradigm* (Philadelphia: Fortress, 1988), p. 106.

[22]Ibid., p. 102.

[23]Ibid.

[24]Ibid., p. 94.

[25]Ibid., p. 101.

[26]Ibid., p. 94.

[27]For a surprisingly sympathetic treatment of the New Age movement by Christian theologians see *New Age Spirituality,* ed. Duncan Ferguson (Louisville, Ky.: Westminster John Knox, 1993).

[28]Dietrich Bonhoeffer, *No Rusty Swords,* trans. Edwin H. Robertson and John Bowden (New York: Harper & Row, 1965), p. 335.

[29]For my further discussion of confessions of faith see pp. 265-87.

[30]For a perceptive critique of entertainment evangelism and so-called contemporary worship see David W. Fagerberg, "Was the Cathedral of Notre Dame a Megachurch?" *Pro Ecclesia* 6, no. 2 (Spring 1997): 141-45. Fagerberg contrasts traditional Catholic worship, which is focused on "the eucharistic event" with

the contemporary worship of the megachurch, which he contends revolves around "the kerygmatic event." In my opinion it is not preaching that commands the attention of the avant-garde worshiping community but music and art forms. Both traditionalist or liturgical worship and contemporary worship are oriented about the visual, not the audible.

[31]See Donald G. Bloesch, "What's Wrong with the Liturgical Movement?" *Christianity Today* 12, no. 7 (1968): 6-7.

[32]Karl Barth, *The Knowledge of God and the Service of God,* trans. J. L. M. Haire and Ian Henderson (London: Hodder & Stoughton, 1938), p. 191.

[33]P. T. Forsyth, *The Church and the Sacraments* (1917; 2nd ed., London: Independent Press, 1947), p. 141.

[34]Joseph Martos, *Doors to the Sacred: A Historical Introduction to Sacraments in the Catholic Church,* expanded ed. (Tarrytown, N.Y.: Triumph, 1991), p. 458.

[35]Bernard J. Cooke, *The Distancing of God: The Ambiguity of Symbol in History and Theology* (Minneapolis: Fortress, 1990), p. 350.

[36]Martos, *Doors to the Sacred,* p. 459.

[37]Michael Green, *I Believe in the Holy Spirit* (Grand Rapids, Mich.: Eerdmans, 1975), p. 110.

[38]Theodore Stylianopoulos, *The Good News of Christ* (Brookline, Mass.: Holy Cross Orthodox Press, 1991), p. 24.

[39]Tony Philpot, "We've Got to Have Good Preaching," *Catholic Digest* 59, no. 12 (Oct. 1995): 42.

[40]See James M. Reese, *Preaching God's Burning Word* (Collegeville, Minn.: Liturgical Press, 1975).

[41]Karl Barth, *The Epistle to the Romans,* trans. Edwyn C. Hoskyns (1933; reprint, London: Oxford University Press, 1975), p. 333.

[42]Karl Barth, *The Word of God and the Word of Man,* trans. Douglas Horton (1957; reprint, Gloucester, Mass.: Peter Smith, 1978), pp. 97-135.

[43]Irenaeus, *Against Heresies* 3.24.1. *Ante-Nicene Fathers* (reprint, Grand Rapids, Mich.: Eerdmans, 1953), 1:458.

[44]Jürgen Moltmann, *The Church in the Power of the Spirit,* p. 65.

[45]John Calvin, *Commentary on the Book of Psalms,* trans. James Anderson (Edinburgh: Calvin Translation Society, 1845), 1:388-89.

[46]Pannenberg, *Systematic Theology,* 3:19.

[47]Ibid.

[48]Nathaniel Micklem, *What Is the Faith?* (Nashville: Cokesbury, n.d.), p. 215.

[49]Dulles, *Models of the Church,* p. 122.

[50]Ibid.

[51]Ibid., pp. 149-50.

[52]For my further discussion see pp. 258-59.

[53]P. T. Forsyth, *The Principle of Authority* (2nd ed., London: Independent Press, 1952), p. 335.

[54]Christoph Blumhardt, *Action in Waiting* (Farmington, Penn.: Plough, 1998), p. 197.

[55]Paul Evdokimov, *L'Orthodoxie* (Neuchâtel: Delachaux et Niestlé, 1959), p. 343.

[56]Among these scholars are Walter Kasper, Karl Rahner, Avery Dulles and Hans Küng.

[57]See Charles Colson and Richard John Neuhaus, eds., *Evangelicals and Catholics Together: Toward a Common Mission* (Dallas: Word, 1995); and "The Gift of Salvation," *Christianity Today* 41, no. 14 (Dec. 8, 1997): 35-38.

[58]See Art Moore, "Does 'The Gift of Salvation' Sell Out the Reformation?" *Christianity Today* 42, no. 5 (April 27, 1998): 21.

[59]Jeffrey C. Silleck, "A More Radical Proposal," *Lutheran Forum* 32, no. 1 (Spring 1998): 28-31. See esp. p. 29.

[60]Ibid., p. 31.

[61]See Carl Braaten, *Mother Church: Ecclesiology and Ecumenism* (Minneapolis: Fortress, 1998).

[62]See esp. Forsyth, *Church and the Sacraments;* Philip Schaff, *The Principle of Protestantism,* trans. John Nevin (Philadelphia: United Church Press, 1964); and Schaff, *What Is Church History? A Vindication of the Idea of Historical Development* (Philadelphia: Lippincott & Co., 1846). This last is reprinted in *Reformed and Catholic: Selected Historical and Theological Writings of Philip Schaff,* ed. Charles Yrigoyen Jr. and George Bricker (Pittsburgh: Pickwick, 1979), pp. 17-144.

[63]Stephen R. Graham, *Cosmos in the Chaos: Philip Schaff's Interpretation of Nineteenth-Century American Religion* (Grand Rapids, Mich.: Eerdmans, 1995), p. 231.

[64]P. T. Forsyth, *The Justification of God* (1917; reprint, London: Independent Press, 1948), p. 38.

[65]Forsyth, *Church and the Sacraments,* p. 6.

[66]See Trevor Hart, ed. *Justice the True and Only Mercy* (Edinburgh: T. & T. Clark, 1995), p. 140.

[67]See James S. Cutsinger, ed., *Reclaiming the Great Tradition* (Downers Grove, Ill.: InterVarsity Press, 1997).

[68]Throughout his career Schaff remained skeptical of Mormonism. See Graham, *Cosmos in the Chaos,* pp. 224-25.

[69]P. T. Forsyth, *The Person and Place of Jesus Christ* (Philadelphia: Westminster Press, 1910), p. 84.

Chapter 3: The Church in the Plan of Salvation

[1]Cyprian *On the Unity of the Church* (6). Quoted in Otto W. Heick, *A History of Christian Thought* (Philadelphia: Fortress, 1965), 1:104.

[2]Cyprian *Letters* 73.21, in Heick, *History,* 1:104.

[3]See "The Church," in *Documents of Vatican II,* ed. Walter M. Abbott, trans. Joseph Gallagher (Chicago: Follett, 1966), pp. 9-106.

[4]Karl Adam, *The Roots of the Reformation,* trans. Cecily Hastings (New York: Sheed & Ward, 1951), p. 91.

[5]Ibed.

[6]Pope John Paul II, *Crossing the Threshold of Hope,* ed. Vittorio Messori (New York: Alfred A. Knopf, 1994), p. 140.

[7]Ibid.

[8]Francis Fernandez, *In Conversation with God* (London: Scepter, 1990), 3:31. See Thomas Aquinas *Summa Theologica* 2-2.177.1.

[9]Fernandez, *In Conversation with God,* 3:162-3.

[10]Thomas F. Torrance, *Theology in Reconciliation* (Grand Rapids, Mich.: Eerdmans, 1975), p. 101.

[11]*The Table Talk of Martin Luther,* ed. Thomas S. Kepler (New York: World, 1952), p. 143.

[12]*Luther's Works,* ed. Hans J. Hillerbrand (Philadelphia: Fortress, 1974), 52:39.

[13]*Luther's Works,* trans. Paul D. Paul, ed. Jaroslav Pelikan (St. Louis: Concordia, 1970), 6:329.

[14]*Luther's Works,* ed. Jaroslav Pelikan (St. Louis: Concordia, 1957), 22:55.

[15]*Luther's Works,* trans. and ed. Jaroslav Pelikan (St. Louis: Concordia, 1963), 26:387.

[16]John Calvin, *Institutes of the Christian Religion,* trans. John Allen (Philadelphia: Presbyterian Board of Christian Education, 1936), 3.2.31 (1:632).

[17]John Calvin, *Commentary on the Book of the Prophet Isaiah,* 33:24, trans. William Pringle (Edinburgh: Calvin Translation Society, 1852), 3:42-43.

[18]John Calvin, *Commentaries on the Epistle of Paul the Apostle to the Romans,* trans. and ed. John Owen (Edinburgh: Calvin Translation Society, 1849), p. 424.

[19]Calvin, *Sermons on the Epistle to the Ephesians* (Edinburgh: Banner of Truth, 1973), p. 156.

[20]For a discussion of irresistible grace, see Donald G. Bloesch, *Essentials of Evangelical Theology* (1978; reprint, San Francisco: HarperCollins, 1991), 1:205-8.

[21]Brunner was influenced by Rudolf Sohm, who contended that the worship and organization in the early church was fluid and characterized by love and spontaneity more than by law. See James Luther Adams' Introduction in Rudolf Sohm, *Outlines of Church History,* trans. Mary Sinclair (1895; reprint, Boston: Beacon, 1958), pp. ix-xv. See esp. xiii.

Also see Brunner, *The Christian Doctrine of the Church, Faith, and the Consummation,* trans. David Cairns (Philadelphia: Westminster Press, 1962), pp. 30-31, 71; and *The Misunderstanding of the Church,* trans. Harold Knight (Philadelphia: Westminster Press, 1953), p. 73.

[22]Brunner, *Misunderstanding of the Church,* p. 72.

[23]Ibid., p. 52.

[24]Ibid., p. 68.

[25]Ibid., p. 65.

[26]Emil Brunner, *Our Faith,* trans. John W. Rilling (New York: Charles Scribner's Sons, 1954), pp. 127-28.

[27]Brunner, *Misunderstanding of the Church,* p. 118.

[28]See Donald G. Bloesch, "Moral Re-Armament," in *Evangelical Dictionary of Theology,* ed. Walter Elwell, rev. ed. (Grand Rapids, Mich.: Baker, 2001), pp. 790-91.

[29]Brunner, *Christian Doctrine of the Church, Faith and the Consummation,* p. 112.

[30]Karl Barth, *Church Dogmatics,* ed. G. W. Bromiley and T. F. Torrance, trans. G. W. Bromiley (Edinburgh: T. & T. Clark, 1969), 4(4):32.

[31]This appears to contradict Mk 13:11 where Jesus tells his followers to "say whatever is given you in that hour, for it is not you who speak, but the Holy Spirit." Cf. Lk 1:70; 10:16; Acts 28:25.

[32]*Karl Barth's Table Talk,* ed. John D. Godsey (Edinburgh: Oliver & Boyd, 1963), pp. 33-34.

[33]Ibid., p. 87

[34]Karl Barth, *Göttingen Dogmatics,* vol. 1, trans. G. W. Bromiley (Grand Rapids, Mich.: Eerdmans, 1991). From Foreword by Daniel L. Migliore, p. lvi.

[35]Karl Barth, *Church Dogmatics,* ed. G. W. Bromiley and T. F. Torrance, trans. G. W. Bromiley (Edinburgh: T. & T. Clark, 1962), 4(3):563.

[36]Dawn DeVries, *Jesus Christ in the Preaching of Calvin and Schleiermacher* (Louisville, Ky.: Westminster John Knox, 1996), pp. 18, 101.

[37]Barth, *Church Dogmatics,* 4(3):563.

[38]Torrance, *Theology in Reconciliation,* p. 87.

[39]Ibid., p. 99.

[40]Ibid.

[41]Ibid., p. 101.

[42]Ibid.

[43]Ibid., p. 99.

[44]Ibid.

[45]Torrance, *The Ministry and the Sacraments of the Gospel* (London: Lutterworth, 1960), p. 141.

[46]See Fanny Crosby's celebrated hymn, "Rescue the Perishing," in *The Worshiping Church: A Hymnal* (Carol Stream, Ill.: Hope, 1990), no. 736.

[47]See Daniel L. Migliore in Karl Barth, *Göttingen Dogmatics,* 1:xxvii.

[48]See Harry Blamires, *Knowing the Truth About Heaven and Hell* (Ann Arbor, Mich.: Servant, 1988), p. 159. These words have been attributed, probably mistakenly, to both Catherine of Siena and Teresa of Ávila. They surely reflect themes in late modern Catholic spirituality.

[49]See Rudolf J. Ehrlich, *Rome: Opponent or Partner?* (Philadelphia: Westminster Press, 1965), pp. 131-36; 142-49; 166-68; 185-89.

[50]For my earlier discussion see Donald G. Bloesch, *Jesus Christ: Savior & Lord* (Downers Grove, Ill.: InterVarsity Press, 1997), p. 258.

[51]P. T. Forsyth, *Faith, Freedom and the Future* (1912; reprint, London: Independent Press, 1955), p. 220.

[52]While not yet a dogma of the church, this interpretation is part of the general teaching of the church.

[53]See Elliot Miller and Kenneth R. Samples, eds., *The Cult of the Virgin* (Grand Rapids, Mich.: Baker, 1992), p. 48.

[54]Martin Luther, Christmas Homily, 1529. Cited in Max Thurian, *Mary Mother of the Lord, Figure of the Church,* trans. Neville B. Cryer (London: Faith, 1963), p. 173.

[55]It should be noted that Thurian converted to Roman Catholicism toward the

end of his life.

[56]Thurian, *Mary,* p. 137.

[57]Ibid., p. 147.

[58]Fernandez, *In Conversation with God,* 3:214.

[59]Thurian, *Mary,* p. 197.

[60]Ibid., pp. 197-98. Also see Thomas A. O'Meara, *Mary in Protestant and Catholic Theology* (New York: Sheed & Ward, 1966), pp. 143-44.

[61]It is well to note that the Second Vatican Council included Mary in the section on the church.

[62]See *Service Book and Hymnal* (Philadelphia: United Lutheran Publication House, 1958), no. 437.

[63]The Apology of the Augsburg Confession allows the saints as intercessors for the church but not as propitiators or mediators. See *The Book of Concord,* trans. and ed. Theodore G. Tappert (Philadelphia: Fortress, 1959), pp. 229-36. It makes a place for thanksgiving for the witness of the saints but not for invoking them for salvation.

For my earlier discussion of Mary, see Bloesch, *Jesus Christ: Savior & Lord,* pp. 107-120.

Chapter 4: The Church and the Kingdom

[1]Wolfhart Pannenberg et al., *Spirit, Faith and Church* (Philadelphia: Westminster Press, 1970), p. 115.

[2]Jürgen Moltmann, *The Church in the Power of the Spirit,* trans. Margaret Kohl (New York: Harper & Row, 1977), p. 196.

[3]Christoph Blumhardt, *Action in Waiting* (Farmington, Penn.: Plough, 1998). See esp. pp. xxvi-xxvii, 4-5, 74-5.

[4]Augustine *The City of God,* trans. John Healey (London: J. M. Dent & Sons, 1945), 20.9, 2:283.

[5]*Luther's Works,* ed. and trans. Theodore G. Tappert (Philadelphia: Fortress, 1967), 54:57.

[6]*Luther's Works,* ed. and trans. John W. Doberstein (Philadelphia: Muhlenberg, 1959), 51:167.

[7]Friedrich Schleiermacher, *The Christian Faith,* ed. H. R. Mackintosh and J. S. Stewart (New York: Harper Torchbooks, 1963), 2:678.

[8]Ibid.

[9]Ibid., p. 691.

[10]Barth offers this illuminating description of Schleiermacher's position: "Civilization as the triumph of the spirit over nature is the most peculiar work of Christianity, just as the quality of being a Christian is for its own part the crown of a thoroughly civilized consciousness. The kingdom of God, according to Schleiermacher, is utterly and unequivocally identical with the advance of civilization." K. Barth, *Protestant Theology in the Nineteenth Century* (Valley Forge, Penn.: Judson Press, 1973), p. 435.

[11]Dietrich Bonhoeffer, *The Cost of Discipleship,* trans. R. H. Fuller, rev. ed. (New York: Macmillan, 1963), p. 269.

[12]Ibid., p. 271.

[13]Ibid., p. 290.

[14]Ibid., p. 269.

[15]See Paul Tillich, *Systematic Theology* (Chicago: University of Chicago Press, 1963), 3:162-220.

[16]Karl Barth, *Church Dogmatics*, ed. G. W. Bromiley and T. F. Torrance, trans. G. W. Bromiley (Edinburgh: T. & T. Clark, 1958), 4(2):655-57.

[17]Markus Barth, *The Broken Wall* (Chicago: Judson Press, 1959), p. 118.

[18]See pp. 51-53.

[19]Emil Brunner, *The Divine Imperative,* trans. Olive Wyon (Philadelphia: Westminster Press, 1947), p. 538.

[20]Vladimir Lossky, *The Mystical Theology of the Eastern Church* (Crestwood, N.Y.: St. Vladimir's Seminary Press, 1976), p. 184.

[21]Archimandrite Vasileios of Stavronikita, *Hymn of Entry,* trans. Elizabeth Briere (Crestwood, N.Y.: St. Vladimir's Seminary Press, 1984), p. 46.

[22]Vladimir Rodzianko, "Baptism and Redemption," in *Crisis for Baptism,* ed. Basil S. Moss (London: SCM Press, 1965), pp. 78-79.

[23]*Humani Generis,* n. 44. See Richard P. McBrien, "Vatican II or Pius XII—Which One is It?" *National Catholic Reporter* 34, no. 25 (April 24, 1998): 19.

[24]Ibid. Roman Catholic triumphalism is also apparent in the more recent *Dominus Iesus* (August 6, 2000), which describes Protestant church bodies as "ecclesial communities," not "churches." See 3.17.

[25]Thomas F. Torrance, *Theological Science* (London: Oxford University Press, 1969), pp. 351-52.

[26]Schleiermacher, *Christian Faith,* 2:532.

[27]P. T. Forsyth, *The Church and the Sacraments* (1917; 2nd ed., London: Independent Press, 1947), p. 95.

[28]Ibid., p. 95.

[29]Ibid., p. 92.

[30]P. T. Forsyth, *The Church, the Gospel and Society* (London: Independent Press, 1962), p. 12.

[31]Avery Dulles, *Models of the Church* (New York: Doubleday, 1974), p. 125.

[32]Michael Horton, *We Believe* (Nashville: Word, 1998), p. 220.

[33]P. T. Forsyth, *The Justification of God* (1917; new ed., London: Independent Press, 1948), p. 158.

[34]Forsyth, *Church and Sacraments,* p. 99.

[35]Ibid., p. 103.

[36]For perspicacious critiques of Ritschl see H. R. Mackintosh, *Types of Modern Theology* (1937; reprint, London: Nisbet & Co., 1949), pp. 142-80; Emil Brunner, *The Mediator,* trans. Olive Wyon (Philadelphia: Westminster Press, 1947), pp. 56-71, 96-97; and Barth, *Protestant Theology in the Nineteenth Century,* pp. 654-61.

[37]Forsyth, *Church and Sacraments,* p. 6.

[38]For an earlier discussion of Niebuhr, see Donald G. Bloesch, *Freedom for Obedience* (San Francisco: Harper & Row, 1987), pp. 100-103; and *Jesus Christ:*

Savior & Lord (Downers Grove, Ill.: InterVarsity Press, 1997), pp. 219-20.

[39]Dietrich Bonhoeffer, *No Rusty Swords,* trans. Edwin H. Robertson and John Bowden (New York: Harper & Row, 1965), p. 188.

[40]For my continuing discussion of the church militant and the church triumphant, see pp. 96-98.

[41]Moltmann, *The Church in the Power of the Spirit,* p. 163.

Chapter 5: Authority in the Church

[1]Hans Küng, *Christianity* (New York: Continuum, 1995), p. 467.

[2]Ibid.

[3]Ibid., p. 470.

[4]Ibid., p. 471.

[5]Ibid.

[6]See my chapter "A Confessing Church," esp. pp. 271, 274-75.

[7]Pope John Paul II has described himself as "a servant of the servants of the Word." Yet an unsurpassable gulf remains between Catholics and evangelicals so long as the pope is not willing to be corrected even in substantial or doctrinal matters.

[8]John Meyendorff, "Light from the East? 'Doing Theology' in an Eastern Orthodox Perspective," in *Doing Theology in Today's World,* ed. John D. Woodbridge and Thomas Edward McComiskey (Grand Rapids, Mich.: Zondervan, 1991), p. 342.

[9]Ibid.

[10]John Albert Bengel, *Gnomon of the New Testament,* trans. Charlton T. Lewis and Marvin R. Vincent (Philadelphia: Perkinpine & Higgins, 1862), 1:xiii.

[11]Philip Schaff, *The Principle of Protestantism,* trans. John Nevin (Philadelphia: United Church Press, 1964), p. 39.

[12]P. T. Forsyth, *The Person and Place of Jesus Christ* (Philadelphia: Westminster Press, 1910), p. 140.

[13]P. T. Forsyth, *The Principle of Authority* (1913; 2nd ed., London: Independent Press, 1952), p. 329.

[14]Ibid., p. 326.

[15]P. T. Forsyth, *The Charter of the Church: Six Lectures on the Spiritual Principle of Non-Conformity* (London: Alexander & Shepheard, 1896), p. 38.

[16]Karl Barth, for example, can speak of the church as infallible. See Barth, *Theology and Church,* trans. Louise Pettibone Smith (New York: Harper & Row, 1962), p. 283.

[17]Ibid., p. 277.

[18]Yves Congar, *I Believe in the Holy Spirit,* trans. David Smith (New York: Seabury Press, 1983), 2:46.

[19]Jaroslav Pelikan, *The Christian Tradition* (Chicago: University of Chicago Press, 1971), 1:333.

[20]Ibid., pp. 319-24.

[21]See Thomas F. Torrance, *The Doctrine of Grace in the Apostolic Fathers* (Edinburgh: Oliver & Boyd, 1948).

[22]See Anders Nygren, *Agape and Eros,* trans. Philip S. Watson (Philadelphia: Westminster Press, 1953). Also see Donald G. Bloesch, *God the Almighty* (Downers Grove, Ill.: InterVarsity Press, 1995), pp. 219-21; cf. pp. 224-28.

[23]See Oscar Cullmann, *Peter,* trans. Floyd V. Filson (Philadelphia: Westminster Press, 1953).

[24]See Küng, *Christianity,* p. 314.

[25]Eduard Schweizer, *The Good News According to Matthew,* trans. David E. Green (Atlanta, Ga.: John Knox Press, 1975), p. 341.

[26]Ibid., p. 344.

[27]For an intriguing discussion of John 20:23, see Leon Morris, *The Gospel According to John* (Grand Rapids, Mich.: Eerdmans, 1971), pp. 847-50.

[28]Dietrich Bonhoeffer, *The Cost of Discipleship,* trans. R. H. Fuller (New York: Macmillan, 1963), p. 324.

[29]Ibid.

[30]Karl Barth, *Ethics,* trans. Geoffrey W. Bromiley, ed. Dietrich Braun (New York: Seabury Press, 1981), p. 443.

[31]See Paul Tillich, *The Protestant Era,* trans. James Luther Adams (Chicago: University of Chicago Press, 1948), pp. 44-48, 56-65.

[32]For my earlier discussion, see pp. 19-23.

[33]*Luther's Works,* ed. and trans. Theodore G. Tappert (Philadelphia: Fortress, 1967), 54:94.

[34]Forsyth, *Principle of Authority,* p. 334.

[35]Ibid., p. 331.

[36]Cited in Carter Lindberg, *The Third Reformation?* (Macon, Ga.: Mercer University Press, 1983), p. 159.

[37]Dietrich Bonhoeffer, *A Testament to Freedom,* ed. Geffrey B. Kelly and F. Burton Nelson (San Francisco: Harper Collins, 1990), p. 191.

[38]William Walsham How, "For All the Saints Who from Their Labors Rest," *Service Book and Hymnal* (Minneapolis: Augsburg 1958), no. 144.

[39]S. Ralph Harlow, "O Church of God, Triumphant," *The Covenant Hymnal* (Chicago: Covenant Press, 1973), no. 481.

[40]Eberhard Arnold, ed., *Inner Words* (Rifton, N.Y.: Plough, 1975), p. 78.

[41]Ibid., p. 43.

[42]See pp. 69-81.

[43]Isaac Watts, "Lord of the Worlds Above," *Service Book and Hymnal,* no. 238.

Chapter 6: Marks of the Church

[1]Hans Küng, *The Church,* trans. Ray and Rosaleen Ockenden (New York: Sheed & Ward, 1967), p. 269.

[2]Avery Dulles, *Models of the Church* (New York: Doubleday, 1974), p. 122.

[3]P. T. Forsyth, *The Church and the Sacraments* (1917; 2nd ed., London: Independent Press, 1947), p. 39.

[4]Martin Luther, *A Commentary on St. Paul's Epistle to the Galatians,* rev. ed. (Westwood, N.J.: Fleming H. Revell, n.d.), p. 40.

[5]John Calvin, *Institutes of the Christian Religion,* 2 vols., ed. John T. McNeill,

trans. Ford Lewis Battles (Philadelphia: Westminster Press, 1960), 4.1.17 (2:1031).

[6]Paul Tillich, *Systematic Theology* (Chicago: University of Chicago Press, 1963), 3:167.

[7]Küng, *The Church,* p. 325.

[8]Ibid., p. 303.

[9]Ibid., p. 310.

[10]Dulles, *Models of the Church,* p. 122.

[11]Küng, *The Church,* p. 355.

[12]Jürgen Moltmann, *The Church in the Power of the Spirit,* trans. Margaret Kohl (New York: Harper & Row, 1977), p. 359.

[13]See Küng, *The Church,* p. 268.

[14]Ibid., p. 265. In Roman Catholicism these signs are identified with the four classical attributes of the church. In Protestantism they signify in addition a wide variety of indicia including the pure preaching of the Word and the right administration of the sacraments.

[15]Besides the Word as a medium of the Spirit, Luther envisaged other marks employed by the Spirit including baptism; the observance of Holy Communion; the keys or the power of discipline; public worship with prayer, praise and thanksgiving; and the cross of persecution and temptation. Cf. Philip Watson, *Let God Be God!* (London: Epworth, 1947), pp. 165-72; and Carl E. Braaten and Robert W. Jenson, eds. *Marks of the Body of Christ* (Grand Rapids, Mich.: Eerdmans, 1999), pp. vii-xii. Also see Gerhard O. Forde, "The Word That Kills and Makes Alive," in Braaten and Jenson, *Marks,* pp. 1-12.

[16]Calvin, *Institutes,* ed. and trans. John Allen, 2 vols. (Philadelphia: Presbyterian Board of Christian Education, 1936), 4.1.9 (2:281).

[17]Martin Luther, *A History of Christian Doctrine,* ed. Hubert Cunliffe-Jones and Benjamin Drewery (Philadelphia: Fortress, 1978), p. 347.

[18]See note 18 in Calvin, *Institutes,* trans. Ford Lewis Battles, 4.1.9 (2:1023).

[19]See David S. Yeago, "The Office of the Keys: On the Disappearance of Discipline in Protestant Modernity," in *Marks of the Body of Christ,* ed. Braaten and Jenson, pp. 95-122.

[20]Friedrich Schleiermacher, *On Religion: Speeches to its Cultured Despisers,* trans. John Oman (New York: Harper & Row, 1958), p. 213.

[21]John Chrysostom *Homilies on the Acts of the Apostles,* 20. Cited in Francis Fernandez, *In Conversation with God* (London: Scepter, 1990), 3:228.

[22]Forsyth, *Missions in State and Church,* pp. 12, 250. Cited in Trevor Hart, ed. *Justice the True and Only Mercy* (Edinburgh: T. & T. Clark, 1995), p. 142.

[23]J. Heinrich Arnold, *Discipleship* (Farmington, Penn.: Plough, 1994), p. 19.

[24]See Donald G. Bloesch, *The Struggle of Prayer* (1980; reprint, Colorado Springs: Helmers & Howard, 1988), pp. 1-10, 67-96. Cf. Friedrich Heiler, *Prayer,* trans. and ed. Samuel McComb (New York: Oxford University Press, 1958).

[25]Küng, *The Church,* p. 290.

[26]See Eberhard Bethge, *Dietrich Bonhoeffer,* trans. Eric Mosbacher, Peter and Betty Ross, Frank Clarke and William Glen-Doepel (New York: Harper & Row,

1977), pp. 298, 300, 301, 309, 344.

[27]At the beginning the heretic will be expelled from the fellowship of the church, but this separation is intended to be only temporary, depending on whether that person renounces the views that are the point of contention and is willing to be corrected by the congregation of faith.

[28]For my further discussion see pp. 135-40.

[29]Wolfhart Pannenberg, *Christian Spirituality* (Philadelphia: Westminster Press, 1983), p. 40.

[30]Christof Gestrich, *The Return of Splendor in the World,* trans. Daniel W. Bloesch (Grand Rapids, Mich.: Eerdmans, 1989), p. 326.

[31]Ibid.

[32]Ibid., p. 327.

[33]See Second Helvetic Confession, Chapter 1, *Book of Confessions* (Louisville, Ky.: Office of the General Assembly, Presbyterian Church [U.S.A.], 1991), 5.004.

[34]Dietrich Bonhoeffer, *No Rusty Swords,* trans. Edwin H. Robertson and John Bowden (New York: Harper & Row, 1965), p. 148. These words are from a catechism devised by Bonhoeffer and Franz Hildebrandt.

[35]Arnold, *Discipleship,* p. 250.

Chapter 7: Worship in Spirit and Truth

[1]Edward Farley, "A Missing Presence," *The Christian Century* 115, no. 9 (March 18-25, 1998): 276.

[2]Ibid.

[3]P. T. Forsyth, *God the Holy Father* (London: Independent Press, 1957), p. 74.

[4]In *One Church* 13, no. 1-2 (1959): 24. Cited in *Reclaiming the Great Tradition,* ed. James S. Cutsinger (Downers Grove, Ill.: InterVarsity Press, 1997), p. 129.

[5]Karl Barth, *The Knowledge of God and the Service of God,* trans. J. L. M. Haire and Ian Henderson (London: Hodder & Stoughton, 1938), p. 198.

[6]Karl Barth, *The Epistle to the Romans,* trans. Edwyn Hoskyns, 6th ed. (1933; reprint, London: Oxford University Press, 1975), p. 452.

[7]See Rudolf Otto, *The Idea of the Holy,* trans. John W. Harvey (1958; reprint, New York: Oxford University Press, 1964).

[8]See Alfred North Whitehead, *Religion in the Making* (New York: Macmillan, 1926), pp. 16-17. For Whitehead we begin with God the void and then proceed to God the enemy and end in God the companion.

[9]This note may seem to be contradicted by Paul's words in Rom 12:1-2, which clearly distinguish between cultic worship and spiritual worship. Paul's point is to underline the fact that the essence of true worship is the conformity of our will with the will of God, and the sacrifices that we are called to make are the sacrifices of our very lives. The spirit of worship will permeate not only the formal acts of worship but also daily life. Paul does not insinuate that life can take the place of worship or that worship is nothing other than ethics.

[10]Michael Horton, *In the Face of God* (Dallas: Word, 1996), p. 216.

[11]See Paul Tillich, *Biblical Religion and the Search for Ultimate Reality* (Chicago:

University of Chicago Press, 1955), p. 85.

[12]Alfred North Whitehead, *Process and Reality* (New York: Macmillan, 1929), p. 532.

[13]See my earlier discussion in Donald G. Bloesch, *God the Almighty* (Downers Grove, Ill.: InterVarsity Press, 1995), pp. 145-52, 219-21.

[14]I do not deny that the living God of the Bible delights in himself, but this too takes the form of *agape,* for it is a delight in which each person in the Godhead is taken out of himself into the other. It is a serving love as well as a rapturous love. God is not superciliously enwrapped in himself, but in each of his persons he unremittingly flows out of himself. This interminable process is evident both within his triune life and in his relationship to the world. He wills to go out of himself by creating and sustaining other beings with whom he can interact. God does not seek the satisfaction of his supposed longings (as in eros love), but he does seek to share his glory with his angelic and human creation and receive glory from them.

[15]See Albrecht Ritschl, *Geschichte des Pietismus,* 3 vols. (Bonn: Marcus, 1880-1886). The mainstream of Pietism regarded the vision of God as a wholly eschatological reality.

[16]John Calvin, *Institutes of the Christian Religion,* ed. John T. McNeill, trans. Ford Lewis Battles (Philadelphia: Westminster Press, 1960), 1.11.12 (1:112).

[17]J. I. Packer, *Knowing God* (Downers Grove, Ill.: InterVarsity Press, 1973), pp. 40-41.

[18]Ibid., pp. 40-41.

[19]Ibid., p. 40.

[20]See Jacques Ellul, *The Humiliation of the Word,* trans. Joyce Main Hanks (Grand Rapids, Mich.: Eerdmans, 1985), pp. 5-47, 100-2.

[21]Luther, Sermon delivered in Merseburg, 1545. Cited in Karl Barth, *Church Dogmatics,* 1(1), 2nd ed., ed. G. W. Bromiley and T. F. Torrance, trans. G. W. Bromiley (Edinburgh: T. & T. Clark, 1975), p. 135.

[22]Cited in Karl Barth, *Theology and Church,* trans. Louise Pettibone Smith (New York: Harper & Row, 1962), p. 317.

[23]See Karl Barth, *The Word of God and the Word of Man,* trans. Douglas Horton (1928; reprint, Gloucester, Mass.: Peter Smith, 1978), pp. 183-217.

[24]Packer, *Knowing God,* pp. 42-44.

[25]P. T. Forsyth, *The Church and the Sacraments* (1917; 2nd ed., London: Independent Press, 1947), p. 40.

[26]On the positive confession movement in Pentecostalism, see D. R. McConnell, *A Different Gospel,* new ed. (Peabody, Mass.: Hendrickson, 1995).

[27]Harold Bloom, *The American Religion: The Emergence of the Post-Christian Nation* (New York: Simon & Schuster, 1992).

[28]See Donald G. Bloesch, *The Struggle of Prayer* (1980; reprint, Colorado Springs: Helmers & Howard, 1988), pp. 67-96.

[29]See Eugene H. Peters, *The Creative Advance: An Introduction to Process Philosophy as a Context for Christian Faith* (St. Louis: Bethany Press, 1966).

[30]See Otto, *The Idea of the Holy,* pp. 210-14.

[31]For my earlier discussion, see pp. 17-26.

[32]G. C. Berkouwer, *The Church,* trans. James E. Davison (Grand Rapids, Mich.: Eerdmans, 1976), p. 251.

[33]See G. A. Pritchard, *Willow Creek Seeker Services: Evaluating a New Way of Doing Church* (Grand Rapids, Mich.: Baker, 1996). Cf. Kimon Howard Sargeant, *Seeker Churches: Promoting Traditional Religion in a Non-Traditional Way* (New Brunswick, N.J.: Rutgers University Press, 2000).

[34]Lyle Schaller, *Worship Leader* (July-August 1995), p. 34. Cited in Michael Horton, *In the Face of God* (Dallas: Word, 1996), pp. 143, 145.

[35]See Martin E. Marty, "Feed My Sheep—Twinkies?" *Context* 29, no. 13 (July 1, 1997): 1.

[36]Michael Horton, *We Believe* (Nashville: Word, 1998), p. 240.

[37]*Context* (July 1, 1997), p. 2.

[38]For example, in Eddie Espinosa's "The Only One" we find this tribute:

> And Lord You are the One
> > that I desire,
> Your love for me has set
> > my heart on fire.

Worship Bulletin, Third Presbyterian Church, Dubuque, Iowa (May 24, 1998).

[39]*Maranatha! Music: Praise, Hymns and Choruses* (1984; expanded 4th ed., Nashville: Word Music, 1997), p. 89. In the Bible, Israel is the apple of God's eye, but the reverse is not found (cf. Deut 32:10; Ps 17:8; Zech 2:8). In Proverbs 7:2 we as believers are to regard the teachings of God as the apple of our eyes. The emphasis in the Bible is not on the possession of God in ecstasy (as in mysticism) but on obedience to his commandments in love and gratitude. Our hope is to rejoin the people of God in the praise of his name (Ps 42:4-5). Our delight is to do the will of God and to speak of the salvation that he has wrought (Ps 40:8, 10). An allegorical interpretation of the Song of Songs yields the picture of an amorous relationship between God and the believer, but the scholarly consensus is that this book exalts the value of human love. See notes of NJB, pp. 1027-29.

[40]"Our God Reigns" is far superior to "Lord We Praise You," which consists exclusively in repetition of that particular phrase. The former might be acceptable if it were conjoined with hymns that explicitly retell the biblical story of salvation through the work of Jesus Christ.

John Frame, who mounts an impressive defense of contemporary worship music, acknowledges that repetition can be a problem in the new praise songs, but he reminds us that traditional liturgy is also characterized by repetition of words and phrases. He does not sufficiently acknowledge, however, that all repetition can easily become vain repetition, thereby contradicting the biblical mandate that true prayer springs from an alert mind and a chastened heart (cf. Col 4:2 NEB). See John M. Frame, *Contemporary Worship Music* (Phillipsburg, N.J.: Presbyterian & Reformed Publishing, 1997). Frame is alert to the danger of confusing worship and entertainment.

[41]For a cogent analysis of the secularizing thrust of the new praise choruses in

the church today, see Kenneth Laudermilch, "Musical Integrity in the Church," *Reformation and Revival* 7, no. 1 (Winter 1998): 79-100. See also Frank Burch Brown, "A Matter of Taste?" *The Christian Century* 117, no. 25 (September 13-20, 2000): 904-11; and Larry D. Harwood, " 'Praise Worship': Sharing a Pillow with God," *New Oxford Review* 69, no. 2 (February 2002): 43-45.

[42]Tim Stafford, "God Is in the Blueprints: Our Deepest Beliefs are Reflected in the Ways We Construct our Houses of Worship," *Christianity Today* 42, no. 10 (1998): 81.

From my Reformed perspective the sacraments are to be included as symbols of communication and not simply treated as ceremonies or rituals. The kerygmatic proclamation is central, but it attains its goal through sacraments as well as through personal faith.

Chapter 8: Rethinking Sacraments

[1]See Ronald S. Wallace, "Sacrament," in *Evangelical Dictionary of Theology,* ed. Walter A. Elwell (Grand Rapids, Mich.: Baker, 1984), p. 965.

[2]P. T. Forsyth, *The Church and the Sacraments* (1917; 2nd ed., London: Independent Press, 1947), p. 226.

[3]*Spiritual Works,* pp. 52ff., cited in *Drinking from the Hidden Fountain: A Patristic Breviary,* ed. Thomas Spidlik, trans. Paul Drake (Kalamazoo, Mich.: Cistercian Publications, 1994), p. 80.

[4]Cited in Joseph Martos, *Doors to the Sacred: A Historical Introduction to Sacraments in the Catholic Church,* expanded ed. (Tarrytown, N.Y.: Triumph, 1991), p. 167. From Augustine *On the Gospel of John* 80.3.

[5]Ibid.

[6]Bernhard Lohse, *A Short History of Christian Doctrine,* trans. F. Ernest Stoeffler, rev. ed. (Philadelphia: Fortress, 1985), p. 138.

[7]Augustine *Sermons* 227. Cited in Martos, *Doors to the Sacred,* p. 223.

[8]Phillip Cary, "Where to Flee for Grace: The Augustinian Context of Luther's Doctrine of the Gospel," *Lutheran Forum* 30, no. 2 (May 1996): 20.

[9]Wolfhart Pannenberg, *Systematic Theology,* trans. G. W. Bromiley (Grand Rapids, Mich.: Eerdmans, 1998), 3:354.

[10]Martos, *Doors to the Sacred,* p. 237.

[11]Thomas Aquinas *Summa Theologica* 3.73.3, 3.79.4; quoted in Martos, *Doors to the Sacred,* p. 237.

[12]See Martos, *Doors to the Sacred,* p. 67.

[13]See Lohse, *A Short History of Christian Doctrine,* p. 152.

[14]A contemporary Catholic theologian Leon McKenzie calls us to transcend the twin fallacies of symbolism and literalism and to affirm the sacramental reality of Christ coming to us by means of the sign. See his *Pagan Resurrection Myths and the Resurrection of Jesus* (Charlottesville, Va.: Bookwrights, 1997), pp. 125-28. "To affirm the Eucharist according to a crude literalism means, for me, to argue that the bread of the Lord's Supper is the physical equivalent of the body of Jesus. Thus, if one would put the bread under a microscope, one might expect to see human skin cells. This interpretation, I

suggest, is not only crude but also frivolous" (p. 127).

[15]The Reformers did not deny the objective reality of Christ's gift of the Spirit in the sacrament of baptism, but they were insistent that this gift does not reach its goal except in the dawning of faith.

[16]While Calvin alluded to a real spiritual presence of Christ in the eucharist, his meaning was that we are raised by his Spirit into living communion with the whole Christ, divinity and humanity, spirit and body. "Christ does not simply present to us the benefit of his death and resurrection, but the very body in which he suffered and rose again." John Calvin, *Commentary on the Epistles of Paul the Apostle to the Corinthians,* 1 Cor 11:24, trans. John Pringle (Edinburgh: Calvin Translation Society, 1848), 1:379.

[17]Martin Bucer, *The Lord of the Journey,* ed. Roger Pooley and Philip Seddon (1986; reprint, London: Collins, 1987), p. 201.

[18]Forsyth, *The Church and the Sacraments,* p. 244.

[19]Ibid., p. 176.

[20]Ibid., p. 143.

[21]Ibid., p. 223.

[22]Ibid., p. 226.

[23]Ibid., p. 218.

[24]Karl Barth, *The Knowledge of God and the Service of God,* trans. J. L. M. Haire and Ian Henderson (London: Hodder & Stoughton, 1938), p. 191.

[25]Karl Barth, *The Teaching of the Church Regarding Baptism,* trans. Ernest A. Payne (1948; reprint, London: SCM Press, 1954), p. 23.

[26]Karl Barth, *The Christian Life,* trans. Geoffrey W. Bromiley (Grand Rapids, Mich.: Eerdmans, 1981), p. 46.

[27]H. Wheeler Robinson, *The Christian Experience of the Holy Spirit* (London: Nisbet, 1928), pp. 192-98.

[28]Ibid., p. 194.

[29]Michael Green, *Baptism* (Downers Grove, Ill.: InterVarsity Press, 1987), p. 120.

[30]W. Harold Mare, "1 Corinthians," *Expositor's Bible Commentary,* ed. Frank E. Gaebelein (Grand Rapids, Mich.: Zondervan, 1976), 10:265-66.

[31]Francis W. Beare, "The Epistle to the Colossians," *Interpreter's Bible* (Nashville: Abingdon, 1955), 11:197.

[32]Paul M. Quay, *The Mystery Hidden for Ages in God* (New York: Peter Lang, 1995), p. 17.

[33]Pannenberg, *Systematic Theology,* 3:246.

[34]See John Baillie's helpful discussion of this position in his *Baptism and Conversion* (London: Oxford University Press, 1964), pp. 32-37.

[35]According to Joachim Jeremias the practice of infant baptism goes back to the apostolic church. See Jeremias, *Infant Baptism in the First Four Centuries,* trans. David Cairns (Philadelphia: Westminster Press, 1960). Arguing on the other side is Kurt Aland in his *Did the Early Church Baptize Infants?* trans. G. R. Beasley-Murray (Philadelphia: Westminster Press, 1963).

[36]For a sterling attempt to build bridges between pedobaptists and those who hold to believers' baptism, see Donald Bridge and David Phypers, *The Water*

That Divides: The Baptism Debate (Downers Grove, Ill.: InterVarsity Press, 1977).

[37]See my earlier discussion in Donald G. Bloesch, *The Reform of the Church* (Grand Rapids, Mich.: Eerdmans, 1970), pp. 87-95.

[38]Daniel Jenkins, "Baptism and Creation," in *Crisis for Baptism,* ed. Basil S. Moss (London: SCM Press, 1965), p. 58.

[39]See Bloesch, *Reform of the Church,* pp. 87-95.

[40]In my view, which is consonant with the mainstream of Reformed Christianity, Christ by his Spirit makes himself present in the eucharistic celebration, but this rite does not re-present Christ or his sacrifice.

[41]See Bloesch, *Reform of the Church,* pp. 44-56.

[42]See François Wendel, *Calvin,* trans. Philip Mairet (London: Collins, 1963), pp. 329-55. Also see *Calvin: Theological Treatises,* ed. and trans. J. K. S. Reid (Philadelphia: Westminster Press, 1954), pp. 144-46. Calvin could even say, "It is indeed true that this same grace is offered us by the gospel; yet as in the Supper we have a more ample certainty and fuller enjoyment, it is with good reason that we recognize such a fruit as coming from it." *Calvin: Theological Treatises,* p. 145.

[43]Hans Urs von Balthasar, *Prayer,* trans. A. V. Littledale (New York: Paulist, 1961), p. 96.

[44]Edward Schillebeeckx, "Transubstantiation, Transfinalization, Transfiguration," *Worship* 40, no. 6 (June-July 1966): 337.

[45]Hans Küng, *The Church,* trans. Ray and Rosaleen Ockenden (New York: Sheed & Ward, 1967), p. 219.

[46]See Vernard Eller, *In Place of Sacraments* (Grand Rapids, Mich.: Eerdmans, 1972), pp. 106-18.

[47]John Polkinghorne, *Science and Providence* (Boston: Shambhala, 1989), p. 93.

[48]My position is also to be contrasted with a ritualistic view in which spiritual reality is necessarily conveyed through the ritual actions of the priest.

[49]From his "First Apology." See *Eerdmans' Book of Christian Classics,* ed. Veronica Zundel (Grand Rapids, Mich.: Eerdmans, 1985), p. 13.

[50]For Calvin we receive the body of Christ as the gift of salvation only through faith. Without faith we are confronted by the living Christ who becomes our judge rather than our Savior. See Ronald S. Wallace, *Calvin's Doctrine of the Word and Sacrament* (Grand Rapids, Mich.: Eerdmans, 1957), pp. 212-13.

[51]I here share the Catholic view that intercommunion between Catholics and Protestants should be postponed until we arrive at an overall doctrinal consensus.

[52]C. F. W. Walther's admonition to a fellow pastor is still relevant: "Above all things be careful not to arrange for the celebration of the Lord's Supper too quickly. Hold those who desire the Lord's Supper off for a while, till you see that you have a small congregation, that there really is a communion there." In *Voices from the Heart,* ed. Roger Lundin and Mark A. Noll (Grand Rapids, Mich.: Eerdmans, 1987), p. 182. We must be careful, however, not to make the Lord's Supper too small, for it should be open to all persons who believe in Jesus Christ and who have truly repented of their sin.

[53]I here take issue with Arthur C. Cochrane, who identifies the Lord's Supper

with the Agape meal. See Cochrane, *Eating and Drinking with Jesus* (Philadelphia: Westminster Press, 1974).

[54]See *The Book of Concord,* ed. and trans. Theodore G. Tappert (Philadelphia: Fortress, 1959), pp. 34, 182-211.

[55]Second Helvetic Confession, chapter 14, *The Book of Confessions* (Louisville, Ky.: Office of the General Assembly, Presbyterian Church [U.S.A.], 1991), 5.093-5.095. Note that Calvin recommended that the ordained minister or pastor be the confidant for the troubled soul. *Institutes* 3.4.12.

[56]The idea of penance as a second floating plank by which sinners can be rescued after the shipwreck of sin goes back to the church fathers including Tertullian (c. 200) and Jerome (fifth century). See *Westminster Dictionary of Church History,* ed. Jerald C. Brauer (Philadelphia: Westminster Press, 1971), pp. 645-46.

[57]Cited in James Atkinson, *Martin Luther and the Birth of Protestantism* (Atlanta, Ga.: John Knox Press, 1968), p. 149.

[58]For a helpful analysis of the critique of confession by Luther and Calvin, see Max Thurian, *Confession* (London: SCM Press, 1958), pp. 23-39. At the time Thurian was still a Reformed theologian, a member of the Taizé community. He later converted to Roman Catholicism.

[59]Bertram Lee Woolf, ed., *Reformation Writings of Martin Luther* (London: Lutterworth, 1952), p. 285.

[60]See John M. Todd, *Luther: A Life* (New York: Crossroad, 1982), p. 240.

[61]Pannenberg, *Systematic Theology,* 3:81.

[62]See Walter Houston Clark, *The Oxford Group: Its History and Significance* (New York: Bookman Associates, 1951).

[63]Eduard Thurneysen points to the crucial difference between Catholic and Evangelical approaches to overcoming sin in the life of the Christian: "Evangelical confessional conversation is distinguished from Catholic confession precisely by the absence of requirements the fulfillment of which will bring about forgiveness." See Thurneysen, *A Theology of Pastoral Care,* trans. Jack A. Worthington and Thomas Wieser (Richmond, Va.: John Knox Press, 1962), p. 297.

[64]Hans Urs von Balthasar, "Jesus and Forgiveness," *Communio* 11, no. 4 (Winter 1984): 322.

[65]*Catechism of the Catholic Church* (United States Catholic Conference, 1994), no. 1459.

[66]In the situation where the sinner seeks the aid of a Christian counselor, proclamation will involve both a declaration of forgiveness and an admonition to walk the pathway of righteousness.

[67]On Thurneysen's perceptive analysis of the psychological basis of modern pastoral counseling, see Eduard Thurneysen, *A Theology of Pastoral Care,* pp. 213-14. Also see L. Gregory Jones, "The Psychological Captivity of the Church in the United States," in *Either/Or: The Gospel or Neopaganism,* ed. Carl E. Braaten and Robert W. Jenson (Grand Rapids, Mich.: Eerdmans, 1995), pp. 97-112; and Jones, *Embodying Forgiveness: A Theological Analysis* (Grand Rapids, Mich.: Eerdmans, 1995).

[68]Relevant books and articles on the relation of theology and psychotherapy include E. Brooks Holifield, *A History of Pastoral Care in America: From Salvation to Self-Realization* (Nashville: Abingdon, 1983); Shirley C. Guthrie Jr., "Pastoral Counseling, Trinitarian Theology and Christian Anthropology," *Interpretation* 33, no. 2 (April 1979): 130-43; Thomas C. Oden, *Kerygma and Counseling* (Philadelphia: Westminster Press, 1966); Oden, *Care of Souls in the Classic Tradition* (Philadelphia: Fortress, 1984); Oden, *Contemporary Theology and Psychotherapy* (Philadelphia: Westminster Press, 1967); Eduard Thurneysen, *A Theology of Pastoral Care;* Thurneysen, "Evangelical Confession," in Walter Lüthi and Eduard Thurneysen, *Preaching. Confession. The Lord's Supper,* trans. Francis J. Brooke III (Richmond, Va.: John Knox Press, 1960), pp. 39-77; Ana-Maria Rizzuto, *The Birth of the Living God: A Psychoanalytic Study* (Chicago: University of Chicago Press, 1979); Paul Tillich, *The Courage to Be* (London: Nisbet, 1952); Tillich, *The Meaning of Health,* ed. Perry LeFevre (Chicago: Exploration Press, 1984); Deborah van Deusen Hunsinger, *Theology and Pastoral Counseling* (Grand Rapids, Mich.: Eerdmans, 1995); and L. Gregory Jones, *Embodying Forgiveness* (Grand Rapids, Mich.: Eerdmans, 1995).

I am closer to those authors who basically hold to an asymmetrical relationship between theology and psychotherapy, viz., Thurneysen, Guthrie, Jones and to a lesser extent Deborah Hunsinger. The last tries to do justice to both the discontinuity and the continuity between the two disciplines. The theology of Karl Barth is conspicuous in varying degrees in the four persons mentioned above. In Barthian theology both the goal and the subject matter of the two disciplines are quite different though not unrelated. Paul Tillich, by contrast, sees psychotherapy and priestly ministry as having a common goal, "full self-affirmation," the attainment of "the courage to be" (*Courage to Be,* p. 73). At the same time Tillich drew sharp distinctions between existential anxiety, an object of priestly help, and pathological anxiety, an object of medical healing. He warned that the functions of the two methods should not be confused, nor should their representatives try to replace one another (*Courage to Be,* p. 73).

[69]Lewis Smedes, in his much acclaimed *Forgive and Forget* (San Francisco: Harper & Row, 1984), offers a measure of biblical wisdom, but the therapeutic model is dominant in his exposition. Forgiveness is a means by which we heal ourselves. "Even the worst of us can find the power to set ourselves free" (p. 74). He leaves the impression that we can more readily forgive others by first learning to forgive ourselves and even God. But Scripture says nothing about forgiving self or God. It seems that Smedes envisions forgiveness as primarily need love, a love that satisfies the human yearning to be free from distress, rather than a gratuitous gift love that goes out to the other person without regard for our own welfare or interests.

For a penetrating critique of Smedes' position by an evangelical theologian, see Robert C. Roberts, "Forgiveness as Therapy," *The Reformed Journal* 36, no. 7 (1986): 19-23; and Roberts, "Therapies and The Grammar of a Virtue," in Richard H. Bell, ed., *The Grammar of the Heart* (San Francisco: Harper &

Row, 1988), pp. 149-70. Roberts rightly discerns that in Smedes's theology of pastoral care the characteristic motive for forgiveness is "the forgiver's desire to heal himself or herself of hatred" (*Grammar of the Heart*, p. 155). For Smedes's response see "Lewis Smedes Replies," *The Reformed Journal* 36, no. 7 (July 1986): 23-24. For an equally devastating criticism of Smedes and the ideology of therapeutic forgiveness, see Jones, *Embodying Forgiveness*, pp. 35-69.

[70]Here Smedes diverges from the therapeutic model by sharply distinguishing between acceptance and forgiveness (pp. 45-46). Yet he says that we can forgive only those who personally wrong us. But as Christians are not we authorized to declare God's forgiveness to anyone seeking help in this area?

[71]We must be baptized into the death of Christ before we can "walk in newness of life" (Rom 6:3-4). Yet we can only be baptized into Christ's death by first being confronted by God's love in Christ (Rom 5:1-11).

[72]This note is especially evident in God's forgiveness of us. The remission of sins is attained through the dethroning of the powers of darkness by the cross and resurrection victory of Jesus Christ. But we also see the conquest of sin in our forgiveness of others. When we extend the hand of forgiveness to others we are recognizing that a sin has been committed. Forgiveness expels the burden of guilt that sin produces so long as the wrongdoer receives our forgiveness in sincere repentance.

[73]I am thinking here of both the forgiveness that comes from God and that which comes from God's representative, the believing Christian. Concerning the woman caught in adultery, Jesus not only assures her of God's forgiveness but leaves her with this admonition: "Go and sin no more" (Jn 8:11 NKJ).

[74]Dietrich Bonhoeffer, *The Cost of Discipleship*, trans. R. H. Fuller (New York: Macmillan, 1963), p. 325. Cf. Bonhoeffer, *Life Together* and *Prayerbook of the Bible*, ed. Geffrey B. Kelly, trans. Daniel W. Bloesch and James H. Burtness (Minneapolis: Fortress, 1996), pp. 108-18.

[75]Dietrich Bonhoeffer, *Ethics*, trans. Neville Horton Smith, ed. Eberhard Bethge (New York: Macmillan, 1949), pp. 292-93.

[76]In evangelical confession the confessor may give an improvised declaration of pardon or one that has the official sanction of the church. The church should probably make available to its pastors and elders a formula or reading that would guide the counselor in this situation.

[77]The divine commandment is not a law in the abstract but a personal address given by God in a concrete situation. We must never commit ourselves to a course of action unless we are inwardly persuaded that this is God's express will for us. For my earlier treatment of the divine commandment see Donald G. Bloesch, *Freedom for Obedience* (San Francisco: Harper & Row, 1987), pp. 64-66, 132-35.

[78]Thomas à Kempis, *The Imitation of Christ*, trans. Leo Sherley-Price (London: Penguin, 1952), p. 205.

[79]I state this against the sacramentalist view that it is the rite of baptism that engrafts us into Christ.

⁸⁰See James Hastings Nichols, *Romanticism in American Theology: Nevin and Schaff at Mercersburg* (Chicago: University of Chicago Press, 1961), pp. 236-58. See esp. p. 245.

⁸¹*Forum Letter* 27, no. 6 (1998): 8.

⁸²Philip Schaff, *The Principle of Protestantism,* trans. John W. Nevin (Philadelphia: United Church Press, 1964), p. 131.

⁸³"Sacraments," in *Encyclopedia of the Reformed Faith,* ed. Donald K. McKim (Louisville, Ky.: Westminster John Knox, 1992), p. 334.

⁸⁴Michael Horton, *In the Face of God* (Dallas: Word, 1996), p. 146.

⁸⁵Ibid., p. 219. I must hasten to add that the sacrament in and of itself does not confer forgiveness, but the Spirit working through the sacrament brings salvation.

⁸⁶Quoted in Martos, *Doors to the Sacred,* p. 3. For Tillich's discussion of sacraments and sacramentalism see Tillich, *Systematic Theology* (Chicago: University of Chicago Press, 1963), 3:120-28.

⁸⁷In biblical prophetic religion holiness has to do with personal relations. The human person becomes holy by being set apart by the holy God. Scripture is holy not as a book but as a personal address by the living God to his people. Baptism is holy not because of holy water but because of the holy God who reaches out to us through baptism. People are holy not because they have a greater measure of infused grace but because they are called by God to embark on a holy vocation. Material things are not intrinsically holy, but they may be set apart for a holy use.

⁸⁸*Baptism, Eucharist and Ministry* (Geneva: World Council of Churches, 1982). Also see Max Thurian, ed., *Churches Respond to BEM* (Geneva: World Council of Churches, 1986); and *Baptism, Eucharist and Ministry 1982-1990* (Geneva: WCC Publications, 1990).

⁸⁹*Baptism, Eucharist and Ministry* (1982), p. 3.

⁹⁰Ibid., p. 10.

⁹¹BEM appears to affirm the complementarity of Word and eucharist rather than the subordination of eucharist to Word.

⁹²Ibid., p. 11.

⁹³BEM is clear that Christ's sacrifice is unique and cannot be repeated or prolonged, but its benefits are effectively communicated through the eucharist. Evangelicals would insist that the efficacy of this sacrifice is realized only where faith and repentance are present. This note is also contained in the document.

⁹⁴Ibid., p. 29.

Chapter 9: The Demise of Biblical Preaching

¹Barth sometimes suggested that the Reformers regarded preaching as the only sacrament. See Karl Barth, *The Word of God and the Word of Man,* trans. Douglas Horton (1957; reprint, Gloucester, Mass.: Peter Smith, 1978), p. 114. Also see Karl Barth, *The Göttingen Dogmatics,* ed. Hannelotte Reiffen, trans. Geoffrey W. Bromiley (Grand Rapids, Mich.: Eerdmans, 1991), 1:23-41.

[2]*The Book of Confessions* (Louisville, Ky.: Office of the General Assembly, Presbyterian Church [U.S.A.], 1991), chap. 1. no. 5.004. The Reformation position is well stated by D. G. Hart: "Preaching is not simply a common act of speech where the minister tries to put across a particular moral or doctrinal truth. It is a holy activity that God has ordained to reveal himself in worship." "Rediscovering Mother Kirk," *Touchstone* 13, no. 10 (December 2000): 24. Hart's emphasis is on recovering a liturgy of Word and sacrament, but he downplays the necessity for heartfelt experience. In a truly Reformed theology both the preaching of the Word and liturgical forms are united with heartfelt experience.

[3]See Dietrich Bonhoeffer, *The Cost of Discipleship,* rev. ed., trans. R. H. Fuller (New York: Macmillan, 1963), pp. 45-60.

[4]*Luther's Works,* trans. and ed. Jaroslav Pelikan (St. Louis: Concordia, 1963), 26:387.

[5]See my discussion of law and gospel in Donald G. Bloesch, *Jesus Christ: Savior & Lord* (Downers Grove, Ill.: InterVarsity Press, 1997), pp. 198-209. Also see Bloesch, *Freedom for Obedience* (San Francisco: Harper & Row, 1987), pp. 106-49.

[6]See esp. David F. Wells, *No Place for Truth* (Grand Rapids, Mich.: Eerdmans, 1993); and Wells, *Losing Our Virtue* (Grand Rapids, Mich.: Eerdmans, 1998).

[7]Barth makes this astute observation: "There is no lack of good preachers and sermons, but a lack of sermons that are meant to be God's Word and are received as such." *Göttingen Dogmatics,* 1:31.

[8]Karl Barth, *The Epistle to the Romans,* trans. Edwyn C. Hoskyns (1933; reprint, New York: Oxford University Press, 1975), p. 333. For my earlier discussion of Barth's uneasiness with sacramentalism see pp. 53-56.

Chapter 10: A Socio-Theological Typology

[1]See James Luther Adams, *On Being Human Religiously,* ed. Max L. Stackhouse (Boston: Beacon, 1976). See esp. Adams' critique of Max Weber, Karl Marx, Rudolf Sohm and Ernst Troeltsch.

[2]Ernst Troeltsch, *The Social Teaching of the Christian Churches,* 2 vols, trans. Olive Wyon (1931; reprint, New York: Macmillan, 1950). See esp. 2:993ff.

[3]Ibid., 2:994.

[4]Ibid., 2:996.

[5]Ibid., 2:993.

[6]Ibid.

[7]Ibid., 2:994.

[8]See H. Richard Niebuhr, *The Social Sources of Denominationalism* (New York: Henry Holt, 1929).

[9]Troeltsch, *Social Teaching,* 2:994.

[10]See my further discussion of Troeltsch on pp. 240-44.

[11]Troeltsch, *Social Teaching,* 2:994.

[12]A "state church" is officially sponsored and supported by the secular reigning authority, as is the case with Catholic, Orthodox and Protestant churches in a number of European countries. It could also be referred to as a "folk church,"

since it forms an integral part of the ethos of a particular people. A "folk church" is more comprehensive in meaning because it can exist where official governmental support is lacking.

[13]P. T. Forsyth, *The Church and the Sacraments* (1917; 2nd ed., reprint, London: Independent Press, 1947), p. 40.

[14]Emil Brunner, *The Misunderstanding of the Church,* trans. Harold Knight (Philadelphia: Westminster Press, 1953), p. 98.

[15]Johann Arndt, *True Christianity,* trans. Peter Erb (New York: Paulist, 1979), p. 173.

[16]Pentecostalism as a worldwide movement now constitutes the second largest family of churches after Roman Catholicism.

[17]See H. Richard Niebuhr, *Christ and Culture* (New York: Harper & Bros., 1951).

[18]Frederick B. Tolles and E. Gordon Alderfer, eds., *The Witness of William Penn* (New York: Macmillan, 1957), p. 48.

[19]See discussion in Donald G. Bloesch, *The Holy Spirit* (Downers Grove, Ill.: InterVarsity Press, 2000), pp. 145-46; 173-78.

[20]In the way I use these words, heterodoxy connotes a slight imbalance in the church's teaching. Heresy refers to an attack on the vitals of the faith.

[21]A good example is the Plymouth Brethren who, while carrying sectarian trappings, identify themselves as orthodox in the Reformation and evangelical tradition.

[22]For an excellent overall analysis of the believers' church through Christian history, see Donald F. Durnbaugh, *The Believers' Church: the History and Character of Radical Protestantism* (New York: Macmillan, 1968). According to Durnbaugh the believers' church fuses the concerns of sects and spiritualist or mystical movements.

[23]Emil Brunner, *Truth as Encounter,* trans. Amandus W. Loos and David Cairns, rev. ed. (Philadelphia: Westminster Press, 1964), pp. 78-79.

[24]On the Pietistic roots of Kierkegaard's faith, see Vernard Eller, *Kierkegaard and Radical Discipleship* (Princeton, N.J.: Princeton University Press, 1968), pp. 31-40.

[25]Robert Bretall, ed., *A Kierkegaard Anthology* (Princeton, N.J.: Princeton University Press, 1947), p. 397.

[26]Brunner, *Truth as Encounter,* pp. 65-129.

[27]Ibid., p. 175.

[28]Ibid., p. 169.

[29]See Martin Marty, "Headline News," *The Christian Century* 117, no. 27 (2000): 1023.

Chapter 11: The Diversity of Ministries

[1]M. H. Shepherd Jr., "Bishop," in *Interpreter's Dictionary of the Bible,* ed. George A. Buttrick (Nashville: Abingdon, 1962), 1:441.

[2]Walter Brueggemann, "Rethinking Church Models Through Scripture," *Theology Today* 48, no. 2 (July 1991): 129. For a vigorous defense by evangelical authors of the position that the NT teaches a normative form of church gov-

ernment, see David J. MacLeod, "The Primacy of Scripture and the Church," and John H. Fish III, "The Life of the Local Church," *Emmaus Journal* 6, no. 1 (1997): 3-96.

[3]*Baptism, Eucharist and Ministry,* Faith and Order Paper No. 111, preface by William H. Lazareth and Nikos Nissiotis (Geneva: World Council of Churches, 1982), p. 24.

[4]Hans Küng, *The Church,* trans. Ray and Rosaleen Ockenden (New York: Sheed & Ward, 1967), p. 410.

[5]Ibid., p. 363.

[6]Ibid., p. 401.

[7]M. H. Shepherd Jr., "Christian Ministry," in *Interpreter's Dictionary of the Bible,* 3:386.

[8]Küng, *The Church,* p. 439.

[9]P. T. Forsyth, *The Church and the Sacraments* (1917; reprint, London: Independent Press, 1947), p. 133.

[10]See Brother Lawrence, *The Practice of the Presence of God* (Westwood, N.J.: Fleming H. Revell, 1958).

[11]The church is, of course, both a fellowship and an institution, but the former has a certain precedence. If the church had no institutional manifestation, it would lack tangibility and would be threatened by dissolution. If the church were only an institution, it would no longer be the holy catholic church, for it would lack vitality and animation. For my earlier discussion see pp. 70-75.

[12]See Donald G. Bloesch, *Wellsprings of Renewal* (Grand Rapids, Mich.: Eerdmans, 1974), pp. 36-37.

[13] Ibid. pp. 38-51.

[14]See Donald G. Bloesch, *Centers of Christian Renewal* (Philadelphia: United Church Press, 1964); *Wellsprings of Renewal* (1974); Lydia Präger, ed. *Frei für Gott und die Menschen* (1959; rev. ed., Stuttgart: Quell-Verlag, 1964); François Biot, *The Rise of Protestant Monasticism,* trans. W. J. Kerrigan (Baltimore, Md.: Helicon, 1963); Siegfried von Kortzfleisch, *Mitten im Herzen der Massen* (Stuttgart: Kreuz-Verlag, 1963); Olive Wyon, *Living Springs* (Philadelphia: Westminster Press, 1963); and Arthur Paul Boers, "Learning the Ancient Rhythms of Prayer," *Christianity Today* 45, no. 1 (2001): 38-45.

[15]The Jesus Fellowship Church, the New Creation Christian Community and *Jesus Life* magazine all belong to the same renewal movement in the United Kingdom.

[16]One cannot help but observe that the religious community in the Protestant context gravitates in the direction of sectarianism. A community can successfully meet this threat by seeking for its board of directors or council of advisors leaders and theologians in the historic Christian churches who share their vision.

[17]The Community of Taizé is suspect in the eyes of many evangelicals for focusing the service of worship on the eucharist rather than on the Word. Exegetical, kerygmatic preaching is rare at Taizé. Ecumenical Bible study is, however, very much encouraged. For a positive appraisal of both Taizé and Iona, see

Belden C. Lane, "The Whole World Singing: A Journey to Iona, and Taizé," *The Christian Century* 117, no. 10 (2000): 336-41.

[18]Ernst Troeltsch, *Christian Thought: Its History and Application,* ed. Baron Von Hügel (New York: Meridian, 1957), p. 143.

[19]Ibid.

[20]R. Lejeune, ed. *Christoph Blumhardt and His Message* (Rifton, N.Y.: Plough, 1963), p. 81.

[21]D. Elton Trueblood, *Signs of Hope in a Century of Despair* (New York: Harper & Bros, 1950), p. 122.

[22]See Werner Neuer, *Man and Woman in Christian Perspective,* trans. Gordon J. Wenham (Wheaton, Ill.: Crossway, 1991), pp. 67-68.

[23]Gerhard von Rad, *Genesis,* trans. John H. Marks (Philadelphia: Westminster Press, 1961), p. 80.

[24]Quoted in Neuer, *Man and Woman,* p. 92.

[25]Ibid.

[26]The similar advice of Paul in 1 Cor 14:34 is possibly aimed at controlling glossolalia in the assembly of the congregation. It seems that more women than men were involved in this practice.

[27]Cf. Markus Barth: "'Subordination' can be an attitude and action of free equal agents, not the breaking of will and the submission to shameful thralldom." *Ephesians 4-6* (1974; reprint, New York: Doubleday, 1982) p. 710.

[28]R. Paul Stevens, "Breaking the Gender Impasse," *Christianity Today* 36, no. 1 (1992): 31.

[29]Christ exercises his lordship in the role of a servant (Mk 10:42-45; Lk 22:27; Mt 20:26-28), so it can be said that in his life and teachings he transforms, even overturns, the cultural meaning of lordship.

[30]With Teresa of Ávila and Thérèse of Lisieux, Catherine of Siena has been named a doctor of the church and therefore a trustworthy teacher of both men and women.

[31]Karl Barth's position seems to be that the order of relationship in which man and woman are created remains the same even when their social roles may vary somewhat. Whatever the circumstances of life man and woman remain interlocked. Both remain dependent on each other, but in different ways.

[32]Wayne G. Boulton, *Out of Step: The Family, American Society, and the Christian Gospel* (Lanham, Md.: University Press of America, 1992), p. 44.

[33]Cf. Markus Barth: "In Paul's teaching the oneness of 'male and female in Christ' (Gal 3:28) means their union and peace, not their intermixture and amalgamation." Barth, *Ephesians 4-6,* p. 753.

[34]Jacques Ellul, *What I Believe,* trans. Geoffrey W. Bromiley (Grand Rapids, Mich.: Eerdmans, 1989), p. 82.

[35]Tertullian, *Treatises on Marriage and Remarriage,* trans. William P. Le Saint (Westminster, Md.: Newman Press, 1956), p. 35.

[36]Stevens, "Breaking the Gender Impasse," p. 28.

[37]I affirm that with the coming of Christ the command to be fruitful and multiply is superseded by the command to preach the gospel to the whole creation. In

the order of redemption we are children of Abraham not by blood or race but by faith. The purpose of marriage in the Christian context is to beget spiritual children for Jesus Christ. Children of the flesh are still great blessings, but unless they are born anew through the Spirit, they do not inherit the promises of God to his people.

[38]This passage clearly indicates that not only celibacy but marriage in the Lord is a gift of grace.

[39]Quoted in Paul Evdokimov, *The Sacrament of Love,* trans. Anthony P. Gythiel and Victoria Steadman (Crestwood, N.Y.: St. Vladimir's Seminary Press, 1985), p. 120.

[40]In both Lutheran and Reformed Orthodoxy celibacy was not depreciated but regarded as an exceptional or extraordinary gift imparted only to a few. See Arthur Carl Piepkorn, "The Theologians of Lutheran Orthodoxy on Polygamy, Celibacy and Divorce," *Concordia Theological Monthly* 25, no. 4 (April 1954): 276-83. According to Piepkorn, in the Age of Orthodoxy theologians commonly held that celibacy was "a greater work and a more eminent gift than matrimony" (p. 276). Also see the Second Helvetic Confession, *Book of Confessions* (Louisville, Ky.: Office of the General Assembly, Presbyterian Church [U.S.A.], 1991), 5:245.

[41]Ernst Troeltsch, *The Social Teaching of the Christian Churches,* trans. Olive Wyon (1931; reprint, New York: Macmillan, 1950), 2:865.

[42]See *Luther's Works,* ed. and trans. Theodore G. Tappert (Philadelphia: Fortress, 1967), 54:23, 25, 223, 324, 444.

[43]Outstanding examples of how marriage can be translated into partnership in ministry are George Fox and Margaret Fell, luminaries of Quakerism; William and Catherine Booth, cofounders of the Salvation Army; Francis and Edith Schaeffer, who organized and directed L'Abri Fellowship; and Archer and Jane Torrey, who together put into tangible form the vision of Jesus Abbey, an evangelical renewal community in South Korea. In Catholicism we can point to Dorothy Day and Peter Maurin, who spearheaded the Catholic Worker movement, though these two worked together not as a married couple but as brother and sister in the Lord.

[44]In Ruth A. Tucker, "'Unbecoming' Ladies," *Christian History* Issue 52 (vol. 15, no. 4): 30.

[45]See Karl Barth, *Church Dogmatics,* ed. G. W. Bromiley and T. F. Torrance, trans. A. T. Mackay et al. (1961; reprint, Edinburgh: T. & T. Clark, 1978), 3(4):116-240. See esp. 141ff.

[46]Ibid., p. 223.

[47]Ibid., p. 189.

[48]Ibid., p. 188.

[49]Ibid., p. 148.

[50]See Max Thurian, *Marriage and Celibacy,* trans. Norma Emerton (London: SCM Press, 1959).

[51]Ibid., pp. 114-15.

[52]Ibid., p. 105.

⁵³Ibid., p. 11.

⁵⁴Contra Thurian, celibacy does not necessarily free one for service, though this may be the ideal. It can burden people with new cares. The arduous work of maintaining a religious community may actually allow little time for mission to the world outside. Celibates who try to fend for themselves are sometimes less available for service to the world than their married counterparts who have the loving support of a family. On the other hand, celibates (and also childless couples) who devote themselves to the cause of the kingdom may be blessed with spiritual brothers and sisters and spiritual children, all of whom may even help provide for their material needs. It is only the divine command that actually gives people freedom for service, and if this command is lacking, neither marriage nor celibacy will make us free, but only lead us into greater bondage.

⁵⁵Robert Bretall, ed., *A Kierkegaard Anthology* (Princeton, N.J.: Princeton University Press, 1947), pp. 116-29.

⁵⁶Quoted in Barth, *Church Dogmatics,* 3(4):141.

⁵⁷Alexander Schmemann, *For the Life of the World* (New York: National Student Christian Federation, 1963), p. 67.

Chapter 12: The Gospel in a Syncretistic Age

¹For my earlier discussion, see Donald G. Bloesch, *Essentials of Evangelical Theology* (San Francisco: Harper & Row, 1978), 2:155-73; *Jesus Christ: Savior & Lord* (Downers Grove, Ill.: InterVarsity Press, 1997), pp. 229-49.

²Friedrich Schleiermacher, *On Religion: Speeches to its Cultured Despisers,* trans. John Oman (New York: Harper & Row, 1958), p. 242.

³Ibid., pp. 174-75.

⁴In H. R. Mackintosh, *Types of Modern Theology* (1937; reprint, London: Nisbet, 1949), p. 183.

⁵Ibid., p. 184.

⁶For a powerful affirmation of a new kind of Christianity interpreted through the lens of pluralism, see Gordon D. Kaufman, *God—Mystery—Diversity* (Minneapolis: Fortress, 1996). Kaufman claims that he is more consistently pluralistic than John Hick (see p. 225).

⁷Quoted in Hendrik Kraemer, *Religion and the Christian Faith* (London: Lutterworth, 1956), p. 61.

⁸S. Radhakrishnan, *The Heart of Hindustan* (Madras: G. A. Natesan & Co., 1983), p. 3.

⁹Gerald Heard "The Philosophia Perennis," in *Vedanta for the Western World,* ed. Christopher Isherwood (New York: Viking, 1945), p. 297.

¹⁰Quoted by Parker T. Williamson, "Sophia Upstages Jesus Christ at the 1998 ReImagining Revival," *Presbyterian Layman* 31, no. 3 (1998): 17.

¹¹Sylvia Dooling, "ReImagining 'Gospel' Is a Message Without Hope," *Presbyterian Layman* 31, no. 3 (1998): 18.

¹²Rosemary Radford Ruether, "Feminism and Jewish-Christian Dialogue," in *The Myth of Christian Uniqueness,* ed. John Hick and Paul Knitter (Maryknoll, N.Y.: Orbis, 1987), p. 141.

[13]Diogenes Allen, *Christian Belief in a Postmodern World* (Louisville, Ky.: Westminster John Knox, 1989), p. 9.

[14]Richard Rorty, *Consequences of Pragmatism* (Minneapolis: University of Minnesota Press, 1982), p. xlii.

[15]Alister E. McGrath, "The Challenge of Pluralism for the Contemporary Christian Church," in *Proceedings of the Wheaton Theology Conference: The Challenge of Religious Pluralism* (Spring 1992) 1:241.

[16]Ibid., p. 245.

[17]Mackintosh, *Types of Modern Theology*, p. 185.

[18]Clark Pinnock, *A Wideness in God's Mercy: The Finality of Jesus Christ in a World of Religions* (Grand Rapids, Mich.: Zondervan, 1992), p. 158.

[19]Quoted in Robert J. Rubanowice, *Crisis in Consciousness: The Thought of Ernst Troeltsch* (Tallahassee: University Presses of Florida, 1982), p. 50.

[20]Ibid., p. 51.

[21]Mackintosh, *Types of Modern Theology*, pp. 190-91.

[22]Ibid., p. 199. Note that this is Mackintosh's interpretation of Troeltsch.

[23]See Paul Tillich, "Symbol and Knowledge," *The Journal of Liberal Religion* 2, no. 4 (Spring 1941): 204.

[24]Ernst Troeltsch, *The Absoluteness of Christianity and the History of Religions*, trans. David Reid, introduction by James Luther Adams (Richmond, Va.: John Knox Press, 1971), p. 114.

[25]Ibid., p. 126.

[26]Ernst Troeltsch, *The Christian Faith*, ed. Gertrud von le Fort, trans. Garrett E. Paul (Minneapolis: Fortress, 1991), p. 299.

[27]Quoted in Rubanowice, *Crisis in Consciousness*, p. 35. From "Die Mission in der modernen Welt" (1906).

[28]*Crisis in Consciousness*, p. 98.

[29]Troeltsch was a syncretist in the sense that he believed that Christianity borrowed much of its theology and social philosophy from the Greco-Roman world, esp. Platonism and Stoicism.

[30]For the residue of nationalism in Troeltsch's thought see Rubanowice, *Crisis in Consciousness*, pp. 99-130. It should be noted that Troeltsch was not numbered among the ninety-three intellectuals who lent official support to the Kaiser's war policy. See *Ernst Troeltsch: Writings on Theology and Religion*, trans. and ed. Robert Morgan and Michael Pye (Atlanta: John Knox Press, 1977), p. 41 n. 200. At the same time it seems that he succumbed to the nationalistic fervor at the beginning of World War I when he exhorted his fellow countrymen: "Be German, remain German, become German!" *Crisis in Consciousness*, p. 102.

[31]Jürgen Moltmann, "Christianity in the Third Millennium," *Theology Today* 51, no. 1 (1994): 89.

[32]See Jürgen Moltmann et al., *A Passion for God's Reign*, ed. Miroslav Volf (Grand Rapids, Mich.: Eerdmans, 1998), p. 51.

[33]Moltmann, "Christianity in the Third Millennium," p. 89.

[34]Moltmann, *A Passion for God's Reign*, p. 61.

[35]Ibid., p. 62.

[36]Ibid., p. 63.

[37]Ibid., p. 62.

[38]Ibid.

[39]Ibid., p. 2.

[40]Ibid., p. 71. These are Nicholas Wolterstorff's words.

[41]Ibid., p. 72. Wolterstorff here gives his interpretation of Moltmann, which I believe to be correct.

[42]Jürgen Moltmann, *The Power of the Powerless,* trans. Margaret Kohl (San Francisco: Harper & Row, 1983), p. 120.

[43]Ibid., p. 142.

[44]Ibid., p. 161.

[45]Ibid.

[46]For my earlier discussion, see Donald G. Bloesch, *Essentials of Evangelical Theology,* 2:155-73; and *Freedom for Obedience* (San Francisco: Harper & Row, 1987), pp. 153-65.

[47]James R. Edwards, "A Confessional Church in a Pluralistic World," *Proceedings of the Wheaton Theology Conference,* 1:95.

[48]P. T. Forsyth, *The Church and the Sacraments* (1917; 2nd ed., London: Independent Press, 1947), p. 38.

[49]Karl Barth, *Church Dogmatics,* ed. G. W. Bromiley and T. F. Torrance, trans. G. W. Bromiley (1962; reprint, Edinburgh: T. & T. Clark, 1980), 4 (3/2):874.

[50]Ibid., p. 846.

[51]Karl Jaspers, *Philosophical Faith and Revelation,* trans. E. B. Ashton (New York: Harper & Row, 1967), p. 317.

[52]Rubanowice, *Crisis in Consciousness,* p. 85. Note these are the words of Rubanowice.

[53]See Kaufman, *God—Mystery—Diversity,* p. 66. Against Kaufman I would argue that while our religious reflection is assuredly never a direct expression of divine revelation, it can be a faithful rendition of this revelation.

Chapter 13: Toward the Reunion of the Churches

[1]See "WCC Celebrates 50th Anniversary," *The Christian Century* 115, no. 24 (1998): 817.

[2]Quoted in Carl Braaten, *Mother Church: Ecclesiology and Ecumenism* (Minneapolis: Fortress, 1998), p. 96. Dietrich Bonhoeffer, *Gesammelte Schriften* (Munich: Kaiser Verlag, 1966), 3:206.

[3]Harold O. J. Brown, "Repentance or Ruse?" *The Religion and Society Report* 15, no. 9 (1998): 3.

[4]Jaroslav Pelikan, *The Riddle of Roman Catholicism* (Nashville: Abingdon, 1959), pp. 45-57.

[5]See *The Oxford Dictionary of the Christian Church,* ed. F. L. Cross, 2nd ed. (New York: Oxford University Press, 1983), p. 1160.

[6]*Luther's Works,* ed. Jaroslav Pelikan (St. Louis: Concordia, 1958), 1:254.

[7]*Johannes Calvini Opera, Corpus Reformatorum,* 13.487. Cited in G. C. Berkou-

wer, *The Church,* trans. James E. Davison (Grand Rapids, Mich.: Eerdmans, 1976), p. 66.

[8]John Calvin, *Institutes of the Christian Religion,* ed. John T. McNeill, trans. Ford Lewis Battles, 2 vols. (Philadelphia: Westminster Press, 1960), 4.2.12 (2:1052).

[9]See Jack Miller, "Waking up the Lutherans, Evangelical," *The Concord* (March 12, 1994):5.

[10]Jeffrey C. Silleck, "A More Radical Proposal," *Lutheran Forum* 32, no. 1 (1998): 31.

[11]See James Hastings Nichols, *Romanticism in American Theology* (Chicago: University of Chicago Press, 1961).

[12]Thomas Hopko, *All the Fulness of God* (Crestwood, N.Y.: St. Vladimir's Seminary Press, 1982), p. 100.

[13]In Trevor Hart, ed., *Justice the True and Only Mercy* (Edinburgh: T. & T. Clark, 1995), p. 140.

[14]Friedrich Schleiermacher, *On Religion: Speeches to Its Cultured Despisers,* trans. John Oman (New York: Harper & Row, 1958), p. 175.

[15]Quoted in William Kuhns, *In Pursuit of Dietrich Bonhoeffer* (Dayton, Ohio: Pflaum, 1967), p. 66.

[16]Joseph Fitzmyer, *Romans,* Anchor Bible (New York: Doubleday, 1993), pp. 117-18.

[17]Wolfhart Pannenberg, *Christian Spirituality* (Philadelphia: Westminster Press, 1983), pp. 20-30.

[18]*Catechism of the Catholic Church* (United States Catholic Conference, 1994).

[19]See Max Thurian, *Mary, Mother of the Lord, Figure of the Church,* trans. Neville B. Cryer (London: Faith Press, 1963), pp. 172-73; and Thomas A. O'Meara, *Mary in Protestant and Catholic Theology* (New York: Sheed & Ward, 1966), pp. 111-45.

[20]See *Luther's Works,* ed. and trans. John W. Doberstein (Philadelphia: Muhlenberg, 1959), 51:115. Cf.: "Let the monks fast, pray, and dress differently from the rest of the Christian people. Let them do this, that is, and even more to tame the flesh and put it to death. But let them not attribute to these disciplines the function of justifying in the sight of God." *Luther's Works,* ed. Jaroslav Pelikan (St. Louis: Concordia, 1963), 26:308.

[21]Hans Küng, *The Church,* trans. Ray and Rosaleen Ockenden (New York: Sheed & Ward, 1967), p. 34.

[22]Paul Tillich, *Systematic Theology* (Chicago: University of Chicago Press, 1963), 3:239, 245.

[23]Emil Brunner, *Our Faith,* trans. John W. Rilling (New York: Charles Scribner's Sons, 1954), p. 126.

[24]Dietrich Bonhoeffer, *No Rusty Swords,* trans. Edwin H. Robertson and John Bowden (New York: Harper & Row, 1965), p. 117.

[25]See Heiko Oberman, *The Harvest of Medieval Theology* (Grand Rapids, Mich.: Eerdmans, 1967), pp. 361-422.

[26]Richard P. McBrien, "Tradition Still in Shadow of Scripture," *National Catholic Reporter* 32, no. 13 (Jan. 26, 1996): 16.

[27]This does not imply that a creedless church is superior to a creedal church, only that the creed should serve rather than cloud the message of faith.

[28]Quoted in Braaten, *Mother Church*, p. 13.

[29]Philip Schaff, *Christ and Christianity* (New York: Charles Scribner's Sons, 1885), p. 16.

[30]Michael Horton, *We Believe* (Nashville: Word, 1998), p. 195.

[31]P. T. Forsyth, *The Church and the Sacraments* (1917; 2nd ed., London: Independent Press, 1947), p. 38.

[32]*The Book of Confessions* (Louisville, Ky.: Office of the General Assembly, Presbyterian Church [U.S.A.], 1991), 5:141.

[33]Barth sees the two basic dimensions of sin as pride and sloth. While he wishes to regard them as equally important, Barth especially in his later phase highlighted the sin of sloth. He can even entertain the notion that sloth lies at the heart of pride and is its final basis, though he cautions against subordinating one kind of sin to another. He acknowledges that sloth has often been neglected in Protestantism, which tends to focus attention on the heroic, Promethean form of sin—pride and arrogance. See *Church Dogmatics,* ed. G. W. Bromiley and T. F. Torrance, trans. G. W. Bromiley (Edinburgh: T. & T. Clark, 1958), 4(2):403-4.

Chapter 14: A Confessing Church

[1]"The Theological Declaration of Barmen," *The Book of Confessions* (Louisville, Ky.: Office of the General Assembly, Presbyterian Church [U.S.A.], 1991), 8.01-8.28. Also see Rolf Ahlers, *The Barmen Theological Declaration of 1934* (Lewiston, N.Y.: Edwin Mellen, 1986); Arthur C. Cochrane, *The Church's Confession Under Hitler* (Philadelphia: Westminster Press, 1962); and Ulrich Mauser, "The Theological Declaration of Barmen Revisited," *Theology Matters* 6, no. 6 (November/December 2000): 1-16.

[2]See Arthur C. Cochrane, *The Church's Confession Under Hitler,* pp. 181, 187; Cochrane, "Barmen: The Church Between Temptation and Grace," *On the Way* 3, no. 1 (Summer 1985): 2-11; and *UCC-EKU Newsletter* 16, no. 1 (November 1998).

[3]See Thomas A. Schafer, "The Beginnings of Confessional Subscription in the Presbyterian Church," *McCormick Quarterly* 19, no. 2 (1966): 114.

[4]For the UCC Statement of Faith see Arthur C. Piepkorn, *Profiles in Belief* (New York: Harper & Row, 1978), 2:669.

[5]Cf. Cochrane: "A Confession of Faith is a confession of *the one, holy, catholic, and apostolic Church.* It is not the Confession of an individual theologian, of a party within the Church, or even of a particular denomination or group of denominations. It speaks for the whole Church to the whole Church." *Church's Confession Under Hitler,* p. 185.

[6]Karl Barth, *The Word of God and the Word of Man,* trans. Douglas Horton (Gloucester, Mass.: Peter Smith, 1978), p. 225.

[7]Arthur Cochrane, "Barmen and the Confession of 1967," *McCormick Quarterly* 19, no. 2 (January 1966): 138.

[8]*The Orthodox Evangelicals,* ed. Robert Webber and Donald Bloesch (Nashville: Thomas Nelson, 1978), p. 77.

[9]*The Book of Confessions* (1991), 8.06.

[10]Cochrane, *Church's Confession Under Hitler,* p. 215.

[11]For my earlier discussion, see Donald G. Bloesch, *The Holy Spirit* (Downers Grove, Ill.: InterVarsity Press, 2000), pp. 144-46.

[12]Brian Gerrish, "The Confessional Heritage of the Reformed Church," *McCormick Quarterly* 19, no. 2 (1966): 131.

[13]Cochrane, *Church's Confession Under Hitler,* p. 210.

[14]Ibid., p. 182.

[15]Bruce McCormack of Princeton Seminary contends that the church today is confronted by a heresy that "constitutes as great a threat as the church has seen since second century Gnosticism." Yet he believes that in the present situation the best approach is to describe the nature of a *status confessionis* and allow people "to draw their own conclusions" (letter to Donald Bloesch, Oct. 13, 1998). Ralph Wood of Baylor University opines that we need a new Barmen Declaration that will counter "the soft-core spirituality that saps much of contemporary Christianity, especially in its evangelical expression." Ralph C. Wood, "In Defense of Disbelief," *First Things* no. 86 (Oct. 1998): 28-33. Also see Gabriel Fackre, *Restoring the Center* (Downers Grove, Ill.: InterVarsity Press, 1998), pp. 31-32.

[16]This motto originated among Reformed Christians of the Netherlands in the early seventeenth century and belongs to the ethos of proto-Pietism. See Jean-Jacques Bauswein and Lukas Vischer, eds., *The Reformed Family Worldwide* (Grand Rapids, Mich.: Eerdmans, 1999), p. 32. The fuller expression of this motto includes *secundum verbum Dei* (according to the Word of God).

[17]H. Richard Niebuhr, Wilhelm Pauck and Francis P. Miller, *The Church Against the World* (Chicago: Willett, Clark & Co., 1935).

[18]Jacques Ellul, *Living Faith: Belief and Doubt in a Perilous World,* trans. Peter Heinegg (San Francisco: Harper & Row, 1983), p. 230.

[19]See Donald G. Bloesch, *Freedom for Obedience* (San Francisco: Harper & Row, 1987), pp. 248-86.

[20]Alvin Toffler, *The Third Wave* (New York: Morrow, 1980).

[21]John Paul II, *Fides Et Ratio* (Boston: Pauline Books & Media, 1998).

[22]See my in-depth critique of the papal encyclical in *The Princeton Theological Review* 6, no. 4 (Fall 1999): 30-31.

[23]Adolf von Harnack, *Thoughts on the Present Position of Protestantism,* trans. Thomas Bailey Saunders (London: Adam & Charles Black, 1899), p. 59.

[24]Gerrish, "Confessional Heritage of the Reformed Church," p. 127.

[25]Cochrane, "Barmen and the Confession of 1967," p. 138.

[26]Cochrane, *Church's Confession Under Hitler,* p. 212.

[27]Ibid., p. 193.

[28]See James Montgomery Boice and Benjamin E. Sasse, eds., *Here We Stand! A Call from Confessing Evangelicals* (Grand Rapids, Mich.: Baker, 1996), pp. 14-20. For my earlier discussion, see Donald G. Bloesch, *The Holy Spirit* (Downers

Grove, Ill.: InterVarsity Press, 2000), pp. 340, 344.

[29]Cf. Cochrane: "A Confession of Faith, as the voice of the one, holy, catholic Church, *reflects its unity and continuity with the Church of the Fathers.*" *Church's Confession Under Hitler,* p. 187.

[30]Boice and Sasse, eds., *Here We Stand!* thesis 1, p. 16.

[31]Ibid., p. 20.

[32]French Catholic theologian Louis Bouyer wrote a helpful book, *The Spirit and Forms of Protestantism,* trans. A. V. Littledale (Westminster, Md.: Newman, 1961), in which he presented a credible case that the essential principles of the Reformation, including the sovereign authority of Scripture, are authentic Catholic beliefs as well.

To hold that the barriers between the two communions are insuperable, especially with regard to the doctrine of justification, would be to hold that a renowned theologian like Augustine is not a brother in Christ. Admittedly Augustine's emphasis was more on the mystical than the forensic side of justification.

[33]See George Hunsinger, *How to Read Karl Barth* (New York: Oxford University Press, 1991), pp. 185-224.

[34]Cf. Cochrane: "A Confession of Faith not only is relevant for the Church's own doctrine and life but *bears definite implications for concrete social and political issues.* This is the *ethical* character of a Confession. It possesses both ecclesiastical and secular significance." *Church's Confession Under Hitler,* p. 206.

[35]Regrettably the Declaration fails to come to grips with the issue of the role of weapons of mass extermination in warfare. Ervin Duggan questions the wisdom of treating nuclear disarmament as a major moral issue (Boice and Sasse, eds., *Here We Stand!* p. 50), but surely this is an issue that Christians committed to right to life must address. A critique of postmodernity is welcome, but it needs to be expanded to cover the nihilism inherent in nuclear war.

[36]In one or other of the eight papers that support the Cambridge Declaration there is some awareness of these problems. Yet even where radical feminism is countered, the issue of language about God is not dealt with at all. See Boice and Sasse, eds., *Here We Stand!*

[37]A genuine confession of faith will not simply repeat what the church said in the past but articulate a new vision of the faith that nevertheless stands in continuity with what has gone before.

[38]"The Gospel of Jesus Christ: An Evangelical Celebration," *Christianity Today* 43, no. 7 (1999): 51-56. Also see *This We Believe: The Good News of Jesus Christ for the World,* ed. John N. Akers, John H. Armstrong and John D. Woodbridge (Grand Rapids, Mich.: Zondervan, 2000); Robert H. Gundry, "Why I Didn't Endorse 'The Gospel of Jesus Christ: An Evangelical Celebration,'" *Books and Culture* 7, no. 1 (2001): 6-9; and Thomas C. Oden, "A Calm Answer," and Robert H. Gundry, "On Oden's 'Answer'," *Books and Culture* 7, no. 2 (2001): 12-15, 39. I share Oden's discomfort with Gundry's attack on "Celebration."

[39]Roger E. Olson and Gabriel Fackre, "Evangelical Essentials? Reservations and Reminders," *Christian Century* 116, no. 23 (1999): 816-19.

[40]The writers of this document are in my opinion correct in contending that out-right rejection of truths like the incarnation of God in Christ places the soul in jeopardy (cf. Jn 8:24; 12:48; 1 Jn 4:2-3). But we cannot thereby assert that sub-scription to this or any doctrine is a necessary condition for salvation. Nor can we hold that explicit denial of certain doctrines insures the damnation of the person in question. I particularly differ from the authors in their assertion that anyone who refuses to treat the sinlessness of Jesus as an essential of the faith cannot be saved. I regard this doctrine as an integral truth of faith, but someone who has theological difficulties with this doctrine and yet who accepts Jesus as the incarnate Lord and Savior surely is still called by God and justified by his blood. At least we must not deny the possibility that such a per-son may indeed be saved! What finally saves is being in a personal relation-ship with Christ based on trust in his mercy.

[41]Fackre is willing to affirm the particularity of the claims of the gospel but within "the context of raised awareness of religious pluralism" ("Evangelical Essentials?" p. 818).

Appendix 1

[1]"The Cambridge Declaration," in *Here We Stand! A Call from Confessing Evangelicals,* ed. James Montgomery Boice and Benjamin Sasse (Grand Rapids, Mich.: Baker, 1996).

Name Index

Adam, Karl, *18, 47, 310*
Adams, James Luther, *190, 328, 334*
Ahlers, Rolf, *337*
Akers, John N., *305, 339*
Allen, Diogenes, *238, 334*
Althaus, Paul, *233*
Ames, William, *18, 306*
Ankerberg, John, *305*
Anselm, *285*
Aquinas, Thomas, *48, 128, 149, 150, 311*
Aristotle, *125, 150*
Armstrong, John, *305, 339*
Arndt, Johann, *196*
Arnold, Eberhard, *97*
Arnold, Emmy, *316*
Arnold, Gottfried, *95, 106*
Arnold, J. Heinrich, *106, 115, 317, 318*
Atkinson, James, *324*
Augustine, *57, 69, 71, 90, 147, 149, 151, 229, 313, 339*
Baillie, John, *322*
Balthasar, Hans Urs von, *46, 323, 324*
Barth, Karl, *1, 17, 20, 21, 24, 28, 29, 30, 31, 36, 38, 46, 53, 54, 57, 60, 72, 78, 89, 93, 114, 118, 152, 153, 188, 224, 230, 231, 232, 243, 244, 249, 259, 260, 269, 272, 279, 282, 307, 308, 309, 312, 314, 316, 318, 322, 327*
Barth, Markus, *73, 314, 331*

Battles, Ford Lewis, *317, 319, 336*
Beare, Francis W., *155*
Beasley-Murray, G. R., *322*
Behan, Hugh, *173*
Beissel, Johann Conrad, *212*
Bengel, Johann Albrecht, *87, 315*
Berkouwer, G. C., *13, 265, 320, 336*
Bethge, Eberhard, *317, 326*
Bianchi, Eugene, *32, 308*
Biot, François, *330*
Blamires, Harry, *312*
Bloesch, Daniel, *326*
Bloom, Harold, *131, 319*
Blumhardt, Christoph, *41, 70, 217, 235, 309*
Boers, Arthur Paul, *330*
Boff, Leonardo, *28*
Boice, James Montgomery, *339*
Bonhoeffer, Dietrich, *13, 25, 35, 72, 80, 92, 95, 106, 116, 170, 171, 181, 202, 203, 252, 257, 260, 261, 265, 279, 307, 308, 313, 315, 316, 317, 318, 326, 328, 336*
Booth, Catherine, *223, 332*
Booth, Evangeline, *223*
Booth, William, *105, 332*
Boulton, Wayne, *224, 331*
Bouyer, Louis, *339*
Bowden, John, *308*
Braaten, Carl, *1, 43, 255, 274, 306, 310, 317, 324, 335*
Bretall, Robert, *329, 333*

Bridge, Donald, *322*
Bromiley, G. W., *306, 312, 319, 328, 335*
Brown, Frank Burch, *321*
Brown, Harold O. J., *335*
Brueggemann, Walter, *205, 329*
Brunner, Emil, *13, 27, 28, 51, 52, 53, 73, 99, 189, 196, 199, 200, 261, 311, 329, 336*
Bucer, Martin, *104, 151*
Bullinger, Johann Heinrich, *67, 259*
Cairns, David, *322, 329*
Calvin, John, *1, 17, 21, 50, 51, 55, 60, 71, 82, 101, 104, 105, 126, 151, 155, 157, 161, 231, 254, 282, 309, 311, 316, 317, 319, 322*
Campenhausen, Hans von, *27*
Carmichael, Amy, *213*
Carson, D. A., *305*
Cary, Phillip, *321*
Catherine of Siena, *223, 331*
Christian, C. W., *306*
Chrysostom, John, *229, 317*
Clark, Walter Houston, *324*
Cochrane, Arthur C., *269, 274, 278, 279, 324, 337, 338, 339*
Colson, Charles, *310*
Colyer, Elmer, *306*
Congar, Yves, *31, 89, 315*
Cooke, Bernard J., *309*
Cox, Harvey, *32, 308*
Crosby, Fanny, *312*
Cullman, Oscar, *90, 316*

Cutsinger, James S.,
310, 318
Cyprian, 310
Davy, Keith, 305
Day, Dorothy, 332
Descartes, René, 241
De Vries, Dawn, 55,
312
Doberstein, John W.,
336
Duggan, Ervin, 339
Dulles, Avery Cardinal,
40, 77, 100, 102, 307,
309, 310, 314, 316,
317
Dunnam, Maxie, 305
Durnbaugh, Donald F.,
329
Edwards, James R.,
178, 248, 335
Ehrlich, Rudolf J., 312
Eller, Vernard, 323, 329
Ellul, Jacques, 275, 319,
331, 338
Elwell, Walter A., 311,
321
Espinoza, Eddie, 320
Evdokimov, Paul, 41,
309, 332
Fackre, Gabriel, 283,
285, 286, 338, 340
Fagerberg, David, 308
Farley, Edward, 116,
318
Fell, Margaret, 332
Ferguson, Duncan, 308
Fernandez, Francis, 48,
66, 311
Finney, Charles, 167
Fitzmyer, Joseph, 257,
336
Florovsky, Georges, 46,
73, 117
Forsyth, Peter T., 1, 13,
17, 24, 27, 36, 41, 43,
45, 46, 64, 69, 76, 77,
78, 79, 82, 88, 95, 100,
105, 116, 117, 147,
151, 152, 178, 189,

195, 204, 207, 235,
249, 256, 263, 265,
307, 310, 312, 314,
315, 316, 318, 319,
321, 322, 329, 335
Fox, George, 332
Frame, John M., 320
Frederick William III,
King, 256
Gandhi, Mahatma, 237
George, Timothy, 42,
305
Gerrish, Brian, 272,
278, 338
Gestrich, Christof, 114,
318
Giertz, Bo, 178
Graham, Billy, 264
Graham, Stephen R.,
310
Green, Michael, 37,
155, 309, 322
Gregory the Great,
Pope, 210
Guinness, Os, 185
Gundry, Robert H., 339,
340
Guthrie, Shirley C., Jr.,
325
Hafemann, Scott, 305
Harlow, S. Ralph, 97,
316
Harnack, Adolf von,
278
Hart, D. G., 328
Hart, Trevor, 310, 317,
336
Harwood, Larry D., 321
Heard, Gerald, 237, 333
Hegel, Georg Wilhelm
Friedrich, 79, 96, 240,
244
Heick, Otto W., 310
Heiler, Friedrich, 317
Heyward, Carter, 237
Hick, John, 236, 308,
333
Hodgson, Peter, 32, 33,
308

Holifield, E. Brooks,
325
Hopko, Thomas, 255,
336
Horton, Michael, 69,
78, 122, 136, 174,
263, 314, 318, 320,
327
How, William
Walsham, 316
Hunsinger, Deborah
van Deusen, 325
Hunsinger, George,
282, 325, 339
Huxley, Aldous, 237
Ignatius of Antioch, 99
Irenaeus, 99, 120, 309
Jaspers, Karl, 249, 335
Jenkins, Daniel, 159,
323
Jenson, Robert, 43,
255, 317, 324
Jeremias, Joachim, 322
Jerome, 229
Joachim of Flora, 80
John of the Cross, 307
John Paul II, Pope, 47,
310, 315, 338
John XXIII, Pope, 262,
277
Johnson, Kevin Orlin,
308
Jones, L. Gregory, 324
Justin Martyr, 163
Kant, Immanuel, 240
Kasper, Walter, 40, 310
Kaufman, Gordon D.,
236, 250, 333, 335
Kavanagh, Aidan, 306
Kelly, Geffrey B., 307,
326
Kierkegaard, Søren, 96,
199, 232, 329, 333
Knitter, Paul, 236, 308
Kraemer, Hendrik, 333
Kuhns, William, 336
Küng, Hans, 27, 28, 29,
31, 74, 84, 99, 100,
101, 102, 104, 147,

162, 204, 206, 252,
260, 308, 310, 316,
317, 323, 330, 336
Laudermilch, Kenneth,
321
Lawrence, Brother,
209, 254, 330
Lazareth, William, *330*
Le Fevre, Perry, *325*
Lee, Mother Ann, *212*
Leo X, Pope, *84*
Lindbeck, George, *244,*
308
Lindberg, Carter, *316*
Littledale, A. V., *22*
Lohse, Bernhard, *321*
Lombard, Peter, *148,*
150
Lossky, Vladimir, *73*
Lubac, Henri de, *28, 29,*
307
Luther, Martin, *21, 42,*
48, 49, 50, 60, 65, 67,
71, 82, 90, 94, 104,
151, 166, 167, 178,
182, 230, 254, 259,
265, 307, 311, 313,
316, 319, 332
Lutzer, Erwin, *305*
Mackintosh, H. R., *20,*
21, 239, 306, 314, 333
MacLeod, David J., *330*
Mare, W. Harold, *155,*
322
Martos, Joseph, *37,*
309, 321, 327
Marty, Martin, *329*
Maurin, Peter, *332*
McBrien, Richard P.,
261, 337
McComiskey, Thomas
Edward, *315*
McConnell, D. R., *319*
McCormack, Bruce,
338
McGrath, Alister E.,
239, 334
McKenzie, Leon, *321*
McKim, Donald K., *327*

McPherson, Aimee
Semple, *223*
Meyendorff, John, *87,*
315
Micklem, Nathaniel,
309
Migliore, Daniel L., *312*
Miller, Elliot, *312*
Miller, Jack, *336*
Möhler, Johann Adam,
29
Moltmann, Jürgen, *27,*
39, 70, 81, 96, 99,
103, 189, 244, 245,
248, 309, 317, 334,
335
Moore, Art, *310*
Morton, T. Ralph, *232*
Moss, Basil, *314*
Myra, Harold, *305*
Neff, David, *305*
Nelson, F. Burton, *307*
Neuer, Werner, *331*
Neuhaus, Richard, *42,*
310
Nevin, John, *173*
Newman, John Henry,
87
Nichols, James Hast-
ings, *327, 336*
Niebuhr, H. Richard,
190, 192, 328, 329, 338
Niebuhr, Reinhold, *79,*
96, 189, 275, 314
Noll, Mark, *185, 323*
Nygren, Anders, *316*
Oden, Thomas C., *305,*
325, 339, 340
Offner, Kevin, *28, 307,*
308
Okholm, Dennis, *274*
Olson, Roger, *283, 284,*
340
Oman, John, *306, 317,*
333
O'Meara, Thomas, *29,*
307, 336
Osterhaven, M.
Eugene, *174*

Otto, Rudolf, *118, 133,*
318, 319
Owen, John, *311*
Packer, James I., *126,*
127, 305, 319
Panikkar, Raimundo,
308
Pannenberg, Wolfhart,
29, 39, 69, 96, 133,
156, 167, 258, 309,
318, 321, 322, 336
Pascal, Blaise, *1, 123*
Pauck, Wilhelm, *338*
Pelikan, Jaroslav, *253,*
311, 315, 328, 335
Penn, William, *198*
Peters, Eugene H.,
319
Philpot, Tony, *309*
Phypers, David, *322*
Piepkorn, Arthur Carl,
332
Pinnock, Clark, *27, 29,*
240, 307, 334
Pius, XII, Pope, *73*
Polkinghorne, John,
162, 323
Power, David, *22, 306-*
07
Pritchard, G. A., *320*
Quay, Paul, *156, 322*
Rad, Gerhard von, *331*
Radhakrishnan, S.,
237, 333
Rahner, Karl, *74, 310*
Rapp, George, *213*
Ratzinger, Joseph Car-
dinal, *90*
Rauschenbusch,
Walter, *248*
Reese, James M., *309*
Rice, Craig, *135*
Riley, John, *68*
Ritschl, Albrecht, *78,*
79, 126, 314, 319
Roberts, Robert C., *325,*
326
Robinson, H. Wheeler,
154, 322

Rodzianko, Vladimir, 73
Rorty, Richard, 238
Rubanowice, Robert J., 334, 335
Ruether, Rosemary Radford, 237, 334
Sargeant, Kimon Howard, 320
Sasse, Benjamin, 339
Schaeffer, Edith, 332
Schaeffer, Francis, 214, 332
Schafer, Thomas A., 337
Schaff, Philip, 17, 43, 45, 88, 173, 262, 310, 315, 337
Schaller, Lyle, 135, 320
Schelling, Friedrich Wilhelm, 240
Schillebeeckx, Edward, 323
Schleiermacher, Friedrich, 19, 20, 22, 71, 75, 105, 217, 236, 240, 256, 306, 313, 314, 317, 333, 336
Schmemann, Alexander, 233, 333
Schmidt, Herman, 306, 307
Schüssler Fiorenza, Elisabeth, 28
Schweizer, Eduard, 90, 91, 316
Shepherd, M. H., 330
Silleck, Jeffrey C., 42, 310, 336
Smedes, Lewis, 325, 326
Sohm, Rudolf, 311, 328
Spidlik, Thomas, 321
Sproul, R. C., 305

Stackhouse, Max L., 328
Stafford, Tim, 321
Staupitz, John, 166
Stevens, R. Paul, 331
Stewart, J. S., 306
Stylianopoulos, Theodore, 309
Tappert, Theodore G., 332
Tavard, Georges, 252
Taylor, J. Hudson, 230
Teresa of Ávila, 331
Teresa, Mother, 204
Tertullian, 227, 331
Tetzel, Johann, 166
Thérèse of Lisieux, 331
Thomas à Kempis, 172, 254, 326
Thomson, John, 267
Thurian, Max, 66, 231, 232, 312, 313, 324, 327, 332, 333, 336
Thurneysen, Eduard, 324, 325
Tillich, Paul, 72, 93, 94, 101, 123, 241, 260, 306, 314, 317, 318, 325, 334, 336
Todd, John M., 324
Toffler, Alvin, 276, 338
Torrance, Thomas F., 13, 48, 57, 58, 74, 306, 307, 311, 314, 315, 332, 335
Torrey, Archer, 332
Tozer, A. W., 116
Troeltsch, Ernst, 190, 191, 193, 195, 197, 217, 235, 236, 240, 241, 242, 243, 244, 312, 328, 331, 334
Trueblood, D. Elton, 218
Tucker, Ruth A., 332

Vasileios, Archimandrite, 73
Vischer, Lukas, 338
Vincent of Lérins, 89
Volf, Miroslav, 3, 308, 334
Wallace, Ronald S., 323
Walther, C. F. W., 323
Watson, Philip S., 316, 317
Watts, Isaac, 98, 316
Webber, Robert, 338
Weber, Max, 190, 192, 328
Weborg, John, 21, 22, 23, 306
Weiss, Johannes, 236
Wells, David, 185, 328
Wendel, François, 323
Wesley, John, 164, 167, 182, 189
Whitehead, Alfred North, 132, 318, 319
Wieman, Henry Nelson, 132
Wieser, Thomas, 324
Williams, D. H., 308
Williamson, Parker T., 333
Wolterstorff, Nicholas, 335
Wood, Ralph C., 338
Woodbridge, John, 305, 339
Woolf, Bertram Lee, 324
Wyon, Olive, 328
Yeago, David S., 317
Zinzendorf, Count Nicholas von, 212
Zwingli, Ulrich, 55, 67, 151, 153, 259

Subject Index

abortion, *275, 276*

Alliance of Confessing Evangelicals, *281*

Anabaptists, *106, 152, 153, 162, 191*

angels, *49*

Anglicanism, *156, 167*

Anglo-Catholicism, *82, 87, 273*

animism, *244*

anxiety, *171, 325*

apologetics, *33, 35, 113, 134*

apostolic succession, *40, 102, 103, 176, 210*

asceticism, *229*

assurance, *25, 59, 109, 172*

Augsburg Confession, *165, 267, 278, 313*

autonomy, *94, 209, 223*

baptism, *14, 36, 50, 52, 55, 57, 58, 60, 106, 108, 115, 146, 148, 152, 154, 156, 157, 160, 172, 173, 176, 207, 274, 281, 323, 326, 327*

Baptists, *153, 191, 196*

Barmen Declaration, *266, 267, 270, 271, 278, 286, 337, 338*

Barmen Mission, *213*

Basel Mission, *213*

biblicism, *93, 94*

Book of Common Prayer, *165*

Brethren of the Common Life, *198*

Brethren of the Free Spirit, *198*

Bruderhof, *97, 106*

Calvinism, *51, 177, 191*

Cambridge Declaration, *280-83, 288-94, 339*

Camps Farthest Out, *198*

Catholic Worker movement, *332*

Celebration of the Gospel, *283-87, 339*

celibacy, *214, 228, 229, 231, 232, 233, 234, 332, 333*

charismatic movement, *28, 207, 208, 209, 214*

Chicago Call, *269*

Christian unity, *41, 44, 211, 252-63*

church
 catholicity of, *40*
 marks of, *39-41*
 unity of, *40*

church growth movement, *35, 42*

collectivism, *13*

Community of Little Gidding, *212*

Confessing Church, *35, 266, 271, 272, 315*

confession of sin, *141, 165, 166-72, 326*

confessions of faith, *17, 34, 35, 106, 135, 265-87, 339*

confirmation, *108, 148, 159*

conversion, *18, 41, 42, 56, 152, 172, 227, 242, 245, 255, 263, 281, 322*

Council of Chalcedon, *189*

Council of Constance, *83*

Council of Florence, *148*

Council of Trent, *148, 150*

credalism, *85, 94, 109, 187, 262*

cults, *192, 198, 201, 202, 203*

death, *26*

deism, *277*

demons, *208, 326*

Disciplined Order of Christ, *198*

dispensationalism, *211*

docetism, *75*

doctrine, *18, 19, 163, 273, 300*

Dohnavur Fellowship, *213*

eclecticism, *195*

ecumenism, *14, 111, 173, 175, 253, 254, 255, 256, 262, 264, 281*

egalitarianism, *224, 227, 277*

election, *58, 65, 73, 157, 158, 159, 191*

Enlightenment, *79, 235, 238, 241, 254, 277*

enthusiasm, religious, *49, 83, 95, 109, 182, 201*

Ephrata community, *212*

eschatology, *20, 81, 160, 203, 232, 236, 247*

eucharist, *42, 54, 55, 59, 106, 108, 114, 115, 142, 148, 160, 161, 162, 163, 173, 175, 176, 177, 205, 207, 208, 321, 322, 323, 330*

Evangelical Sisterhood of Mary, *213*

evangelicalism, *14, 15, 23, 34, 41, 42, 45, 83, 86, 216, 273, 280, 283*

evangelism, *63, 106, 204, 208, 209, 216, 222, 246, 247, 248, 274, 294, 304* excommunication, *112*

existentialism, *18, 23, 249*

experience, *15, 17, 20, 22, 24, 25, 26, 33, 56, 83, 86, 93, 94, 96*

experientialism, *24, 93, 94, 95*

faith, *14, 17, 18, 19, 23, 35, 41, 50, 55, 60, 71, 95, 96, 102, 131, 148, 158, 175, 182, 245, 286, 300*

feminism, *34, 224, 225, 228, 237, 253, 273, 275, 334, 339*

Fifth Lateran Council, *84*

forgiveness, *25, 51, 59, 63, 92, 166-72, 174, 282, 324, 325, 326*

foundationalism, *236*

fundamentalism, *244, 268, 273*

globalism, *256*

gnosticism, *131, 169, 181, 220, 221, 226, 229, 277, 338*

grace, *25, 26, 28, 29, 36, 45, 48, 54, 56, 61, 62, 63, 66, 80, 109, 122, 153, 172, 177, 190, 214, 218, 253, 284, 286, 291, 292*

guilt, *169, 326*

Harmony Society, *213*

hell, *26, 55, 90, 165, 249*

heresy, *34, 45, 85, 111, 112, 181, 196, 202, 203, 237, 270, 272, 318, 329*

Herrnhut community, *212*

heterodoxy, *34, 45, 111, 136, 202, 272, 329*

heteronomy, *94, 209, 226*

Hinduism, *237*

historicism, *193, 240, 250*

holiness, *67, 100, 103, 111, 229, 281, 282, 286, 290, 297*

Holy Spirit, *15, 16, 24, 25, 26, 29, 30, 32, 38, 39, 41, 47, 49, 51, 56, 58, 59, 64, 66, 74, 79, 83, 84, 85, 87, 94, 97, 100, 108, 120, 121, 129, 140, 147, 161, 173, 177, 179, 182, 188, 194, 205, 211, 247, 264, 280, 281, 286, 289, 290, 296*

homosexuality, *253, 275, 283*

humanism, *170, 274, 277*

iconoclasm, *127*

idealism, *193, 200, 243, 276*

ideology, *13, 15, 253, 266, 273, 274, 275, 326*

idolatry, *122, 129, 130, 145, 197, 245, 260, 283*

inclusivism, *110, 199, 236, 239, 242, 273, 274, 283*

individualism, *13, 24, 42, 137, 193, 236, 290*

insularism, *109*

intercession, *14*

Iona community, *213, 331*

Jehovah's Witnesses, *196*

Jesus Abbey, *214, 332*

Jesus Christ
  his cross, *28, 32, 44, 45, 46, 56, 76, 78, 80, 92, 120, 153, 159, 186, 249, 285*
  his incarnation, *15, 57, 96, 243, 285, 340*

his Lordship, *58, 75, 76, 255, 265, 273, 276, 340*

his resurrection, *28, 32, 44, 45, 46, 51, 56, 76, 78, 80, 92, 97, 150, 207, 249, 285, 302*

justification, *42, 44-45, 67, 110, 166, 180, 184, 215, 252, 253, 257, 258, 282, 284, 285, 290, 298, 299, 302, 303, 304, 310, 339*

kingdom of God, *14, 26, 29, 32, 33, 60, 61, 68, 69, 70, 72, 73, 76, 77, 78, 79, 80, 91, 97, 106, 139, 154, 181, 183, 203, 207, 218, 226, 228, 231, 242, 247, 264, 286, 299, 313*

Koinonia Farm, *213*

L'Abri Fellowship, *214*

Lateran Council, Fourth, *150*

latitudinarianism, *89, 110, 111, 256, 267, 274, 284*

Lee Abbey, *213*

legalism, *110, 197, 214, 215, 284*

Levellers, *191*

liberalism, *15-16, 45, 180, 270, 273, 275, 278*

liberation theology, *107, 185, 273*

liturgical movement, *36*

Lord's Supper. *See* eucharist

love, *40, 63, 78, 102, 125, 169, 319*

Lutheranism, *42, 43, 128, 156, 161, 162, 191, 200, 253*

Manichaeism, 229
Marxism, 254
Mary
  assumption, 42, 67,
    258
  immaculate concep-
    tion, 42, 259
  motherhood, 64, 65,
    66
  perpetual virginity,
    67, 258
Mercersburg move-
  ment, 255
Methodism, 191
militarism, 33
millennial kingdom,
  80, 81, 197
miracles, 107, 148
Möllenbeck monas-
  tery, 212
monasticism, 144, 199,
  208, 211, 212, 216,
  226, 336
monergism, 62
Moody Bible Institute,
  213
Moral Re-Armament,
  53, 214, 217, 311
moralism, 42, 79, 146,
  180, 183, 235, 284
Moravians, 191, 215
Mormonism, 196, 310
multiculturalism, 185
mysticism, 14, 70, 83,
  94, 95, 100, 108, 123,
  126, 131, 133, 134,
  169, 172, 187, 191,
  192, 198, 237, 256,
  265
National Socialism,
  254, 271, 338
nationalism, 243, 334
naturalism, 94, 131,
  276
neo-orthodoxy, 15, 24,
  185
Neoplatonism, 13, 259
neo-Protestantism, 20,
  78, 95

Nestorianism, 75
New Age movement,
  33, 34, 198, 237, 257,
  308
Nicene Creed, 39, 100,
  278
nihilism, 238, 251, 277,
  339
obedience, 20, 51, 55,
  65, 84, 100, 121, 148,
  157, 176, 218, 268,
  275, 302
objectivism, 24, 58,
  156, 157, 200, 201
Operation Mobiliza-
  tion, 213
orthodoxy, 14, 15, 16,
  17, 45, 111, 133, 187,
  201, 270, 273, 280,
  332
Orthodoxy, Eastern, 28,
  30, 37, 38, 41, 42, 62,
  73, 83, 86, 87, 100,
  107, 117, 156, 177,
  215, 229, 252, 253,
  255, 273, 329
Oxford Group, 53, 167.
  See also Moral Re-
  Armament
pacifism, 275
paganism, 277, 321
papacy, 42, 82, 210,
  257
Parliament of World
  Religions, 236, 237
patriarchalism, 219,
  220, 222, 225-27, 229,
  230
patristic theology, 21
penance. See confes-
  sion of sin.
Pentecostalism, 40,
  106, 138, 196, 319,
  329
Pietism, 13, 18, 20, 21,
  24, 70, 87, 95, 105,
  106, 157, 169, 172,
  173, 191, 199, 200,
  212, 217, 230, 306,

329, 338
Pius XII, Pope, 73
Platonism, 13, 149, 334
pluralism, 236, 238,
  239, 244, 246, 250,
  274, 283, 284, 300,
  333, 334
Plymouth Brethren,
  213, 329
politics, 64, 183
pornography, 275
postmodernism, 30,
  236, 238, 250, 251,
  277, 283, 334, 339
prayer, 14, 21, 22, 63,
  107, 108, 110, 121,
  131, 142, 165, 209,
  214, 229, 247, 260,
  275, 319
preaching, 14, 19, 29,
  37, 38, 51, 53, 114,
  127, 140, 146, 153,
  178-88
predestination, 51, 250,
  260
Presbyterian Confes-
  sion of 1967, 269
process theology, 94,
  125, 277, 319
propositionalism, 18,
  24, 37, 94, 133
Protestantism, 13, 36,
  37, 38, 87, 89, 101,
  138, 143, 181, 218,
  233, 253, 259, 270,
  317, 337
psychotherapy, 169,
  325
purgatory, 45, 257
Puritanism, 13, 105,
  128, 191, 230, 306
Quakerism, 108, 191,
  198, 218, 332
rationalism, 19, 37, 93,
  94, 99, 113, 133, 173,
  281, 301
Reformation, Protes-
  tant, 13, 20, 27, 30,
  34, 38, 39, 42, 52, 60,

84, 94, 99, 139, 145,
150, 165, 180, 187,
211, 253, 288
Reformed tradition, *41,*
51, 58, 86, 128, 143,
274, 328
regeneration, *18, 21,*
24, 29, 49, 58, 76, 77,
79, 148, 149, 152,
154, 156, 169, 176
Regensburg Confer-
ence, *254*
relativism, *193, 236,*
238, 241, 251, 284,
286, 300
religious orders, *211-*
18
revelation, *15, 20, 22,*
56, 94, 118, 123, 181,
183, 193, 239, 243,
247, 251
revivalism, *13, 14, 24,*
167, 261
ritualism, *14, 36, 118,*
151, 172, 175, 194,
320, 321
Roman Catholicism,
20, 21, 28, 29, 30, 36,
38, 40, 41, 45, 47, 59,
61, 68, 83, 86, 87,
100, 106, 133, 161,
168, 169, 177, 191,
212, 229, 259, 312,
317, 329
Romanticism, *44, 236,*
241, 255, 336
sacerdotalism, *49, 52,*
148, 151, 195
sacramentalism, *55,*
148, 155, 156, 160,
195, 207, 327
sacraments, *14, 27, 28,*
36, 37, 40, 44, 45, 48,
52, 56, 58, 61, 74, 88,
95, 101, 108, 114,
146, 147-77, 190, 200,
201, 257, 264, 321
St. Chrischona Pilgrim
Mission, *213*

St. Julian's community,
213
saints, *13, 14, 39, 64,*
66, 67, 71, 96, 169,
187, 229, 259, 283
salvation, *27, 28, 29,*
34, 46, 47, 49, 55, 56,
58, 60, 62, 65, 68,
105, 110, 111, 118,
138, 140, 155, 157,
165, 176, 179, 190,
211, 215, 231, 254,
277, 284, 291, 297,
320
Salvation Army, *45,*
105, 108, 223
sanctification, *71, 92,*
157, 282, 284, 299,
303
Second Helvetic Con-
fession, *114, 165,*
264, 318, 324, 332
sectarianism, *35, 156,*
191, 203, 267, 279,
280, 329, 330
sects, *35, 190, 191,*
192, 194, 195-98, 201,
202, 203, 329
semi-Pelagianism, *89*
Seventh-day Advent-
ism, *196*
Shakerism, *212*
signs and wonders, *40,*
41, 106, 107
sin, *59, 60, 77, 92, 110,*
163, 165, 166, 167,
168, 169, 174, 176,
195, 202, 233, 239,
249, 259, 298, 302,
326, 337
Society of Separatists,
213
spiritual gifts, *28, 207,*
208, 209
Spiritualism, *198*
spirituality, *22, 33, 130,*
131, 132, 134, 135,
169
Stoicism, *334*

subjectivism, *20, 24,*
34, 200, 201
Swedenborgianism,
198
syncretism, *192, 195,*
236, 237, 238, 239,
240, 242, 246, 249,
265, 267, 277
synergism, *62, 157,*
227, 282
Taizé community, *66,*
213, 330, 331
Ten Articles of Reli-
gion, *165*
theology, *19, 21, 78*
Theosophical Society,
198
Torchbearers, *214*
transubstantiation, *42,*
150, 152, 323
Trevecka community,
212
Trinity, *57, 133, 224,*
268, 299, 302
truth, *96, 109, 157, 175,*
246, 301
unitarianism, *277*
United Church of
Christ, *256, 268*
universalism, *249, 277*
Vatican Council I, *46,*
84
Vatican Council II, *40,*
47, 73, 84, 261
weapons of mass
extermination, *276,*
282, 339
Willow Creek Commu-
nity Church, *35, 135*
women's liberation.
See feminism
World Council of
Churches, *252, 253*
worship, *35, 36, 37,*
113, 116-46, 184-85,
188, 191, 280, 293,
296, 308

Scripture Index

Genesis
1:27, *219*
1:28, *228*
2:18, *219*
2:18-25, *215*
3:16, *219*
9:1, *228*
9:7, *228*

Exodus
15:20, *219*
20, *127*
20:4-6, *126*

Numbers
6:2, *219*

Deuteronomy
5, *127*
5:8-10, *126*
32:10, *320*
32:30, *188*

Judges
4:4, *219*
5:7, *219*
5:12, *219*
13:23, *219*

1 Samuel
2:6, *188*
15:22-23, *118*

2 Samuel
14:1-20, *219*
20:14-22, *219*

2 Kings
22:14, *219*

1 Chronicles
16:29-30, *116*

2 Chronicles
20:21, *119*

Nehemiah
6:14, *219*
8:2, *219*

Psalms
17:8, *320*
40:8, *320*
40:10, *320*
42:4-5, *320*
51:17, *118*
78:58, *126*

Proverbs
7:2, *320*
31:10-31, *219*
31:20, *219*

Isaiah
12:5, *295*
29:13, *118*
40:18, *126*
55:8-9, *129*
55:11, *125*
56:3-5, *228*

Jeremiah
6:16, *125*

Hosea
6:6, *118*
11:9, *130*

Joel
2:13, *119*
2:28-29, *220*

Amos
5:21-24, *118*
8:11, *178*
8:11-12, *178*

Micah
6:7-8, *118*

Nahum
1:8, *124, 125*

Habakkuk
2:20, *133*

Zephaniah
1:7, *133*

Zechariah
2:8, *320*
2:13, *133*

Matthew
5:16, *234*
5:17, *125*
7:15, *203*
7:16-20, *105*
9:2, *171*
9:17, *53, 112*
10:40, *92*
12:33, *105*
13:33, *234*
16:13-19, *90*
16:18, *1, 26*
16:19, *82*
18:15-17, *171*
18:18, *91*
19:3-12, *228*
19:11-12, *233*
20:25-28, *207*
20:26-28, *222, 331*
20:28, *298*
23:10-11, *222*
24:11, *203*
24:24, *203*
25:31-32, *296*
26:26-29, *160*
26:29, *160*
28:18-19, *301*
28:18-20, *154*
28:19-20, *63, 198, 210*
28:20, *247*

Mark
1:14, *301*
10:42-45, *207, 331*
13:11, *91, 312*
13:22, *107, 203*
14:22-25, *160*
14:25, *160*
14:61-62, *299*

16:15, *63*
16:15-16, *154*
16:17-18, *107*

Luke
1:30, *67*
1:45, *65*
1:47, *68*
1:48, *65, 220*
1:70, *312*
3:8, *61*
5:37-39, *53, 112*
6:26, *203*
10:16, *91, 92, 187, 312*
11:20, *78*
12:31, *234*
12:32-48, *92*
15:11-32, *125*
15:22-24, *63*
17:21, *73, 78*
18:29-30, *232*
22:14-20, *160*
22:18, *160*
22:24-27, *207*
22:27, *206, 331*
24:44-53, *63*
24:47, *198, 301*

John
1:1, *302*
1:5, *145*
1:12, *299*
1:14, *302*
1:18, *127*
3:5, *155*
3:16, *295*
4:20-24, *119*
4:23-24, *118*
4:24, *116*
8:11, *326*
8:24, *340*
12:31, *298*
12:48, *340*
13:13-15, *206, 222*
13:34-35, *300*
14:6, *35, 250, 297, 301*
16:13, *89*
16:33, *145*
17:15, *234*

17:15-18, *234*
17:20-21, *300*
17:23, *252*
19:26-27, *65*
20:22-23, *168*
20:23, *91, 92, 316*

Acts
1:8, *63*
1:14, *65, 221*
2:17-18, *221, 227*
4:12, *240, 297*
5:12, *107*
6:1-5, *209*
8:4-6, *220*
18:26, *220*
19:11-12, *107*
20:28, *205*
21:5, *229*
21:9, *222*
28:25, *312*

Romans
1:1, *301*
1:3, *302*
1:16, *184, 301*
1:17, *298, 299*
1:18-32, *297, 298*
3:4, *249*
3:9-20, *298*
3:21-24, *298*
3:23, *67, 258*
3:23-25, *298*
3:25, *258*
3:25-26, *298*
3:28, *303*
4:1-8, *298*
4:5, *258, 298, 303*
5:1-2, *298*
5:1-11, *326*
5:9, *258*
5:17, *299*
6:1-4, *156*
6:3-4, *115, 326*
6:12-14, *122*
7:6, *299*
8:4, *304*
8:9-17, *299*
8:13-14, *304*

8:26, *107*
10:3, *258*
10:17, *127, 144, 216*
11:33-36, *129*
12:1, *110, 118*
12:1-2, *318*
12:3-8, *227*
12:4-8, *205*
13:12-14, *110*
14:1—15:13, *300*
15:18-19, *107*
16:1, *220*
16:7, *220*

1 Corinthians
1:18, *301*
1:21, *144, 301*
1:22-24, *274*
1:23, *183, 186*
2:1-5, *301*
2:2, *186*
3:2, *139*
3:11, *91, 92*
6:7-11, *122*
7:29, *232*
7:32-35, *228*
7:39, *230*
9:5, *222, 229*
9:19-22, *301*
10:14, *122*
10:16, *160*
11:3, *225*
11:7, *225*
11:23-26, *160*
11:24, *322*
11:26, *160*
11:27-30, *163*
12:1-31, *227*
12-14, *205*
12:13, *155*
14:34, *331*
15, *298*
15:14, *302*
15:22, *297*

2 Corinthians
5:18-19, *135*
5:18-21, *298*
5:19-21, *303*

5:21, *285, 299*
6:17, *198*

Galatians
1:1-11, *301*
1:6-9, *303*
2:16, *303*
3:2, *144*
3:5, *144*
3:13, *285,
302*
3:28, *221,
331*
3:28-29, *300*
4:4-7, *298*
4:5, *302*
4:10, *118*
5:1, *171*
5:16-21, *122*
5:16-24, *110*
5:22, *105*
5:22-25,
304
6:14, *113*

Ephesians
1:21, *123*
2:1-3, *298*
2:4-10, *298*
2:8, *66*
2:8-9, *303*
2:12, *298*
2:20, *91, 92*
3:9-10, *63*
4:5, *155, 274*
4:11-12, *204,
205*
4:11-16, *227*
4:13, *299*
4:17-32, *122*
5:21, *227*
5:21-33, *224*
5:25, *226*

Philippians
1:21, *299*
2:2, *300*
3:9, *299*

Colossians
1:13, *78*
1:13-14, *248*
1:15, *127*
1:20, *298*
2:11-12, *155*
2:13-14, *298*
2:15, *298*
3:16-17, *221*
4:2, *132, 320*

1 Thessalonians
4:13-16, *296*

1 Timothy
2:5, *301*
2:8-15, *221*
2:15, *221*
3:11, *221*

2 Timothy
3:5, *118*

Titus
1:5-7, *205*
3:5, *147, 155, 303*

Hebrews
1:1-4, *298*
1:3, *134, 302*
2:1-18, *298*
2:4, *107*
2:17, *302*
4:14-16, *298*
6:1-12, *299*
7:1—10:25, *298*
7:26-28, *302*
9:11-14, *285*

9:11-28, *207*
9:25-28, *59*
9:28, *285, 299*
10:11-14, *59*
10:14-18, *207*
12:2, *35*
12:28-29, *119*

James
2:14-26, *299*
5:16, *168, 170*

1 Peter
1:1, *205*
1:14-17, *122*
2:5, *91, 207*
3:1-7, *224*
3:18, *298*
3:21, *155*
5:1, *205*

2 Peter
1:11, *78*
2:1, *203*
3:12, *62*

1 John
4:1, *203*
4:2-3, *302, 340*
4:10, *135*
4:14, *297*

Revelation
1:6, *91, 207*
1:18, *92*
3:7, *92*
3:16, *111*
5:9, *299*
5:10, *91, 207*
7:9, *301*
14:9-10, *122*
22:1-5, *299*